Contemporar

Canadian Curriculum

Principles, Portraits, & Practices

Edited by

Darren Stanley & Kelly Young

DETSELIG
ENTERPRISES LTD

Calgary, Alberta, Canada

Contemporary Studies in Canadian Curriculum:
Principles, Portraits, and Practices
© 2011 Darren Stanley & Kelly Young

Library and Archives Canada Cataloguing in Publication
    Contemporary studies in Canadian curriculum : principles, por-
traits, and practices / edited by Darren Stanley and Kelly Young.

Includes bibliographical references.
ISBN 978-1-55059-399-0

    1. Education--Curricula--Social aspects--Canada. 2. Curriculum
change--Canada. I. Stanley, Darren II. Young, Kelly, 1969–

LB1564.C3C67 2011   375.000971   C2011-901026-7

Detselig Enterprises, Ltd.
210-1220 Kensington Rd NW
Calgary, Alberta T2N 3P5
www.temerondetselig.com
temeron@telusplanet.net
Phone: 403-283-0900
Fax: 403-283-6947

We recognize the support of the government of Canada through the
Canada Books Program for our publishing program.

We also acknowledge the support of the
Alberta Foundation for the Arts for our
publishing program.

Cover art: *Trent University Landscape* (2006) by Margrit Bohart
        Watercolour – 350 cm x 275 cm
SAN 113-0234
ISBN 978-1-55059-399-0
Printed in Canada.

Contents

FOREWORD

William F. Pinar

IN THIS IMPORTANT NEW COLLECTION, several key concerns – summarized in Cynthia Chambers's (2003) invaluable survey of the field – continue to characterize Canadian curriculum studies. Prominent among these are questions of the indigenous peoples. In this collection these are not confined to the indigenous peoples themselves, but are "exported" to the mainstream Canadian curriculum (see, for instance, the Battiste and Bell chapters). In part due to the ecological crisis, in part due to the calamities of economism, in part due to the indigenous character of Canada (Saul, 2008), these questions reverberate not only in environmental education but in science as well as in literature, the arts, politics, and history, as these chapters testify. The concept of decolonization – not only of indigenous peoples but of Canadians of European descent as well – seems to summarize this pressing curricular concern. Clearly, contemporary scholars have responded to Chambers's (p. 223) complaint that indigenous education was "underrepresented." As this invaluable collection testifies, on this key concern the field's progress has been dramatic.

Also evident in this collection is progress on the other (often intersecting) concerns and concepts that Chambers (2003) construed as central to the Canadian field. Prominent among these are (1) *politics* (p. 223), evident in the Balzer, Iannacci, Phelan, and Smith chapters; (2) *wisdom* (p. 225), evident in the Riley and Rich as well as Smith chapters; (3) *subjectivity* (p. 229), resounding in the Jardine, Luce-Kapler, and Ng-A-Fook chapters; (4) *place* (p. 233), discernible in the Alsop and Fawcett, the Sumara, Davis, and Laidlaw, and the Kulnieks, Longboat, and Young chapters; and (5) *arts-based inquiry* (p. 235), evident in Luce-Kapler's close writing and Smits's invocation of fugue and nocturne in his chapter. In advancing our understanding of these key curricular concerns and adding others (like queer questions of sex education in the Cavanagh chapter and the curricular significance of complexity theory in the Stanley chapter), the essays collected here extend the "third way" that Chambers (p. 246) identified as distinctively Canadian. Neither European nor American (as in the U.S.), but incorporating each in its decolonizing indigenous emphasis, contemporary Canadian scholarship recalibrates the curriculum in a new key (Aoki, 2005).

Despite these achievements, there remains disciplinary work to do. In this outsider's view, one next step is the updating and revision of George Tomkins's (2008) canonical study of Canadian curriculum history. Key pieces of this reconfigured puzzle are already on the table in this collection. What remains to be done is the integration of this work with scholarship on "new" immigrants as well as curriculum studies in Québec (which Chambers [2003, pp. 236–237] references) and, of course, continuing historical research (see, for instance, Christou, 2009). Supplementing such revision and updating of Tomkins's history of the Canadian curriculum and the updating of Chambers's insightful survey of the contemporary field should be, I suggest, a more specific stream of scholarship on the intellectual history of Canadian curriculum studies, resembling, perhaps, work underway in other countries (see, for instance, Pinar, 2011). Working from and through these histories will enable that continuing intellectual advancement prerequisite for the field to address the daunting challenges Canadians have inherited from the past and face in the future.

References

Aoki, T. T. (2005 [1978]). Toward curriculum inquiry in a new key. In William F. Pinar and Rita L. Irwin (Eds.), *Curriculum in a New Key* (pp. 89–110). Mahwah, NJ: Lawrence Erlbaum.

Chambers, C. (2003). "As Canadian as possible under the circumstances": A view of contemporary curriculum discourses in Canada. In William F. Pinar (Ed.), *International Handbook of Curriculum Research* (pp. 221–252). Mahwah, NJ: Lawrence Erlbaum.

Christou, T. M. (2009). *Exploring the meanings of progressive education in two Ontario journals, 1919–1942* (Unpublished doctoral dissertation). Queens University, Kingston, Ontario.

Pinar, W. F. (Ed.). (2011). *Curriculum studies in Brazil: Intellectual histories, present circumstances.* New York, NY: Palgrave Macmillan.

Saul, J. R. (2008). *A fair country: Telling truths about Canada.* Toronto, ON: Viking Canada.

Tomkins, G. S. (2008 [1986]). *A common countenance: Stability and change in the Canadian curriculum.* Vancouver, BC: Pacific Educational Press.

INTRODUCTION:
PRINCIPLES, PORTRAITS, AND PRACTICES IN CONTEMPORARY CANADIAN CURRICULA

Darren Stanley & Kelly Young

THE IMPETUS FOR THIS COLLECTION comes from our conversations exploring schooling and Canadian curriculum theory and practice. We conceptualize our book through three interconnected and overlapping approaches addressing the topic of contemporary Canadian curriculum studies in terms of principles, portraits, and practices. By principles we include dialogues that consider ideologies, conventions, assumptions, and beliefs about Canadian curriculum. By portraits we include discussions and approaches that consider the relevance of landscapes and place, stories, profiles, and depictions of Canadian curriculum. By practices we include methodological approaches, conventions of curriculum enactment, and performances of Canadian curriculum.

Further, we divide our book into three broadly defined sections: Canadian Curriculum and Social Identities, Canadian Curriculum and Culture, and Canadian Curriculum and Indigenous and Ecological Perspectives. This book is unique in that it offers a variety of perspectives, inviting the reader to engage in a conversation about the multiple dimensions of the relationship between contemporary Canadian curriculum theory and practice in terms of social justice and ecological and Indigenous perspectives.

In the first section, Canadian Curriculum and Social Identities, we begin with Dennis Sumara, Brent Davis, and Linda Laidlaw's chapter, as they develop a thesis that curriculum studies work in Canada might be characterized in terms of some persistent and consistent theoretical commitments, ones that they suggest might have been prompted in part by the nation's history and by popular commentaries on national identity. They draw on ecological and postmodern discourses in an effort to conceptualize and describe a relationship between Canadian culture(s) and the development of theories of curriculum within the Canadian context.

The question of possibility for Canadian curriculum studies, through the metaphors of nocturne and fugue, is the focus of Hans Smits's chapter. Nocturne suggests the difficult – perhaps dark – terms, in Hannah Arendt's historical view, that challenge purposes for curriculum. The notion of fugue suggests the complex and contradictory forms that curriculum can take. The challenge for a "Canadian" curriculum, it is argued, is not in terms of identity, but in terms of a creative and ethical way of enacting our responsibilities as educators.

Humans make sense through story, but how we can learn through interrupting story? How does trying to write in another's style offer different interpretations? In Rebecca Luce-Kapler's chapter, she explores how close writing challenges the syntax of narrative and brings the attention of the curriculum theorist to the details of the text. We learn that it is in the interruption – the uncomfortable – where one comes to know what it was we missed or were not ready to hear. Close writing as an ethical practice interrupts normative experience and brings one to appreciate the complexity of experience and to recognize moments of possibility for learning.

In Tasha Riley and Sharon Rich's chapter, they juxtapose the story of a young woman discovering her whiteness and difference with the development of an understanding of co-learning as a curricular construct. They use the story to demonstrate the ways in which curricular theorizing can be complemented by an understanding of who we are and of the ways in which we act in the world. In this chapter, the authors explore curriculum as a story that unfolds and helps us to understand who we might become as teachers, co-learners, and as human beings. They juxtapose a story of self-discovery with a story of creating a co-learning and reflexive classroom curriculum to indicate the ways in which the personal informs the public to create new spaces for learning.

Geraldine Balzer examines the service learning program of one high school in her contribution to this text. She contextualizes the story of the program of Academy High School by first presenting a brief history of the service learning movement, the benefits of participation in service learning, and its connections to social and ecological justice. Balzer introduces narratives, created from the interviews and journals of the researcher and participants, to provide a personal glimpse into the transformative impact of the service learning experience. To be sure, international service learning seeks to empower communities, connect peoples, and facilitate personal and physical border crossings. And, while not perfect, the program Balzer speaks about facilitates the transformation of Canadian youth into globally aware and caring citizens of the world.

In the second section of the book, Canadian Curriculum and Culture, we begin with David Smith's chapter which addresses the current global financial crisis that marks the end of the legitimacy of *neoliberalism*, or market determinism, as a basis for education, including curriculum and pedagogy. What source of value and valuing might guide the education of the future? Three characteristics of global wisdom traditions are discussed – meditative sensibility, a kairotic understanding of time, and the unified field of birth and death – as an antidote to the pathologies of market logic. This discussion follows a genealogical tracing of how the market has been understood by both its supporters and detractors and an examination of the specific economistic roots of much educational practice today.

In Anne Phelan's chapter, she considers how politics as a form of culture within a profession suggest a space of tolerance, respect, and difference. It is a space wherein teachers, coming from a plurality of standpoints, can engage one another and their leaders in discussion about educational matters. Such engagement, she argues, enables educators to produce a strongly articulated sense of shared professional and social-political purpose. Is it possible to cultivate such a political culture among educators who are inevitably caught between their own judgments and authoritative constraints of policy, professional culture, and school leadership? Drawing on the work of Hannah Arendt, she explores the individual teacher's will as both an anti-political and political force in the teaching profession.

Consumer identities and how they are fostered and subverted among early years culturally and linguistically diverse (CLD) children through early years literacy curricula is the topic for Luigi Iannacci's chapter. He develops ecojustice-informed curricula that provide teacher educators and teachers with principles and practices that may forward pedagogies that resist furthering consumer rituals and identities. Narratives constructed from field data are offered as a way of demonstrating the current context and to facilitate follow up discussion intended to conceptualize this curricula. He adds to the recent growing body of work in early years literacy research grounded in sociocultural theory and reconceptualist curriculum theorizing as it informs early literacy and as such, draws on ecojustice perspectives to develop an analytic lens and curricular principles.

In her chapter, Sheila Cavanagh uses queer theory to analyze the recent public debate about the 2010 Ontario sex education proposal. The proposed changes to the Health and Physical Education curriculum were retracted by Premier Dalton McGuinty due to a public campaign launched by socially conservative religious groups. Religious leaders raised moral concerns about the introduction of topics like gender identity and sexual orientation into the curriculum. She considers how the anti-sex education campaign is structured by linguistic tropes conjuring up images of bodily disorientation and irrational ideas about childhood sexual innocence. She argues that education is about how we position ourselves in relation to others socially coded as different or non-normative.

In Darren Stanley's chapter, he explores how a particular kind of language is required to frame and understand landscapes. He argues that such a language can be drawn from the contemporary, transdisciplinary framework known as "complexity theory," which offers a way of understanding a wide range of diverse phenomena. While the field of education may reflect an indefinite plurality of disciplinary perspectives and concerns, a complexity theory framework extends well beyond the usual concerns and activities of individual and collective knowledge to embrace a notion of embedded "bodies of knowledge." Although these bodies of knowledge include biological subsystems, the biologic body, social collectives, the body politic and cultural bodies, local ecologies, and the biosphere, at the dynamical heart of each of these bodies is a collection of principles, portraits, and practices that underlie a view of learning and learning organizations.

In the third section of our book, Canadian Curriculum and Indigenous and Environmental Perspectives, we begin with Marie Battiste's chapter, in which she provides a background, context, and perspective that may inform current decision makers in a revisioning of curriculum, beginning with an overview of the obligations and commitments made to First Nations in the treaties, and more recently as Aboriginal rights to education have been affirmed in the United Nations Declaration on the Rights of Indigenous Peoples (2007) and finally affirmed in Canada in 2010. She considers the ways in which federal and provincial school systems have not translated these constitutionally protected rights into current models of education, but rather the discursive modes of analysis have led to various models of education that focus on students' perceived deficits and that ignore systemic racism and structural failures of the educational systems. Eurocentric approaches to curricula reform in most educational systems continue to have a conceptual bias that ignores the system and structure and relies on the dispositional self of individual children as central to understanding their educational failure and tragic circumstances.

In Nicholas Ng-A-Fook's chapter, he explores the ways in which we, as curriculum theorists, educators, and teacher-candidates, reread the Ontario curriculum and often continue to narrate historical slights and insults that disinherit indigenous knowledge and language by ignoring the potential pedagogical value they might have within contemporary educational contexts to help us commit our eco-civic relational responsibilities to the land. Taking indigenous thought seriously as a form of curriculum theorizing asks us to consider alter/native intergenerational teachings of place. In response to such teachings, he shares narrative visions of how curriculum theorists, teacher-candidates, and indigenous communities can collaborate together to create, develop, and engage participatory social action community service learning projects. In turn, he examines how such social action curriculum projects provide curricular and pedagogical opportunities for teachers and students to develop praxial narrative strategies for rereading colonial narrative artifacts scarred into the very material fabric of the land, as an aesthetic form of métis/sage-ing.

In David Jardine's chapter, he explores the ecological and pedagogical images hidden within a tale of the author's returning to the place he was raised and going for a birding walk with some old friends. He takes his reader on a "birding lesson" and imagines mathematics conceived as a living discipline, a living topography, a living place, full of ancestors, full of tales told and tales to tell. He then imagines mathematics education as an open, generous invitation to our children into the intimate ways of this old, mysterious, wondrous place.

Andrejs Kulnieks, Dan Roronhiakewen Longboat, and Kelly Young's contribution considers how conceptions of curriculum have historically been theorized through a scientific model since the early twentieth century in relation to and development of environmental education. They then turn to an analysis of contemporary environmental education curriculum policies. Specifically, they examine recent environmental educational policies developed by the Ontario Ministry of Education that are embedded in a scientific inquiry model in relation to our personal beliefs that all education should lead toward environmental learning. To this end, they consider core principles such as the ways in which language often impedes an understanding that the earth is a living being. They conceptualize environmental learning by turning their attention to successful examples of models of Indigenous curriculum and pedagogy that can inform all aspects of environmental education to move toward a more holistic approach toward education.

In Nicole Bell's chapter, she speaks to the need for the education system to address the needs of Indigenous students, in particular their identity needs and the cross-cultural educational needs of non-Indigenous students in understanding the perspectives, experiences, and histories of Canada's First Peoples. She draws upon medicine wheel pedagogy to demonstrate that a distinct learning environment needs to be created for the transmission of Indigenous knowledge and worldview. The learning environment needs to be multifarious, circular, longitudinal, and integrative. She argues that educational spaces need to be inclusive of the experiences, histories, and voices of those on the "margins," including Indigenous people. While the new Ontario Curriculum has attempted to include First Nation, Métis, and Inuit content into the curriculum, it is offered through an "added-on" approach that does not serve the cultural needs of its Indigenous students.

Leesa Fawcet and Steve Alsop explore science, schooling, and education. They draw on selected literature in science technology studies and feminist postcolonial theories to offer some acts of resistance through local environmental knowledges as sciences. They chart these meanderings using a series of nautical metaphors, building on the archetypical ghost ship the Mary Celeste and discuss science and education both within the curriculum and its cultural influences on the curriculum. They draw on selective literature in science and technology studies (STS) and feminist postcolonial theories to offer some acts of culture jamming through local situated environmental knowledges and practices as sciences. They posit that contemporary curriculum questions cannot easily escape discussion of science and its effects on the curriculum, but some of the curriculum discussions in the sciences relating to situated environmental knowledges might offer insight and opportunities to act.

PART ONE

CANADIAN CURRICULUM & SOCIAL IDENTITIES

Canadian Identity and Curriculum Theory: An Ecological, Postmodern Perspective

1

Dennis Sumara & Brent Davis, University of Calgary
Linda Laidlaw, University of Alberta

Reproduced with permission from *Canadian Journal of Education* 26 (2001): 144–163.

Part 1: As Canadian As . . .

IN A 1960s RADIO CONTEST, Peter Gzowski of the Canadian Broadcasting Corporation challenged the nation: "Complete the adage, As Canadian as . . ." Apparently most listeners heard the contest as a quest for something quintessentially Canadian – a symbol to fit our nation the way the adage "mom and apple pie" describes the American character. Most submissions were predictable: a fresh snowfall; eh?; the Mounties. The contest judges, however, were not convinced that "Canadianism" could be captured by a single image; The winner was "As Canadian as possible under the circumstances."

The winning adage hints that an essential quality of Canada is a lack of essential qualities. At least, Canadians would prefer not to identify those qualities that we imagine might pin us to a particular way of identifying ourselves. To appreciate the sort of curriculum theorizing that has occurred in Canada, one must first have a sense of the deliberate diversity that is represented among the nation's peoples, its territories, its climates, and so on.

We frame this effort at redescription with the idea of "ecological postmodernism." Both *ecology* and *postmodernism* have risen to considerable prominence in academic circles over the past few decades. Although deriving from somewhat different sources – ecology principally from the sciences and postmodernism principally from the arts and humanities – some interesting compatibilities among these frames exist.

Over the past two decades, postmodern and ecological perspectives have figured prominently in curriculum-theory literature. As Pinar, Reynolds, Slattery, and Taubman (1995) develop, these and a host of other contemporary discourses have been taken up recently, for the most part, in the service of a broad critique of the unified, logical, and totalized conceptions of reality that modernist and analytic philosophies project. As might be expected, there are critics of this shift in sensibility (Muller, 2000; Wraga, 1999). Announced concerns revolve around the tentativeness and self-imposed constraints of emergent discourses. Detractors worry that such delimited perspectives risk a descent into an "anything goes" relativism.

Such criticisms and concerns appear to have some justification, especially as postmodern, ecological, and other discourses have been used in conjunction with, for example, trivialized constructivist accounts of learning (see von Glasersfeld's 1995 critique) or populist versions of critical and emancipatory pedagogies (see Ellsworth's 1988 critique). As educational researchers, we share this concern that an overzealous embrace of radically different ways of thinking has contributed to the rise of new, but not necessarily more informed, classroom orthodoxies.

However, at the same time, we find ourselves taken aback at the sometimes virulent responses of some educational researchers to emergent theoretical discourses. This puzzlement is re-emphasized each year as we contrast the topics and manners of presentation at academic conferences inside and outside Canada. Although meetings of Canadian educational researchers are not without their heated moments, we are under the strong impression that the sorts of ongoing territorial disputes and border skirmishes that we witness at American meetings simply do not occur with the same frequency in Canada – despite the fact that the conceptual diversity among Canadian theorists is at least as broad as that of Americans. (This point is underscored by the disproportionate representation of Canadians in such synoptic texts as Pinar et al., 1995.[1])

We have developed a working hypothesis to help account for the different ways that such ideas seem to be taken up on opposite sides of the Canada–U.S. border. This difference might have something to do with popular habits of Canadian self-identification. In this article, we develop this hypothesis by foregrounding and tracing some of what might be described as Canadian cultural mythology. More specifically, we draw on popular mythologies to understand how they might be knitted through the sorts of curriculum theorizing that Canadian educators have taken up and developed.

In identifying this project, we do not mean to essentialize or reify a Canadian identity. Our intention is quite the opposite, in fact. While we do draw on stereotypes, established histories, and popular media depictions, the aim is not to interrogate, validate, or uncritically embrace such representations, but **to investigate the work that they do with regard to the issue of Canadian self-identification.** The premise is not that popularized conceptions of Canadian identity can capture the complexity of Canadian history and culture, but that they are part of a common sense that is influential.

In other words, **we do not imagine there to be a quintessential Canadian identity.** Nor is it our intention to map out a conclusive argument or a linear narrative that specifies relationships among historic, geographic, or political circumstances and curriculum theory. However, while we explicitly reject the suggestions that theory is *determined* by situation, we believe theory to be *dependent on* situation. Therefore, we are interested in useful (re)description, not totalized explanation.

On that count, we do not invoke ecology and postmodernism to account for a Canadian identity (or lack thereof). Such discourses do not offer explanatory principles. Instead, we are trying to show how the discourses of postmodernism and ecology offer interesting vocabularies for redescribing and reconceptualizing a relationship between Canadian history and culture, and curriculum theory in Canada. Although we offer a number of examples of persons working in the field of curriculum theory in Canada, we have not aimed to provide synoptic review. Rather than providing a comprehensive overview of curriculum theory in Canada, we use citations to support our central thesis.

Postmodernism and the Example of Canada

Neither ecology nor postmodernism can be construed as a consistent or fully coherent discourse. This is particularly the case with postmodernism, which tends to be defined more in terms of what it isn't than what it is. That is, postmodernism isn't modernism (Borgmann, 1992; Madison, 1988; Taylor, 1991). It is thus a rejection of the belief that the universe is unified, finished, and available to a totalized explanation through analytic method. Instead, postmodernism posits that we live in a world of partial knowledge, local narratives, situated truths, and evolving identities (Lyotard, 1984).

The world of the postmodern is relentlessly temporary and endlessly contemporary. It is a constantly emerging reality; one in which metaphor, rather than the logical proposition, is the main means of dealing with collisions between history and memory, language, and geography. As such, postmodern theories are primarily interested in how humans continuously adapt to new conditions of experiences and, at the same time, reinterpret the past. A postmodern sensibility demands endless reinterpretation of conditions and antecedents. There are, it seems, no universal truths and no grand unifying themes in this postmodern world except for one: The diversity of postmodern discourses and practices join in a rejection of modernist claims to reductive and totalizing truths.

On one level, this point of agreement announces a generously diverse range of conceptual possibilities. In repudiating the quest to locate a single narrative to represent conditions of humanity, postmodernists have either rediscovered or invented important interpretive tools (see, for example, Lather, 1991). On another level, however, an uncritical embrace of interpretive multiplicity can quickly take on the character of naïve relativism. In a world still dominated by modernist sensibilities and structures, this latter interpretation is most often assigned to anything postmodern: unanchored, uninformed, incoherent.

Within this frame, an interesting parallel emerges between postmodern discourse and attempts to characterize Canada and Canadian identity. As might be interpreted from the CBC contest, the issue of "who we are" receives a good deal of air play in Canada. Despite the endless discussion, there seems to be only one point of real consensus. While Canadians can't seem to agree on what they are, they have no trouble at all agreeing on what they're not. That is, Canadians seem to define themselves in very much the same terms as postmodernism is defined. This practice of differentiation is not limited to national identities; regional and other forms of variation among Canadian groups and individuals are noticed and represented. Indeed, as will be developed, such variations are inscribed into our legal and educational systems.

To state it concisely, discussions around Canadian identity tend to cluster around claims that Canadians are not overbearing, not totalizing, not monolithic, not unified, not static: or, put more bluntly, Canadians are not Americans. Just as postmodern thought represents an explicit rejection of modernism's two-way mirror of inward-looking rationalism and outward-looking empiricism, so popular Canadian self-definition might be read as an explicit rejection of what is seen as Americanism's two-way mirror of inward-looking nationalism and outward-looking imperialism.

This point was underscored in a highly successful beer advertisement appearing several years previously, which, as such televised commercials often go, had nothing to do (explicitly) with beer. Referred to as "The Rant," the ad featured a young man demonstrating the very Canadian habit of defining national identity in terms of what it is not. Midway through he declares, "I believe in peace-keeping, not policing. Diversity, not assimilation." Although never overtly stated, Canadians did not miss the implication that the nation more given to policing and assimilation was the United States of America.

Ecology and the Example of Canada

"The Rant" begins with, "I'm not a lumberjack or a fur trader. And I don't live in an igloo, or eat blubber, or own a dogsled." This is, of course, a statement about popular Canadian perceptions of the typical American's knowledge of Canada. Anyone who has visited the Canadian Pavilion at the Epcot Center in Florida's Disneyworld would appreciate this objection. There, Canada is represented by a trading post staffed by people clad in the familiar red and black plaid of lumberjacks. The trinkets for sale are mainly coon-skin hats, plush beavers and moose, plastic Mounties, toy rifles with eagle feathers, snowshoes, mittens, maple syrup, and the like. This image of Canada is complemented by a 20-minute 360° movie, given to sweeps over mountains, forests, tundra, and prairie.

Stereotypical representations aside, it is no surprise that climate, geography, and natural resources figure so prominently in these instances of cultural marking. Canada is a resource-rich, geographically diverse, northern country. The topic of the weather, in particular, never seems far from mind. Such references are not simply matters of environmental awareness. They are, rather, indicative of a certain ecological sensibility. To draw an important distinction, *environmental* and *ecological* announce two very different ways of thinking. "Environmental" implies a separation of observer and observed, as it points to concerns with surroundings. In contrast, "ecological" is about relationships, with particular attention to the complex co-evolutions of humans and the more-than-human world (Abram, 1996). The ecologist is interested in the continually evolving relationships of biological and phenomenological worlds, an attention that Merleau-Ponty (1962) described as double-embodiment.

The intertwinings of human and more-than-human have particular relevance to Canadians, for whom physical contexts occupy a large part of our attention. Historically, the European settlers who first tried to hunt and farm these lands were dismayed to learn that Canadian winters were longer and much more severe than those they had known, and that things only seemed to become worse as they pressed westward. Much of the early journal writing by explorers, fur traders, lumberjacks, and homesteaders focused on the challenges of accommodating to the Canadian climate. Despite the fact that we can now control our exposures to such conditions, our habit of talking about the weather continues. As Chambers (1999) notes, an enduring theme in Canadian literature is how physical setting is woven into the psyche. The unpredictable, uncontrollable, and unrelenting characters of landscape, climate, and weather are particularly present in novels and memoirs written in Canada.

In Canadian literature, many works reflect strong interests in the physical, particularly with how human bodies are tied to environmental circumstances. Many of our most prominent works, for example, Ondaatje's *The English Patient* (1992), Michaels's *Fugitive Pieces* (1996), and Urquhart's *The Underpainter* (1997), are developed around the struggles of characters to maintain a coherent personal and collective sense of identity as they age and ail within unforgiving environmental conditions. While this theme is not restricted to Canadian writers, Canadian literary workers tend to share interests in the complex ways that the biological, the geographical, and the phenomenological co-develop.

Ecological Postmodernism and the Example of Canada

With an emphasis on examining the evolving web of interactions that constitute human relations within the more-than-human world, postmodern discourses provide support for ecological discourses. Some postmodern theorists and philosophers regard the field of ecology as a subdiscourse of postmodernism (White, 1998). This move, however, is not always embraced by ecologists themselves, as reflected in contemporary work in ecology that has provided a potent criticism of some postmodern thought. Such discourses, it is argued, tend to be too narrowly focused on the social and the cultural, that is, on the bounded realm of immediate human concern and activity, on the already noticed objects of consciousness (Merchant, 1994). This criticism is especially relevant when it comes to questions of personal knowing and collective knowledge. In particular, ecological thought rejects the mantra of what might be considered *postmodern social constructivism*: All knowledge is socially constructed.

The postmodern social constructivist formulation has figured prominently in the academy since the late 1960s, so much so that it is now regarded in many circles to be commonsense. Many ecologists have noted, however, that such an assertion implies a narrow conception of knowledge, one in which all knowing is seen to occur within realms of human sociality. That is, if all knowledge is understood to be socially constructed, then it makes no sense to suggest that hearts know how to beat, beavers know how to build dams, ecosystems know how to recover from unexpected perturbations, and so on. These examples of knowing and knowledge compel an elaboration of contemporary postmodern discourses, an awareness which in turn should broaden the ways that learning and schooling are discussed.

We offer these linguistic moves, that is, the distinction between *environmental* and *ecological* and the elaboration of *postmodern* concerns through *ecological* discourses, to characterize what we perceive as trends in curriculum theorizing in Canada. For many persons working in the field of curriculum theory in Canada, there is an attention to the complex, co-specifying, mutually affective relationships between actor and circumstance (Chambers, 1999; Jardine, 1992; Smith, 1999; van Manen, 1990). Curriculum theorists in Canada, then, are not so much interested in representing the objects, personalities, or content of their inquiries. Rather, they seem to be fascinated by projects showing the usually invisible relations among these.

It is our impression that much curriculum theorizing in Canada might be described as representing a sort of ecological postmodernism. In addition to curriculum theory, cultural studies, various critical discourses, and continental and pragmatist philosophies – which are domains that have drawn from and influenced postmodernist discourse – ecological postmodernism includes developments in biology, meteorology, geography, geology, neurology, immunology, cognitive studies, and mathematics. The term ecological postmodernism in itself represents an attempt to refuse a dissociation of the biological and the phenomenological, an effort reflected in such recently invented terms as geoepistemology, ecosophy, biomythography, bioethics, neurotheology, ecopsychology, and ecopolitics.

This embrace of theories to account for the complexity of human interaction with the more-than-human world has been represented in curriculum theory in Canada in many ways. In Canada, the moment one raises issues of identity, knowledge, and history – the subject matters of curriculum – one enters the realm of the contextually dependent, the negotiated, and the compromised. Following a long history of learning to create a nation by stitching together geographies, climates, cultures, ethnicities, and languages, curriculum theorists in Canada seem to have learned that meanings and identities are not discovered, nor can they be fully represented. As Canadian historian and political analyst John Ralston Saul (2001) notes, Canada embraced organizing ideas that have only recently been supported by both postmodernism and complexity theories:

> Canadians still see themselves as a society of minorities. They are constantly balancing the centre, the regions, the language groups, and even the importance of the population versus the land. It seems that they believe that taking responsibility for minorities is one of government's principal jobs. (p. A13)

For Canadians, this has meant being prepared to live with a certain sense of ambiguity, a belief that the nation and the identities of Canadians are continually being created. As Saul suggests, the country's continued success in maintaining a nation state has been Canadian's embracing of the idea that nations are made of collections of minority groups and interests, whose identities are continually shaped by the overlappings of history, geography, memory, and language. This point might be better framed by a brief tour through some popular interpretations of moments in Canada's knotted past.

Part 2: . . . Possible, Under the Circumstances

Because we, the authors, have lived significant parts of our lives in different regions of Canada, it has become clear to us that the experience of Canadian identity shifts with changes in geography and language. In Canada, we might not be able to say much about what it means to be a Canadian, but we can, and often do, make clear distinctions among ourselves in terms of region, language, history, and culture. To name only a few examples: Atlantic Maritimers, Francophones in Quebec, Manitoba, New Brunswick, or Ontario, central Canadian urbanites, Aboriginal Canadians (distinguished by region, history, language, and culture). The particularly Canadian patchwork of identities is also alluded to in the descriptive terms "cultural pastiche" or "vertical mosaic" (Porter, 1965), often used to set us apart from the more American melting pot.

The suggestion here is that the noted lack of essential qualities to Canada and Canadian identity may be linked to a certain extent to circumstances of both history and geography. Canada is a post-colonial country, where significant institutional structures may be traced to their associations with Britain. For example, Canadian federal government is a parliamentary structure inherited from this history, in addition to a continued recognition of the British monarchy. At the same time, the effects of proximity to the United States have also provided a pervasive influence. Canada maintains strong economic, political, and cultural relationships with the United States. In contrast to the typical American's general knowledge about Canada (or lack thereof), it is not unusual for Canadians to be up to date on the Dow Jones and the NASDAQ, the latest American presidential election and political scandal, or current Hollywood movies and Billboard charts. Of course, affiliations with the United States extend beyond economic ties, political leanings, and/or pop culture. Those of us involved in the Canadian academy conduct much of our intellectual work within structures that are American or, at least, shared with Americans.

But it would be a mistake to think that our primary identifications and affiliations are with the United States. We are also aligned with other nations. The vitae of a curriculum theorist in Canada will likely include presentations at American conferences and publications in American journals alongside publications and presentations in such countries as England, Australia, South Africa, France, or the Netherlands. Such tendencies toward European (and, to a lesser extent, Asian and African) academic identifications are as much rooted in family lineage, through our history of immigration, as in our history of relationships with the United States.

On the Emergence of Canada

The history of Canada's development as a nation, at least in terms of post-European contact, is one that differs considerably from that of the United States. When the American Civil War ended in 1865, the residents of the lands north of the 49th parallel felt that the Union armies might soon turn their expansionist attentions to resource-rich territories of what is now Canada. Confederation in 1867, then, was prompted in part by worries that the smaller colonies in Central Canada and in the Eastern Maritimes were vulnerable to American intrusion. This was not an unwarranted paranoia; a series of border disputes and American attempts at military invasion punctuated Canada's pre-confederation history.

Much of this wariness was linked to Canadian perceptions of the American attitude toward cultural difference. A century before Canada achieved nationhood, for instance, American commentators such as Benjamin Franklin took no pause in their criticisms of the liberal British attitudes that allowed French to be spoken and Roman Catholicism to be practised in an English colony. Franklin, along with others, advocated an invasion of the territories known as Canada, confident that the population would quickly be incorporated into the norms of American culture. Indeed, the "Quebec Act" of the British parliament, which legislated rights of language and religion for Canada's French population, was one of the final straws, prior to revolution, for Americans set on independence from England.

Canada's cultural and legal commitments to two languages and to distinct cultures predate its official nationhood. Such commitments have given rise to some of the most progressive multicultural policies in the world. With its brief history and its explicit acknowledgment of multilinguistic and ethnic minorities, Canada has never fallen into the error that it is an ethnic nationalist state, nor has it attempted to project an image of a singular or unified nation. As Ignatieff (2000) and Gwynn (1996) have explained, Canada's national identity has not emerged from a long history of shared ethnic or linguistic experiences, but instead has arisen from complex and innovative rights frameworks, social infrastructures, and government services. While an ethnic nationalist state defines its citizens on the basis of common ancestry, language, religion, customs, and rituals – and, in consequence, places a heavy emphasis on the assimilation of other groups into dominant cultural trends – a nation state like Canada derives its unity from common principles rather than common origins.

We do not suggest that common origins cannot be historically traced, nor that these are not officially recognized. The difficulty for Canada has been that it is a country that has emerged from French and English colonial experiments. Although the British North America Act of 1867 is commonly portrayed as the defining moment for Canada as a country, confederation was more a culmination of long processes of negotiation with French, English, and various independent First Nations, including, for example, the Cree, the Ojibway, the Salish, the Blackfoot, and the Shuswap. Canadian Confederation, then, was not so much prompted by shared ethnic experiences or desires for cultural uniformity or independence. Rather, it emerged from ongoing processes of conflict, co-operation, and conciliation. Embedded in the confederation-defining British North America Act of 1867 are historical traces of the ways in which the Dominion of Canada was pieced together through negotiation. Because the colonial powers and the numerous First Nations could not draw on shared language or ancestry as bases for common understanding, they were compelled to develop policies and principles that would be useful in the ongoing challenges of maintaining a national unity, and which might, at the same time, embrace linguistic and ethnic diversity.

Although Canada is a relatively young nation, members of the colonizing nations have lived in parts of what is now Canada since the 1600s. The French settling of Canada, which originally consisted of the territory along the St. Lawrence River and, later, around the Great Lakes, occurred alongside the British colonization of the east coast of North America. These two colonial projects met in what the French called Acadia and what the English called Nova Scotia, a region that passed back and forth between the colonizing nations.

During these imperialist expansions, many First Nations groups who had occupied such areas participated actively in alliances with either British or French colonists and sometimes with both, especially under threat of American expansion. While this article is not the place to provide details, it must be noted that the borders separating Canada from the United States were settled through combinations of disputes between the French and the British, other wars to defend Canada from the Americans, and numerous overlapping skirmishes between and among First Nations groups, rebel groups, and soldiers representing France and England. The very existence of the British and French communities depended in large part on alliances and relationships with First Nations groups. The dependencies were more than that of economic relations through the fur trade; early settlers were also heavily reliant on indigenous peoples' knowledge of how to survive the Canadian climatic extremes. Settlers also enlisted warriors who made pivotal contributions in many military campaigns. Despite this, Aboriginal nations were largely forgotten by both the French and the British at the time of confederation, when the founding nations of the country were officially named as England, Scotland, Ireland, and France.

Canada's early history of nation-making began with compulsions to pay attention to the relationships between national identity and attachments to language, history, ethnic ritual and memory, and the material world (including geography) that comprise or contribute to personal identity. Although not made explicit at the time, a principle in the founding of Canada as a nation was that experiences of individuality were inescapably social experiences. To succeed as a nation, Canada needed to develop a system of governance that embraced the notion that identities, individual and collective, were not pre-given or discovered but were continually invented, including the invention of a national character. It is not surprising, then, that Canadians have some difficulty answering the question of what might be considered as quintessentially Canadian. This is not so much because Canadians lack a sense of who they are, but instead, a logical hesitation that emerges from a long history of having to first look around and interpret current circumstances, and compare these to the remembered and the imagined, before attempting to represent current experiences of identity. Canadian identity is not unified or seamless, but shifts according to the particularity of language, geographical affiliations, and historical circumstances.

On the Emergence of Canadian Curriculum

The history of efforts and events in Canadian curriculum is also inextricably tied to Canada's particular history of nationhood. As Canadian curriculum historian Tomkins (1981) concluded, cultural conflict has been a noticeable theme from the historical beginnings of Canadian schooling, with "bitter social, political and religious controversies which ultimately have hung on the objectives and content, including the materials, of the curriculum" (p. 135). Many examples of struggles have emerged within the history of Canadian schooling: controversies over religion and language, such as demands for separate schools in Upper Canada (the issue of funding for separate schools continues to be controversial in the province of Ontario today); the establishment, and subsequent dismantling, of denominational schools in Newfoundland; the Manitoba Schools Act of 1890.

As with other national institutions mentioned earlier, history and geography have also influenced Canadian educational institutions. Historical trends in curriculum have often mirrored those of the United States or reflected British or French colonial ties. Until after the 1930s, the cultural content of curriculum in English-speaking areas of Canada generally provided a British imperialist or colonial perspective at the expense of addressing Canadian contexts or content (Chambers, 1999). However, the pervasive influence of American curriculum theories began to emerge as Canadian curriculum took up the call of the scientific movement in education in the 1920s, embracing the models of efficiency offered by Ralph Tyler and Franklin Bobbitt (Tomkins, 1979). Here, however, it is also interesting to note a Canadian reluctance to acknowledge this reliance on American ideas; for example, "both in Ontario and British Columbia, the famous British Hadow report of 1926, which ironically acknowledged its own debt to American progressive ideas, was cited in the 1930s as the source of those same ideas" (Tomkins, 1979, p. 9).

In large part the desire to accommodate nations within nations has prompted the formation of formal education in Canada as a shared responsibility of federal and provincial governments, with specific accommodations for local ethnicities, religions, and languages. Public school and post-secondary education in Canada are funded federally, through negotiated transfer payments from the federal government to the individual provincial governments, and provincially, largely through property taxes and, in the case of post-secondary education, through tuition fees. Each province has a minister of education who is responsible for overseeing educational structures and processes, including the development of curriculum content. While implementation of these structures varies from province to province, in most there are processes of collaboration regarding matters of education among representatives from the ministry of education, provincial teachers' organizations, local and provincial teachers' unions, and local school boards and districts. For the most part, and to varying extents, university-based faculties of education also provide input, and, in most provinces, these faculties are also responsible for pre-service, in-service, and post-graduate programs in education.

In the authors' home province of Alberta, for example, there is a long history of co-operation and collaboration among a variety of agencies and institutions. The development of school curricula, for example, has been carried out by teams, with representatives from Alberta Learning (the provincial ministry of education), teachers and consultants from school districts across the province, members of the Alberta Teachers' Association, subject area specialists representing organized councils, and professors from university teacher-education institutions. The resulting curriculum documents usually represent the interests and expertise of these groups, with attention given to the most recent research studies in particular learning and teaching areas. Notable as well is Canadian researchers' proclivity for interdisciplinarity and for cross-cultural and international interests.[2] The current English language arts curriculum in Alberta, for example, includes innovations drawn from research in North America, Great Britain, Western Europe, Australia, and New Zealand. As well, reading lists include reviewed and approved fiction (in both the English and French languages) from many countries worldwide.

Historically, Alberta's curriculum path has involved multiple influences, echoing a number of the themes we have discussed earlier, in terms of their significance to a Canadian sense of nationhood, or, more accurately, the lack of a definitive sense thereof. Events outside the province as well as those of a more regional nature have, over the years, shaped the development of curriculum.

After joining Confederation in 1905, Alberta acquired a school organization, a program of studies, and financial organization from the North-West Territories. The British-oriented curriculum was one that had originated in Ontario, developed by David C. Goggin, who became superintendent of Alberta in 1893 (Sheehan, 1986). Palmer (1982) notes as well that this imperialistic curriculum was, in part, directed by a fear of the immigrant, in a time when record wheat production and an economic boom invited an increase in population through migration.

By the 1920s, curriculum in Alberta, as in schools elsewhere in Canada, attempted to move away from its focus on the Empire. However, as Stamp (1971) suggests, the variety and availability of American resource materials and textbooks was influential. Although American influences in curriculum might not be actively acknowledged, they were ever-present in the classroom and on school library shelves.

Although education is provincially controlled in Alberta and elsewhere in Canada, curriculum has also been influenced by federal interests and decisions. For example, the 1971 national policy on multiculturalism and the focus on national bilingualism led to an increased emphasis on multiculturalism for instruction in Alberta, and affected curriculum in terms of support for French language instruction across the nation (Sheehan, 1986). These efforts have continued to underline the importance of recognizing and supporting diversity within curriculum.

On the Emergence of Canadian Curriculum Theory

One of the earliest and most influential explications of postmodern thought, *The Postmodern Condition* by Jean-François Lyotard (1989), was commissioned in 1979 by Conseil des Universitiés of the government of Quebec. That Quebecers should have enlisted the assistance of a French philosopher for a report on knowledge is indicative not only of strong Canadian ties to Europe, but of Canadians' history of incorporating new threads of thought into the socio-cultural and economic fabric.

On this point, it often seems that writings of Canadian curriculum theorists echo the historical contingencies of Canada's emergence (Aoki, 1991; Barrow, 1979; Egan, 1978; Milburn & Herbert, 1973; Tomkins, 1986). As well, the language used by these theorists tends toward themes of diversity (rather than the bifurcating Otherness) and considered compromise (rather than the domination-seeking standard of the rational argument) – linguistic moves through which writers have attempted to avoid (or at least to trouble) some of the commonsense dichotomies that frame popular discourse. There is also a tendency to embrace what Lyotard (1989) names *"les petits-récits"* (p. xxiv) (roughly translated, small or personal accounts, narratives, or stories, including interpretive cultural histories) rather than grand narratives (Clifford & Friesen, 1993; Connelly & Clandinin, 1988; Leggo, 1997).

While curriculum theory in Canada continues to be developed by persons from a wide array of theoretical positions, a diversity that resists simplistic attempts at summary,[3] this theoretical diversity is accommodated, in part, because Canadians have emerged from their history with a sensibility that resonates with postmodern thought. There are deep commitments to the notions that history is layered in the present, that language cannot represent experience, and that translation is difficult.

Put differently, we could say that that ecological postmodern thought has presented a vocabulary that helps Canadians express an already well-developed sensibility, one that is woven through our national character. In refusing to say with finality who or what we are, Canadians are able to operate in and through what Rorty (1999) calls final vocabularies – the words we can find at this moment to define ourselves and our situation, but that are constantly at risk of being replaced by new final vocabularies. In academia, this license to use whatever final vocabulary presents itself might appear as a certain opportunism, as Canadian theorists seem to draw readily from emergent and divergent discourses. However, not only have Canadian curriculum theorists been willing to incorporate new vocabularies into the study of educational experience, they have also demonstrated an innovative and rigorous interdisciplinarity.

Canada, it seems, has been uniquely positioned to take advantage of theoretical tools from the United States and from western Europe. In most of our university faculties of education, one finds interdisciplinary theoretical work in which North American and European thought is mixed in provocative ways. Of course, these academic tendencies are not restricted to Canadians. However, our informal comparisons of writing that emerges from Canadian-based curriculum scholars to those from other nations indicate a decidedly more pronounced attention to cross-cultural interdisciplinarity. Indeed, one of the difficulties we have encountered in this writing is one of categorization. The work of some of the theorists mentioned in this article has shifted in terms of how it might be categorized and often changed along with geographical moves. As well, we note that a number of individuals we classify as Canadian curriculum theorists originate from roots outside of Canada, though currently doing their work here, or have left for other geographical contexts, often American. The irony of the difficulty in pigeonholing Canadian curriculum theorists in light of our discussions of Canadian identity does not escape us. However, we also expect that these difficulties further underscore the complexity of notions of Canadian identities and thought.[4]

As commentators such as Rorty (1999) and Said (1994) have noted, ideas emerge from people who are situated in particular contexts and who are influenced by particular histories. Images and ideas emerging from fields of postmodernism and ecology emphasize this theme. In this article we have used the example of Canada to emphasize the usefulness of vocabularies emerging from an ecological postmodern sensibility. In so doing, we have been able to create an interpretive shape – a useful fiction – for representing relationships among history, memory, language, and geography, and the ways these interact to form a nation, personal identities, and intellectual work.

For us, this manner of representing curriculum experiences with small, contextually and historically specific narratives is more than an interesting academic exercise. It also operates as a cautionary tale. In times when international projects are popular, as is the case in our home university, and when calls to internationalize curriculum intensify, we are reminded that ways of organizing and interpreting curriculum are always rooted in local needs, worries, desires, and imaginings.

Notes

1   To provide one typical example, in the chapter "Understanding Curriculum as Institutionalized Text," Pinar et al. refer heavily to the work of Canadian curriculum theorists including Robin Barrow, Ted Aoki, Terry Carson, Peter McLaren (who later established himself in the U.S.), Richard Butt, Kieran Egan, John Willinsky, Max van Manen, David Jardine, John Goodlad (another relocated Canadian), Michael Fullan, Jean Clandinin, Michael Connelly, Clermont Gauthier, Andy Hargreaves, Warren Crichlow (originally from the U.S., but now living in Toronto) Hugh Munby, Antoinette Oberg, and Ivor Goodson, among others.

2   Hunsberger (1992), Jardine (1992, 1993), and Smits (1997) are curriculum theorists who provide such examples.

3   To provide only small evidence of this range, we note the work of
     Canadian curriculum theorists working in the areas of psychoanalysis
     (Britzman, 1998; Jagodzinski, 1997; Simon, 1992), Aboriginal education
     (Battiste & Barman, 1995; Haig-Brown, 1995), poststructuralism (Aoki,
     1991; Daignault & Gauthier, 1982; Graham, 1991), gender (de Castell &
     Bryson, 1997; Khayatt, 1992) hermeneutics and phenomenology (Martel
     & Peterat, 1994; Smith, 1999; van Manen, 1990), peace education (Smith
     & Carson, 1998), postcolonialism (Willinsky, 1998) among many other
     areas of possible categorization.

4   We recognize the impossibility of including *all* Canadian curriculum the-
     orists within the space of an essay and apologize to those theorists and col-
     leagues who may not find themselves mentioned here. We believe that the
     purpose of this article, however, is not to provide a compendium of "who's
     who" in Canadian curriculum theory.

References

Abram, D. (1996). *The spell of the sensuous: Perception and language
    in a more-than-human world.* New York, NY: Pantheon Books.

Aoki, T. (1991). *Inspiriting the curriculum: Talks to teachers.*
    University of Alberta Press.

Barrow, R. (1979). *The Canadian curriculum: A personal view.*
    Faculty of Education, University of Western Ontario.

Battiste, M., & Barman, J. (Eds.). (1995). *First Nations education in
    Canada: The circle unfolds.* University of British Columbia Press.

Borgmann, A. (1992). *Crossing the postmodern divide.* University of
    Chicago Press.

Britzman, D. (1991). *Practice makes practice: A critical study of learn-
    ing to teach.* State University of New York Press.

Britzman, D. (1998). *Lost subjects, contested objects: Toward a psy-
    choanalytic inquiry of learning.* State University of New York
    Press.

Chambers, C. (1999). A topography for Canadian curriculum theo-
    ry. *Canadian Journal of Education, 24*(2), 137–150.

Clifford, P., & Friesen, S. (1993). Teaching and practice: A curious plan; Managing on the twelfth. *Harvard Educational Review, 63*(3), 339–357.

Connelly, M., & Clandinin, J. (1988). *Teachers as curriculum planners: Narratives of experience.* New York, NY: Teachers College Press.

Daignault, J., & Gauthier, C. (1982). The indecent curriculum machine. *Journal of Curriculum Theorizing, 4*(1), 177–196.

de Castell, S., & Bryson, M. (Eds.). (1997). *Radical in(ter)ventions: Identity, politics, and difference/s in educational praxis.* State University of New York Press.

Egan, K. (1978). What is curriculum? *Curriculum Inquiry, 8,* 65–72.

Ellsworth, E. (1988). Why doesn't this feel empowering? Working through the repressive myths of critical pedagogy. *Harvard Educational Review, 59,* 297–324.

Gillmor, D., & Turgeon, P. (2000). *Canada: A people's history.* Toronto, ON: McClelland & Stewart.

Graham, R. (1991). *Reading and writing the self: Autobiography in education and the curriculum.* New York, NY: Teachers College Press.

Gwynn, R. (1996). *Nationalism without walls: The unbearable lightness of being Canadian.* Toronto, ON: McClelland & Stewart.

Haig-Brown, C. (1995). *Taking control: Power and contradiction in First Nations adult education.* University of British Columbia Press.

Hunsberger, M. (1992). The time of texts. In W. F. Pinar & W. M. Reynolds (Eds.), *Understanding curriculum as phenomenological and deconstructed text* (pp. 64–91). New York, NY: Teachers College Press.

Ignatieff, M. (2000). *The rights revolution.* Toronto, ON: House of Anansi Press.

Jagodzinski, J. (1997). *Postmodern dilemmas: Outrageous essays in art & art education.* Mahwah, NJ: Erlbaum Erlbaum Associates.

Jardine, D. (1992). Reflections on education, hermeneutics, and ambiguity. In W. F. Pinar & W. M. Reynolds (Eds.), *Understanding curriculum as phenomenological and deconstructed text* (pp. 116–127). New York, NY: Teachers College Press.

Jardine, D. (1993). *Speaking with a boneless tongue*. Bragg Creek, AB: Makyo Press.

Khayatt, M. D. (1992). *Lesbian teachers: An invisible presence*. State University of New York Press.

Lather, P. (1991). *Getting smart: Feminist research and pedagogy with/in the postmodern*. New York, NY: Routledge.

Leggo, C. (1997). *Teaching to wonder: Responding to poetry in the secondary classroom*. Vancouver, BC: Pacific Educational Press.

Lyotard, J. (1984). *The postmodern condition: A report on knowledge* (G. Bennington & B. Massumi, Trans.). University of Minnesota Press.

Madison, G. (1988). *The hermeneutics of postmodernity: Figures and themes*. Indiana University Press.

Martel, A., & Peterat, L. (1994). Margins of exclusion, margins of transformation: The place of women in education. In R. Martusewicz & W. M. Reyolds (Eds.), *Inside out: Contemporary critical perspectives in education* (pp. 151–166). New York, NY: St. Martin's Press.

Merchant, C. (Ed). (1994). *Ecology*. Atlantic Highlands, NJ: Humanities Press.

Merleau-Ponty, M. (1962). *Phenomenology of perception* (C. Smith, Trans.). London, England: Routledge and Kegan Paul.

Michaels, A. (1996). *Fugitive pieces*. Toronto, ON: McClelland & Stewart.

Milburn, G., & Herbert, J. (Eds.). (1973). *National consciousness and the curriculum: The Canadian case*. Toronto: Ontario Institute for Studies in Education.

Muller, J. (2000). *Reclaiming knowledge: Social theory, curriculum and education policy*. London, England: Routledge.

Ondaatje, M. (1992). *The English patient: A novel.* Toronto, ON: McClelland & Stewart.

Palmer, H. (1982). *Patterns of prejudice: A history of nativism in Alberta.* Toronto, ON: McClelland & Stewart.

Pinar, W. F., Reynolds, W. M., Slattery, P., & Taubman, P. M. (1995). *Understanding curriculum: An introduction to the study of historical and contemporary curriculum discourses.* New York, NY: Peter Lang.

Porter, J. (1965). *Vertical mosaic: An analysis of social class and power in Canada.* University of Toronto Press.

Rorty, R. (1999). *Philosophy and social hope.* New York, NY: Penguin.

Said, E. (1994). *Representations of the intellectual: The 1993 Reith lectures.* New York, NY: Pantheon Books.

Saul, J. R. (2001, March 9). My Canada includes the North. *The Globe and Mail,* p. A13.

Sheehan, N. M. (1986). Education, the society and the curriculum in Alberta, 1905–1980: An overview. In N. M. Sheehan, J. D. Wilson, & D. C. Jones (Eds.), *Schools in the West: Essays in Canadian educational history* (pp. 39–56). Calgary, AB: Detselig Enterprises.

Simon, R. (1992). *Teaching against the grain: Texts for a pedagogy of possibility.* Toronto: Ontario Institute of Studies in Education Press.

Smith, D. G. (1999). *Pedagon: Interdisciplinary studies in the human sciences, pedagogy, and culture.* New York, NY: Peter Lang.

Smith, D., & Carson, T. R. (1998). *Educating for a peaceful future.* Toronto, ON: Kagan and Woo.

Smits, H. (1997). Living within the space of practice: Action research inspired by hermeneutics. In T. R. Carson & D. Sumara (Eds.), *Action research as a living practice* (pp. 281–297). New York, NY: Peter Lang.

Stamp, R. M. (1971). Canadian education and national identity. *Journal of Educational Thought, 5,* 133–141.

Taylor, C. (1991). *The malaise of modernity.* Concord, ON: Anansi.

Tomkins, G. S. (1979). Towards a history of curriculum development in Canada. In *The curriculum in Canada in historical perspective, sixth yearbook 1979.* Vancouver, BC: Canadian Society for the Study of Education.

Tomkins, G. S. (1981). Stability and change in the Canadian curriculum. In J. D. Wilson (Ed.), *Canadian Education in the 1980s* (pp. 135–158). Calgary, AB: Detselig Enterprises.

Tomkins, G.S. (1986). *A common countenance: Stability and change in the Canadian curriculum.* Scarborough, ON: Prentice-Hall Canada.

Urquhart, J. (1997). *The underpainter.* Toronto, ON: McClelland & Stewart.

van Manen, M. (1990). *Researching lived experience: Human science for an action sensitive pedagogy.* London, ON: The Althouse Press.

von Glasersfeld, E. (1995). *Radical constructivism: A Way of knowing and learning.* London, England: Falmer Press.

White, D. R. (1998). *Postmodern ecology: Communication, evolution, and play.* State University of New York Press.

Willinsky, J. (1998). *Learning to divide the world: Education at empire's end.* University of Minnesota Press.

Wraga, W. G. (1999). Extracting sun-beams out of cucumbers: The retreat from practice in reconceptualized curriculum studies. *Educational Researcher, 28*(1), 4–13.

NOCTURNE AND FUGUE:
CANADIAN CURRICULUM THEORY AS POSSIBILITY[1]

2

Hans Smits, University of Calgary

Nocturne ...

In dark times, we need to resist the temptation to miniaturize the human spirit. (Cornell, 2010, p. 221)

In this crisis of our present lives in North America, an effort is required to think what we have become. (Grant, 2008/1969, p. 213)

Nocturne: from the Latin *nocturnus*, "of the night"

IN HIS *NOCTURNES* (2009), the novelist Kazuo Ishiguro relates "five stories of music and nightfall." Each of the five stories represent, in achingly melancholic terms, the lives of singular but identifiable individuals and their losses of fleeting and contingent opportunities set against horizons of fading moral and redemptive possibilities. In some ways, they are stories of broken lives and broken relationships and represent troubling glimpses of possibilities that only stay at the margins of everyday life. Yet, glimmers of hope reside in the creative impulse to create music, to make something new and different, even if it cannot make things whole again. Ishiguro's stories are ones of melancholy, that sense of loss that is "hard to tolerate or explain" (Sanchez-Pardo, 2003, p. 215). *Nocturne*, then, is evocative of both the night, what we experience in dark times, and the creative urge to make sense of our feelings of loss.

Ishiguro's stories resonate with my thinking about curriculum and, to borrow a term from music, its contrapuntal qualities. The contrapuntal – the play of counterpoint suggesting the sometimes melodic interweaving of diverse chords and voices but also discordance or dissidence – offers complexity and the invitation to hear differently. Like Ishiguro's nocturnes, curriculum also lives between the difficulties and radical contingencies of life and the hope embodied through the creation of the new. The core mission of curriculum, it could be justifiably argued, is indeed to "think anew" and consider "what we have become," and in educational terms, where we might lead our young, to relate to them "the collective story about our past, present and future" (Grumet, 1981, p.115). It is this question of what is "collective" that is at the heart of any question about possibilities for curriculum, and if anything, what might be Canadian about that.

Thinking about my own career as a teacher in both secondary and post-secondary institutions, I would have found it difficult, if not entirely meaningless, to teach without the sense of curriculum of which Madeleine Grumet writes, without trying to identify what made up my own identity as teacher, and not without, as Ishiguro's nocturnes suggest, the experiences of both loss and hope in being a teacher. Several years ago in a course I took with her when I was then a junior high school teacher, and through her writings, Grumet (1988) provoked the importance of subjectivity – "who we are" (and more challenging, "who was I") – and how that is deeply shaped by gender and our relations to others. My own curriculum journey, so to speak, has revolved around the questions about the difficult relationships between the contexts in which we work and the sources for thinking about what makes one's life possible as a teacher, as someone with responsibility to introduce the world to succeeding generations.

"My work in curriculum theory has emphasized the significance of subjectivity to teaching" (2004, p. 4), William Pinar wrote, and his work has both emphasized and exemplified curriculum theorizing as the complex intertwining of subjectivity, society, culture, and critically, history. Like the characters in Ishiguro's stories, our own lives as teachers can be represented in curricular terms: how we are both shaped by and can shape our work within and against the historical boundaries which are necessarily part of what Grumet and Pinar have named as currere. In thinking about possibilities for curriculum, one of those boundaries – or constellations of boundaries – is the context (e.g., Canada) in which we live and labour.

This chapter was written towards the end of my career as an educator, at least in terms of institutional affiliation and obligations. It represents an attempt to be neither hubristically prescient about what we need in curriculum, nor nostalgic about past achievements in our field. In discussing the idea of "possibility," the ensuing discussion is not a historical overview of curriculum in Canada, nor a synoptic discussion of the contributions of specifically Canadian curriculum theorists.[2] In raising the question about possibilities for "Canadian curriculum theory" it is to accept, in Hannah Arendt's terms, that **we always are caught between the past and the future.** Neither our remembrances of the past nor our predictions for the future can reliably guide our current needs for understanding and actions, as several recent educational writers thinking with Arendt's work have emphasized in their discussions about purposes and aims in education.[3] While it may be debatable in historical terms to suggest that our times are more particularly "dark" with reference to Arendt's work,[4] there is nonetheless the required effort to locate ourselves historically, to go beyond a simple recounting, and to understand that "always there is something that begins and ceases" (Ricoeur, 2004, p. 33). This "effort to recall" and not just espouse a "simple evocation," as Ricoeur (p. 19) suggests, seems to me to be at the heart of thinking about possibilities for curriculum in both historical and spatial terms.

However, what should guide that thinking? Slavoj Žižek's (1993) counsel to eschew more fully our reliance on a "big Other" was written in the shadow of the fall of the Berlin Wall in 1989 and the subsequent demise of the Warsaw Bloc nations and the ideological underpinnings of official communist ideology – one of the "big Others." But the demise of big Others was already underway, as pre-figured in Jean Lyotard's *The Postmodern Condition* (1984) and his announcement of the death of overarching ideologies – such as official communism, but also nationalism and the enlightenment's confidence in endless progress: "a process that releases us from the status of 'immaturity'"; in Kant's terms "enlightenment is defined by a modification of the preexisting relation linking will, authority, and the use of reason" (Foucault, 1984, p.32). The reliance on reason as a way to become more fully human and become engaged in the world through the exercise of will and freedom and along a teleological movement of history is central to the modernist project. The heart of the postmodern critique is the bold questioning of that modernist project, disturbing our certainties about curriculum, its narrative arc of purpose, and the possibilities for engendering sustainable meaning and action in the world. It is a sense of darkness implied by nocturne, a kind of lament for, or melancholia about, engendering strong subjectivities in a failing world (Sanchez-Pardo, 2003, p. 13).

Although it may seem almost passé now to talk about postmodernism in Lyotard's or Žižek's terms, and we may indeed be exhausted by the toll on hope and action that incredulity towards metanarratives may occasion, thinking about "what we have become" in George Grant's words, remains a substantive and urgent task for curriculum theorists and educational workers in general. The question is, what is the nature of that thinking about what we have become? And what, historically and spatially, does that entail?

It is perhaps a naïve question to ask who we are as "Canadian" educators and about the "Canadianness" of our curriculum work. The question suggests a particular form and substance for agency and how we take up our subjectivities within historical context. However, with regard to those possibilities for human agency, two historically dominant narratives: the idea of limitless progress ("the conviction that history has reason, purpose, and direction" [Brown, 2001, p. 5]) and the idea of the "sovereign self" ("fiction of the autonomous, willing, reasoning, rights-bearing subject" [p. 10]) seem to me to be at work in much of curriculum. Like others responding to the postmodern challenge, Wendy Brown asserts that such narratives nonetheless have, over the past century, faltered as foundations for guiding human action and judgment in progressive and remedial ways. Yet, questions of purpose and subjectivity are central to the work of curriculum and cannot escape questions of history nor "psychic significance" (Pinar, 2007, p. xviii).

Arguably, both the idea of progress and the development of sovereign selves are integral, or have been, to the core vision and purposes of Western education, particularly in Canada (Richardson, 2002). In broad terms, education has depended on narratives that link purposes to the idea of progress, enlightenment, and possibilities for individual human enhancement.[5] But as Brown (2001) writes about her experience with students, "Without a notion of progress, my students invariably lament, 'what is the purpose of working for a better world'" (p. 15).[6]

It is a kind of lament echoed by other philosophers concerned about education. In a conversation with Joseph Dunne, Alisdair MacIntyre is quoted as having written the following in an earlier work:

> "The moral content of our educational system is simply a reflection of the moral content of our society," and that "the task of the educator is to stand against a current which will in fact probably overwhelm him"; This was written forty years ago, and later MacIntyre wrote that "teachers are the forlorn hope of the culture of western modernity . . . the mission with which they are entrusted is both essential and impossible." (MacIntyre & Dunne, 2002, p. 1)

In the conversation, Dunne asks MacIntyre, given this rather bleak view, how teachers are to "find truth . . . in this characterization of their task to respond to both sides of it?" – that is, what is "both essential and impossible"?[7]

What MacIntyre and Dunne are referring to as both "essential and impossible" can be interpreted as having to do with a larger crisis: in Arendtian terms, "the crisis of world estrangement" or alienation. As Levinson (2010) and others emphasize, Hannah Arendt's notion of world-alienation is deeply and historically embedded in Western culture and societies and has to do with humans' increasing estrangement from the world through forms of knowledge and organization that have marked the historical development of our societies. Critically, Arendt also addresses the quality of public life, and to what extent what she calls thoughtful "action" is fully possible, when much of life and work has become oriented in instrumental ways – with an ensuing sense of "worldlessness." In a discussion of this, Stephanie Mackler (2010) describes the problem of world alienation and its implications for thinking about education:

> At first glance, such talk of the disappearance of the world might seem hyperbolic, if not simply bizarre. One way to get an immediate feel for this idea . . . is to consider another of Arendt's terms, world alienation. In modern, Western society, there is a widespread feeling of isolation and disconnectedness from both our physical and social world. (p. 510)

Arendt's worldlessness means that we cannot simply assume that there is a world for which we can confidently and unproblematically prepare future generations of young people. To simply accept the world as it is, or as we think it might or ought to be, can be an act of irresponsibility. Arendt's counsel is to think more historically and to ask what our own contemporary world offers or not for the purposes and practices of education and curriculum.

From that perspective, the problem of "world alienation" and what MacIntyre noted as the difficult, if not impossible, "task of the educator is to stand against a current which will in fact probably overwhelm him" has been intensified by more recent historical developments in Canada and other Western societies, namely the development of globalization in its current forms and the adoption of "neoliberal" economic and social policies. As Sennett (2006) has argued, neoliberal policies have severely constrained possibilities for forms of association and human action other than oriented to individual and economic gain. From a recent discussion on the impact of neoliberalism on everyday life, the following provides a broad definition, contributing to a further sense of what is meant by "worldlessness":

> "Neoliberalism" broadly means the agenda of economic and social transformation under the sign of the free market that has come to dominate global politics in the last quarter century. It also means institutional arrangements to implement this project that have been installed, step by step, in every society under neoliberal control. . . . The most dramatic form of commodification is the privatization of public assets and institutions.[8] (Connell, 2010, p. 22–36)

To discuss fully the impact of neoliberal policies on education would require a much greater treatment than I can provide here. Briefly, however, discussions by various authors of the dominance of economic and instrumental thinking has addressed not only questions of the commodification of educational services, but also a greater stress on quantifiable forms of productivity, testing, competition, and narrowed standards of accountability.[9] The "worldlessness," in Arendtian terms, occasioned by neo-liberal policies and their impacts on life, would refer to the limits created on possibilities for human flourishing, and the narrowing of, for example, teaching and learning, to more instrumental and economic ends. Further, the change in institutional contexts and expectations for the work of educators limits the fuller development of what some writers have termed as "capabilities."[10]

Within the framework of neoliberal reforms of institutions, it can be asked how that changes, distorts, or even forecloses on certain possibilities for curriculum that offer hope and imagination.[11] The discussions about world alienation and the limiting of possibilities through narrowed economic interests throw into question the kind of world for which we educate, and realizing possibilities for engendering good teaching.[12] If we accept, or at least are willing to consider, Arendt's historical framing for education and MacIntyre's pessimism about the possibilities for teachers to make the world better, we are left with fundamental questions about the historical role of curriculum. In other words, however arguable our perspectives and interpretations of the current world and what the future might hold, there is nonetheless always the imperative to situate our purposes and to articulate what those might be, to always "think anew," in Arendt's (2003) terms.

In thinking about possibilities for curriculum in Canada, then, Arendt's counsel, and that of Ricoeur, involves the difficult work of historical narration and deciding what both constrains us and what may provide sources for our imagination. "The duty of memory consists essentially in a duty not to forget" Ricoeur suggests (2004, p. 30). Nocturne as a movement in curriculum may be wistful, then, as a recognition or even longing for what is lost, but also a move to strengthen the work of memory, to decide, in a sense, what ought not to be forgotten in our work as educators.

Fugue . . .

Music: a contrapuntal composition in which a short melody or phrase (the subject) is introduced by one part and successively taken up by others and developed by interweaving the parts. Psychiatry: a state or period of loss of awareness of one's identity, often coupled with flight from one's usual environment (*New Oxford American Dictionary*)

"The need to think can be satisfied only through thinking, and the thoughts which I had yesterday will satisfy this need today only to the extent that I can think anew." (Arendt, 2003, p. 163)

Fugue suggests a complex interplay of diverse themes and reflections on identity. There is an inherent ambiguity and ambivalence at work in fugue in that it cannot be reduced to only one chord, motif, or identity. I suggest that such an idea of fugue is consistent with the forms of inquiry that curriculum theorizing invites: the very idea of fugue suggests resistance to closure and provocation to memory in its complex structure and openness to interpretation. Hence the usefulness of Žižek's (1993) term "tarrying." To tarry means to delay, to resist closure, but also, in the origins of the word, to be "against identity." In the form of fugue, to be "against identity" suggests resisting closure to simple representation, allowing instead the interplay of diverse perspectives and voices. Like the complexity of fugue as a musical form, with its interweaving of multiple voices, curriculum, too, lives in such complex form.

In his book, *What is Curriculum Theory?* (2004), the curriculum theorist William Pinar wrote: "The short answer [to the question, 'what is curriculum theory?'] is that *it is the interdisciplinary study of educational experience*" (p. 2; italics in original). Thinking about curriculum as "fugue" by definition invites interdisciplinary inquiry and conceiving of curriculum studies as an interweaving and complex arrangement of diverse narratives and perspectives, particularly the play of subjectivity and society. As those of us who work in the field of curriculum studies appreciate, Pinar has been principally responsible for both the use of the term "currere" and deepening our understandings of what it means to live educational experience.

The contribution of currere has been to complicate the notion of "educational experience." I would cite particularly the work of Hans-Georg Gadamer and his critique of experience as something that we just do, or its reduction to merely technical acts. Relevant to my discussion is the responsibility to develop experience as "an articulation of the world" and to encourage "a form of knowing that presents the missing other half of the truth, a truth that stands alongside the great monologue of the modern sciences" (Gadamer, 2007, p. 273). It is experience as a form of knowing that is central to thinking about curriculum and how it is also historically situated and practised. History is central to experience as currere; as Ricoeur (2004) noted:

> One does not simply remember oneself, seeing, experiencing, learning; rather one recalls the situations in the world in which one has seen, experienced, learned. These situations imply one's own body and the bodies of others, lived space, and . . . the horizon of the world and worlds, within which something has occurred. (p. 36)

Ricoeur's emphasis on the historical qualities for understanding self and relation to others is central to discussing possibilities for curriculum theory in Canada, the terms in which we might describe curriculum theorizing as particularly Canadian, and indeed whether or not it even makes sense to ask that question. In doing so, Pinar's and Ricoeur's stress on the conditions for and of subjectivity are critical to the discussion of that question. In taking up the possibilities for curriculum theory, it is even more important to stress the historical conditions for such work and to consider, as Pinar citing Dwayne Huebner suggests, that "many of us seem to have forgotten the past, and we are unable to imagine the future" (2004, p. 3). The tension that is involved in forgetting and remembering, the flight from questions of who and where we are, are also, metaphorically, conditions of fugue.

The discussion of Hannah Arendt's work by education scholars is important to the discussion of curriculum because it causes us – or should – to think about purposes and frameworks for our thinking and how our ideas and practices are deeply embedded within historical circumstances and change. However, to attempt to situate curriculum as possibility in the Canadian context is not to simply assert one's Canadian identity. As you will see from my reference list and the discussion in this paper, I do try to appeal to some literature that is "Canadian," but also to a much broader set of references. The point is not to be parochial, but to ask how we might read our experiences differently and, at the same time, be open to the absences in our own understanding – about our sources of memory (and how and what we choose to remember) and our sources of forgetting and why.[13] What is at work in complicated conversations is a play between forgetting and memory, a relation that represents " fear of having forgotten, of continuing to forget, of forgetting tomorrow to fulfill some task or other, for tomorrow, one must not forget . . . to remember (Ricoeur, 2004, p. 30).

The very question of sources for complicated conversations – and the work of memory – is critical. **Even though we have great curriculum theorists and practitioners in Canada, arguably our references** – philosophical and theoretical for understanding our lived experiences – **generally come from elsewhere.** Further, as Celia Haig-Brown (2008) reminded us, curriculum in Canada is often wilfully ignorant about indigenous peoples' knowledge. The desire to situate curriculum in Canadian terms requires us to identify our relationships to the historical colonization of First Nations peoples. As well, and again in historical terms, we have also in complicated fashion lived and developed as a nation under American imperial hegemony.

It is interesting that Tomkins (2008) makes fleeting comments on Americanization of curriculum in Canada, but never provides a deeper analysis of the qualities and impacts of that relationship. He does recognize the periodic reactions to Americanization as a desire on Canadians' part for cultural survival. In any event, the question today is perhaps more appropriately understood in terms of globalization and the complex interplay of identity and difference (Jameson, 2009). Globalization can be understood, as I touched on earlier, as the hegemony of a certain kind of free-market capitalism, in line with American interests in the world, or as the celebration of difference occasioned by the democratization of forms communication (Jameson, 2009, p. 436).

Resistance to forms of external hegemony through the articulation of strong and imagined identities or as a looser sense of diversity and difference, nonetheless, poses the risk of fantasizing about a "big Other," in Žižek's terms: that there is a coherent narrative that overshadows our work as educators in Canada or our regions of Canada. Given the overwhelming conditions of globalization, and what that both offers and denies, I am not sure that an argument for Canadian curriculum theory can be made in the name of nationalism, for example. It could be that Canadian nationalism, or the striving to be a nation in conventional terms, is an incomplete project at best and perhaps ultimately something that requires different terms of understanding and possibility – something that George Richardson (2002) argued in his book *The Death of the Good Canadian*. Richardson's study is significant from a curriculum perspective because, as he shows, the resources on which teachers can draw for their work with children around questions of identity is either suspect in terms of hidden or not so hidden hegemonic biases, but also, and perhaps necessarily so, filled with ambiguity.

In wanting to tarry, I also want to say that my response is not comfortably based on a postmodernist stance. Evoking the term "to be against identity" does suggests a fundamental opposition to the rule of any "big Other" or master narrative, but for curriculum studies and curriculum theory, the question of identity is nonetheless central, as I noted earlier. The postmodern response to identity carries with it the temptation even in its deconstruction of a "big Other," to posit other, albeit fragmentary and uncertain, situated identities (Borgmann, 1992; White, 2000). Žižek (2008) parodies various responses to the triumph of capitalism (e.g., from New Ageism to forms of spirituality and ecological movements), which reintroduce forms of identity which are perhaps "weaker" in character, but nonetheless create subject positions in individualistic terms. Such subject positions, in Žižek's analysis, demonstrate the limitations of discourses that celebrate experience without a more rigorous narrative of oppositional and more collectively oriented critique.

One of our challenges in curriculum is that even as we have appealed to postmodern perspectives we have not yet addressed fully the legacy and ongoing impacts of modernism in our cultural and educational lives (e.g., the critique of schooling and notions of the public that have roots in modernist notions of space, time, development, and enlightenment). In two significant discussions of curriculum in Canada, Chambers (2003) and Sumara, Davis, & Laidlaw (2001),[14] I found it interesting that in asking the question about the identity of Canadian curriculum theory, both essays appeal to the phrase "possible, under the circumstances." I interpret it as a kind of implied limit situation for a Canadian curriculum theory, but the nature of that limit or limits are not fully explored. More evident in Chambers, but only implicit in Sumara et al., are suggestions about American hegemonic influences, the impacts of geography, and more generally the diverse regional realities and histories that characterize Canada as a nation. The idea that Canadian curriculum is possible, but within limits, raises questions for what that means and for defining "what we have become," to echo George Grant.

This question of meaning in the context of difficult and complex cultural and historical situations is something addressed very thoughtfully by Jonathan Lear in his masterful essay *Radical Hope* (2006). Although he is not a curriculum theorist, Lear's questions are profoundly pertinent to curriculum in terms of linking language and concepts to hope and what he calls "longing":

> Part of the sustenance our parenting figures will give us is the concepts with which we can at least begin to understand what we are longing for. This is critical for acquiring a natural language: inheriting a culture's set of concepts through which we can understand ourselves as desiring, wishing, and hoping for certain things. (2006, pp. 122–123)

Thinking in terms of fugue, then, raises questions about how we might remember who we are, in Ricoeur's terms, engaging in the work of memory and history. One example is Chambers's reference to the work of Harold Innis (1956). Innis was best known for his "staples" theory of development and how Canada's dependence on the exploitation and export of natural resources (e.g., the fur trade, lumber, fishing, minerals and arguably carrying on today in terms of mining, oil and gas, and large-scale mono-agriculture) influenced social and cultural development in Canada. The historical importance of Innis to understanding historical context is oriented to looking at the peculiarities of development in Canada, the development of social class structure, and what would be a more recent ecological perspective – the nature of Canadians' relationship to the land, space, and nature. In her paper on Canadian curriculum theory, Chambers (2003) very nicely makes the point that Innis's work in part helps to explain the kinds of relationships European settlers and colonists imposed on First Nations people.

What is the point of raising this with relation to the possibilities for Canadian curriculum theory and the conditions of its possibility? A major part of doing a genealogical history of curriculum in Canada would attempt to contextualize various educational narratives within historical, social, economic, and cultural conditions. Such contexts, while not determinative of subjectivity, nonetheless provide contingent conditions for our sense of place, identity, and social structure. In other words, to conduct a historical inquiry into curriculum would be to focus on the sources for self and subjectivity that characterize our contemporary lives, to raise questions about the qualities and relationships that Canadian communities have to the land, and the qualities of social class and cultural relations unique to Canada (or specific regions of Canada). Questions like those do not make us very different from other peoples around the globe, whose lives and economies depend on the exploitation of resources. But it is worth asking what is particularly Canadian about that and, more pertinently, how it allows for understanding ourselves.

Raising the question about what is "possible under the circumstances" can, however, lead us to consider that the answers are not only in alternative theories, but that they can also be understood in terms of the kinds of questions posed by Lear: *"for what may we hope?"* and *"what ought I to do?"* (2006, p. 103; italics added).

Framing the question about possibilities for Canadian curriculum studies in terms of those kinds of questions suggest further avenues of inquiry, which would start with questions like those offered by Lear. Such questions suggest the complexity of fugue as a structure for curriculum inquiry and its possibilities. I will mention three related themes or motifs of such a fugue: the historical, the nature of understanding place, and globalization as a challenge.

First of all, there is the question of the adequacy of our historical knowledge and the quality of historical inquiry in curriculum work in Canada. I recall speaking on a panel to a group of social studies teachers about the new social studies program in Alberta and the question of assessment; what struck me about that is that our histories as educators can be so quickly erased – a loss of memory, the meaning of fugue in its psychic sense: a forgetting who we are. Few of the teachers present at the session I spoke at had any memory of the struggles that went on in Alberta (by practicing teachers) to insist on making inquiry-based learning, with an emphasis on encouraging children to engage in meaningful social action, a central part of the social studies program. In Pinar's (2007) terms, there is both a loss of the sense of "verticality" in curriculum (that curriculum always has deep history, embedded in sometimes unwritten practices), but also a kind of thrall to the present, and that curriculum is always presented as something about what is needed now, a kind of thrall to the new. Thus, I realize in posing the question of Canadian curriculum studies that there is much work to be done in both recovering – and I will put this in the plural – various histories, but to also see them in terms of the complex relationships between groups of people, social forces, and the structure and content of the stories which are told – or sometimes not.

Building on Chambers's work, what would need to be articulated are not only the contributions of curriculum theorists in Canada but also a more extensive genealogy of the content of that work and how it is oriented. Pinar's (2007) recent work on "verticality" and "horizontality" in curriculum inquiry provides a framework and examples for engaging in such work; he suggests the urgent need to understand curriculum theories and our understanding of the disciplines in the complex intersections between history and current contexts.[15]

Secondly, it may well be that there is a history of public schooling that is unique to Canada or at least visions and experiences of public life that are peculiar to the places and regions in which we live in Canada. Whether or not one can appeal to certain aspects of the ethos of national or regional cultures, whether mythical or not – such as the more collectivist roots of Canadian life as opposed to individualist forms south of the border – curriculum theory has an obligation to bring forward and explore the roots or, to use Charles Taylor's (1989) term, "sources of the self."

The question of our relationships to place and the way that it has been taken up in some recent curriculum writing is something I find problematic. I understand the impulse to locate ourselves in and through identifications with the places in which we find ourselves and through that to claim something more primordial about our relationships to where we live. The romanticization of place in much curriculum writing is perhaps an antidote to our instrumental relation to things. But there is nonetheless what I would call a kind of nostalgia embedded in some of that work (although, more charitably, perhaps a kind of "longing" that Lear identifies as an aspect of our desires to locate and name).[16]

Perhaps alternative narratives, including fiction, can encourage us to re-imagine our lived spaces and our historical connections to them in ways that tug with greater force at the experiences of lived space. I will only offer a very few examples: Guy Vanderhaege's *The Englishman's Boy* (1996); Rudy Weibe's novels about the experiences of Big Bear; Sharon Butala's *Perfection of the Morning* (1995); Aretha van Herk's *Places far from Ellesmere* (1990); and Sinclair Ross's bleak evocation of life in Saskatchewan during the 1930s drought and depression *As For Me and My House* (1957), which acts as an antidote to W. O. Mitchell's much more romantically and nostalgically inclined work *Who Has Seen the Wind* (1947).

What texts like these offer is a rereading of our imagined – or perhaps even ideologically framed – relation to place; both Vanderhaege and Butala, writing about the same geographic area (southeastern Saskatchewan), remind us vividly that First Nations peoples' blood and artifacts are embedded in the earth, literally soaked with blood, but hidden by the stories that non-Native people have privileged as history, a deliberate forgetting, in Ricoeur's terms. It could be that our relationship to place, while remembered romantically, is actually marked by other than care, which the work of Innis reminds us; that is, our relationship to land has been one of exploitation, which has created both limits and possibilities for cultural and social forms and the narratives that we create to represent those.

Nonetheless, there is something to be recovered here. The point is that **stories matter, and how we tell them matters even more**, as Thomas King (2003) suggested in his work on stories. My example of Innis above suggests that our stories about place cannot be told in the absence of understanding the deep impulses of exploitation of the land and the social relations of production that privilege certain people and certain things over others. In the discussion of both history and place, then, the question of knowledge and traditions are paramount. Postcolonial, indigenous, and other counter narratives are critical for understanding possibilities for curriculum; at the same time we might ask what these stories hold in relation; while postmodernism resists totalizing discourses, there is still something which is required to hold things together, or in perspective, or in tension. Jameson (2009) suggests what could be applied to possibilities and imperatives for curriculum theorizing, which involves questioning "the categories themselves, the modes and forms of thought in which we inescapably have to think things through, but which have a logic of their own to which we ourselves fall victim if we are unaware of their existence and their informing influence on us" (p. 454).

Thirdly, there is the question of globalization. It can certainly be argued that globalization has made us, in very real and everyday terms, part of one world. Žižek's point, mentioned at the outset of my discussion, is that while at one time we might have relied on some "big Other" to define ourselves differently – nationalism, Communism, or liberalism, for example – the reality is that to base identification on such master narratives has become problematic at best. However, as both Perry Anderson (2007) and Jameson (2009) have written, globalization is not a unitary process, even as it flattens out the world in the name of capitalism and production. While globalization has its roots (in more recent human history) in the modernist impulse to "conquer" the world and nature, it has also opened both the possibility and need to understand – and indeed take responsibility for – the "other" (Kapus´cin´sky, 2008).

The French philosopher Alain Badiou (2008a, 2008b) has raised provocative questions for the work of critique in our altered world (and this has become even more accentuated by the global financial crisis), which also speak to the work of curriculum theory. He noted, in a way that I think addresses my concern about the conditions of possibility that "the political problem . . . has to be reversed. We cannot start from an analytic agreement on the existence of the world and proceed to normative action with regard to its characteristics. *The disagreement is not over qualities but over existence*" (2008a, p. 38; italics added).

If we are to follow Badiou (and I think also Lear), the direction of our curriculum work must be to "focus on the conditions of existence, rather than just improving its methods" (Badiou, 2008a, p. 37). What has become difficult of course is to find a point, as he argues, "that would stand outside the temporality of the dominant order and what Lacan once called the 'service of wealth'" (Ibid.). Badiou asks what the consequences would be of thinking about globalization as "one world" and responds evocatively:

> A first consequence is the recognition that all belong to the same world as myself: the African worker I see in the restaurant kitchen, the Moroccan I see digging a hole in the road, the veiled woman looking after children in a park. That is

where we reverse the dominant idea of a world united by
objects and signs, to make a unity in terms of living, acting
beings, here and now. (2008a, p. 39)

Badiou describes such possibilities for linking us in the struggle for
understand and building a better world, a "performative unity." For
example, to his assertion that globalization means "there is only one
world," he responds with the statement that "this is not an objective
conclusion. It is performative: we are deciding that this is how it is for
us" (2008a, p. 38). Citing Lacan, he notes that on the one hand we
can turn to the "big Other" for comfort and to assuage our guilt or
depression, or we can turn to the performance of certain virtues or
dispositions as something which might unite us – courage, for example, which "is the virtue which manifests itself through endurance in
the impossible" (2008a, p. 41). Jonathan Lear also writes that our
inquiries "are directed to a future goodness that transcends our current ability to understand what it is" (2006, p. 103). I think that these
ways of defining "theorizing" in terms of performativity is a call to
responsibility.

In referring to nocturne and fugue – the complex interplay of
darkness and a contrapuntal retelling of the world – I am trying to
point to possibilities for curriculum in Canada. Perhaps this does not
make it particularly Canadian, but it can be Canadian in its exemplary reference to the kinds of historical and geographic experiences and
relations to the global that have defined us and offer sources for redefinition.

A possibly compelling way to think about how our work is framed
is reference to Ricoeur's notion of the relation between ideology and
utopia, and the ways in which thoughts and actions are always situated historically between what was, what exists, and what is imminent
or possible. Such a discussion is oriented to understanding the difficulties of our responsibilities and the frames through which we practice our inquiries and develop our responsibilities. Ricoeur (1991)
states, helpfully I think, that examining the relationship between ide-

ology and utopia serves as a "theory of cultural imagination"(p. 308). We can think about curriculum through the interplay of ideology, a recognition of those narratives that both offer opportunities and constraint – and distortions – for understanding, and utopia, which is to think beyond those limits offered to us at any historical moment.

> This interplay of ideology and utopia appears as the interplay of the two fundamental directions of the social imagination. The first tends towards integration, repetition, and a mirroring of the given order. The second tends to disintegration because it is eccentric. But the one cannot work without the other. (p. 323)

Ideology and utopia are counterpoints, a contrapuntal play of diverse themes and possibilities that mark the idea of fugue and the idea of curriculum as what Pinar (2004) has called a "complicated conversation." Ricoeur's notion of the relation between ideology and utopia, the necessary aporia that it presents (in Arendt's terms always caught between the past and future) suggest that in part, at least, our work in curriculum is to inquire into the conditions that limit or enhance possibilities for thinking about what is possible.

In *Radical Hope* (2006), Lear starts with a statement by Plenty Coups, the Chief of the Crow First Nation when it suffered defeat and, therefore, the loss of their livelihood and culture, in the late nineteenth century. Lear cites Plenty Coups saying that after the defeat by colonizing forces and the loss of the buffalo "the hearts of my people fell to the ground, and they could not lift them up again. After this, nothing happened" (2006, p. 2). Lear writes that this statement in its stark enunciation reflected a profound loss of hope, and he asks what this statement, "after this, nothing happened," could possibly mean. He argues that hopelessness arises when commonplace languages, practices, and concepts we know are no longer sustained by the actual conditions of our living, when they no longer make sense. Rethinking our concepts, and finding ways to meaningfully relate those to practices on the other hand, may occasion radical hope. Lear characterizes the practice of radical hope as that of requiring practical reasoning, and the exercise of "virtues" such as courage and imagination.

To conclude, I refer back to the earlier discussion in the paper: the challenges posed by Arendt's concerns about the difficulties of preparing our students for the world but within constraints posed by the historical conditions in which we find ourselves today. The Arendtian critique, as Levinson (2010) and others have noted, is that "preparation" of young people often is narrowly conceived in terms of being prepared in vocational terms to enter the world as it is. So for example, we might emphasize technical proficiency in the use of computers but not engage children in questions about the greater responsibility to live well with others in the world. Curriculum inquiry, then, is not just about designing better methods for educating our young, but also to focus on "conditions of existence" (Badiou, 2008, p. 20).

Focusing on the conditions of existence suggest inquiry that is avowedly utopian in orientation because it asks us to think about what it means to live well and what that means in ethical and socially responsible ways, and particularly so in the contexts of failed or failing principles and narratives. But utopian thinking also needs to understand practice, to take us back to ourselves more fully and to build capacities for ongoing understanding. Perhaps that is where our work in curriculum begins, and how we begin to also dwell productively with others in the conduct of our diverse needs and responsibilities.

The dark side of curriculum is to fall prey to the immediate and to foreclose on other than technique and instrumentality – a melancholy nocturne indeed. Promise and hope lie in the joys and possibilities of creating knowledge, in experiencing the fecundity of social reason, and in glimmerings of what it means to take up responsibility for the world, as difficult and daunting as that sometimes may seem. In Arendtian terms, it is a challenge to live currere in the interest of enhanced human action, generating language for what is necessary, imminent, and celebratory of our relations to other humans, but also the larger world. It is to conduct inquiry as "tarrying with the negative" (Žižek, 1993, p. 237), to think with and against the grain of existing knowledge and practice. Such ways of thinking may define curriculum theory as possibility, and as well, define ourselves in Canadian terms as honouring both the specificity of our locales, but also our openness to the world and the other.

Notes

1   This chapter is a substantial revision and extension of two previously published papers (Smits, 2008, 2010).

2   The best overview to date of the work of Canadian curriculum theorists in my opinion is that of Chambers (2003), which particularly covers the work of Canadian curriculum theorists who were influenced by the reconceptualist movement. More recently, William Pinar has provided a critical and historical introduction to the re-issue of George Tomkins *Stability and change in the Canadian curriculum* (2008) which provides a critical entry point to the historical discussion of curriculum studies in Canada.

3   The February 2010 issue of *Teachers College Record* is dedicated to essays dealing with the implications of Arendt's work for thinking about education, and particularly the conundrum or challenge of teaching in "worldless times," and how educational practices and institutions are deeply implicated in the problem of world alienation.

4   See the recent collection of writings on the influence of Hannah Arendt's work (Berkowitz, Katz, & Keenan, 2010) which represents a conversation around the need for "thinking in dark times." The notion of dark times can be understood as both the overwhelming sense of tragedy that is befalling the world at the time I am writing this – the various ongoing wars, flooding in Pakistan, Sri Lankan refugees, environmental degradation: the general sense of precariousness (Butler, 2004) that such events occasion in our experiences, even where we are nominally safe – but also darkness in Arendt's terms as our collective and individual inabilities to respond more fully to such disasters (disaster means literally to lose one's star [Caputo, 2010]), to be able to recognize and "frame" (Butler, 2009) them in ways that can narrate hope and possibility. The theme of "darkness," a kind of melancholic nocturne about the present, is pervasive in current literature.

Some recent examples include Gilligan and Richards (2009), Žižek (2008), and more recently, Žižek (2010), which takes up the terminal crises of the ecological, economic, and other global situations in the world, seen through the lenses of the stages of mourning. Such discussions can be read as critical laments for the eclipse of emancipatory movements, but a with call for their re-thinking in different terms.

5   For a brief but compelling discussion of what might be termed the humanist purposes of education see Hans-George Gadamer (2001). Gadamer emphasizes, that "the humane capabilities are the ones to stress if one is to educate and to cultivate oneself, and that only then, when we succeed in that, will we also survive without the damage from the progress of technology and technicity." (p. 537). Gadamer's comments were offered in the context of a broader and critical discussion around the notion of understanding education as bildung, a concept that is difficult to translate into current educational practices, but speaks to a form of education that allows for the nurturing of capacities that capture Kant's ideas about linking will, authority, and the use of reason in becoming more fully human. In defense of Gadamer's ideas about self cultivation, he does raise alarms about educational and curriculum outcomes that are narrowly conceived in technicist and utilitarian ways. The critique of what Gadamer writes – and the idea of bildung – involves the broader historical context for supporting certain ways of being, or certain forms of subjectivity, to put it in other words.

6   Brown explores the problem of how "commitments to knowledge, questioning, and intellectual depth [have] been overtaken" by certain kinds of fundamentalism (2001, p. 37). She asks this in the context of weakened social bonds and structures that have emerged as a consequence of neoliberal policies, which I will come back to further on.

7   Both writers are known as "neo-Aristotlean" in their recasting the meaning of practice in contemporary contexts. For example, in his account of virtues, MacIntyre has emphasized the importance of ethical actions and understandings as practices – which is different from the application of knowledge to practice (MacIntyre, 1981). As Dunne (1993) has written, "I have stressed the way in which, with the help of a range of Aristotelean concepts, one can formulate the capacity for appropriate responses to particular situations which is essential to good performance in any practice" (p. 378).

8   A recent collection of essays on the impact of neoliberal policies on institutions and is *Neoliberalism and everyday life* (Braedley & Luxton, 2010). Another very interesting discussion of the impacts of neoliberalism on everyday life and its effects on self and identity – or subjectivity – is the

work of Richard Sennett (2006). Sennett argues that the "new capitalism" has served to weaken social bonds, lessening the possibilities for commitments, common purposes, and ends.

9   The curriculum scholar David Smith (2003, 2006a, 2006b, 2008) (Faculty of Education at the University of Alberta) has written several essays exploring the impact of what he has termed "market fundamentalism" on educational life and practices. Smith's work is important in educing how certain kinds of educational practices and the narrowing of teaching and learning to instrumental and limited ends has deep roots in Western forms of thought, exacerbated in more recent history through the impacts of heightened capitalist globalization and the social forms and restraints that impose on possibilities for education that speaks more truthfully to human ends and needs.

10   For a relevant discussion of the "capability" approach to understanding human practices, see Deneulin, Nebel, & Sagovsky (2006). In the opening essay, Paul Ricoeur speaks to the importance of social arrangements and institutions to the recognition of persons: "The idea is that individuals may be held to be 'great' or 'small' according to the evaluations ruling specific categories of social activities" (Ricoeur, 2006, p. 25). Social and institutional activities are given importance in how human activity is evaluated, how we think about practices, and the kind of world to which they are oriented.

11   Charles Taylor (1991) has discussed this in terms of the "malaise of modernity"; such malaise has intensified under neoliberalism: in Taylor's terms, "the fading of moral horizons," "the eclipse of ends," and a loss of freedom. Examples would include the stress on certain forms of individualism that constrain possibilities for individual authenticity, and intensified forms of instrumental actions, in the absence of more meaningful and overarching narratives of possibility.

12   See a very interesting recent discussion of how two dominant trends within the "neoliberal" construal of education – narrowed forms of testing and quantitative measures and "choice" – have impacted and limited fuller possibilities for teacher professionalism in Hirsch (2010). The article is a review of a recent book by Diane Ravitch (2010). Particularly relevant for the discussion in this paper is what Ravitch claims is the overemphasis on "teacher effectiveness" or quality: "She does not doubt that good teachers are supremely important, but argues that reformers are guilty of an oversimplification when they isolate this variable from the many factors that have made schools ineffective" (Hirsch, 2010, p. 17). Ravitch's new work is somewhat ironic, to say the least, given her previous support for movements like "accountability" and competition in education. But to her cred-

it, her new work recognizes what I am arguing in this paper, namely that certain forms of social and political organization are limiting of broader and deeper aims of education.

13   In his discussion of the relationship between memory and forgetting, Ricoeur (2004) notes especially the problem of assuming that the present can be experienced as having either no history or future. Pinar (2004, 2007) as well writes of the problem of "presentism" in educational practice and theorizing.

14   Another significant set of writings, which particularly address curriculum in terms of Canadian contexts, is that edited by Hasebe-Ludt and Wanda Hurren (2003).

15   Pinar's reintroduction of George Tomkin's work, cited earlier, at once demonstrates the work not only of historical recovery, but also of how we might read such work in the contexts of understanding ourselves and our inquiries in the present. Tomkin's work is exemplary of a certain kind of historical rendering of education, but what it still lacks is the complex discussion of ties between memory, place, and forms of narration (Ricoeur, 2004) – or in Jameson's (2009) terms, a more dialectical reading of history – to account for the interplay of diverse and sometimes opposing forces; for example, that identity and difference are always defined in terms of each other. Globalization, Jameson argues, is a case in point of how its impacts cannot be more fully understood without understanding the play of identity (the drive for sameness) and difference (the possibilities for other than what is). (pp. 454–455).

16   I would consider some of the chapters in Hasebe-Ludt and Hurren (2003) to reflect qualities of the kind of longing that Jonathan Lear identifies as an aspect of radical hope. It is perhaps the quality of the writing and representations that tend to suggest

References

Anderson, P. (2007). Jottings on the conjuncture. *New Left Review*, 48, 5–37.

Arendt, H. (2003). *Responsibility and judgement* (J. Kohn, Ed.). New York, NY: Schocken Books.

Badiou, A. (2008a). The communist hypothesis. *New Left Review*, 49, 29–42.

Badiou, A. (2008b). Roads to renegacy. *New Left Review*, 53, 125–133.

Berkowitz, R., Katz, J., & Keenan, T. (Eds.). (2010). *Thinking in dark times. Hannah Arendt on ethics and politics.* New York, NY: Fordham University Press.

Borgmann, A. (1992). *Crossing the postmodern divide.* University of Chicago Press.

Braedley, S., & Luxton, M. (Eds.). (2010). *Neoliberalism and everyday life.* Montreal, QC: McGill-Queen's University Press.

Brown, W. (2001). *Politics out of history.* Princeton University Press.

Butala, S. (1995). *The Perfection of the morning: An apprenticeship in nature.* Toronto, ON: Harper Perennial.

Butler, J. (2004). *Precarious life: The powers of mourning and violence.* London, England: Verso.

Butler, J. (2009). *Frames of war: When is life grievable?* London, England: Verso.

Caputo, J. (2010, June 23–25). Symposium on radical hermeneutics. Canadian Hermeneutics Institute. Toronto, ON.

Chambers, C. (2003). "As Canadian as possible under the circumstances": A view of contemporary curriculum discourses. In W. F. Pinar (Ed.), *International Handbook of Curriculum Research* (pp. 221–252). Mahwah, NJ: Lawrence Erlbaum.

Connell, R. (2010). Understanding neoliberalism. In S. Braedley & M. Luxton (Eds.), *Neoliberalism and everyday life* (pp. 22–36). Montreal, QC: McGill-Queens University Press.

Cornell, D. (2010). Thinking big in dark times. In R. Berkowitz, J. Katz, & T. Keenan (Eds.), *Thinking in dark times: Hannah Arendt on ethics and politics* (pp. 221–227). New York, NY: Fordham University Press.

Deneulin, S., Nebel, M., & Sagovsky, N. (Eds.). (2006). *Transforming unjust structures: The capability approach.* Dordrecht, Netherlands: Springer.

Dunne, J. (1993). *Back to the rough ground: Practical judgment and the lure of technique.* Notre Dame University Press.

Foucault, M. (1984). What is Enlightenment? In P. Rabinow (Ed.), *The Foucault reader* (pp. 32–50). New York, NY: Pantheon Books.

Gadamer, H.-G. (2001). Education is self-education. *Journal of Philosophy of Education, 35*(4), 529–538.

Gadamer, H.-G. (2007). Greek philosophy and modern thinking. In R. Palmer (Ed.), *The Gadamer reader: A bouquet of later writings* (pp. 266–273). Evanston, IL: Northwestern University Press.

Gilligan, C., & Richards, D. (2009). *The deepening darkness: Patriarchy, resistance, and democracy's future.* New York, NY: Cambridge University Press.

Grant, G. (2008/1969). Time has history. In *More lost Massey Lectures: Recovered classics from five great thinkers* (pp. 210–272). Toronto, ON: House of Anansi.

Grumet, M. (1981). Restitution and reconstruction of educational experience: An autobiographical method for curriculum theory. In M. Lawn & L. Barton (Eds.), *Rethinking curriculum studies* (pp. 115–129). New York, NY: Halsted Press.

Grumet, M. (1988). *Bitter milk: Women and teaching.* University of Massachusetts Press.

Haig-Brown, C. (2008, May 30). Keynote address to the Canadian Association for Curriculum Studies annual pre-conference *Locating Canadian Curriculum Studies in Global Traditions.* University of British Columbia.

Hasebe-Ludt, E., & Hurren, W. (Eds.). (2003). *Curriculum intertext: Place/language/pedagogy.* New York, NY: Peter Lang.

Hirsch, E. (2010). How to save the schools. *The New York Review of Books, 57*(8), 16–19.

Innis, Harold. (1956). *The Fur Trade in Canada: An Introduction to Canadian Economic History* (Rev. ed.). University of Toronto Press.

Ishiguro, K. (2009). *Nocturnes: Five stories of music and nightfall.* Toronto, ON: Alfred A. Knopf.

Jameson, F. (2009). *Valences of the dialectic.* London, England: Verso.

Kapus´cin´sky, R. (2008). *The other.* London, England: Verso.

King, T. (2003). *The truth about stories: A native narrative.* Toronto, ON: House of Anansi.

Lear, J. (2006). *Radical hope: Ethics in the face of cultural devastation.* Cambridge, MA: Harvard University Press.

Levinson, N. (2010). A "more general crisis": Hannah Arendt, world alienation, and the challenges of teaching for the world as it is. *Teachers College Record, 13*(2), 464–487.

Lyotard, J.-F. (1984). *The postmodern condition: a report on knowledge.* University of Minnesota Press.

MacIntyre, A. (1981). *After virtue.* University of Notre Dame Press.

MacIntyre, A., & Dunne, J. (2002). Alasdair MacIntyre on education: In dialogue with Joseph Dunne. *Journal of Philosophy of Education, 36*(1), 1–19.

Mackler, S. (2010). And worldlessness, alas, is always a kind of barbarism: Hannah Arendt and the challenge of education in worldless times. *Teachers College Record, 112*(2), 509–532.

Mitchell, W. O. (1947). *Who has as seen the wind.* Toronto, ON: Macmillan of Canada.

Pinar, W. (2004). *What is curriculum theory?* Mahwah, NJ: Lawrence Erlbaum.

Pinar, W. (2007). *Intellectual advancement through disciplinarity: Verticality and horizontality in curriculum studies.* Rotterdam, Netherlands: Sense Publishers.

Ravitch, D. (2010). *The death and life of the great American school system: How testing and choice are undermining education.* New York, NY: Basic Books.

Richardson, G. (2002). *The death of the good Canadian: Teachers, national identities and the social studies curriculum.* New York, NY: Peter Lang.

Ricoeur, P. (1991). Ideology and Utopia. In K. Blamey & J. Thompson (Trans.), *From text to action: Essays in hermeneutics* (Vol. 2, pp. 308–324). Evanston, IL: Northwestern University Press.

Ricoeur, P. (2004). *Memory, history, forgetting* (K. Blamey & D. Pelletier, Trans.). University of Chicago Press.

Ricoeur, P. (2006). Capabilities and rights. In S. Deneulin, M. Nebel, & N. Sagovsky (Eds.), *Transforming unjust structures: The capability approach* (pp. 17–26). Dordrecht, Netherlands: Springer.

Ross, S. (1957). *As for me and my house.* Toronto, ON: McClelland & Stewart.

Sanchez-Pardo, E. (2003). *Cultures of the death drive: Melanie Klein and modernist melancholia.* Durham, NC: Duke University Press.

Sennett, R. (2006). *The culture of the new capitalism.* New Haven, CT: Yale University Press.

Smith, D. (2003). Curriculum and teaching face globalization. In W. Pinar (Ed.), *The new international handbook of curriculum studies* (pp. 35–51). Mahwah, NJ: Lawrence Erlbaum.

Smith, D. (2006a). On enfraudening the public sphere: The futility of empire and the future of knowledge after "America". In M. Peters & J. Freeman-Moir (Eds.), *Edutopias: New utopian thinking in education* (pp. 65–78). Rotterdam, Netherlands: Sense Publishers.

Smith, D. (2006b). Troubles with the sacred canopy: Global citizenship in a season of great untruth. In G. Richardson & D. Blades (Eds.), *Troubling the canon of citizenship education* (pp. 124–135). New York, NY: Peter Lang.

Smith, D. (2008). From Leo Strauss to collapse theory: Considering the neoconservative attack on modernity and the work of education. *Critical Studies in Education, 49*(1), 33–48.

Smits, H. (2008). Is a Canadian curriculum studies possible? (What are the conditions of possibility?). Some preliminary notes for further inquiry. *Journal of the Canadian Association for Curriculum Studies, 6*(2), 97–112.

Smits, H. (2010). Introduction: The Aporia of ideology and utopia – field experiences in teacher education as peril and promise. In T. Falkenberg & H. Smits (Eds.), *Field experiences in the context of reform of Canadian teacher education programs* (Vol. 1, pp. 51–66). Faculty of Education, University of Manitoba.

Sumara, D., Davis, B., & Laidlaw, L. (2001). Canadian identity and curriculum theory: An ecological, postmodern perspective. *Canadian Journal of Education, 26*(2), 144–163.

Taylor, C. (1989). *Sources of the self: The making of modern identity.* Cambridge, MA: Harvard University Press.

Taylor, C. (1991). *The malaise of modernity.* Concord, ON: House of Anansi Press.

Tomkins, G. (2008). *A common countenance: Stability and change in the Canadian curriculum.* Vancouver, BC: Pacific Educational Press.

Van Herk, A. (1990). *Places far from Ellesmere.* AB: Red Deer College Press.

Vanderhaege, G. (1996). *The Englishman's boy.* Toronto, ON: McClelland & Stewart.

White, S. (2000). *Sustaining affirmation: The strengths of weak ontology in political theory.* Princeton University Press.

Žižek, S. (1993). *Tarrying with the negative: Kant, Hegel, and the critique of ideology.* Durham, NC: Duke University Press.

Žižek, S. (2008). *In defense of lost causes.* London, England: Verso.

Žižek, S. (2010). *Living in the end times.* London, England: Verso.

THE CURRICULUM OF CLOSE WRITING

3

Rebecca Luce-Kapler, Queen's University

Is there any gesture humans make that is not a species of remembering? (Zwicky, 2006, p. 93)

WRITING PRACTICES HAVE BEEN CRITICAL to my work as a curriculum scholar. Writing is how I think best; writing is how I think best with others; writing is how I know that I have learned; writing is how I know there is so much more to learn. A writer has to be careful, though, that the form does not begin to dictate the thinking. I know this happens when I finish an essay or an article and see no change in my ideas. I can point to the argument, the methodology, the representation of data, and even why all this information might be important, but it is merely reporting and not knowing. The "finished" box is checked as it sinks beneath the surface of caring.

In our embrace of the scholarly as erudite and learned, we can forget that scholar at its most basic means "learner" or one who is "taught in school" (OED). Writing as a scholarly activity is about coming to know, and it is this kind of enterprise in which I want to engage. Such an exploration requires an interruption of form to open up the text and acknowledge the tensions. When I push at form, play with the genre, I find my writing adumbrated by the poetic and the lyric. This sensibility is influenced by my work as a poet but also, I would submit, by the way I understand most deeply.

The lyric, while certainly important to poetry, can be understood more broadly than the Romantic traditions. Philosopher-poet Jan Zwicky characterizes lyric as "thought whose *eros* is coherence ... the characteristic formal properties of lyric ... are resonance and integrity; and, as a fundamentally integrative mode of thought [is] a flight from the condition of language" (2003, foreword). We attempt to live, she suggests, in the tension between the lyric and the "objectifying project of tool-use (which includes the use of language)" (fore-word). The lyric is our embodied sense of the rhythms of living and what we ache to articulate in language; but just as language reveals a world, it sets us apart from it. In many of her essays, Zwicky uses poetic attention and the structure of her text to mediate the tension between the lyric and the scholarly (1995, 2003, 2006). In this chapter, inspired by Zwicky, I teeter between the lyric and the scholarly, using structure and form to argue for close writing practices as my way to find a home in curriculum theory.

At sixteen I borrowed a reel-to-reel tape recorder and dragged it to Edmonton to interview my great-aunt Emily who remembered escaping from Russia and emigrating to Canada. I still have that afternoon's conversation, now digitized, where Emily's voice with its rich rolling accent recollects when she was no older than I at the time of the interview, describing the family's travels across the ocean and over half a country to live in the prairies – a landscape that was not yet a province. Before I heard the term "narrative research," before I knew that fascination with learning from others' stories could be called "curriculum theory," I was engaged in the work of understanding experience through the biographies and life histories of those around me. Now, as a researcher, my studies often centre around story – how people understand their experience through literature and how they interpret those understandings through writing. Kerby (1991) writes about how our passion for narrative is a way of "emplotting" our lives. We make sense through story. But I am also interested in how we can learn through interrupting that story. How does the poetic line change what we can know? How does trying to write in another's style offer different interpretations? In changing the tempo of the comfortable narrative rhythm we hear in our head, what does one learn? It is in the interruption; the uncomfortable where one comes to know what it was we missed or were not ready to hear.

While much of my research has been with groups of women across all ages, exploring different forms and technologies of writing (Luce-Kapler, 2004, 2007, 2008), it is my biographical studies where I develop the writing practices to bring to these collectives. I examine the lives of women artists and writers, developing responses to their biographies through poetry and narrative (Luce-Kapler, 2003). The interview with great-aunt Emily signalled this nascent interest, which grew to include Emily Carr, Margaret Bourke-White, Kate Chopin, and others, the most recent being Geraldine Moodie, the first woman to have a photography studio in western Canada late in the nineteenth century.

Finding the Narrative

I begin to piece together the story of Vivia, the photographer. What is known about her seems even less than what is known about Geraldine and that is little enough in itself. I wonder if Geraldine was the female photographer who Vivia described meeting in Calgary at the train station – the one who inspired her to send away for a small camera and begin to record the unspoken of her life. When I search for information about Geraldine, I find men: Ernest Brown, Harry Pollard, Alfred Blyth, Harry Bamber. Only incidentally is there the story of a woman – Gladys Reeves – who worked with Ernest Brown and who recognized that for the work to be known and lauded, she would have to create the story of their photographs. While Ernest was away with his family, Gladys crafted the narrative: "Birth of the West." She shifted and ordered the prints to make connections and tell tales that they did not know they were telling. By morning, bleary-eyed and weary, she spared a few more moments to pen a note to Ernest. "Dear Daddy-Love . . ." she wrote.

This is the problem with Geraldine. Only now are details of her biography emerging, her photographs being collected and traced. There are no big stories. Nothing linking the pictures to the landscape in which they were wrought. No man behind the narrative, except her husband through the NWMP. And there are no surviving notes that tell me that Geraldine was the woman Vivia met on the train platform. Their stories do not have a devoted lover constructing the heroic tale and so the story begins again and again.

I try to reconstruct my own memory. It is fall; combining time. Grandpa and Dad are out in the fields, rushing to get the oats off before the snow comes. Mom is milking cows and doing the chores while Vivia makes supper and watches me and my sisters. That afternoon, with the autumn sun slanting long, she takes the four of us out on the back porch for a photograph. The box camera set firmly on the tripod, she calls our attention to the lens.

For the first time, I think about how often the camera accompanies her. Why do you take so many pictures? I ask.

Vivia glances at the distant horizon where the dust of harvest rises. I was coming here with your grandfather on our honeymoon, she said, to meet his parents. We had been married several weeks before and were taking the train to Ponoka. We stopped in Calgary to change trains. We had several hours to wait in the station, and there I saw an older woman with a camera. She was taking pictures of the trains, the passengers, the architecture. She noticed that I was interested and sat down beside me to talk, asked me where I was going and where I had come from. I told her about my fear as a city girl leaving the United States and coming to a farm, perhaps to stay forever. She told me about her camera and how it had made the difference for her. She understood through her pictures. I didn't forget that.

I think that was the story – one that I heard more than once over her lifetime – but never with the name of the older woman. Was it possible? Somewhere in Geraldine's photographs might be a shot of the young Vivia journeying to the farm and a new life. I remember another picture of Vivia from that era: waves of black hair held up with combs, eyes large and dark, a necklace of jet beads about her neck. A woman who might have met Geraldine.

I work with memoir, narrative, hypertext, poetry, and fiction, exploring the dimensions of the genres as an interpretive practice. To see the possibilities of learning, I depend on writing, drawing on literary practices developed over a number of years of research, engaged in what I have to come think of as "close writing." Close writing hearkens back to close reading, which was the New Critics' call for readers to mine the literary text, to appreciate its complexities, and to understand the workings of its art without focusing only on themes and author biography. When "new criticism" fell out of favour because of its exclusionary approach (only the "best" literature was considered, usually meaning male, white, and western), close reading, by its association, also diminished. Nevertheless, what was and continues to be important about this approach is the deliberate attention the reader must pay to what is actually on the page.

Jane Gallop, in her essay "The Ethics of Close Reading: Close Encounters," argues that close reading is "a technique to make us learn, to make us see what we don't already know, rather than transforming the new into the old" (2000, p. 11). Rather than projecting what readers think the writer is saying, close reading demands they attend to the diction, punctuation, figurative language, footnotes, rhythms, and so on, as they discern what is presented. Readers need to trouble their assumptions to really read the text. Gallop posits that close reading is also an ethical practice that shows respect for the writer's thinking. Close reading, Gallop maintains, encourages one to also become a close listener, really focusing on what people are communicating. In her teaching of the process, she has noticed that her students also become close writers, attentive to how the structure of their sentences, choice of punctuation, use of imagery, and other techniques convey a message.

It is this argument of Gallop's that encouraged me to use the term "close writing"; however, I also use close writing to mean trying different styles and genres, noticing the literary techniques present in other writers' texts then experimenting with them. What I have come to appreciate is the potential for learning through this process as the writer's voice is challenged and a respect for other ideas is engendered. As an ethical practice, close writing interrupts normative representations – what we say and expect to see without questioning – and helps us appreciate the complexity of experience and recognize openings or moments of possibility for learning – what I call the subjunctive spaces.

A figure who is part of it all, though only watching and watching.
(Dorothea Lange in Dyer, 2005, p. 150)

The women sit behind the screen on the outer edge of the Sun Dance tent. They are not part of the inner circle, the mystery that Geraldine feels as the tent billows and ripples in the wind. She too is on the edge – their edge – since most have turned their backs to her. Shrouded in their wraps, they present a dark and solid image: You cannot and will not know. Others look down, caps pulled down to their noses or scarves shadowing their faces. Even those who look at her do not reveal any welcome, their eyes narrowed or stony. They are still and implacable in their resistance to her prying lens.

As Geraldine waits and watches, manipulating her camera only as much as she dares, she refocuses her understanding. They may be on this side of the screen, but she is the only one excluded. Their bodies sink into the earth and in their silence, Geraldine senses some linking, a collective sigh visible only in the light. The intensity flows about her, and for a moment she is drawn; an invitation has been

"Cree women near the
Sun Dance circle"
Credit: Geraldine Moodie,
Library and Archives
Canada, PA-028830.

given. She steps closer, then realizes that she has felt the edge of a powerful circle. A glimpse is the only gift.

Later, when she prints the photograph, she is surprised by the darkness and how the light circles away from her lens.

Gallop elaborates her argument for the ethics of close reading by noting that such a practice encourages a diversity of perspectives, especially those that lie outside the traditional western, white canon of literature. Students genuinely engage with differing viewpoints rather than bringing stereotypical readings to texts. Gallop notes that these include negative and positive stereotypes (e.g., "the noble savage" or the "selfless nurturing mother," p. 15). Close reading interrupts the projection of simplistic political correctness onto readings and the dismissal of texts without the reader having to engage meaningfully with the ideas. As Gallop writes, "Fighting prejudice with prejudice is an all too common practice, but one I don't recommend. To my mind the best way to fight prejudice is in fact close reading, challenging one's pre-judgments through close encounters with the other" (p. 16).

A writer can rely on clichéd expressions or other literary structures without thoughtfully considering their origins or their significance. Close writing signals an ethical responsibility to one's text in that careful attention to the message being communicated can highlight pre-judgments and potential impacts. An important exercise I ask students to do when they have larded their writing with quotations is to have them paraphrase what they believe is being said to be sure the message they are borrowing is one that they wish to promote. Paraphrasing itself is a type of close reading and writing that brings one's attention to the perspective being shared.

Through writing, we can become acutely aware of what Bakhtin describes as the dialogic nature of language. He explains that there are no "neutral" words but that "each tastes of the context and contexts in which it has lived its socially charged life; all words and forms are populated by intentions. . . . The word in language is half someone else's (1981, p. 293). Writing is an immersion into a sea of language whose meanings and character intertwine with the diversity of human understanding and the rhythm of our existence. As an engagement with language, writing becomes part of that larger system, one that reveals traces of interconnection in every word. Like oral language, writing is not solely the public production of a fixed text but rather a "dynamic meeting of reflection and production: a complex and ongoing interplay among personal and public voices" (Welch, 1993, p. 3). The history of meaning associated with words and the shared rhythms of language are part of a writer's work as she attempts to shape that language and engage some of her own history in its use, struggling against the forces that would narrow interpretation and exclude others.

When I think of the ethical quality of close writing, I am meaning the kind of sensitivity that careful attention to language and its usage in the text invokes and the willingness to be troubled by the challenges. Ethical behaviour does not arise from habit or obedience to patterns or rules but from intelligently guiding our actions "in harmony with the texture of the situation" (Varela, 1999, p. 31), by seeing what is arising before us.

Drawing from Buddhism, Varela elaborates how our sense of self emerges from a pattern of activity – an activity such as writing, perhaps – where a self seems to be centrally located even while it is nowhere to be found. Understanding and experiencing the self as virtual or as a selfless self offers a comparison to those occasions when our ego becomes mixed with our concern for other humans, confusing those interactions with a need to satisfy one's cravings for recognition and self-evaluation. Instead, acting wisely and ethically calls for "intelligent awareness, that is, the moment-to-moment realization of the virtual self as it is – empty of any egoistic ground whatsoever, yet filled with wisdom" (1999, p. 73).

In writing, by considering what is to be gained, by relying on habitual response and by closely following a carefully defined and rigid plan, the focus remains on our selves, the writers, and we are less able to perceive what is unfolding before us. The capacity to attend and respond to the place we inhabit in the moment, aware of our mind and imaging those of others, is what Jan Zwicky calls a "sensitivity to resonance" (2003, p. 60). She suggests that such recognition involves a reorganization of experience,

> an act of contextualization, a sensing of connexions of immediate experience and other experiences. Thus the experiences of seeing how an assemblage of parts must go together, recognizing an old friend in an unfamiliar setting, and understanding a metaphor are species of the same phenomenon. They all involve insight, understood as re-cognition; a gestalt shift. (p. 1)

It is in the educating of the imagination, in re-cognition, where there is the possibility for ethical practice and for learning in close writing.

Self-Portrait II

She dreams
    of being in a house
where the floors are never clean
where children beat spoons

    they cry
    for constant attention

She does not remember
    when she knew
the easy swing of limbs slowed
by the first moments of morning

    she floats
    away from desire

She is afraid
    of disappearing
before she can waken knowing
flesh falls from bones

    it hastens
    to leave the body

Self-Portrait III

Staid she has never been but when the men
open studios in Medicine Hat, hang out
their shingles in bars and council meetings
shilling for portraits of wives and lovers
she does not chat up the women, attend
their teas; she is tired of sitters still

in her studio, faces solemn for posterity.
She is a grass widow with J.D. mapping
the Yukon-Edmonton or is it the Edmonton-Yukon
route; fifteen months away as she feels the wash
of time settle about her ankles.
With one studio closed and another slowed
she rides out into the prairie to shoot the hard ride
of the cowboy and the laughter of children.

In joint projects, Dennis Sumara and I have brought our close reading and writing practices together to work with individuals whose
voices have typically been marginalized – gay, lesbian and transgendered teachers and older lesbian and heterosexual women (Luce-
Kapler, 2004; Luce-Kapler & Sumara, 2010; Luce-Kapler, Sumara, &
Davis, 2002; Luce-Kapler, Sumara, & Iftody, 2010; Sumara, 2002,
2006, 2007). As communities whose voices have often been side-
lined, we have noticed that participants tend to respond to reading
literature and to write with well-rehearsed narratives that rely on
stereotypical and normative identifications. Although these self-narratives seemed fixed, critical readings of and responses to contemporary fiction and memoir begin to mediate these identifications.
Individual and collective responses are reformulated into memoir,
epistolary, and creative fiction forms. Through the development of
these specific close reading and writing practices, participants generate responses that show how practices of fictionalizing and narrating
influence the trajectory of self- and cultural learning. The seemingly
fixed identity narratives are transformed through close reading and
writing.

Another aspect I have considered in close writing is the role of
voice – problematic as that conception has been. The suggestion of
"finding one's voice" has been important for those who value the
expressivist (personal expression) writing, especially feminist, queer,

and critical theorists (DeSalvo, 1999; Smith & Watson, 2001) who argue for the importance of hearing from those whose opinions have been suppressed, affecting their sense of self worth and participation in the cultural discourse. For instance, feminists have argued that when women are able to explore their experience through writing, such a process can have a profound effect on their decision-making and sense of confidence (DeSalvo, 1996; Luce-Kapler, 2004; Mairs, 1994). Voice is a synecdoche for the expressive confidence that comes from recognizing that what one thinks and believes is worthy of attention.

Peter Elbow (2007), in part answering the critics who have misinterpreted and dismissed his arguments for voice, suggests that our desire to use the term voice points to the difference between words on the page and the spoken medium of language. He argues that text focuses our attention on the visual and spatial features of language as print – an abstract system that does not take on its nuances of meaning until it is spoken. He posits that we benefit from considering both aspects in our discourse: text and voice. For instance, paying attention to voice in writing helps rhetorical effectiveness. Elbow points out how we recognize when voice in a piece of writing is wrong and by analyzing voice in text and reading those texts and our own drafts aloud, we can learn to hear what are readers are most likely to hear. Many of these textual features are what can be described as style, but Elbow argues that the voice metaphor works better for many.

> Not only do most readers hear voices in texts as they read, they tend to hear people in the texts. Written words may be silent semiotic signs, but when humans read (and write), they usually infer a person behind the words and build themselves a relationship of some sort with that person. (2007, p. 180)

At the same time, Elbow points out how the notion of voice does harm because the term has no stable meaning. He suggests that its "peculiar resonance" comes from its reinforcing "harmful mythic assumptions" where writers can believe that if they find "their own unique voice," they will be good writers and that this belief perpetuates the thinking that we have single and unchanging selves as it foregrounds personal power (p. 183).

Some of my close-writing practices include imitating another writer's style, first by copying a passage out word for word and then substituting words while retaining the rhythms and idiosyncrasies of the original. Another practice asks participants to write letters that adopt the voice of someone they know well. What occurs during this type of practice is that writers close-read their work and become more attentive to the details of the craft that create a sense of voice. In a recent study, older women, writing letters in the voice of women they admired, discovered that they brought a new level of understanding and empathy for their subjects – especially those who chose women with whom they may have had a challenging relationship.

Wildflower

Three days by train to Winnipeg, a long ride in the cart that J. D. procured. Two small babies crying in the nests she made from Hudson Bay blankets. This was not Lakefield where only a few days ago her mother helped with the children. She has been entranced by the enthusiasm of J. D. and his father. When they talked about homesteading, she remembered the stories of Grandmother and Aunt Catherine, embracing the wilderness with just a touch of civility. Now, on this dusty trail away from Brandon, her life unwound as she lost friends and close contact with her mother. There were no large stands of ancient hardwood, only miles of grasses and the fall sky, endlessly blue in the early September light.

One night she dreamt about working in her mother's dining room. The sunlight was mottled by the lace curtains, but bright enough for painting. Her tongue slid between her teeth as she,

Maime, and Alice helped her mother paint five thousand lithographs. Her hands ached as she shaded the stems in green over and over, starting again, starting until J. D. cut through with his plow and draft horse, slicing prairie grass and scattering wildflowers. Geraldine startled awake. She wrapped a cloak around her nightgown and dug for the sketchbook that she belatedly stashed in her satchel the day they left. She hastened away from the small shack toward the rock in the northwest corner of their land where the unbroken ground still nurtured the last plants of summer. The air was chilly with coming frost, and by the time she found the spiky blooms of what Agnes called a Painted Cup, the dew sogged the hem of her gown. Geraldine hoisted herself onto the rock, twisted the wet nightgown off her legs, and turned to a fresh page. In the last gloom of the setting moon, she sketched the shape of the plant with her soft pencil – the contours of the stem and its branches, the leaves. By the time the horizon glowed, she filled in the details – the fiery tongues of colour at the end of each stalk that rose up to meet the sun.

When J. D. touched her shoulder, she gasped. Douglas is crying for your milk, he said, sliding suspenders over his shoulders. Come to the house. She whispered her pencil from the page.

Evening Primrose

Moon catches the white vein
of blossom, draws the eye
to the centre of golden seed
beneath which lies the heart
invisible in darkness

Nest in prairie grass
for a time and you will see
a quiet call to the moth
pink glow of flower
Behind moonlight
real work begins

Close writing can open up the complexity of a text – the aspects of language that make up the style or voice, the references to other voices and texts. Close writing with others makes this more readily apparent. At first those in the group notice when similar themes, images, or language influence each other's pieces. As they read fiction, memoir and poetry alongside, they observe when details of that literature permeate the writing. Then they begin to trouble each other's writing by noting the contradictions and patterns as a history of closely read texts is established.

Understanding the complexity of our writing – what I call an "ecology of language" – means bringing an attentiveness to the text that understands writing as embedded in a system of relationships with the human and the more-than-human world. Yet with our deeply ingrained western cultural beliefs about authorship and how it represents self-expression, it is not surprising that most discussions about writing collectives foreground benefits for the individual. Writer Margaret Atwood criticized this perspective:

> Readers and critics both are addicted to the concept of self-expression, the writer as a kind of spider, spinning out his entire work from within. This view depends on a solipsism, the idea that we are all self-enclosed monads, with an inside and an outside, and that nothing from the outside ever gets in. (1982, p. 342).

Ecology hearkens back to the word for home and habitation: a household, as Capra (1996) noted. A household is a gathering place, a central location, somewhere to come from and go back to. Whether we consider the home of writing being the individual and her text, or the writing group where the text is read, or the larger community of readers and writers, each is a system of relationships among the practices and influences within an environment. Close writing challenges the notion of the individual as singular creator of a text – a conception that Foucault (1984) has critiqued. He argued that what is recognized as the author reflects a historical moment when individualization of ideas was privileged. The author is a discursive creation that is not isomorphic with the writer of the text. Rather, it becomes an identifiable marker that can demarcate the text as being attributable to one source and thereby be containable. Meaning can be smoothed and the perspective narrowed when the responsibility of the text belongs to an individual.

Narratives and the construction of a voice encourage a sense of singularity and the careful connection of details that wrap up the story. We search for an order to make sense. "Narrative addresses us as members of the tribe, it binds us in a common *mythos*. Narrative *makes* things hang together causally; we use it to tame experience so that it does not overwhelm us" (Zwicky, 2006, p. 95). Narrative is important for us to understand, to make sense, to satisfy our pattern-seeking brains, but it can also lull us into thinking that it is the only truth. It is useful to shake up our narratives and notice what can be hidden beneath the temporal linkages: "*Before, after, meanwhile . . . if, so, inspite of . . .*" (Zwicky, p. 93).

Sometimes to see what else is possible, we have to shift to a new genre or break apart the narrative. For instance, writers can follow the pattern of an existing lyric poem to represent an incident they previously narrated. Reconceptualizing the story in this way changes what can be told. Writers find they attend to the affective qualities and the visual elements that can engage the readers' imaginations more deeply. The results feel more like another perspective on the event rather than *the* story.

Another close writing practice follows the work of Frigga Haug (1987). Participants in her group challenged their narratives by making lists of words from their texts and sorting them into actions, feelings, and dreams. By interrupting the logic of syntax, writers found the individual words had greater importance and offered insights different from the narrative's message.

A Stretch of Time

The two days I am in Chicago at a conference, I spend one morning at the Art Institute touring the photograph gallery. I miss the early morning at home with the tin box on my lap, remembering and longing to spend time with pictures. The Institute has a special show featuring Joel Meyerowitz. At the first exhibited photo, I step out of the clock tick of the morning and gasp at the lines of gray and pale blue, ocean meeting shore on Cape Cod as I hover in the scene. Time washes behind me and settles into stillness, the web of moments stopped in the picture.

When I finally move again, sidestepping to the next photograph, I travel through the ocean into my childhood. In this shot, a woman, visiting a resort in the Catskills, makes a phone call. Meyerowitz has caught her in the midst of a life. I think of those around me during that time – ones who have left the earth. For a moment, Vivia is brought to life again. It's as if she is the one speaking on the telephone. I smell the cherry scent of her Jergen's lotion, the fine bones of the 1960s as she speaks on a public telephone in the small alcove. As I step out of the memory, I see the woman is framed by a large portrait of a couple on the wall to her right and a foyer with another guest walking through on her left. She is wearing the flowered shorts, puffy like a skirt skimming her mid-thigh and a white bolero jacket over a dark swimsuit. On her head is a peaked hat, the same straw as her large bag settled by her foot. She is speaking intently, her arm raised in gesture.

The wrist near the mouthpiece becomes Vivia's as she motions me to come closer. My eyes burn and a thread that has been broken for many years trembles in the breeze.

When I return home, I look through the box of photographs, searching for the sensation of time travel that I experienced in the gallery. I find one black and white snapshot of the Christmas bazaar that the Ladies' Aid hosted every December.

The photograph is in the church hall in town with card tables arranged in the center of the room. Each one covered with freshly laundered and pressed linens – the white cotton decorated with embroidery or an edging of crocheted lace. Along the sides of the hall are tables of handicrafts and baking for purchase – woolen slippers, clever Christmas wreaths of white plastic and red ribbon, tiny clothes for dolls with small buttons and crisp waists. One could buy a dozen fresh cinnamon buns or sugar cookies festively iced. After shopping, folks could sit down at a table with friends and be served a cup of tea or coffee; a small plate of squares and cookies would appear in the centre ready for sampling. Often these same treats would be for sale somewhere along the side, and those who particularly loved the Nanaimo Bars could pick up another dozen to take home. Or if you were planning a large Christmas gathering, mincemeat pies were ready for your freezer.

Vivia had taken her camera this year – 1954 was written on the back of the shot – the year of my birth. I wonder how she feels about my arrival – her first grandchild. Does she sense the weight of time passing? She would have been just a couple of years older than I am now, and there are nights when I awake in panic at the disappearing moments of my life.

But maybe with a sense of optimism, she brought her camera along with her lemon squares and coconut macaroons and the Christmas aprons she has sewn. Perhaps she was thinking about the pictures of her life that she might offer to her grandchild.

The photograph shows a woman seated at a card table in a smart black sheath wearing white gloves. She is lifting a teacup to her lips with her small finger crooked just as I have seen in old pictures of etiquette instruction. Beside her is a man dressed in work clothes, his cap resting on the edge of his knee, a beefy hand around his delicate cup. The woman has just called him in from his work to drive her to town for a cup of tea and to attend the bazaar. In her face are all the dreams of refinement and in his body the impatience with decorum. And yet, when you look at his face, he is gazing at the woman, a small and seemingly tender smile hovers. The story floats about the table, blurring the backdrop of Christmas busyness. There is a wistfulness in the picture that I remember shadowed Vivia's demeanour much of her life.

Humans are accustomed to using oral and print narratives to make sense of experience and develop an emerging story where one event seems to arise from another like links in a chain. In fact, we often speak of narratives as "linear," although this is a bit of a misnomer. A closer investigation indicates otherwise. Carol Shields characterizes narrative as a "subjunctive cottage." She writes: "a narrative isn't something you pull along like a toy train, a perpetually thrusting indicative. It's this little subjunctive cottage by the side of the road. All you have to do is open the door and walk in" (2000, p. 54). The subjunctive, as Jerome Bruner (1986) reminds us, opens possibilities rather than settles for certainties. Writing can become a subjunctive space, an "as if" opportunity. What such contingency does is broaden the possibilities for creating and understanding through narrative as well as through genre transposition and other close-writing practices.

In my study of Geraldine Moodie, I have struggled to represent my interpretations of her experience. In the past, I have tended to choose one genre – fiction or poetry – to respond to biographical details. For the Moodie project, I first tried to write a novel. While the narrative I initially wrote worked very well to create a single line out of a multiplicity of alternatives, it was ultimately dissatisfying because I could not seem to illustrate the complex nature of Geraldine's experience. But neither did poetry seem to encompass the breadth I had imagined. Then I began a research project with teenagers using Storyspace – a hypertext writing software where one can create discrete chunks of text and image through multiple linking of "text boxes" (Luce-Kapler, 2007, 2008). To become familiar with the challenges of the program, I decided to use my Geraldine project as an example. What quickly became apparent was that digital linking and visual mapping increased the potential to illustrate the multiple perspectives of Geraldine that I had been attempting to represent because I was no longer trying to create a coherent narrative thread.

While I eventually moved the writing out of Storyspace,[1] what that experiment made possible was my current structure of fragments: photographs and short narratives that are both imagined and quoted from other places such as newspapers, history books, and archives; and poems, some of which are meant to represent photographs. Storyspace interrupted my typical narrative structure, but it also highlighted for me the interpretive potential of juxtaposing poetry and image with narrative.

Zwicky writes that the difference between lyric and narrative memory is the difference between witness and explanation (2006, p. 98). Lyric recognizes the difficulty in rearrangement, in finding an answer. "Lyric knows the answer is nothing more than, nothing less than, the moment itself," that the world is a "resonant whole" (p. 100). Narrative looks for reasons, for the sense in things. "'Why do I remember this?' It is not the *content* of narrative's answer that is important, but the fact that it tries to answer at all" (p. 100).

The tension in writing about Geraldine Moodie is the same tension I inhabit in my scholarly writing – how does one glimpse the "resonant whole," offer readers that shimmering insight of a moment while still addressing the imperative for explanation, a demonstration of understanding. Writing does offer a subjunctive space that invites an exploration of the "as if." I write as if I can describe the reality of a moment or explain an event and as if language did not remove me a step back from that sense of reality. I participate as an imagined narrator or character, a persona that creates an "I" distinct from the writer. Through recognizing this "other," I find myself in a mutual reflection and perception. The writer and reader can explore alternative consciousnesses, experiencing subjectivity in a way that offers a sense of its shifting and changing nature. This thinking about the subjunctive space, though, still focuses on an individual identity and its possibilities for a writer. It is important to remember that at any given moment, who we are cannot be separated from those with whom we share a world. Within such a world, the key to acting appropriately is to be "in harmony with the texture of the situation" (Varela, 1999, p. 31). The challenge for writers is to find ways of doing so. Close writing is one way that we can learn.

Gardening

Red zinnias next to green bells of Ireland and a row of purple
cabbage. Food and flowers, yes, but she loves the colour
from her living room window, winter drapes are replaced with cotton
and drawn from the pane to brighten the room.
Golden sunflowers tower over the lattices of peas
and poppies run wild about the edge. Catnip and parsley.
The blades of onion shoots. She composes the garden
for its late summer photographs, the shadow and light
of shape so pleasing to the eye that she almost forgets
the colour has remained with the plants and not migrated
to her film. In winter, by the late afternoon fire, she examines
her seasonal pictures and plans for the coming spring.
Next year the cauliflower leaves must be gathered up with string
to discourage the moths and the mint moved to the wet end
of the plot. Next year she will photograph children
next to the rose bushes for a sense of scale. Every year
the gardens grow into her dreaming pictures.

Notes

1   I found Storyspace a bit cumbersome for my needs in the end and moved
     back into word processing with a program called Scrivener that still
     allowed a sense of fragments and links.

References

Atwood, M. (1982). *Second words: Selected critical prose.* Toronto,
     ON: Anansi.

Bakhtin, M. M. (1981). *The dialogic imagination* (M. Holquist, Ed.;
     C. Emerson & M. Holquist, Trans.). University of Texas Press.

Bruner, J. (1986). *Actual minds, possible worlds.* Cambridge, MA:
     Harvard University Press.

Capra, F. (1996). *The web of life: A new scientific understanding of living systems.* New York, NY: Doubleday.

DeSalvo, L. (1996). *Vertigo.* New York, NY: Dutton.

DeSalvo, L. (1999). *Writing as a way of healing. How telling our stories transforms our lives.* San Francisco, CA: Harper.

Dyer, G. (2005). *The ongoing moment.* New York, NY: Pantheon
     Books.

Elbow, P. (2007). Voices in writing again: Embracing contraries.
     College English, 70(2), 168–188.

Foucault, M. (1984). What is an author? In P. Rabinow (Ed.), *The
     Foucault reader* (pp. 101–120). New York, NY: Pantheon Books.

Gallop, J. (2000). The ethics of close reading: Close encounters.
     Journal of Curriculum Theorizing, 17(3), 7–17.

Haug, F. (Ed.). (1987). *Female sexualization* (E. Carter, Trans.).
     London, England: Verso.

Kerby, A. (1991). *Narrative and the self.* Indiana University Press.

Luce-Kapler, R. (2003). *The gardens where she dreams.* Ottawa, ON:
     Borealis Press.

Luce-Kapler, R. (2004). *Writing with, through, and beyond the text:
     An ecology of language.* Mahwah, NJ: Lawrence Erlbaum.

Luce-Kapler, R. (2007). Fragments to fractals: The subjunctive spaces of e-literature. *Journal of E-Learning, 4*(3), 256–265.

Luce-Kapler, R. (2008). Thinking in hypertext: Interrupting the mindset of schooling. *Curriculum Matters, 4*, 85–101.

Luce-Kapler, R. & Sumara, D. (2010) Taking shape: How reading (in)forms writing. In M. C. Courtland & T. Gambell (Eds.), *Literature, media & multiliteracies in adolescent Language Arts* (pp. 213–234). Vancouver, BC: Pacific Education Press.

Luce-Kapler, R., Sumara, D., & Davis, B. (2002). Rhythms of knowing: Toward an ecological theory of learning in Action Research. *Educational Action Research, 10*, 353–372.

Luce-Kapler, R., Sumara, D., & Iftody, T. (2010). Teaching ethical know-how in New Literary spaces. *Journal of Adolescent and Adult Literacy, 53*(8), 536–541.

Mairs, N. (1994). *Voice lessons: On becoming a (woman) writer.* Boston, MA: Beacon Press.

Shields, C. (2000). *Dressing up for the carnival.* Toronto, ON: Random House.

Smith, S., & Watson, J. (2001). *Reading autobiography: A guide for interpreting life narratives.* University of Minnesota Press.

Sumara, D. (2002). *Why reading literature in school still matters: Imagination, interpretation, insight.* Mahwah, NJ: Lawrence Erlbaum.

Sumara, D. (2006). Normalizing literary responses in the teacher education classroom. *Changing English: Studies in Reading and Culture, 13*(1), 55–68.

Sumara, D. (2007). Small differences matter: Interrupting certainty about identity in teacher education. *Journal of Gay and Lesbian Issues in Education, 4*(2), 135–149.

Varela, F. (1999). *Ethical know-how: Action, wisdom, and cognition.* San Francisco, CA: Stanford University Press.

Welch, N. (1993). One student's many voices: Reading, writing and responding with Bakhtin. *Journal of Advanced Composition,*

13(2). Retrieved from http://www.jacweb.org/
Archived_volumes/Text_articles/V13_I2_Welch.htm

Zwicky, J. (1995). Bringhurst's Presocratics: Lyric and ecology. In T. Lilburn (Ed.), *Poetry and knowing: Speculative essays & interviews* (pp. 65–117). Kingston, ON: Quarry Press.

Zwicky, J. (2003). *Wisdom & metaphor.* Kentville, NS: Gaspereau Press.

Zwicky, J. (2006). Lyric, narrative, memory. In R. Finley, P. Friesen, A. Hunter, A. Simpson, & J. Zwicky (Eds.), *A ragged pen: Essays on poetry & memory* (pp. 87–108). Kentville, NS: Gaspereau Press.

No More Boundaries:
Narrative Pedagogies, Curriculum, and Imagining Who We Might Become

Tasha Riley, AIDS Vancouver
Sharon Rich, Nipissing University

NOTED ABORIGINAL WRITER Thomas King wrote, "The truth about stories is that's all we are" (2003, p. 5). The truth about us is that we tell stories, and in each of our stories we give a piece of ourselves to our listeners. The truth about us is that we are storytellers who teach, and through our teaching we learn. We like to think that we help our students learn what they know and imagine who they might become. The truth about good teachers is that they know only this – the students who stand beside them and learn will take them places they have never imagined. They will create new worlds, and from their journey together they will learn what human potential can be. In this paper we explore curriculum as a story that unfolds and helps us to understand who we might become as teachers, co-learners, and as human beings. We juxtapose a story of self-discovery with a story of creating a co-learning and reflexive classroom curriculum to indicate the ways in which the personal informs the public to create new spaces for learning.

Look at the face in the mirror. What do you see? A young woman. Wait. Not so young. There are creases around her eyes. What does that mean? She has known happiness. Or maybe too much sun.

And her mouth? Cute mouth. Turns up at the corners. Natural smile. Foul when angry. A nice mouth.

Her nose? What about that? An alright shape. Not perfect. There's a bump at the top. I can see it. Looks like it was broken. It wasn't. It looks like it was. It wasn't. And her forehead? Describe it to me. Clear but three scars. They form a pyramid. What were they from? Chicken pox maybe.

Acne. Does that bother her? Not any more. It did when she was younger. Now she thinks they're magic. How strange. Maybe.

She worries too much. How can you tell? The creases. They bunch up when she's thinking. Like that. I see. And her eyes? Tell me about her eyes? Big eyes. Expressive. There is sadness. I see sadness there. She has seen some things. Haven't we all? That is true. And her eyes? Tell me about her eyes? Big eyes. Expressive. There is laughter. I see laughter there. She has seen some things. Haven't we all? That is true.

What colour is her skin? White skin. There is nothing more to say. What colour is her skin? White skin.

There is so much more to say.

The teachers we try to be are ones who create a safe community in which both the students and the teachers can respond to the passion and subtext of desire that informs our lives. Rather than reducing this subtext to something that is rational and seemingly more easily controlled, we raise issues that matter and treat these as part of the daily classroom texts. Juxtaposing the printed text of the school curriculum with the texts that we as co-learners create fosters a more dynamic setting in which learning can take place, a setting in which wisdom might be fostered.

In 2009, one of us argued that the social imperative for education in contemporary times was the pursuit of wisdom (Rich & McLaughlin, 2009). One year later, as storytellers, administrators, teachers, daughters, and mothers, we are even more convinced that for public education and our planet to survive it is imperative that we seek to develop wisdom in our populace and that our notions of curriculum finally begin to embrace Pinar's (2004) notion that curriculum is the interdisciplinary study of educational experience and not simply a syllabus or a series of documents produced in ever increasing numbers and in ever increasing detail upon which to crucify learners and teachers alike.

Pinar (2004) suggests that there are no easy answers to complex questions and increasingly, as the world is faced with problems of poverty, ecological disasters, and ever growing angst, when rightist governments push for simple–minded notions of globalization, the need for wisdom is ever more apparent. Unfortunately, what seems to have happened in our education system is a failure to acknowledge that the world has moved on as schools remain content with busy work that looks to the past rather than to the future. Learners and teachers have lost the notion of public intellectuals as identified by Richard Posner (2003, p. 18), and recently anyone who suggests that such a creature is needed is open to ridicule. Ours, especially within organized education, is to do as we are told without question. The test scores seem to matter more than the individual, and so we try to extract meaning from an environment that challenges and at times defies us. And we are a part of that environment, and to emerge from it we need to take a journey that makes us question who we are and who we might become.

We swayed our bodies to the disjointed movements of the bus as it bounced steadily along the gravel road. The bus seemed to sway to the rhythm of the jovial beat that rolled through the speakers and danced in the limited space left between our packed-in bodies. I wiped the sweat from my forehead and peeled my back away from the black vinyl seats. I dug through my worn backpack, now covered with dust, and pulled out my map to try and gauge where exactly I was supposed to get off. Three more stops, the driver said. He would let me know. I folded the map and put it into the left pocket of my light sage, durable, cotton twill cargo pants complete with bellowed, self-fastening pockets, including one with a place for a cell phone – the unofficial uniform of the North American tourist. That was it, however. I drew the line at the Tilley hat.

In essence we are experiencing an age of control chic in which the curriculum is largely controlled by those outside of the classroom, and what teachers and learners are expected to do is check progress against a list of predetermined expectations – we don't get to choose, we simply respond to the questions asked. Yet those of us interested in Pinar's sense of curriculum must begin to read or interpret events as a limitless text that can and should be influenced by individual actions As we learn to reread and recast the various texts in which we are embedded, we may be able to become stronger, more self-aware people who are co-learners and who can critically reflect on who we are and who we want to be.

To critically reflect on curriculum and our lives, we need to evidence a willingness to take risks and begin to understand our professional lives differently. In so doing we reconsider our patterns of interaction with students and with colleagues, which have been taken for granted. In schools, critical reflection can challenge the usual assumptions embedded within both our classrooms and our profession. When we assume responsibility both for shaping the curriculum and for determining what type of personal professional development is appropriate, we remove control from external bureaucratic authority and enter into a collaborative relationship with our students. In order to do this, we begin to engage in acts of storying our lives, acts that can begin to restore the human subject to the centre of the curriculum. The restoration creates meaning and acknowledges that through our self-narratives we might be able to devise alternative plots and encourage our co-learners to do the same. In these locations, teachers act in conjunction with, rather than in opposition to, learners and eventually form qualitatively different relationships with students, colleagues, and knowledge since nothing in the classroom remains static or is taken for granted. And at times it needs a change in location to change the orientation and challenge the assumptions that we have always held.

Several years ago I went to Botswana, Africa. I was a developmental worker doing aid work for an organization called Kuru Development Trust. I worked with the San, an indigenous group from the Kalahari. We went there to implement a program on HIV/AIDS awareness. Maybe we succeeded. Maybe we didn't. I guess it depends on how you view success. We succeeded in implementing the program, if that's what you want to know. Whether we made anyone aware can only be determined in time. I'd like to think we made an impact. I'd like to think we helped out in some way. I'd like to think a lot of things. In the Kalahari, I interviewed teachers and students. I interviewed principals and administrators. I interviewed people in the village. We interviewed a lot. We made some proposals. Some good proposals. We set up workshops. We travelled to many different villages. I think it may have helped. I'd like to think it helped. But then I'd like to think a lot of things. We worked together with some local guys in the village. We shared ideas with them. We did some more interviews. I marvelled at another way of living. I hoped to make a difference. I'd like to think I made a difference. You know what's next don't you. I guess I don't need to say it this time. "Do-gooder White girl." I don't think I like that term. Is that who I am? Is that who you'll label me as? Can I choose another label?

You don't get to choose. You talk, and we'll label. Go back in time. Tell us about your experiences. You are being recorded. Just say whatever comes to mind. We will ask questions if we feel it is appropriate. It will be transcribed later. Don't worry about what you say. We will give it back to you. You can make adjustments if you're not satisfied. We only want your story. That is all. Continue.

In a critically reflective stance towards curriculum and towards the self, content knowledge, the micro-knowledge of practices and procedures, and the relationship of knowledge to the broader social and political contexts are questioned and examined. Rather than assuming a morally relativistic stance, we, together with the learners, become responsible for displaying the complexities of any particular piece of knowledge. Thus the relational nature of knowledge is articulated so that inconsistencies can be examined and action taken.

Co-learning is an essential feature of any critically reflective practice. Interactions between classroom members are in flux, with each person assuming alternately teacher and learner roles depending on the specific context of the discussion and content. In such contexts, the teacher and the learners are aware of the implications of the curriculum for the larger community and are aware of the ways in which they are implicated in the curriculum. Further, classroom interaction serves to open rather than limit the possibility of alternative forms of knowledge for individual classroom members.

Suggesting that every classroom context contains the potential for critical reflection only begins to penetrate the rhetoric of educational discourse. In order to understand when a situation creates liberatory learning, we must understand the dynamics surrounding curricular knowledge and the creation of settings for learning, since inherent within any knowledge are notions of power, authority, and expertise. The control of what is taught in school and the reification of particular forms of knowledge within the curriculum maintains particular status roles of society. Certain curricula and individuals are deemed to hold knowledge that may be either privileged or denigrated within the school hierarchy. For example, we note that the present standardized assessments privilege particular forms of literacy and numeracy over others and over other subject disciplines. Some say that literacy and numeracy as measured by the standardized assessments are good and necessary because they provide accountability, yet we know that such measures systematically silence the voices of those whose knowledge is not represented within the assessment and the curriculum. Since their voices are not represented, they are discounted, unheard, and effectively silenced.

The bus continued to meander slowly down the road as I desperately tried to refrain from bopping my head too much to the funky beats wafting out from the radio. Everyone watch out! Crazy White girl dancing straight ahead. Scary stuff. I was already fully aware of the attention my pasty skin had attracted. Not that I minded or anything. I was used to it by now. I recalled the first time I really noticed I was the minority in a place. It was three years earlier, and I was teaching English in Korea. Once again I was on the bus. This time I was standing. It was another hot day but the bus was so packed you not only had to peel yourself off of the seat, you also had to peel yourself away from whoever had been unfortunate enough to stand beside you. Sudden movements became risky as you never knew exactly whose gut you might elbow or foot you could step on. The hot sun poured through the open windows and played against the golden hairs of my arms. Not something I would usually pay attention to except for the fact that the children in the seat beside me were pointing at my arms and giggling uncontrollably. I looked in their direction and they promptly covered their laughing mouths with their hands in a failed attempt to smother another burst of giggles that flew from their mouths in a torrent breaking threw the cracks between their fingers. One brave girl reached out to touch my arm. I felt her fingers press lightly upon my skin, paused for a moment and then darted away like the flick of a snake's tongue. She glanced up at me to gauge my reaction and seeing as I hadn't turned into a ferocious monster in the short time it had taken to pull her hand away, she ventured out again to make a second attempt. Placing her tiny hand upon my arm, she stroked the golden hairs that jetted upward and out of my skin. Soon all the other children began to touch. I remember feeling a little strange, rather like a caged dog in a pet store. A young Korean woman closer to my age noticed my predicament and then snapped sharply at the children. The children stopped abruptly, put their hands between their knees, and cast their eyes down while desperately trying to stifle giggles. The woman turned to me. "They are fascinated by the hair on your arms," she explains. "They have never seen a white person before."

It's funny isn't it? We are blind to our own difference if our own difference is never pointed out to us. I grew up in London, Ontario. The people on the buses were white. The people in my classes were white. The people walking in the mall were white. It was a very white city. Oh, there were exceptions of course. There always are. But then you notice those exceptions. Those exceptions are pointed out to you in subtle or not so subtle ways. But no one ever points out the colour of your own skin when you're a White person living in a dominantly White society. The golden hairs upon your arms are just like the hairs on everyone else.

Keep going. Don't stop now. We're still here. We're listening. Tell us more.

Since curricular knowledge is a cultural product that has been imbued with value, teachers, through their certification, are given the power to convey legally determined curricula to students. We, as critically reflective teachers, demonstrate the ability to carry out the authorized role and at the same time cause our students to question the place of that curricular knowledge. In so doing they, and we, take risks and enter new relationships with students, but in order to do this effectively, we, and they, must be cognizant of our own privileged status within the school.

To teach reflectively, we as teachers need to learn to teach within the culture as we question its fabric. Our actions are not such that they tear the fabric asunder but instead highlight aspects of the culture and of curricular knowledge that need to be questioned. We are moving in two directions at once. First we have the responsibility to the learner to suggest the possibility of opting into the present structure of power, but we also have determined to highlight the features of that structure that potentially have negative consequences for everyday life. Our actions in maintaining the dialectic role demonstrate for students both possibility and limitations of the structures. This enables us to make informed decisions and provide a constant critique of our own interactions.

Bound with the notion of knowledge as relational and contextual is the relationship between our views of knowing and our assessment of students as knowers as well as the students' perceptions of themselves as knowers. In traditional classrooms, teachers and students enter a unique and specialized relationship that has a clear epistemological basis.

We as teachers have power because we have curricular knowledge, but in a critically reflective classroom, this relationship changes, because at different times both we and our students will hold the position of expert. This role of expert contains similar assumptions about knowledge and power in that the expert has specialized knowledge that can be shared with others. When the role of expert shifts from teachers to learners, the teacher assumes the role of learner and the location of power and authority shifts. Since both teachers and students can assume the expert mantle, the context becomes reflexive as we enter a dialectic relationship in which teaching and learning are activities engaged in by all classroom participants. It is not simply a question of the teacher creating the context in which the learner can share particular expertise, but the learner must also consider the implications of holding particular expertise. All of these actions are conducted within the complex social setting of the classroom.

Since our teaching involves close human interactions, the relationship between teacher and learner is complex, shifting, and determined by both sociological and psychological relationships. Many of the dilemmas raised within the teaching/learning situation are not solvable but must be managed, often resulting in solutions which are at best problematic. The co-learner context that we describe here acknowledges a process of persons-in-relation in which, through critical reflection, the participants consider the meaning of alternative voices and roles.

So there I was in Africa, a development worker trying to implement an HIV/AIDS program to an indigenous group living in the Kalahari Desert. I had never known what it was like to live in poverty. I had never known hunger. The truth was, I probably couldn't imagine it if I tried. Of course, I had made some educated guesses about how I might feel. I read works describing indigenous peoples' feelings of displacement and had studied articles on settlement disputes. I could, when asked, repeat in detail the heartbreaking stories of isolation and abandonment felt by First Nation and Inuit peoples. I was aware of these issues. However, could I ever really know what this would feel like for myself? Could I ever really understand? Although I could research, study, and empathize to an extent, I don't think I could ever really know. So now you're wondering what this little White girl was doing there. Good question. What was I doing there?

This was not the first time I had ventured into a different country. For the past four years I had been travelling around, taking whatever job I could find until I felt ready to move on to the next place. I had worked in bars and factories. I had worked as a camp counsellor, an English teacher, a tour guide, and finally a development worker. During this period I had also answered many questions: What was a university-educated student doing working at a bar? Why would a young woman teach English in another country? What was a Western woman doing as a tour guide in the Middle East? Truth is, I could never really answer, because I never knew the answer myself.

I do remember, when I was about five or six, looking past the fence of my childhood playground. I could see that beyond the barbed wire gate was a field, some houses, a few more houses, and then there were many trees in the distance. What lay beyond those trees, I wondered. I thought about it for a while, pondered in my head everything I knew about the world and then finally concluded rather soundly that it was tigers. Yes it must be. Beyond the trees there were always tigers. Satisfied with my own little conclusion, and a little freaked out, I made my way back home.

Is this what you are looking for? Are these the kinds of stories you want? Am I saying the right thing? Should I start over?

Maybe. Maybe not. Do what you wish. Just tell us how you feel.

Silencing has been a part of the taken-for-granted fabric of our educational institutions and of our curricula as students try to determine what the expectations of them are. We rarely challenge our students to look outside of themselves, to ask questions about why they are here in this place at this time. Too often knowledge that is esoteric, arcane, and created elsewhere has the cachet of expertise and is valued for its rarity, but getting outside into the world to understand the other is not part of our everyday learning. We value knowledge that can be controlled in its dissemination, and through that control, those who hold it have power over others. We rarely look beyond the tigers at the end of the garden.

Yet critically reflective teachers argue for the recognition that curricular knowledge is socially constructed and is held relationally, that is, shared with those who participate in the knowledge acquisition process. As noted previously, at different times members of our critically reflective classrooms will assume different roles. Curricular knowledge is not viewed as created elsewhere but is a product of a complex set of interactions with multiple texts and multiple authors in a wide range of contexts. For us, reflective practice is a way of acknowledging the teacher's voice and expertise within the curriculum while at the same time placing practical knowledge within the complex context of historical and social relations that allows our students to share their expertise. There are implications of relational power in who describes and what is described in the classroom setting. All too often, when practical knowledge is celebrated, power relations inherent in the formation of particular practices are not open for analysis. What is missing in both the traditional concept of curricular knowledge as given (outsider knowledge controlled by an elite) and practical knowledge (insider knowledge controlled by practitioners in classrooms) is a balance that would enable either type of knowledge to be subjected to examination and critique. Our critique of teaching and learning in our classrooms includes both ways in which knowledge is constructed, its content and its relational nature.

Who was I to pose these questions to a group of indigenous people on the other side of the world? What gave me the right to investigate this topic? I am a White, middle-class female who grew up and completed public school and university in a dominantly White society. My classes were taught by White, middle-class teachers and academics. As a student I received little information on the background of First Nations groups throughout Canada, although there were tidbits of token information squeezed between paragraphs on White prime ministers and war heroes in the standardized textbooks we used. Field trips consisted of the occasional outing to the "Indian Village" where I was inevitably taught how to make corn bread and flat cakes by an actor with beaded bracelets on her arms and feathers in her hair. I, like so many others in Canada, was spoon-fed the construct of Daniel Francis's "Imaginary Indian" and was painfully unaware of the truth that lay behind the image.

My work abroad has given me the experience of living with other people who have very different circumstances to my own. Through these experiences I became more aware of my own position as a White Western woman living within theses "new worlds." I realized for the first time what it was like to be a minority in a culture. I became consciously aware of the advantages I had had as part of a majority within my own country where I never had to worry about standing out or saying the "wrong thing." Still, I realized how much my own "Whiteness" was revered in countries other than my own. I was assumed by some to be in a position of power and prosperity and would cringe when people offered me their seat or tried to usher me first in line. I realized all the things that I had once taken for granted. While working with other White folks like me, I also became aware of how quickly we could judge people for their "differences," for not being more "like us." Sometimes I was ashamed.

Should I continue? I don't know what you want me to tell you.

Whatever you are willing to tell us. It's your story. We are not going to tell you what to say.

As teachers we are in authoritative positions and because of our positions are imbued with expertise and power vis-à-vis the lived curriculum. We have to take the time to think about our position of privilege with respect to students and knowledge. If expertise is acknowledged by virtue of judgments about what knowledge is important and who owns it, the decision to share responsibility for both ownership and determination of the value of curricular knowledge in the classroom is a fairly radical one and means that we as teachers have to consider who we are and why we hold our positions. Critiquing the system that imbues teachers with status may place them at risk with both colleagues and school districts. Yet as reflective teachers we have taken this risk, and in so doing have entered into new relationships with curricular knowledge and with learners.

When we begin to view curricular knowledge as something that is fluid and that can be created and re-created as we reflect on the contexts and the perspectives in which the knowledge is formed, we can reconcile the opposition between technical or received and practical knowledge. In this acknowledgment, we as teachers recognize that expertise can change depending on both the particular definition of curricular knowledge and on the context in which it is created. The tensions between public and private knowledge that affect every facet of our everyday lives in schools, particularly when a form of private knowledge is not respected or valued by the school curriculum, is highlighted. Thus in some of our language education classes, digital literacies may not be valued by a prescribed curriculum that focuses on print literacy. Yet we know that for many students there is a disjuncture between home and school, since the private knowledge of the home is not accepted by the official curriculum, and we often take up the opportunity to examine the disjuncture and to provide a commentary on the different ways in which languages and cultures value different forms of curricular knowledge.

Many names had been given to the indigenous people of Southern Africa. Being Canadian, I automatically strived to find which name of all theses names was "the most politically correct." (It is indeed a sad Canadian trait of which I am fully aware.) So what was it? Should I address them as "Bushmen," a term used by European colonists, a term in which common usage meant little more than those without domestic livestock and later acquired further derogatory connotations through associations with theft and race, not to mention the fact that the term already excluded half the population? Hmmm. This did not seem right. Well then. Did I use the Nama term "The San?" After all, it did seem the most probable, as it was the term I found most when researching information in various informative texts. Still, even after reading several books and articles on the San, I came no closer to finding out what this term actually meant. As it turned out, neither did the San themselves.

In Botswana, The San or the Bushmen are also referred to as "Barsarwa." Unfortunately this word also contained many negative connotations of being unclean and poverty stricken, much as the term Eskimo is for the Inuit people. (Meaning "eaters of raw meat." Not really what one would like to be referred to in polite conversation.) I was at a loss. "So what do I call you?" I asked Lofa Soso, a local of D'Kar who had agreed to help me with some translation. He replied honestly, "We are called San by many researchers, but I don't really know what that means. You can call us Bushmen. . . . We don't mind as long as you don't use it in a negative context. We call ourselves Ncoak hoe, which means in English 'The Red people,' so you could call us that also." "So what do you prefer?" I asked, slightly perplexed by this stage. "Well," he said with a smile, "You can call me my name."

That's a good story isn't it? It speaks about the dangers of putting real people under categories and our incessant need to label everything. I used it as part of my introduction to the report I did called "Heading West: A Guideline to the Strategic Planning for the Implementation of Total Community Mobilization in Western Botswana." I thought it gave it more of a personal touch. What do you think of that title? It's a good title isn't it? Official but not pretentious. Well, maybe a little pretentious, but not annoyingly pretentious. There is a difference, you know. I do hate pretentious works. All statistics and no substance, I say. I much prefer to tell a story. Don't you?

Go on. We're listening. This is us interviewing you remember. It's your turn now.

Unlike collaborative learning contexts in which the role of the possibility of teachers as co-learners is ignored or not taken seriously, the co-learning context that we create provides an opportunity to critique the structures of power that form the context in which we work. Because the traditional teacher/student, researcher/researched relationship has been turned around, we are faced with a demonstration of the way in which a classroom or a research project can function democratically. There are places and times for authority, but there are also times when all members of the community have their voices heard. In a co-learning context, the teacher and the students have made a deliberate attempt to be transformative and change the basic classroom structure.

As a co-learner, the teacher does not abdicate the role of expert nor does the researcher in the research context. Rather, as teachers/researchers we move between the role of expert disseminating or gathering knowledge into a more fluid, dynamic relationship within the institutional context. Rather than being simple and direct, the moves represent a gradual shifting that is barely perceptible to the outside observer. As teachers we may create a context for learning, involve students in discussion, begin to raise questions, then gradually answer questions posed by students. As we discuss with our students, the traditional lesson format of teacher question, student answer, teacher evaluation of response becomes more like normal conversation. By engaging in real conversation, there is the possibility for a dialogue that relates to the expertise of the learners. In the interactions of the classroom, our role shifts from that of leader to that of member and partner. At different times we and our students negotiate curricular knowledge on equal terms. Thus the traditional expert/novice relationship is reconstructed as co-learning.

In all educational contexts, we stand in relation to our students. At times in both traditional and in co-learning context, we have information to convey which has been deemed necessary by the system. At other times, during independent project work, we may structure a context in which the students work independently, and in so doing create a more independent learner. Over time, students explore a wide range of fields within their independent work and gain expert knowledge at the level of content or the micro level. At this point, we as teachers become the novices in the classroom. In our critically reflective context we acknowledge the position of novice and eschew the role of evaluator in order to be come a co-learner. Both we and our students are on equal footing as we begin to question the structure of the task in which we are engaged. The exploration of the depths and implications of their structural relationship allows us to discover new knowledge and explore the dimensions of what has become the teaching/learning partnership. Together we define not only our new knowledge but the context in which it is created.

Unfortunately, images of power and control are all too often seen as related to the maturity of the learners. Thus in elementary schools, teachers often suggest that it is impossible to negotiate the curriculum because the learners are immature and without expertise. However, when one recognizes that the young learner has already developed a scheme for organizing learning and has acquired expertise in a variety of areas, the problems with the apprentice/master relationship at the elementary level become apparent. What needs to be accepted, and indeed is accepted, is that in any classroom, all players possess different but valid curricular knowledge. The substance of the classroom dialogue becomes acting out the different versions of knowledge, making them explicit and considering what they might mean. This allows all learners, regardless of age or cultural differences, to enter into dialogue and explore possibility.

I clearly recall speaking with a couple of young San men. We got on to the topic of marriage in San culture. We asked them numerous questions regarding tradition and marriage, including whether or not San could choose their own partners. The men thought for a moment and then one of them replied, "Yes, we can choose who we want to marry, but we probably wouldn't marry someone who was black or white." When we asked him why, he shrugged his shoulders and replied, "Because we are inferior to them." The seven of us were visibly shocked; however, it wasn't just what he said that astounded us, but rather it was the manner in which he spoke these words. He expressed neither anger nor frustration but rather seemed to be stating a simple truth. I was incredibly disturbed that someone could ever consider themselves inferior to someone else. This is not to say that this young man didn't respect and value himself. In fact, he seemed to be very confident and self-assured. So if this is the case, how could he say something so derogatory about his own background? Chances are, he probably didn't even think about it. Whilst growing up he had probably become so accustomed to hearing such things said that saying something like this became almost as automatic as saying one's own name.

I later discovered that San children were reported as having low self-worth. The low sense of self-worth tended to be reinforced by teachers and peers at school. As visible minorities, San children were often discriminated against by their peers at school. Name calling and verbal abuse is not an uncommon occurrence for many San children at school largely because there is so little attention given to discussion on topics such as prejudice and social acceptance. When speaking to one student who had completed most of his education, I asked whether he had been discriminated against in school. His response was that his "skin gave him an advantage" because, being the child of a San mother and a Botswanan father, he had taken the physical attributes of his father, which allowed him to "blend" in more and thus be accepted. Many San students with similar circumstances would go to such extremes as changing their San names to English names so that they could escape being recognized as "Sersarwa" at school.

When I asked this same student for suggestions as to how to make the school experience less painful for San children, he suggested that in the provision of school materials for them, care should be taken to be less obvious about the assistance. He stated that when other children see San children getting "hand outs," they are subjected to further discrimination, which can be detrimental to the child's self-esteem. One non-San child I spoke with admitted to feeling some resentment towards San students because he felt they were given special treatment not only by the government but also by "foreigners like you who come in and give them special attention." Foreigners like me. You are not innocent. Remember your own implications in this. Remember you are a guest in this country. Remember who you are.

And who are you?

As human beings we have the capacity to stand outside the self and to objectively view the self in its relation to others. As participants in a socially and historically constructed world, both teachers and learners need to develop the capacity to see the roles in which they have been cast if they are to engage with the curriculum in new ways. The task is one of challenging prior assumptions and beginning to reconstruct a different way of thinking about the world. One of the difficulties is that it is very hard for actors within a context to overcome the socialization process that has been part of the everyday experience. Much research suggests that in daily interactions with students, many teachers systematically reinforce traditional stereotypes and cultural patterns (Riley & Ungerleider, 2008). Until teachers are aware of the ways in which they are implicated in cultural reproduction and of the assumptions they hold about teaching and learning, it is difficult to initiate any change in their practice.

Critically reflective classrooms, whether inside or outside the school, emphasize co-operation, co-learning, and individual rights as the participants question both their own social formation as a class and their position with the larger community context. Talk within the classroom environment leads to the development of a shared language that enables classroom members to make sense of their world and to question problematic aspects. Members of the class negotiate shared meaning as they work through content and interpersonal relationships. The critically reflective classroom offers the dual benefits of providing personal support and a specific reference group in which each person is recognized as possessing diverse strengths and experiences and is capable of assuming diverse but reciprocal roles.

Within the critically reflective classrooms that we advocate and create, people share ideas about learning, about what to learn, and about the ways in which to learn. Eventually they begin to note that many of the concerns that drew them together are not simply practical problems related to the classroom but are those that reflect broader, systemic problems that arise because of inequities in the social structure. Thus, within the classroom there is the dual purpose of mutual personal support and the classroom-identified task of highlighting and articulating the tacitly held assumptions of individual members of the class and of members of society at large. Once the assumptions have been articulated, they can be analyzed, critiqued, and changed.

The reciprocity of the teaching/learning relationship that we have described means that the classroom can operate as a social support network for both teacher and students. In addition, potential conflicts among approaches to teaching or among conflicting sources of knowledge can be safely critiqued as teacher and learners focus on a specific concern then invite each other to consider the potential of that problem in the lives of others. At other times, classroom members point out the ambiguities within particular positions of held or received knowledge. Understanding that the teacher/learner role is reciprocal is essential in order to highlight the ways in which power is inherent in the assumption of various roles.

In the classrooms we advocate, personal and social development are consequences of interaction. Drawn together by systemic pressures (in the case of students assigned to a particular teacher's class) or by choice (as in the self-selected class run by a favourite instructor), the nature of the classroom interaction creates a community in which members can begin to reconstruct their histories and their realities. In these classrooms we establish conditions of trust and openness in order to enable participants to learn what is expected and respect the necessary degree of self-disclosure. Any teachers who enter into critically reflective relationships with students must be cognizant of the historical construction of the nature of power relationships within the school and the classroom. Initially they have to be cautious since both they and the learners have to overcome histories of interdependencies and expectations of teachers as suppliers of knowledge and preservers of culture. Assuming the position of co-learner within the classroom means an acknowledgment of different voices and roles.

A key element in the way in which we operate in our co-learning environment is the focus on talk and interpersonal interaction. Our talk may focus initially on safe topics related to instrumental activities, but over time we begin to highlight the ways in which the instrumental activities are artifacts of a particular world view. In the classroom, we may begin by discussing a shared view of a common problem. By sharing the problem, the participants define what it is that they value through a process of negotiating meaning. Until beliefs are known and assumptions are tested, energy goes into the effort to discover and negotiate surface meaning.

In our classrooms, talk focuses on not only the solution to a problem but the process through which the solution was developed. For example, class members might discuss issues surrounding the identification of students with learning disabilities. In their discussion they attend not only to the solution to the problem of identification but also to the way in which the issue of how and why identification was articulated as an issue. Some might ask why identification is needed at all if students are to be treated individually. In examining institutionally created texts on the issue (rules and regulations that essentially define the term "disabled"), other questions can be asked. Where was the authority in the text? In what ways did the text experience differ from that of the members of the class? What assumptions or stereotypes might be embedded within the process of identification? Within the classroom itself, who had the most to say about this issue? Why? The reflexive relationship between the classroom participants themselves and with the outside texts enables them to consider not only solutions but the dynamics involved in the development of the solution. Over time, as the classroom matures, the processes in the classroom become predictable as it evolves its own culture.

The negotiated classroom culture can centre on any number of issues, but any critically reflective classroom ultimately considers its own behaviour in order to understand why it functions as it does. In any classroom, certain processes and understandings about classroom roles, dynamics, and politics emerge over time and shape the participants' interaction both internally and externally. The impact of the classroom on the individual participant and the way in which members collaborate to form a shared culture can only be determined by opening a window on the lived experience of members.

Essentials for Critical Reflection

We have identified two separate but related issues that surround critically reflective classrooms. The first has to do with issues of knowledge: what it is, its ownership, and its relation to the teaching/learning act. The second has to do with practical issues of managing and creating a classroom that is both personally satisfying and worthy of study and investment. We argue that to create a critically reflective classroom, teachers have to re-contextualize the school context. This means that the traditional classroom response pattern, in which the teacher is always evaluator, yields to the role of co-learner as the teacher builds on the learners' knowledge through interactive discussion that takes into account the relative position of all classroom participants. The teacher then problematizes the issues raised in terms of everyday life. Knowledge can thus be formed, owned, and produced by the members of the classroom who have equal responsibility for creating and participating in the learning community.

In order to fully understand critically reflective classrooms and the way they might function, one must become a part of them by sharing our stories of becoming better learners so that our students will know that we too struggle with tough concepts and big ideas and that some days we wonder whether we are really able to carry on. As teachers we must be ready to give up our authority and stand beside the other who is our student as we listen to their stories with respect. A key part of what happens in the critically reflective classroom is sharing stories of who we are and of what matters in our worlds. The critically reflective classroom becomes a place to share hopes, dreams, and the stories of who we are now and who we might become tomorrow. In such a classroom, perhaps we can accept and create a new way of knowing in which there are no more boundaries.

We swayed our bodies to the disjointed movements of the bus as it bounced steadily along the gravel road. The bus seemed to sway to the rhythm of the jovial beat that rolled through the speakers and danced in the limited space left between our packed-in bodies. I wiped the sweat from my forehead and peeled my back away from the black vinyl seats. I dug through my worn backpack, now covered with dust, and pulled out my map to try and gauge where exactly I was supposed to get off. Three more stops, the driver said. He would let me know. I folded the map and put it into the left pocket of my light sage, durable, cotton twill cargo pants complete with bellowed, self-fastening pockets, including one with a place for a cell phone – the unofficial uniform of the North American tourist. That was it, however. I drew the line at the Tilley hat.

We had made it to the Kalahari. Enchanting and mysterious Kalahari. Go to a library and take out a book on this topic. What will you find? Will it be a romance? A world of mystery and intrigue complete with visions of a tiny people dancing in animal skins and loin cloth around a roaring fire telling tales of hunts on an endless terrain with no boundaries and complete freedom. Or will you find a tragedy? A people lost without an identity, a people with no name searching for a home that has been stolen away from them. Chances are you will find both. Or at least that is what I found when I began my research on the Kalahari, and, to be fair, I didn't have to search for long. The bookstores are filled with contradictory notions of what the Kalahari is. Glossy covers of coffee table books displaying romantic visions of "Bushmen" hunting upon golden sand compete against hard cover copies of intellectual manuscripts holding the tragic tales of the very same "Bushmen" being thrown off the very same sand. Of course, like everything else in this world, the truth lies somewhere in the spaces between.

And who are you?

Maybe I am one of the writers of one of those books. Maybe I am the grey matter in between. Maybe I am a lot of different things. I don't know if I am ready to answer this question. Can you ask me this some other day?

Thank you very much. We have everything we need at this time.

And so the story ends. We understand that together with our students we can create a romance, a fable, a tragedy, a different future. We understand that what we give to them is no more nor no less than what they give to us. We are many different things, and so are our students. What we need to do is provide the time and the space for all of us to be many different things, but at the core, human beings in relation, who are struggling towards wisdom.

References

King, T. (2003). *The truth about stories: A native narrative.* Toronto, ON: House of Anansi Press.

Pinar, W. F. (2004). *What is curriculum theory.* Mahwah, NJ: Lawrence Erlbaum.

Posner, Richard (2003). *Public intellectuals: A study of decline.* Boston, MA: Harvard College Press.

Rich, Sharon J., & McLaughlin, John (2009). Education for the twenty-first century: Putting wisdom on the agenda. *Education Canada, 49*(4), 37–45.

Riley, T., & Ungerleider, C. (2008) The face of achievement: Influences on teacher decision making about Aboriginal students. *The Alberta Journal of Educational Research, 54*(4), 378–387.

WHY GO TO GUATEMALA? INTERNATIONAL SERVICE LEARNING AND CANADIAN HIGH SCHOOL STUDENTS

5

Geraldine Balzer, University of Saskatchewan

*I*N THE PRE-DAWN FEBRUARY MORNING, *a dozen grade 12 students, wearing matching t-shirts, huddle together in a prairie airport, not sure whether they are awake enough to be excited. Gathered near them is a collection of parents and teachers, checking to make sure everyone has passports, tying neon surveyor's tape to all luggage, offering last minute advice. These grade 12 students are en route to Guatemala for a two-week service learning trip, the eighth time students from this school have embarked on this journey and the fourth time I have accompanied them as a participant-researcher. The excitement mounts as we move through security and prepare to board the first of three flights that will carry us from -30C to +20C, from snowy plains to dusty mountains, from English to Spanish. Some of these students have never been on an airplane, others are seasoned travelers, but none have been to Guatemala. They have heard the stories from their peers and siblings who have gone before, they have looked at the photos, and they have raised money to contribute to the projects they will work on. Fifteen hours later we arrive in Guatemala City, fill out the requisite immigration and customs forms, and find our bags. The air is heavy, my hair begins to curl, the excitement and nervousness is palpable, and we move out, a brigade besieged by vendors selling candy, key chains, and scarves, proffering taxi rides and hotel rooms to purple-shirted Canadians. As we step through the doors, our world changes. I scan the street looking for the old grey van that I know will be there to rescue us from this cacophony. I was ready for the onslaught, the students weren't. After a fifteen minute drive through the city, we arrive at the seminary, which will be our home base for the next few days. The gates open and we drive inside, an oasis in the midst of chaos. The students marvel at the orchids in full bloom, the lush green trees, the quietness of this space. They then begin to notice the locked gate,* *the razor wire, the walls enclosing our oasis. Guatemala is a whole new world.*

Social justice issues are becoming an increasingly important part of curricula at all levels of education; many programs are built on the belief that social justice cannot only be an intellectual enterprise but must also encourage students to consider engaging with these issues in the real world. While earlier definitions of social justice often focused on issues related to poverty and economic egalitarianism, over the past few decades social justice education has expanded significantly to include racial, gender, and health inequalities, Aboriginal issues, peace and conflict studies, and of course, the mounting concerns about our environment. Social justice educators realize the need to move beyond theory and provide students with opportunities to see injustice and work toward justice in both the local and global community. In an attempt to make the connection between the classroom and the community, volunteering has become an optional or mandatory part of school programs. Both Ontario (2006) and the Northwest Territories (2002) mandate volunteerism (community service or involvement) as a requirement for high school graduation. High schools in other provinces also encourage students to engage in volunteer opportunities, and, in all likelihood, other programs of study will also mandate community service or volunteerism. To meet curricular demands or because of the pedagogical implications and the connections to civics and citizenry, some schools are including service learning opportunities in their programs.

While the broader aim of my study is to determine how structured service learning opportunities, specifically those with a global focus, impact participants, this paper focuses on the historical and theoretical underpinnings of service learning, the connections to curriculum, and the implementation and execution of effective service learning at the secondary level. This qualitative study is situated in a school that has an established and ongoing service learning program.

Each year, all students of this faith-based grade 10–12 school partic-ipate in structured service learning. The majority of projects are local, although some students have the opportunity to travel to urban centres in neighbouring provinces. Participating in an additional service learning experience in Guatemala has been an option for the past eight years, and three years ago, following Hurricane Katrina, a Mississippi option was developed. The students who participate in the international service learning options, Guatemala and Mississippi, must meet selection criteria and have the financial resources to meet the cost of the trip. This school was chosen because of the structured way in which service learning has been incorporated into the curricula and because of the history of service learning within the school.

What is Service Learning?

While service learning seems to be a very recent phenomenon, the ideals of service have been embedded in American post-secondary education since, as Hutchison (2001) asserts, the founding of Harvard in 1637. She contends that land grant colleges were estab-lished with community needs in mind, and that "colleges and univer-sities have traditionally served as the social conscience of the nation" (p. 1). She continues by describing the ways in which concern about standardization and accreditation have led post-secondary educa-tional institutions to move away from this sense of civic duty. In the early part of the twentieth century, it was not uncommon for univer-sities to have extension programs that served the needs of the com-munity. Students at the University of Saskatchewan, for example, spent time sharing their knowledge with the larger population in order to "extend the resources of the university for the benefit of cit-izens not enrolled as full-time students" (McLean, 2007, p. 7). Over time, the purpose of these extension programs moved from social justice to revenue generation, and service replaced service learning.

The current iteration of service learning has its roots in the notions of experiential education fostered by John Dewey and Jane Addams, and service became popularized in the 1960s with the establishment of organizations such as the Peace Corps. Service learning re-emerged with the establishment and popularization of college work-study programs (Titlebaum, Williamson, Daprano, Baer, & Brahler, 2004) With the proliferation of these programs, a clearer definition of service learning was necessary. Over time, the definition of service learning has been refined to differentiate it from volunteerism, internships, and practica. Bringle and Hatcher (1996) clearly delineate the differences, defining service learning as:

> a credit bearing educational experience in which students participate in an organized service activity that meets identified community needs and reflect on the service activity in such a way as to gain further understanding of the course content, a broader appreciation of the discipline, and an enhanced sense of civic responsibility. Unlike extracurricular voluntary service, service learning is a course-based service experience that produces the best outcomes when meaningful service activities are related to the course material through reflection activities such as directed writings, small group discussions, and class presentations. Unlike practica and internships, the experiential activity in a service learning course is not necessarily skill-based within the context of professional education. (p. 221)

While the definitions for service learning are numerous, all emphasize the need to connect the service projects to curricula, to meet the needs of the community, and to ensure that guided reflection is part of the process (Carpini & Keeter, 2000; Morin, 2009; National Commission on Service-Learning, 2002, 2008; Strom, 2010). Carpini and Keeter (2000), citing Elrich, contend that the experiential aspect of service learning implies that the experience must occur outside the classroom as participants work together with community members to solve a problem. International service learning provides learners with the opportunity to participate in a planned cultural immersion through travel to foreign countries and homestays with local people (Grusky, 2000). In this way, international service learning differs from volunteer or justice tourism which Stoddard and Rogerson (2004) describe as tourists who "volunteer in an organized way to undertake holidays that might involve aiding or alleviating the material poverty of some groups in society, the restoration of certain environments or research into aspects of society and environment" (p. 311). The lines between service learning and voluntary tourism are easily blurred since the majority of participants in both "tend to be young, educated, affluent, and white (Sherraden, Lough, & Mcbride, 2008, p. 398). For this reason, careful planning is at the core of service learning as the international volunteers work together with the local community.

Terry and Bohnenberger (2003) reiterate the connection between community service and academic study in the development of service learning programs. Ideally, there should be a balance between the service and the learning, but that is not always possible. They contend that the continuum of service learning can be classified into three categories. The first level involves increased awareness of the community through volunteerism or community service. This tends to involve a "high degree of service with a lesser degree of learning" (pp. 25–26). Community exploration reverses the balance and emphasizes learning rather than service. Within this category "the students go out into the community or members of the community come into the school, where information from the real world is shared and explored on a more authentic level than the distancing abstraction of a textbook" (p. 26). Elements of experiential education such as internships may be part of this process. Terry and Bohnenberger define the balance between service and learning as community action which "involves students becoming aware of, exploring, and becoming engaged in their community, as well as making a positive difference" (p. 26). Community action involves the greatest degree of service and learning and thus has the greatest impact on the learners and the community. This impact results in a "stronger, safer, more powerful, happier" community where students work toward a larger goal rather than simply completing required volunteer hours (Stoecker & Beckman, 2009). The Alliance for Service Learning in Education Reform, as cited in Terry and Bohnenberger (2003), emphasizes reflection as the framework for the processing and synthesizing of experiences. The transformative potential of service learning is greatly diminished without careful and guided reflection. If students are able to synthesize the information and ideas, the impact of service learning can be life changing.

Why Engage in Service Learning?

Advocates of service learning identify several benefits to the learners and the community: the personal and intellectual growth of the learner, civic engagement of the participants, and opportunity to address issues in the community through a process of reciprocity. The benefit of travel is frequently touted by teachers organizing travel clubs, field trips, and student exchanges. Students who participate in these activities undoubtedly grow in their understanding of the world but are rarely given an opportunity to contribute to the growth of others or the community. Service learning is intentionally designed "to equally benefit the provider and the recipient of the service as well as to ensure equal focus on both the service being provided and the learning that is occurring" (Furco, 1996, p. 5).

Since service learning is integrated into the school curriculum, the personal and intellectual growth of the student is integral to a successful project. Slavkin (2003) identifies several ways that service learning enhances curriculum, learning, and the community, resulting in engaged students who are more likely to see the "dynamic nature of information" (p. 20) since the "experiences often require teachers and students to interact with members of the community to engage in higher-order thinking" (p. 22). Slavkin also notes that engagement in service learning and experiential education disrupts a linear view of curricula and standards. This disruption does not only lead to improved student learning but also builds relationships leading to stronger schools and communities as students become contributors to the community (Kielsmeier, 2010). Lakin and Mahoney (2006) found that students who were "actively involved in their community have a stronger self-image and value themselves more highly than adolescents who do not take part [resulting in] improved interpersonal relationships and skills" (p. 514). Participation in service learning enables teachers to see the assets students bring to a project that may be very different than the assets they bring to the classroom. The sense of accomplishment and the emotional engagement often result in lifelong altruism (Krystal, 1999). Service learning offers youth the opportunity to connect with communities and identify with values and ideologies that have historical continuity. Leming (2001) identifies three development concepts necessary to facilitate adolescent identity formation: agency, personal relatedness, and moral political awareness.

While many of these benefits can be reached through participation in local service learning projects, international service learning has the opportunity to extend the moral political awareness and sense of civic responsibility into a global world view. International service learning exposes students to communities that differ significantly from their own in race, class, culture, and opportunity (Hartman & Rola, 2000; O'Donnell, 2000; Tepper-Rasmussen, 2006). In a world that is increasingly global, Holland (2000) feels educational relationships may be more important in addressing issues of sustainability and social justice than governmental relationships. Service learning projects enable students and teachers to begin building relationships, extending the notion of community. Relationships are no longer defined by proximity. Ultimately, "service learning foregrounds diversity and emancipatory pedagogy. It serves as a vehicle through which to examine in depth personal bias and racism and to better understand the meaning of diversity" (Baldwin, Buchanan, & Rudisill, 2007, p. 315). Better understanding of diversity may result in greater civic engagement.

Declining participation in civic, provincial, and national politics is a cause for concern, and politicians seek ways to invite youth to become involved and interested in civic affairs. Kielsmeier (2000) observed that youth, while distrustful of politicians and adversarial politics, are involved in a new politics of participation and voluntary service, reconceptualizing the role of young people in modern democracies. Owen (2000) also found that while youth are not supportive of established political institutions, and their patriotism and national pride is weak, they are engaged in volunteerism within the community. Youniss and Yates (1997) contend that the "process of reflection, which takes place publicly with peers and adults, as well as privately, . . . allows youth to construct identities that are integrated with ideological stances and political-moral outlooks" (p. 36). Service learning provides the forum for students to engage in volunteerism and reflection. Both Schmidt, Shumow, and Kackar (2007) and Zaff and Lerner (2010) advocate the use of school based service learning to increase civic awareness and engagement.

International service learning ensures that increased civic awareness extends globally rather than remaining local. Reciprocity must be part of the relationship. When North American volunteers travel to developing communities, the power imbalance is obvious (Simonelli, 2000). They come from a place of plenty and can easily be seen as voyeuristic judges, marvelling at the poor but happy villagers, charmed by traditional dress, and discomfited by traditional housing and lack of technologies. They bring with them wealth and power and a desire to re-create communities in their own image. Hartman and Rola (2000) outlines the process that needs to be implemented to ensure that the service learning project does no harm to the international community.

For the host communities where we will learn and serve, we must:
- Recognize the inherent capacity of every human being and of the communities in which they live;
- Realize that within each community, aspirations and needs vary from individual to individual, and household to household;
- Respect each person; you are a guest in someone else's life; and
- Learn to be kind and caring, not controlling and exploitative.

In preparing faculty and students for a service learning experience, we must:
- Observe before coming to conclusions rather than entering a community thinking we already have all the answers to their needs and problems;
- Think analytically and critically by asking real world questions in new environments;
- Learn by doing to connect theory with reality; and
- Be careful to do no harm; seek to understand before seeking to be understood.

After return to our institutions, we must:
- Find appropriate means to share the new understanding of how our former hosts view their world and begin in a modest way to expand the horizons of those who have not yet experienced service learning;
- Continue to carefully cultivate relationships with international communities and seek their feedback about how to improve future experiences for all involved; and
- Recognize that it takes both time and commitment to effect positive change. (p. 8)

Designing and implementing service learning, whether locally or internationally, requires careful planning, the cultivation of partnerships, and opportunities for reflection, transformation, and action on the part of the students.

Guatemala City seems a world away as our micro buses wind ever higher and farther west. The sounds of Spanish have been replaced with Tzutuil and K'iche´, Mayan languages that have resisted the colonizer's tongue. As we travel from town to town, we recognize the changing dress of the women – the brightly embroidered blouses of the Tzutuil, the frilly aprons of the Mam. We are in the western highlands where every patch of arable land holds a home and a family. This is where the Mam and the K'iche´ rebuilt their lives when the Spanish claimed the fertile lowlands for sugar cane, banana, and coffee plantations. After hours of travel, we arrive in San Marcos, the regional centre, a bustling market town. We meet our guide and a local activist who wants to speak to us about Canadian mining interests in Guatemala. Canadians have mines in Guatemala? The students are intrigued. I can see them thinking about the economic possibilities, the jobs, the improved living conditions that prosperity from a gold mine will bring. Alejandro arrives. He does not tell the story the students want to hear. He tells of cracks in houses from blasting and cyanide leaching fields close to homes. He tells of a mine that uses as much water in one hour as a Guatemalan family would use in twenty years. He tells of a community divided by those who fear for their environment and way of life and those who hope the mine will bring employment and prosperity. He asks the students if Canadians know about this mine. The students are embarrassed because they assumed Canadians were benevolent protectors of the environment and people. They leave determined to change the world.

We return to our micros and continue our journey, ever higher. We see the lights of villages and farms scattered across the mountains like stars across the sky. We begin to understand how many people a mine will displace. We arrive at the end of the road, a community of 100 homes at an altitude of 10 000 feet where we are greeted warmly by members of the community, welcomed into their homes, told of their dream. They are worried that more of their young men will leave to work illegally in the U.S. While the money they send home is important, the fabric of the community is strained by the divided families, fathers who are away for three, five, even twelve years. They are worried that another mine will open and their streams will be diverted and their health will be compromised. They have a dream. They have backyard trout farms, an important source of protein for the community, a source of cash when they market the excess. They are building a hatchery so they will no longer need to transport fish stock three hours. They watch tourists come from the city to climb the volcano and dream of being hosts and guides. But they do not only dream – they build and invite us to be part of their dream as we break ground on the tourist cabana, spending two days digging in the mud and working with rebar.

With the energy and optimism of youth, students return to Canada and write letters to mining companies and political leaders. They are told that the information they have is biased, that the mine does no harm. Some of them wonder if they have been too hasty in casting judgments; others are more determined than ever to have their voices heard. It is now the end of June – graduation day. They are being offered words of wisdom and encouragement, challenged to make their voices heard, reminded that they can make a difference. Then they receive this news: On June 24 Guatemalan president Alvaro Colom announced that he is suspending operations at the Marlin mine. A cheer erupts, not just from the letter writers, not just from the thirteen students who travelled to Guatemala, but from their peers and their parents. They believe they have a voice and the power to change the world.

How Do You Develop Effective Service Learning Programs?

Service learning has the potential to change lives, yet in order to meet that potential the programs must be carefully planned and evaluated. Building an effective service learning program involves more than finding a project and booking plane tickets. Over the last decade volunteer tourism has increased in popularity, and a niche market has been built around it (Stoddart & Rogerson, 2004). While some of this "voluntourism" brings needed infrastructure and support to communities, it also has the potential to provide an outside diagnosis and an unsustainable solution to the issue. The potential to alienate rather than build relationships is a danger of service learning. The National Youth Leadership Council (2008) has developed a set of standards and indicators for quality service learning:

- Service-learning actively engages participants in meaningful and personally relevant service activities.
- Service-learning is intentionally used as an instructional strategy to meet learning goals and/or content standards.
- Service-learning incorporates multiple challenging reflection activities that are ongoing and that prompt deep thinking and analysis about oneself and one's relationship to society.
- Service-learning promotes understanding of diversity and mutual respect among all participants.
- Service-learning provides youth with a strong voice in planning, implementing, and evaluating service learning experiences with guidance from adults.
- Service-learning partnerships are collaborative, mutually beneficial, and address community needs.
- Service-learning engages participants in an ongoing process to assess the quality of implementation and progress toward meeting specified goals, and uses results for improvement and sustainability.
- Service-learning has sufficient duration and intensity to address community needs and meet specified outcomes. (pp. 10–11)

Preparing the ground for the tourist cabana at the base of Tacman.

These goals and their accompanying indicators are a useful tool in the assessment of existing service learning programs, identifying the strengths and weakness of those programs, and making recommendations for future projects. I have used the NYLC goals and indicators as a template in assessing my research site.

Meaningful Service

Developing meaningful international service learning experiences for secondary school students poses major challenges. Grade 12 students have limited life experiences, and their understandings of global issues reflect those limitations. However, the Academy has worked together with their Guatemalan partners to participate in suitable projects that often focus on environmental issues. We have worked in several reforestation projects, one of which addressed the societal issue of land ownership. Participating in this project led students to question land distribution issues in Canada and the displacement of Canadian Aboriginals to make way for colonization. Each of the proj-

Building rebar armatures for the foundations of the tourist cabana.

137

ects has been part of a larger project developed by the local community, and the students feel that they worked with, not for, a community.

We arrived in this tiny village in Alta Verapaz – no electricity or running water, two room houses where the women cooked over an open fire. We were welcomed with smiles and hot tortillas, the staple of our diet for the next four days. We assembled on the field, fifteen of us, fifteen of them, and began to uproot vegetation as we prepared the ground for the vivero. By the end of the day, we had a fenced plot of land. We spent the next two days building nursery beds and filling tree bags with soil. We sat in a big circle, Canadian students and Qe'qchi men whose work in the coffee plantations taught them to be expert tree planters. They were patient teachers as they showed us time and again how to fill the bags perfectly. Each of these bags would contain a pine seedling; 800 000 seedlings would satisfy the government reforestation program, and many families would own the land their ancestors had farmed for centuries. Over the days we worked together, we transitioned from visitors and bystanders to co-workers, and I began to understand that I have a responsibility to serve, to help others even when it is not in my best interest. On our last morning we met to bless the land and the trees; grown men cried as they thanked us for helping to change their world. I had no idea planting trees could mean so much. Participating in this project has helped me grow into the person I want to become.

Link to Curriculum

The curricular links of the Academy's service learning program is the real strength of this project. Because students are involved in service learning each year, understanding service and context are built into a variety of courses. Elective course have been developed which focus on peace and justice; colonialism is critiqued through history and native studies classes. The faculty ensure that the students understand why service learning is important and prepare them to be thoughtful listeners and respectful guests. I have listened to students who describe the way an experience in Guatemala helped them understand their unearned advantage or the effect of colonialism on Aboriginal people in Canadian contexts.

We were standing by the big fountain in Parque Central, the oldest part of Guatemala City. Our guide explained to us that all Spanish colonial cities and towns had the same structure, a square bordered by the government, the church, the military or police, and the market. He called these the four powers and explained how these powers had taken the land away from the Mayan people and continued to suppress them through the long civil war. We saw these murals in the National Palace illustrating the Spaniards bringing civilization to the Mayans, and I suddenly realized that I had seen similar paintings in Canada. Suddenly, I realized that Canada had a colonial history, and the winner gets to write the history.

There is garbage everywhere – along the side of road, in the ravines, and the dump is disgusting. People live and work there with the vultures

The students spent four days building a tree nursery or *vivero*. One year later, the next participants were able to see the seedlings and walk the land that again belonged to the Qe'qchi Mayan. They had lost ownership of the land when the nineteenth-century government sold it to coffee plantation owners, but the reforestation project provided the finances to purchase the land.

and the toxic garbage, and it stinks. Why don't Guatemalans have a recycling program or something to deal with this garbage. Then our teacher talked about the infrastructure that supports our waste management programs in Canada, and I realized that we have a garbage problem, we just don't see it. When I think about everything we consume, we might even have a bigger garbage problem than Guatemala.

Reflection

Initially I thought that reflection was a weaker aspect of the Academy's service learning program. The students are encouraged to keep journals while on their trip, and there are plenty of opportunities to enter into conversations with peers, teachers, guides, and hosts. Most of the participants leave Guatemala with good intentions but later admit that the business of school soon derails their plans. Peers who have not participated in the project have limited interest, and life interferes with their goals. Those students enrolled in the Peace and Justice elective have an opportunity for guided reflection, and many other courses enable them to reflect indirectly, but "multiple challenging reflection activities" are not formalized. However, when conducting follow-up interviews with the students, I began to realize how deeply they continue to reflect.

Going to Guatemala was a life changing experience for me, and I don't see the world in the same way anymore. I've come to understand that our life experiences depend on where we were born, not on how hard we work. I've become much more conscious of my consumption and think about where products were made and whether there is a fair trade option. I don't use as much water, and I try to recycle more things. I've realized that we are privileged to worry about things that aren't important, and the people of Guatemala worry about things like food and housing. But in spite of everything we have and they don't, they showed us how to be community. I realize that my career will have some aspect of service in it; I have to give back to the world.

Diversity

Participating in service learning in Guatemala disrupts the students' comfort levels in profound ways. They are suddenly a visible minority without the language skills necessary to survive, reliant on their guides and hosts. This experience enables them to empathize with the foreign students in their school and the recent immigrants to their communities. They learn to value the skills of their hosts who patiently teach them how to bend rebar, fill seedling bags, or make tortillas. Their perception of "the other" changes.

Before I went to Guatemala, I had a "World Vision" view of poverty, starving children with flies crawling on them, waiting to be saved by donations. My view of poverty changed. I now know that poverty and impoverished are not the same thing, and sometimes I think we are the impoverished people. They have a richness of community and family that we seem to have lost. There is more to people than what you see on TV. I think experiences like this can reduce racism.

I was shocked by the billboards. They only had white people on them. Who do the Mayans look up to? White people aren't The People. Why has the American form of beauty enveloped everyone?

Listening to stories.

Youth Voice

International travel and working with international partners sets limitations; however, within those limitations, students are given a voice. Students at Academy plan and organize an annual fundraising drive that generates capital for the service projects. This year, they distributed over $10 000 to Guatemalan projects, the local food bank, and to Haitian earthquake relief. Students travelling to Guatemala were asked by the local partners to work in the preschool and the after school programs. They chose activities and were responsible for acquiring the supplies and teaching the children. Students are given opportunity to take leadership in a safe and nurturing environment. Their evaluation of the quality and effectiveness of the project is limited by their age and experience, but their enthusiasm is boundless.

We can change the world! When we get back home, we need to tell everyone these stories because we can make a difference. It's important that other youth have these experiences because we are young, and we have more time to be involved in these kinds of projects. When we are older, it will be harder to change the way we see the world. I now know that people who have the most have the most responsibility to improve the situations of others. I am definitely going to do more of this when I am older – maybe Doctors without Borders or Engineers without Borders or one of the other volunteer programs. I feel as if I have made a difference because they trusted me to do the job I was given. I think it is unusual for high school students to be trusted in this way, and I am lucky to go to this school and participate in these projects.

Partnerships

International partnerships are difficult to develop and maintain. A two-week annual visit and a language barrier curtail the development of personal relationships. And the program would be impossible to

mount if not for the partnership with the hosting organization who are locally based and have established credibility with the communities. We are the beneficiaries of the trust they have established. The positive behaviour of each participating student group ensures that the new group is welcomed into the community. The stories told by participating students introduce grade 11 students to names and faces. The students wonder if their unskilled labour will be a valued resource. The work is often laborious and tedious.

I am wondering why I spent all this money to come here and do monkey work, work that local people could have done and done with more skill. I talked to my teachers about that and they helped me see the bigger picture. Because we worked on the project, community members don't have to. They can go work in their fields or pick coffee or go to their regular jobs. Our sixty hours of labour means that the project is sixty hours closer to completion. But maybe this isn't about me serving them. Maybe the service is just part of the learning. Maybe the community is serving me as I grow in understanding. I now understand that the community doesn't want my charity; they don't want us to work for them or to work for us – they want us to work together for a common goal. My host mother said that every time an international volunteer stays with her, her family gets bigger. This is all about empowerment, not charity. It has taken me a while to understand that.

Duration and Intensity

Ideally service learning should occur over an extended period of time in order to have the greatest impact. Universities and colleges are able to implement service terms, secondary schools cannot. The Academy, however, addresses the issue of duration by incorporating service learning into each year as part of the extended curriculum. The Guatemalan experience provides students with duration and intensity appropriate to their age and maturity. While two weeks is a relatively short period of time, it is sufficient to make an impact. During this time, the students are besieged by new experiences, a new culture, strange food, and hard work. Most of the students are ready to return home to those things that are familiar, but many of them plan on returning to Guatemala or embarking on another adventure. Indeed, over the years of the program, a significant number of alumni have chosen to engage in short- or long-term volun-

Teaching art in the preschool.

teerism. Some have returned to Mississippi or Guatemala, others have ventured to new places.

I wanted to do more work! At first I felt too much like a tourist. I couldn't understand anything, and we had to communicate with our host families through sign language. But then the kids really helped. We created a picture dictionary, and now I have some words. At first, all I could see was the dirt floor, the smoke filled kitchen, and chickens in the house. And the latrine really creeped me out. But after a day or two, I began to see that this family wasn't so very different from my own. The big difference is the amount of time they have to be family. Once it is dark, everyone is home for the evening. We sat around the fire getting the corn ready for the next day's tortillas. I can't believe how many they make and how many they eat. I would be tired of tortillas three times a day every day. In fact, I am tired of them. I don't think I will ever complain about food again. Staying here this long has helped me see past the initial problem to the root problem. It's easy to say that they need more education or better nutrition. I now realize that they need their land. There is no short-term way to fix past hurts. I wonder if that is the way victims of Canadian residential schools feel?

Painting the school damaged by a mudslide.

145

Conclusion

International service learning is a complex, resource intensive, experiential learning strategy that few secondary schools engage in. The question is whether or not the student experience and learning are worth the additional cost and risk. In my assessment, they are well worth the additional resources. As Baldwin, Buchanan, and Rudisill (2007) note, "Service learning foregrounds diversity and emancipatory pedagogy. It serves as a vehicle through which to examine in depth personal bias and racism and to better understand the meaning of diversity" (p. 315). The majority of Academy students who have participated in these experiences have had their personal biases challenged, and they have returned to Canada with new understandings of the local situations. Tepper-Rasmussen (2006) concludes that the most important aspect of the international experience "is opening students' eyes to those who have lived totally different lives, without the luxuries to which we are accustomed, to allow them to see that we are not really so different" (p. 25).

These new perceptions lead to a new interest in world events and empower students to become involved in local, national, and global issues. Students who participate in international service learning are more likely become politically engaged (Owen, 2000) – as evidenced by the Academy students' commitment to expose the human rights abuses of Canadian mining interests in Guatemala – discuss land tenure of Aboriginal peoples, or consider environmental issues associated with consumption. However, this knowledge would not be possible without the careful scaffolding of committed teachers and the development of long term partnerships. Goals and objectives need to be firmly established, and the curricular links must be clear. Students who embark on international travel, while wooed by the romance of the exotic, must also understand that cultural and physical discomfort is part of the experience. I concur with Krystal (1999) who believes that

Service learning should be at the core of every school's curriculum because it gives young people purpose and nurtures their spirit as few experiences can. How is the spirit nurtured? From the feeling of accomplishment; from the rewards of giving and realizing how much they have received; from knowing they have made a difference in someone's life or in the community; from discovering their special talents; from having fun and learning at the same time; from the tears shed at the end of the service experience; from knowing they are part of their community and will perform service in some form the rest of their lives. (p. 61)

In the pre-dawn February morning, a dozen grade 12 students, again wearing matching t-shirts, load their packs into the big grey van and prepare for the journey to the airport. The walls and razor wire no longer seem so alien as the gate opens and we leave our oasis. We catch our last glimpses of the volcanoes surrounding the city, and breathe deeply of the moist warm air. The vendors attempt to sell us a few more souvenirs for our already bulging packs, but we have learned to ignore their persistent cries. We enter the airport, pass through security, and enter a familiar world that seems strangely foreign. By nightfall, we are back in the prairie airport, greeted by family. The air is cold, but we don't notice because we have stories to tell, experiences that have changed the way we see the world. When we hear the news of a volcanic eruption, mudslides and sinkholes caused by tropical storms, it matters. Are Juan and his family okay? Did our freshly painted school survive the floods? Have they put a roof on the preschool? Will the group next year see a finished cabana at the base of Tacman? We care because we know the people. We can cheer when a mine closes and we can cry when we hear of natural disasters. In two weeks, our world has gotten smaller but our hope for the world has grown. We believe that we can make a difference by doing our part.

References

Baldwin, S., Buchanan, A., & Rudisill, M. (2007). What teacher candidates learned about diversity, social justice, and themselves from service-learning experiences. *Journal of Teacher Education,* 58(4), 315–327.

Bringle, R. G., & Hatcher, J. A. (1996). Implementing service-learning in higher education. *Journal of Higher Education,* 67(2), 221–239.

Carpini, M., & Keeter, S. (2000). What should be learned through service learning? *PS: Political Science and Politics,* 33(3), 635–637.

Furco, A. (1996, Fall). Service-learning and school to work: Making the connections. *Journal of Cooperative Education,* 32(1), 7–14.

Grusky, S. (2000). International service learning: A critical guide from an impassioned advocate. *The American Behavioral Scientist,* 43(5), 858–867. doi:10.1177/00027640021955513

Hartman, D., & Rola, G. (2000). Going global with service learning. *Metropolitan Universities: An International Forum,* 11(1), 15–23.

Holland, B. (2000). From the editor's desk. *Metropolitan Universities: An International Forum,* 11(1), 3–6.

Hutchison, P. (2001) Service learning: Challenges and opportunities [Online article]. Retrieved from http://www.newfoundations.com/OrgTheory/Hutchinson721.html

Kielsmeier, J. C. (2000). A time to serve, a time to learn: Service-learning and the promise of democracy. *Phi Delta Kappan,* 81(9), 652-657.

Kielsmeier, J. C. (2010). Build a bridge between service and learning. *Phi Delta Kappan,* 91(5), 8–15.

Krystal, S. (1999). The nurturing potential of service learning. *Educational Leadership,* 56(4), 58–61.

Lakin, R., & Mahoney, A. (2006). Empowering youth to change their world: Identifying key components of a community service program to promote positive development. *Journal of School Psychology, 44*(6), 513–531.

Leming, J. (2001). Integrating a structured ethical reflection curriculum into high school community service experiences: Impact on students' sociomoral development. *Adolescence, 36*(141), 33–45.

McLean, S. (2007). University and social change: Positioning a university of the people in Saskatchewan. *Adult Education Quarterly, 58*(1), 3–21.

Morin, E. (2009). Service learning pitfalls: Problems you didn't see coming. *College Teaching Methods & Styles Journal, 5*(1), 43–51.

National Youth Leadership Council. (2002). *Learning in deed: The power of service-learning for American schools.* Available from http://www.nylc.org

National Youth Leadership Council. (2008). *Growing to greatness 2008: The state of service learning.* Available from http://www.nylc.org

O'Donnell, K. (2000). Building intercultural bridges. *Metropolitan Universities: An International Forum, 11*(1), 25–33.

Owen, D. (2000). Service learning and political socialization. *PS: Political Science and Politics, 33*(3), 638–640.

Schmidt, J., Shumow, L. & Kackar, H. (2007). Adolescents' participation in service activities and its impact on academic, behavioral, and civic outcomes. *Journal of Youth and Adolescence, 36*(2), 127-140.

Sherraden, M., Lough, B., & Mcbride, A. (2008). Effects of international volunteering and service: Individual and institutional predictors. *Voluntas, 19*(4), 395–421.

Simonelli, J. (2000). Service learning abroad: Liability and logistics. *Metropolitan Universities: An International Forum, 11*(1), 35–44.

Slavkin, M. (2003). Service learning and brain-based strategies are natural partners to keep standard-based curricula from promoting passive, rote learning. *Principal Leadership Magazine, 3*(9), 20–25.

Stoddart, H., & Rogerson, C. M. (2004). Volunteer tourism: The case of Habitat for Humanity South Africa. *GeoJournal, 60*(3), 311–318.

Stoecker, R., & Beckman, M. (2009). Making higher education civic engagement matter in the community [Online article]. Retrieved from http://www.compact.org/wp-content/uploads/2010/02/engagementproof-1.pdf

Strom, S. (2010, January 3). Does service learning really help. *New York Times.* Retrieved from http://www.nytimes.com/2010/01/03/education/edlife/03service-t.html

Tepper-Rasmussen, M. (2006). Weaving service into adolescent lives. *Montessori Life, 18*(3), 22–25.

Terry, A., & Bohnenberger, J. (2003). Service learning: Fostering a cycle of caring in our gifted youth. *Journal of Secondary Gifted Education, 15*(1), 23–32.

Titlebaum, P., Williamson, G., Daprano, C., Baer, J., & Brahler, J. (2004). Annotated history of service learning: 1862–2002 [Online article]. Retrieved from http://www.servicelearning.org/what_is_service-learning/history

Youniss, J., & Yates, M. (1997). *Community service and social responsibility.* University of Chicago Press.

Zaff, J., & Lerner, R. (2010). Service learning promotes positive youth development in high school. *Phi Delta Kappan, 91*(5), 21–23.

PART TWO

CANADIAN CURRICULUM & CULTURAL PERSPECTIVES

Can wisdom trump the market as a basis for education?

6

David Geoffrey Smith, University of Alberta

The wise are mightier than the strong. (Proverbs 24:5)
The tongue of the wise brings healing. (Proverbs 12:18)

O
N THE MORNING OF February 17th, 2010, a distinguished professor of business at one of Canada's leading research universities made a remarkable suggestion. Market regulators, he said, would do well to practice Buddhist philosophies. His comment came after his keynote speech, entitled "Why Markets Fail," during a symposium sponsored by the university and the Social Sciences and Humanities Research Council (SSHRC) of Canada. The symposium was designed to help people better understand the contemporary collapse of global markets and, perhaps, to allay their fears for the future (Morck, 2009).

As a professor of education who has been studying global wisdom traditions, including Buddhism, for over twenty years, my ears suddenly pricked up. Buddhist philosophies may be helpful, the professor surmised, because the Buddha spoke of the impermanence of life, of the dialectical relation of pleasure to suffering, and because markets might be analogous to the Buddhist concept of illusion. So far so good. He continued, the temptation to regulate markets, which always follows a collapse, may in fact impede the "natural ability of the market to recover" (a presumption, surely), and indeed make matters worse in the long run. So the argument went, and just as suddenly my ears resumed their flopped position. Why? Because the professor's logic appropriated the Buddha's wisdom for a predetermined purpose, namely the survival of the market, rather than letting that wisdom interrogate market logic itself, and perhaps thereby transform it into a better practice of social and cultural healing, if in fact that might be possible.

That last point about healing is relevant insofar as the earliest for-mulations of market logic in the eighteenth century were indeed designed to encourage personal and social healing, especially healing of the wounds of ethnic, religious, and political strife. Repudiating existing religious and monarchical traditions for their propensity to produce enmity, Voltaire (1734/1980), a leading French *philosophe* of the European Enlightenment, pointed to the London Stock Exchange as "a place more respectable than many a court," where "you will see assembled representatives of every nation for the bene-fit of mankind. Here, the Jew, the Mohametan and the Christian deal with one another as if they were of the same religion, and reserve the name 'infidel' for those who go bankrupt"(Letter Six).

It's a fairly long journey from the establishment of the first Stock Exchange in Antwerp Belgium in 1460 to the collapse of the global market in 2008 – a time of an immense inversion of human val-ues – when, for example, the Seven Deadly Sins (SDS) of medieval Christendom (anger, greed, sloth, pride, lust, envy, and gluttony) gradually morphed into the easier virtues of contemporary capital-ism (self-righteous rage against another in the name of personal rights, consumerism, leisure, self-esteem, recreational sex, wanting what the other has, and insatiability. (Brainstorming with a class the binary opposites of the SDSs is an interesting pedagogical activity.) Responsibility for this inversion of values may rest with traditional religious institutions themselves, if "sin" means "missing the point" of life (Gk. *hamartia*), and there has been a persistent failure to trans-late consciousness of sin into the one quality celebrated above all others by the new Enlightenment rationality, namely human happi-ness. The enshrinement of the right to pursue happiness in the new American constitution of 1789 marked a determination that had been evolving for almost two hundred years that worldly happiness was a good thing, that the status of life beyond death was something undecidable in human terms and hence of less immediate concern. By the mid-eighteenth century, the word "civilization" had taken on a new and very specific meaning, identified as *refinement*, a kind of moral rehabilitation of luxury (Febvre, in Burke 1973, p. 229). The Scottish philosopher David Hume (1751/1983), in his 1742 essay "On Luxury," denounced what he called "the monkish virtues" of asceticism and self-denial, and Voltaire, in his 1734 poem "The Worldling" (1734/1901), assailed the "poor Doctors of the Church" (p. 84) for their hypocrisy in failing to appreciate their dependence on the material welfare supplied by the new wealth of urban luxury. In all of this, the market was seen to play *the* pivotal role in producing what the godfather of modern economics, Adam Smith, in 1776 anticipated as "universal opulence," but also a new form of social control based on the self-control necessary to succeed in a world based on commercial relations. Indeed, the word "Proprietor" entered the English language to describe the "propriety" of the new business man (Muller, 2003, p. 72).

Smith (1780/1982) was sanguine enough about human nature to recognize that "The wise and virtuous" were inevitably "a small party" (p. 62), with the new logic of self-interest capable of leading to what a century later the philosopher Hegel called "bad infinity," from Aristotle's *pleonexia*, a seduction into infinite desire incapable of restraint (Muller, 2003, p. 159) It is worth noting too, as an aside, that Smith foresaw how the division of labour, or specialization, he recommended as part of production efficiency for market success would lead to new forms of isolation and alienation for workers. His antidote was "education," so people could engage with understandings of the world broader than the one inflicted on them by their working conditions. Smith was thus a forebear of mass public education in capitalist societies.

Today, the market has assumed the status of what Buddhist social theorist David Loy (2003) has termed "the world's first transcendental logic." To question it is to invite derision, especially from those who most profit from it, which includes not just those involved in production, trade, and finance, but also so-called academics who make their reputations in faculties and schools of business while refusing to critically examine their underlying presuppositions. It is important to remember, however, that in the classical republican traditions of Greece and Rome, merchants were stigmatized as being involved in practices that, while necessary for material provisioning, for that very reason were somehow "lesser" on the scale of human dignity. Mind and spirit were always more important in the classical world to such a degree that being a merchant actually disqualified one from citizenship in the republic (Muller, 2003, p. 61). In the Christian tradition too, at least until the Protestant Reformation of the sixteenth century, self-interest, the very basis of market logic, was regarded as a passion, thus part of a person's bodily *animal* nature rather than true human nature (Ibid.).

All these foregoing contextualizing remarks reinforce what in recent days social theorist Samir Amin (2004) has stressed, specifically the importance of understanding capitalism as a "parenthesis" in the human story, not its final end, a remark intuitively understood, perhaps, by a group of MBA students at Canada's University of Western Ontario subsequent to the current market crash. "The paradigm has broken" said one student (Grant, 2008). More on this point later.

What I wish to attempt in this paper is both genealogical and pedagogical. As has been well established in recent scholarship, since the middle of the 1990s, public education policy and indeed practice have fallen under the formidable influence of what is usually termed *neoliberalism*. Basically, the era beginning in the late 1970s/early 1980s with Margaret Thatcher in the United Kingdom and Ronald Reagan in the U.S. was a time when Western economies were floundering under pressures of economic stagnation, and the Thatcher/Reagan solution was to invoke the economic ideas of Friedrich von Hayek (and his American disciple Milton Friedman) by way of solution. These ideas included ending the welfare state that had been constructed since World War II, privatization whenever possible of public institutions like schools and hospitals, holding all public institutions accountable to severe standards of economic efficiency, and ending state "interference" in the operation of the "free market." New terms in education were born, such as "the new knowledge economy," which attempted to reduce all knowledge to commodity form for international trade in a conceived new "borderless" world of "globalization." Knowledge production itself became an "industry" subject to the efficiency requirements of industrial production, with universities held to new management rules of accountability and stricture. Because market logic is structured on a foundation of human competitiveness, education became articulated as the task of preparing students, defined as "human capital," for "global competitiveness." Schools and universities became subject to global ranking measures, with those "falling behind" subject to threat of state de-funding. The language of "excellence" appeared as a coverall term used by institutions to legitimize themselves as both worthy and desirable within an increasingly stringent fight for resources, customers, clients, and recruits. Cornell University even devised an "Excellence in Parking" award for its parking services department (Peters, 2007). In the United States, those who drafted the *No Child Left Behind* policy seemed unaware of the apocalyptic nature of the policy's title. To this day all these reforms have had enormous effect on life in educational institutions, and in pedagogical terms most of it has been negative. Teachers are being asked to teach more and more students with fewer and fewer resources. Education faculty members are pressed to publish more and more, since in the new performance measures it is the number of publications that counts, not their quality, with most of the new scholarship being unenlightening as time for deep study is reduced by increases in institutional responsibility and teaching. Students at both school and tertiary levels have come to see educational institutions as "service providers" for which they themselves are clients or customers with highest priority rights for personal satisfaction. As a consequence, teachers and professors have lost much of their former professional authority over both curriculum and pedagogy. The list could go on.

What is relevant here, and it is a development that has received scant attention in virtually all educational research literature to date, is that *the contemporary collapse of the global market signifies the end of neoliberalism as a legitimate basis for educational and practice.* The principles of "deregulation," the aggressive economic imperialism masked by the euphemism of "globalization," the myth of education as the conduit to personal wealth creation, all of these assumptions now lie in shambles. Because mainstream media (newspapers, television, Hollywood cinema, etc.) are controlled by those now desperately trying to manage the collapse, information about the collapse and its impending intensification is hidden behind veiled language of economic recovery. The facts of the matter, however, are such that a recovery to some pre-recessionary levels of economic health is a delusional idea. Basically this is because the global economy has been constructed on a foundation of U.S. public and state indebtedness, designed to finance the failed imperial wars in Iraq and Afghanistan, wars which, undertaken in the heady, swaggering years of post-communism, in turn were undertaken to ameliorate the already perilous condition of Western economies. (For a more detailed discussion of these claims, see various articles at http://globalresearch.ca/, and particularly the work of the GlobalEurope Anticipation Bulletin, available online). That perilousness today calls for a new kind of social and political vigilance by all those concerned for public welfare, especially perhaps educators, whose unique vocational responsibility is to stand for an open future so that the young, the special charge of educators at all levels, may indeed have a future.

Vigilance is one thing, but relevant vigilance requires a particular kind of attention. In this case, education can no longer be left to the economists, neither can economists alone be trusted to guide the public sphere as they have done, basically since the eighteenth century, but in a uniquely heightened and ideologically driven way since the 1970s. If, however, educators are to creatively resist the oppressive obsessions of the economists, they have no alternative but to engage the operating assumptions of economists themselves. Educators have to study economics, but actually in a unique way, a hermeneutic way. By this I mean they/we have to study economics not as a set of inert ideas requiring only effective implementation, but rather as a historically derived field that constituted itself in response to particular questions and issues arising in the public domain. Robert Heilbroner (1999), an economic historian, once described economics as work of "human provisioning." The origin of the word in the Greek *oikos*, meaning "household," points to how economics must be concerned with the overall welfare of the human household and not tied, as it has become today, to ideological posturing and divisive politics. What makes the current situation particularly elusive yet decisive is the fact that most, if not all, economists simply do not know what to do. Because the global economy is now, well, global – integrated in a way unprecedented in human history, conventional economic theory, based on forms of rationality rooted in the eighteenth-century European Enlightenment – this economic theory is inadequate for interpreting the intricacies and requirements of truly global times. In this essay, my point is that today, economics needs to be put in its place, basically to where it belonged before the industrial revolution of the nineteenth century. As economic historian Karl Polanyi (2001) argued in his classic book *The Great Transformation*, before the nineteenth century the economy served society; since then society has served the economy. It is this latter condition that needs to be revisited, but, as noted, responsible social theorists of all stripes need to educate themselves regarding the assumptions of the field they wish to revise. It is in that spirit that this present paper proceeds. What is market logic, and what have been the debates about it historically? How can market logic today be engaged creatively, not just critically? It is in that last respect that I turn to global wisdom traditions for assumptions about how priorities in human living might be established beyond the currently dogmatic formulations of global monetarism. In what follows I undertake a kind of genealogy of "capitalism," a term which entered the English language in the nineteenth century, before which Adam Smith simply referred to "commercial society," later embellished by G. F.Hegel as "civil society" (Muller, 2003, p. 166).

In the modern period, concerns about "commercial society" go back to writers like Justus Moser (Knudsen, 1986) of the late eighteenth century who saw the market as a "destroyer of culture," the concomitant need being to protect indigenous traditions of social wellness. In the nineteenth century, philosopher G. F. Hegel (Hardimon, 1994) saw the arbitrariness of "free choice" in a culture of consumption as a sign of "unfreedom" leading to entrapment in subjectivity. For Karl Marx in the last century, capitalism was seen to produce human alienation from self, others, and the natural world, inevitably leading to war and the polarization of rich and poor. Hungarian Georg Lukacs (Kadarkay, 1991) regarded modern capitalism as "an age of absolute evil" and a "system of illusion" that produces passivity, mental torpor, and "thingification" with *reification* as the failure to see the relations produced by capital as historically constructed. Indeed, for Lukacs, so enmeshed can we become within the operations of the market that to become conscious of this would be "to commit suicide," the result being that most people prefer "false consciousness." In the 1960s and 70s, Herbert Marcuse (1964; Katz, 1982) became famous for his suggestion that capitalism produces totalitarianism without terror by producing a form of "one dimensional thought" that reduces everything to a single logic. He coined such terms as "stupefaction" and "moronization," with true economic freedom meaning "freedom *from* the economy" (Marcuse, 1964, pp. 2–4).

Even supporters of the market have recognized its downsides, though sometimes interpreting the negatives as positives. In his classic work *The Philosophy of Money*, Georg Simmel (Wolff, 1965) explored the effect on the mind of living in a capitalist society. The calculating consciousness that develops in a market-dominated culture produces tendencies toward abstraction and removal of personal emotional investment from the affairs of daily life, along with indifference to others, which, ironically, Simmel regarded as a good thing, with people left alone to go about their own business. Today's epithet "mind your own business" is an echo of what Simmel was suggesting. Simmel also referred to "the tragedy of culture" within capitalist societies when people are frustrated by dreams of what they *could* do in life but simply can't by force of circumstances. While the competition fostered by market relations "achieves what usually only love can do: the divination of the wishes of the other, even before he himself becomes aware of them," inevitably this produces "A fight *of* all, *for* all" (Wolff, 1965, p. 62).

Simmel's contemporary Max Weber was interested in a similar question of "What human type is promoted by modern capitalism?" In *Economy and Society* (1978) he argued that the modern huge corporation has produced an entirely new class of persons, namely "managers," who operate at all levels throughout a large company and now, indeed, society. As bureaucratic functionaries, their necessary preoccupation is with an instrumental rationality to match "means" with predetermined "ends," resulting in a "disenchantment of the world," since the capacity to imagine a different world has been subverted by the need to keep the present order of things running smoothly. This in turn leads to an experience of living within the "iron cage" of one's own subjectivity (Scaff, 1989), an interpretation inspired perhaps by Hegel.

In a way, the title of this chapter is misleading if it is taken as a rhetorical invitation to condemn market logic as a completely negative phenomenon, perhaps especially with respect to providing a basis for education. As argued by von Hayek, today all of life's requirements are mediated through the market, so in fact to criticize the market is anti-life (Muller, 2003, p. 367). Even to go to a spiritual retreat that considers alternatives to market logic requires all the benefits that a market society has produced – a mode of transportation to get there, books and reading materials produced by commercial publishing houses, electricity for illumination at night, blankets produced by textile companies, clothing by garment industries, etc. It is impossible to live *outside* of market relations today, and indeed one of the main points of pro-market theorists right from the beginning (Voltaire through von Hayek) has been that the market produces creative possibilities in human relations that have eluded every other historically constituted institution to date. Nation, state, church, mosque, synagogue, tribe, race – all these eventually invert into a phenomenology of regression built on assumptions of exclusion and/or self-superiority. The market has been the great leveller of the human condition, has been the suggestion, and the reason, why it must be continually promoted as a path to world peace based on equality and a common rule of law. Of course, this is a rhetorical argument in itself, completely based on a selective interpretation of facts that hides the true cost of market relations taken as an ultimate truth form. That is where the question of wisdom enters the picture, consideration of which will be taken up later.

In the meantime, I wish to outline the key ideas of two of the most important economic thinkers to have shaped our current circumstances both in the West as well as more globally, namely Joseph Schumpeter and von Hayek, already mentioned. If there is going to be any meaningful engagement over the question of human futures in a more cosmopolitan and internationally equitable sense, then it is essential in my view that Schumpeter and von Hayek be better understood than they presently are, since their ideas are largely responsible for how contemporary market assumptions have been shaped.

Schumpeter published his landmark book *Capitalism, Socialism and Democracy* in 1942 (recently republished 2008) when he was a professor of economics at Harvard, after emigrating from Germany in the thirties. The title of the book itself signals one of Schumpeter's foremost interests as being to delegitimize Marxist "socialism" as, ironically, a "substitute religion" which inevitably ends up repressing the very working classes it proclaims to emancipate, since success of the socialist system is built on a closed totalitarian model that cannot abide its own critics. What is important here for our own purposes is to identify how the argument between capitalism and socialism, that has defined economic theory first in the Western tradition but now also globally since the early twentieth century, sets up a logic of choice which may indeed be a false choice. Today my argument is that this choice is an anachronism that wisdom traditions may help to rectify. The requirements of human survival demand a more catholic (L. *universal*) deliberation on questions of human provisioning, including education. Again, more later.

In a sense, Schumpeter was an heir to the iconoclasm of Friedrich Nietzsche (1844–1900) who repudiated the "God-hypothesis" of conventional religion in favour of a more naturalistic interpretation of human life and necessities. This world, he argued, perpetually organizes and re-organizes itself within a fundamental disposition he called "will to power," which gives rise to successive iterations of power relationships. "This world," he proposed, "is the will to power and nothing besides, and you yourselves are also this will to power – and nothing besides!" (Kaufmann, 2000, p. 70). Often characterized as nihilist, Nietzsche's vision was actually one of human possibility and especially creativity, which he described as the unique possession of gifted individuals who should be given privileged responsibility for human leadership, a task which cannot, indeed must not, be left to "the herd." Hence Nietzsche's theory of the "superman" (Ger. *Ubermensch*), the leader who leads but who also in that role inevitably inspires resentment (Ger. *Ressentiment*) from lesser mortals.

All of these themes found a place in Schumpeter's economic theory, and later that of von Hayek. Schumpeter emphasized the importance of entrepreneurship as the engine of economic innovation, which required a class of elites who shared "the joy of creating." According to Schumpeter, people with "supernormal brains" move towards business not just because of the lure of great profits, but also because of the ability of business to engage their creative powers through research, marketing, and organization theory. Schumpeter was a defender of big corporations since they provided support and opportunity for the creatively superior. Inevitably, though, such elitism inspires resentment from those "below": "that feeling of being thwarted and ill treated which is the auto-therapeutic attitude of the unsuccessful many." While Schumpeter agreed that capitalism "effectively chains the bourgeois stratum to its tasks," nevertheless, the habits of mind within capitalism, especially "rationalistic individualism," have produced significant social advances such as the emancipation of women and a more generalized pacifism. Schumpeter was also famous for his description of capitalism as a "veritable whirlwind of creativity and destruction." Market logic perpetually creates new products and services but in that process destroys old ones, creates new cultures while traditional ones fall before it. Needless to say, this is not a happy picture for the fallen, who historically rise in resistance, as evidenced in much of the world today.

What makes Schumpeter important for educators is the way his ideas serve as a prelude to those of Friedrich von Hayek, who in turn is the intellectual godfather of the most important influence on public policy in the West since the late 1970s and 1980s, namely *neoliberalism*, and it is through the ideas of von Hayek that we can trace the transformation of educational policy from a more balanced, humanistically oriented practice to the distorted, less mindful market-oriented activity that it has become today. Actually, as noted earlier, the collapse of global markets in 2008 marks, in my view, the end of legitimacy for neoliberalism, and that is one reason why the times are auspicious for re-theorizing public policy, including that of education. Economic historian Jerry Z. Muller has identified von Hayek's philosophies as "the crystal-clear vision of the one-eyed man"(2003, p. 386), and for that reason alone a strenuous deconstruction of von Hayek's ideas is a necessary for the defence of a world free from the kind of economic determinism for which he is responsible.

Like Schumpeter, von Hayek, in his seminal 1944 book *The Road to Serfdom* (see 2007 edition), defined his work against socialism, celebrating individual achievement over "collectivism." Furthermore, he saw democracy as a threat to the liberal order that functioning free markets require, and during the rise of neoliberalism in the 1990s, there were many calls for the scaling back of democracy, for example by Prof. Ian Angell of the London School of

Economics. For one thing, democracy holds functioning governments to ransom through the operation of what von Hayek called "special interests," people who use democratic politics to push their own limited agendas. He was especially critical of groups who operated in the name of "social justice," a concept he termed "a quasi-religious superstition" that only makes sense in small self-contained communities, but is too vague and amorphous to be of value in global times. The only legitimate meaning of justice is "protection" against those who would thwart individual self-effort and the efforts of individual companies and corporations. Ironically, said von Hayek, democracy could destroy liberalism, such that means need to be put in place to limit the range of questions to be decided by political process. Similarly, while market relations make cultural pluralism possible, this requires vigilance against those who in the name of their own self-interest would impose their own specific agenda on everyone else. Of course there is a certain hypocrisy in this view, since market logic itself serves a very specific agenda and very specific groups of persons.

Like Schumpeter, von Hayek also believed in leadership by elites, and that the gifted few should be entitled to the special privileges that their creative hard work has accomplished: "Whoever leaves to others the task of finding some useful means of employing his capacities must be content with a smaller reward" (Muller, 2003, p. 358). Indeed, it is the dynamic and resourceful few who must force the less resourceful to adapt, a kind of "impersonal compulsion" created by the laws of competition. This is related to his theory of the state, which he regarded as amoral, as simply a "piece of utilitarian machinery," having no ethical duties or responsibilities nor any "educative" function. The responsibility of the politician is only to ensure that market relations can operate without fetter. Because politicians don't have time for truly creative thinking, they must rely on intellectuals, of which there are two kinds, (a) "Originals," a very rare breed who can think out and through genuinely new paradigms, and (b)

"Second hand dealers in ideas" who can operationalize the work of Originals into new forms of social functioning.

It is easy to discern how the basics of von Hayek's ideas translated into the realm of education. The system of rewards and punishments implicit in his paradigm is revealed in new kinds of bullying ("impersonal compulsion") by school and university administrators to goad teachers and professors into forms of performance the implicit value of which is believed beyond their right to debate, since the registers of value are predetermined by institutional officials themselves. Those who succeed in satisfying the registered requirements are thereby rewarded for "excellence," the implicit meaning of which is actually indeterminable, a fact that is taken as irrelevant except to the degree that excellent performance can fold into a comparative institutional accounting of the same irrelevances.

If the state has no educative function, what becomes of the function of education within the state? Insofar as the value of *all* social practices is determined by market logic, only forms of education that serve the market have value. Hence the recommendation of Hon. Mike Harris, Premier of Ontario, at the beginning of Hayekian reforms in that province in 1989: "The humanities should be removed from the university, since they serve no economic benefit." More recently, the Social Sciences and Humanities Research Council of Canada has passed policies that give priority funding to proposals that directly serve the interests of the business community (SSHRC, 2009).

For a teacher, the most important consequences of the von Hayek vision may be more intangible, but perhaps all the more powerful for being so. This has to do with the kind of person produced by the vision, reflected in the personalities of students who enter classrooms and study halls, in people driving cars, riding buses, performing on playgrounds and in stadia, and otherwise behaving in public spaces. In fine, the Hayekian vision produces individuals who are self-serving, self-justifyingly violent against others in the name of seeking competitive advantage, and whose pursuit of happiness comes at the price of others' happiness. In broader terms, the Hayekian vision has produced heightened conflict in the international sphere as Anglo-American powers since the 1990s have seized the moment of the fall of communism to assert new forms of global "Full Spectrum Dominance" (Mahajan, 2003) through constructing the "War on Terror" as a device to serve their predetermined agenda (Chossudovsky, 2005; McMurtry, 2002; Petras & Veltmeyer, 2001). As mentioned, though, this agenda has been implemented at enormous cost to the ordinary public, a cost that has in fact bankrupted the economy of the world's heretofore most dominant economy, that of the United States of America. The social, cultural, and political implications of this bankruptcy around the world have only just begun to be felt, but the effects will be irreversible, long-term, and of enormous global consequence. Real unemployment in America stands today at about 30% (Global Research, 2010). The rise of "surveillance culture" (hidden cameras, bar coding, "security chips" in automobiles, Google street and community videoing, etc.) operating under the cover of the new Department of Homeland Security is not a feature of the war on terrorism, as if terrorism means a strike from the outside; no, the Department of Homeland Security is designed as a defence against impending civil violence as more people lose their jobs, their homes, and their sense of a possible future (see http://globalresearch.ca/). Insofar as Canada not only borders the U.S. but is also its most significant trading partner, all Canadian citizens should be cognizant of the forces that will inevitably shape their own future.

So, if the times are auspicious for a "paradigm change" in the manner in which economics is appreciated and assessed within the broader social realm, including education, how might this be characterized? It is here that a turn to global wisdom traditions may be relevant, and in the remainder of this chapter I hope to work out some possible ways of how this might be so. As a beginning it may be helpful to remember that there was in fact a fully operational social, cultural, and political world before "the market" became its definer beginning somewhere around the sixteenth century. To say this is not to advocate a nostalgic return to the days of feudalism, medieval theology, and pre-science, although indeed it was the fracturing of the medieval taboo against lending money at interest (condemned as "usury") that became the cornerstone of contemporary market logic yet which is also now the root cause of the market's collapse, since it is the lending of money and the creation of "credit society" that has led to the present unsustainable rate of public and state indebtedness. A related point is also relevant: credit and debt are a form of social control by the holders of debt, a condition of significant human un-freedom and hence profoundly resisted by the religion of Islam, for example. The point is, though, that it is possible to imagine a world of healthy, creative human relations that is not dependent on, nor indeed tolerant of, the kinds of human abuses that rule the day today in the name of market inevitabilities. This could be a world where culture and the arts are celebrated as contributing to the nurturance of human character instead of producing products that are humanly demeaning and foolish, a world where marketing experts are forbidden to use the insights of child psychology to "brand" children in the name of consumer loyalty, a world no longer stuck in automobile traffic jams in the name of civilization and hence perpetually trapped in wars conducted in the name of a civilization based on petroleum. To imagine all this is to understand that the form of the world that is *sold* to the average person as a normal world is in fact a *constructed* world based on assumptions about how life should be lived and evaluated. It is precisely those assumptions that demand an urgent, open, and sustained debate in today's world. The old dialectical reasoning of nineteenth-century Europe, a legacy which presents the false choice between capitalism and collectivism as the *only* choice available for social theorists and policy makers today, is simply silly yet dangerous, as the political divisiveness it sponsors is taken to be resolvable only through war over one side or the other of the argument.

In the history of economic theory, two themes relevant to the present discussion recur significantly. One is an admission that market logic produces an ossification of concern for *means* rather than ends. In philosophical terms the result is the collapse of *teleology*, or the study of ends. What is the market *for*, apart from concern for its own survival as the world's first transcendental logic? As noted at the beginning of this chapter, originally the market was an icon of hope for human happiness against the failures to produce that happiness by the traditional guardians of human conduct. What would the record show today regarding the market's ability to produce human happiness? In North America, mental illness, especially depression, is the fastest growing medical condition (Whitaker, 2010). The market is indeed spectacularly successful in producing an endless variety of material goods, but many of these are actually unnecessary for human welfare in any deep sense; then too, what should the purpose of life be when all material requirements are met? Furthermore, the global inequity in the production and distribution of these goods is constructed on a template of world order rooted in nineteenth-century European, and later American, imperialism, a situation at the heart of much global conflict today (Bello & Mittal, 2001). Indeed it is the very devolution of that imperial order now that implicitly announces new possibilities for human futures, deliberation over which writings such as this are attempting to contribute.

A second recurrent theme in economic history is a recognition that the kinds of human behaviour argued as essential for success in a market-driven world are actually unworkable in the day-to-day functioning of a healthy society. In essence, to be successful in the market requires of entrepreneurs, financiers, marketers, salespersons, etc. actions that are exploitative in basic essence, since personal or corporate profit is the guiding motive. Human relations only matter to the degree that money can be made from them or some other form of capital. A most striking example of this is in the powerful documentary film *Merchants of Cool* (PBS Frontline, 2001), a detailed revelation of how marketing is undertaken by advertising agencies to get inside the minds of young people to discover their primary interests, drives, and determinations which are then "sold" back to them in the form of packaged products directly connected to those interests, drives, and determinations. The sophistication of this is well described by Michael Budde (in Erlendson, 2003).

> Marketing/advertising power does not operate in a (simple) "hyperdermic" fashion, implanting ideas and desires into the minds of countless passive individuals. Nor does it assume that people are stupid, easily duped, or incapable of choice. Its dynamic is more closely akin to a seduction than assault. It involves actor A knowing things about B that B doesn't realize A knows. It is like playing poker against someone who has already seen your hand, unbeknownst to you. . . . In such a context, the actor under surveillance chooses, she is acting freely, but she does so in a context constructed to advance the priority of others. So long as asymmetry in information persists, and so long as the player under surveillance is unaware of the degree of contextual manipulation and structuring, the one-sided interaction can continue indefinitely." (p. 42)

In other words, behind the shadows of "normal" human interaction lie persons manipulating that interaction for their own predetermined purposes. After watching the film *Merchants of Cool*, it is difficult for parents and teachers to restrain their desire to have the manipulators of the adolescent subconscious criminalized as corruptors of public morals, at least such is the common response when I have shown the film in university classes. The question is, could a school or university class, or a family, survive if the values purveyed by such requirements of market success were taken as the norm? The most likely result would be to turn families and classrooms into places of deep paranoia, distrust, and ultimately forms of aggression that would destroy each entity. Market-dominated society, then, survives only through the creation of a secret schizophrenia whereby the public rhetoric of freedom, democracy, and personal agency operate *in front of* a mask that hides the agents of human control and manipulation. When it comes to the question, then, of whether the market can produce human happiness, the answer can only be that the happiness produced by the market is grounded in *dissociation* – i.e., the "happy" person is psychically dissociated from the agency actively constructing the conditions of that happiness – such that the happiness is essentially without power or agency itself. It cannot "go" anywhere without permission of the market agents, who would always deny it as a threat to their own survival or subvert it into yet another more sophisticated manipulative turn. The only place that normal human agency can go, psychically and indeed physically, under market domination, is inward, into narcissism and ever-increasing self-enclosure (psychic privatization), the long-range consequences being various forms of self-destruction then later anarchy as inarticulate disorientation explodes in public violence.

It is on this point alone that a global discussion may begin about wisdom and the requirements of healthy living and human well-being, since it is a mark of all wisdom traditions that the world inheres in a fundamental unity that cannot be broken except artificially as an act of human will. Human well-being depends on a unity between word and act, between self and other, between the human and natural worlds, and between life and death. It is a call for a recovery of that sense of unity that inspires the remarks that follow.

To speak of "wisdom" is difficult, since the term seems so amorphous and ambiguous. Instead one may speak of "wisdom traditions" which may be more easily identifiable and then accessible for their specific recommendations, which must be taken up not uncritically but at least openly. Every civilization has its sages and wisdom figures, and there is an emerging interest in the field globally (Ferrari & Potworoswski, 2009; Kornfield, 2001; Miller, 2006). The Hebrew tradition has its sapiential literature in Proverbs, Ecclesiates, Job, the Book of Wisdom, etc. Classical Greece had the concept of *phronesis* as practical philosophy, with "philosophy" meaning love of wisdom

(Gk. *philo* + *sophia*). Asia holds the inheritances of Taoism, Buddhism, Confucianism, and the yogic traditions of Hinduism, especially Yoga. Islam has its Sufi traditions. Today, Africa is in the process of recovering its wisdom in the form of *Unhu/ubuntu*, a theory of *being* based on the primacy of community and togetherness over individualism (Connel, 2007). Aboriginal and indigenous wisdom is also finding new respect in Western academies (Battiste, 2000).

Open the "BOOKS" link on Amazon.com and enter the words "education and wisdom" and revealed will be a burgeoning domain literature. The most striking feature of this literature, however, is the way it treats wisdom as a kind of prosthetic device to help teachers and students survive the travails of contemporary education. Practice meditation and mindfulness so as a teacher you may more calmly orchestrate the pedagogical and curricular necessities of daily life (MacDonald & Shirley, 2008). This approach is exactly wrong since it merely sponsors and nurtures the kind of happy dissociation, or cultural schizophrenia, that is at the heart of the problems outlined in this chapter. No, what is required is something much more difficult and challenging. Wisdom must critically and forcefully *address* the conditions of our time, revealing their non-sustainability, deconstructing their underlying *mythos*, and thereby providing a "Way" to human happiness that is fully integrated, psychically speaking, with an understanding of the ways of the world. Wisdom can never be an enclave *against* the world but an invitation to live fully *in* the world in a healthy, life-giving way. The reason why the distinguished professor of business noted at the beginning of this chapter is in error regarding Buddhism is that he proposes to use Buddhism to predeterminatively preserve the market, whereas a correct understanding of the Buddha's teaching would be to challenge the human propensity to cling to and reify *any* construct of the human imagination. Hence neither can wisdom be *against* the market, since that too would be predeterminative. No, the virtue of wisdom is its ability to see the market for what it is – capable of doing much good in the provisioning of human need, but also, in its present form, addled with assumptions that are humanly destructive.

It would be impossible to survey all of the wisdom traditions noted above, but here will be an attempt to identify a few common themes with their relevance for educational theory and practice. What is the source of Wisdom? The Hebrew tradition puts it this way: "Reverence (or awe) for the Lord is the beginning of wisdom" (Proverbs 9:10). This language can be de-theologized phenomenologically to express the human experience of the world as being charged with a creative energy that is not subject to human will or rationality alone. Life is always greater than any interpretation human beings give it, including this one, so that while indeed sometimes human interpretations can penetrate, at least superficially, aspects of the worldly condition, any attempt to make permanent those interpretations ends in disaster. This is the case for example with the discoveries of science, experience showing that when such discoveries become absolutized in human confidence, they usually turn into monstrous deformities of one kind or another. Same with all political theories. Wisdom thus teaches that the appropriate response to the world is one of reverence and awe, since no matter how confident we may become in our knowledge of the world, such knowledge is miniscule compared to the vastness of our ignorance relative to the entirety of what is. Hence, the Hebrew writer asserts that to eschew this insight is a mark of foolishness: "fools despise wisdom" (Proverbs 1:7). The marks of wisdom are modesty, genuine humility (hence L. *humus*, "earth," as the derivation of "human"), and openness to the unfolding of larger pictures of human experience in the world rather than quick dismissal of them in the name of foregone opinion.

Putting the matter thus aligns the Hebrew tradition with most other wisdom traditions of the world, where *meditative sensibility*, as it might be best described, is the foundation of this kind of deep understanding of the human condition. Meditative sensibility is cultivated through the practice of stillness, directed to finding what in

Taoism is called the "stillpoint," in Islam "the eternal now" (Arabic *waqt*), in Buddhism "equipoise" (Gyatso, 1985). Meditation operates as the silent awareness of the immensity of the cosmos in which we find ourselves, and the foolishness of all false confidence and braggadocio. The silence, too, marks a *finding* of oneself *in* the world and not alienated from it, with alienation being what arises when time-bound interpretations supplant any sense of timelessness or eternity.

The great Tibetan teacher Chogyam Trungpa (1990) described meditation as "the art of making friends," which points to a recovery of the essential unity of the world that has been lost under the hyper-individualist rubrics of Western rationality. Again, the Hebrew writer declaims "To gain wisdom is to love oneself" (Proverbs 19:19), a love very different from the kind of narcissism described earlier as symptomatic of the dissociative personality, instead pointing to a recovery of the alienated self into a new unity of being. Indeed it is this very unity of being that is the authority undergirding and permeating all Life, as evidenced in the Mosaic experience of divinity as "pure being" (Lit. "I am", Exodus 3:14).

Instead of meditation, the great Trappist monk Thomas Merton (1975) sometimes used to speak of "wordless prayer," which creates a space "open to others" and "rooted in a sense of common illusion and criticism of it." This acknowledgment of criticism as a function of meditative sensibility, a concern for our common illusions, is linked in Catholic tradition to an understanding of "evil," taken to mean "the privation of a good that should be present. It is the lack of a good that essentially belongs to nature: the absence of a good that is natural and good to a being. Evil is therefore the absence of what ought to be there" (Hardon, 1985, p. 136). Putting the matter as strongly as possible, what signifies the triumph of commercial values to a transcendent logic as evil is precisely the way such a triumph causes a privation of any other manner of being human. Within such a logic, there is no "other," or as Margaret Thatcher ignorantly declaimed following von Hayek: "There is no alternative."

In the domain of curriculum and pedagogy, therefore, what forms of practice would be inspired by the wisdom perspective so far outlined? In general terms, wisdom-guided curriculum and pedagogy must begin by pushing away any interpretation that exclusively sees education as preparation for the competitive global market. Instead, such education should be guided by helping students recover the unity of their being, a unity that has been shattered by virtue of their formation within capitalist culture. Distractedness, inability to focus and concentrate, aggressiveness in human relations, self-interested conflict as virtue – increasingly these qualities have come to define the lives of young people, which the wisdom curriculum may serve to heal. A primary requirement for such healing is for young people to learn to be still, which arises naturally not from some enforced artificial discipline, but from forms of curriculum and pedagogy that are a genuine invitation to see the immensity of the world as an open place with an open future, indeed an "awesome" place, to use current vernacular. It is precisely the fact that so many students experience school as a place sponsoring a future that is so predictable that drives so many into narcissism and despair.

The invitation to see the world as an open place has its own requirements. One is to understand how the received human world is a constructed world, which means learning to see it as "readable" or interpretable, and hence not fixed and static. Such a world can be engaged creatively and moved forward by forms of insight disciplined by a comprehensive understanding of the past. Human stillness, indeed peacefulness, arises through a balance of relations between acts of withdrawal (in Catholic tradition the practice of "recollection") and acts of genuine engagement, as experienced for example in the art studio, the music room, or shop class. In Confucian traditional curriculum, the Chinese word wen denotes "the arts of peace" (Waley, 1992, p. 39), and they include music, calligraphy, archery, etc., all designed to assist in the overall formation of human character. One of the first reforms inaugurated by the neoliberal assault on public education was to consistently abolish arts programs in schools, and in wisdom terms, this is best understood as an evil act, i.e. the privation of an inherent good.

A second characteristic of global wisdom traditions concerns their understanding of time, or what might more formally be described as the temporal enframements of human action. This is related to the first point above in that time, in a cosmological sense, is very different from how time is experienced under the rule of capital. In the Western tradition, there are two basic concepts of time, with one privileged to the unfortunate loss of the other. Chronological time (Gk. *chronos*) is the measured time of industry, efficiency, and day-to-day routine. In Greek mythology, Chronos was the god who ate his own children, so one might wonder how the rule of chronological time in schools and classrooms serves to deliver the young to the platter of adult intention rather than providing a place where the young can learn to *be*, then better able to serve the broader community from the creative reservoir of their free maturity. East Indian social theorist Ashis Nandy (1987) has suggested that in technical rational cultures like that of the West, childhood has been rationally idealized and taken over by various forms of social engineering, the consequence being the disappearance of the "real" child.

The concept of time silenced by market logic is translatable from the Greek word *kairos*, denoting the sense of things having their time beyond the capacities of specific measurement. In English, there is the expression, "in the fullness of time, such and such occurred," meaning that the event could not have been specifically forecast in advance, but when the time was right, it happened. This relates to the earlier understanding of awe and wonder. What genuinely impresses us, humanly speaking, usually takes us by surprise, since it breaks through routine contingencies to reveal something about life that we could never have imagined based on previous logics and understandings.

As part of wisdomly understanding, the kairotic sense of time is of enormous relevance in teaching, but again, unrecognized in almost all educational theory today. It involves a recognition that things have their time in a way that cannot be delivered chronometrically. Some students simply take longer to appreciate some things than others. The son of a personal friend was repeatedly diagnosed in elementary school as having a "reading disability" and suffered the inevitable humiliation of such a diagnosis. Eventually my friend firmly told school authorities, "Just leave him alone!" Today the son is completing his PhD.

Furthermore, some things *reveal themselves on their own terms*, when they are ready, not simply under the duress of a formal curriculum requirement at 10:30 Tuesday morning. This is now well understood in the realm of ecology, for example, and the study of (so-called) wildlife. The best way to see animals in their natural habitat is simply to sit still; then the animals will come out of hiding and show themselves. How often do the young hide themselves because they intuit that conditions are not safe for their self-revelation? How much cultural rejuvenation is lost because being "juvenile" has taken on a pejorative meaning? Attention to juvenile behaviour might indeed teach us a lot about ourselves if we could better understand it rather than predeterminatively condemn it. Mahatma Gandhi used to speak of the young as "the barometers" of culture, who express its pressures and tensions in ways superseding conventional interpretation.

In many wisdom traditions, the hiddenness of things is well appreciated. The Hebrew prophet Isaiah (45:15) declared of the God of Israel, "Truly you are a God who hides himself." Again, this language can be de-theologized phenomenologically to express the human experience of cosmological uncertainty, even anxiety, in the face of realizing that what once had inspired confidence seems to have disappeared. It also expresses the way in which so often life is experienced as a mystery, that something inscrutable draws us deeper into an examination of our own ignorance and limitations. In the Buddhist tradition, philosophers have suggested that there are times and places where the Buddha will not reveal himself. Usually this is because of a perception on the part of the Buddha that the times are not right, that any revelation would be rejected, not seen, or even ridiculed.

In curriculum and pedagogy, these understandings of hiddenness can teach us that not only do things reveal themselves on their own terms, in their own good time, but also that certain things are impossible under certain conditions. Deep truth cannot be seen when overlaid with the obsessions of ideology, politics, or dogmatic agendas of self-survival. More concretely one might ask, why does so much educational "research" today seem so unenlightening, repetitive, and incapable of moving beyond itself? Wisdomly, the answer must be "because it is paradigmatically stuck," and cannot see beyond the parameters of its current imaginal space. Historically this problem goes back to the eighteenth century and the death of metaphysics inspired by *The Critique of Pure Reason* (1781/2008) of Immanuel Kant. Kant argued that philosophy was incapable of describing life as it actually exists in its wholeness or universality since the philosopher is subject to his own perceptions which are bound in time and place. Philosophy says more about the philosopher than the world he is philosophizing about. All we can do is point to the operation of Reason itself and make assessments based on what later became known as the "historico-critical method" whereby everything from Kant onwards, in the Western tradition at least, can only be understood in its historical and spatial context. This was a pivotal moment in the Western tradition because the final bi-product of the Kantian argument was the self-enclosure of human subjectivity and the loss of the world as something that addresses me from beyond myself. The world as a Whole lost any form of pedagogical function, with description of things in their time and space boundedness the only recourse left to scholarship.

Historically, the solution to solving problems of global "development" has been controlled by the subjectivity of Western powers to turn the rest of the world into an image of itself. Today, the global education agenda seems almost universally directed to re-creating

Western self-understanding everywhere. Today's national *Globe and Mail* newspaper (Church, 2010) reports on how Canadian universities need to see India as a "land of opportunity" for developing satellite campuses there, with the Schulich School of Business of York university celebrated as a prototype. A recent $12 million grant from the Canadian International Development Agency was designed to help China turn its entire educational system from a (so-called) Confucian model of authoritarian teaching and rote-based learning into one of Western styled child-centred pedagogy. Sitting in on one of the earliest planning meetings for the project, I was simply stunned by the presumptions being made by my well-meaning Canadian colleagues. Where is "the world" in the context of contemporary educational scholarship, in the sense of how a new appreciation of Others might penetrate the enclosed subjectivity of the Western tradition to open a genuine dialogue regarding human futures? What might the necessary conditions be for a truly global discussion about this, beyond Western self-replication? One might hope that teacher education institutions see the implications of contemporary global requirements. In the Canadian context of curriculum and pedagogy, two young scholars are engaged in work worthy of note, Jackie Seidel (2006) and Sandra Wilde (2007), both currently at the University of Calgary.

In Buddhism there is a concept of "Dharma Cycles" used to describe the manner in which geopolitical and cosmological forces converge in the creation and devolution of mass formations of one kind or another. In Sanskrit, dharma means "that which sustains us" and refers generally to a sense of the Law of Life, or the rule of life that lies beyond our human desire or intent, even though such desire and intent may indeed play a role in the unfolding of that rule, a paradox of freedom and fate well understood in Greek tragedy. A dharma cycle is a historical period of approximately five hundred years, from the early inception of a new idea or development through its maturation and eventual decline. Reading the Western tradition backwards from the present identifies the European conquest of the

Americas as the inception of Euro-American modernity (Dussel, 1995, 1996). As Enrique Dussel argues, it was the new wealth that flowed into Europe from that conquest that gave rise to the Renaissance (recovery of the human body from its Greek neglect theologized by the Christian Church), to the new individualism of the Protestant Reformation inspired by the boldness of the new mercantile class, to the subjectivist rationalism of the Enlightenment and the consequent rise of "rational" science, to industrialism, democracy, and eventually America, which British philosopher John Gray (1998) names "the world's last Enlightenment regime."

Inevitably, concepts such as the Dharma Cycle can only be speculative, but their value is to serve in reminder that nothing lasts forever, that things are always in motion, and that the phenomenon of death is built into the phenomenon of birth. Ironically, Joseph Schumpeter argued that the very success of (European) capitalism may result in its own destruction because by "rationalizing the human mind" it creates "a mentality and style of life incompatible with its own fundamental conditions" (Muller, 2003, p. 299). In his classic work *Denial of Death* (1973), Ernest Becker argued that the Western tradition, based on Christian languages of hope and eternal life, has been unable to face mortality as fundamental to the human condition, and yet it is a universal insight of wisdom that one cannot truly live until life and death are appreciated in their essential unity. Thai master Achaan Chah (2002) provides a powerful description of training in this understanding in the Theravada tradition. Learning to sleep in the "charnal grounds" (burial grounds) is part of the curriculum for novices. At first there is nothing but terror over unusual sounds, echoes, fear of spirits, ghosts, etc. Eventually, through perseverance, comes peace as acceptance of death produces freedom from clinging to understandings of life that are self-preservational in a very limited sense. The basic achievement of wisdom, therefore, is not cleverness or knowledge or even strength in the usual manner. No, the basic achievement of wisdom is freedom – freedom from fear, freedom from delusion, freedom from the limitations of parochial culture. In the Mosaic tradition, the call of pure being is to freedom from enslavement, so in the context of this paper, the main pedagogical challenge is to invite consideration of the ways that teachers, students, parents, and professors have become enslaved to understandings that prohibit dreaming of a better world, and to lay them down in an act of great relinquishment so that freedom may prevail and we may be born again.

In conclusion, the following point can be made. The ascendance of Market Logic to a place of transcendence relies on a conceit unique to the Western tradition itself, namely an assumption of the very possibility of universal logic. It is that very conceit that is dying today. As Adam Smith recognized back in the eighteenth century, the world has always been a multicultural place, and his projected vision of "universal opulence" would therefore depend on good communicative relations between cultures, especially between East and West, as well as firm regulation by moral and self-disciplined states. As Giovanni Arrighi (2009) suggests, the fact that China is now rearticulating how market logic might function to serve a more just distribution of goods and services rather than only individual wealth creation is symptomatic of how market relations are being rethought in global times.

So, can Wisdom trump the market as a basis for education? Because ignorance of wisdom prevails so widely, response to the question might be pessimistic. Fortunately life is not a poker game, and wisdom actually has no interest in winning or losing but only in living well. Considering what that might mean in an increasingly complex and conflicted world may now be a special charge to educators.

References

Amin, S. (2004). *Obsolescent capitalism: Contemporary politics and global disorder.* London, England: Zed Books.

Arrighi, G. (2009). *Adam Smith in Beijing: Lineages of the 21st century.* London, England: Verso Books.

Battiste, M. (2000). *Reclaiming indigenous voice and vision.* University of British Columbia Press.

Becker, E. (1973). *Denial of death.* New York, NY: Free Press.

Bello, W., & Mittal, A. (2001). *The future in the balance: Essays on globalization and resistance.* Oakland, CA: Food First Books.

Burke, P, (1973). *A new kind of history: From the writings of Febvre.* New York, NY: Routledge and Kegan Paul.

Chah, A. (2002). *Food for the heart: The collected teachings of Ajahn Chah* (A. Amaro & J. Kornfield, Eds.). Boston, MA: Wisdom Publications.

Chossudovsky, M. (2005). *America's "War on Terrorism".* Available from http://www.globalresearch.ca/globaloutlook/truth911.html

Church, E. (2010, July 3). For Canadian universities, India is a land of opportunity. *Globe and Mail,* p. A1.

Connell, R. (2007). *Southern Theory.* Cambridge, MA: Polity Press.

Dussel, E. (1995). *The inventions of the Americas: Eclipse of 'the Other' and the myth of modernity* (M. Barber, Trans.). New York, NY: Continuum.

Dussel, E. (1996). *The underside of modernity: Apel, Rorty, Taylor and the philosophy of liberation.* Atlantic Highlands, NJ: Humanities Press.

Erlendson, R. (2003). *Without a map: Teaching business in an age of globalization* (Unpublished doctoral dissertation). University of Alberta, Edmonton.

Ferrari, M., & Potworowski G. (2009) (Eds.). *Teaching for wisdom: Cross-cultural perspectives on fostering wisdom.* New York, NY: Springer.

Global Research. (2010). *Systemic crisis of the world economy: Geopolitical dislocation.* Retrieved from http://www.globalresearch.ca/PrintArticle.php?articleId=19814

Grant, T. (2008, Oct 27). What happened to my dream job? *Globe and Mail.* Retrieved from http://www.globecampus.ca/in-the-news/article/what-happened-to-my-dream-job/

Gray, J. (1998). *False Dawn: The delusions of global capitalism.* London, England: Verso.

Gyatso, T. (1985). *Kindness, clarity and insight* (J. Hopkins & E. Napper, Trans. & Eds.). Ithica, NY: Snow Lion Press.

Hardimon, M. (1994). *Hegel's social philosophy: The project of reconciliation.* New York, NY: Cambridge University Press.

Hardon, J. (1985). *Pocket Catholic Dictionary.* Garden City, NY: Image Books.

Heilbroner, R. (1999). *The worldly philosophers: The lives, times and ideas of the great economic thinkers.* New York, NY: Simon and Schuster.

Hume, D. (1751/1983). *An enquiry concerning the principles of morals* (J. B. Schneedwind, Ed.). Indianapolis, IN: Hackett Publishing.

Kadarkay, A. (1991). *Georg Lukacs: Life, thought and politics.* Cambridge, MA: B. Blackwell.

Kant, I. (2007). *Critique of Pure Reason* (M. Weigelt & M. Muller, Trans. & Eds.). London, England: Penguin Classics.

Katz, B. (1982). *Herbert Marcuse and the art of liberation: An intellectual biography.* London, England: Verso.

Kaufmann, W (Trans. & Ed.). (2000). *Basic Writings of Nietzsche.* New York, NY: Modern Library Press.

Knudsen, J. (1986). *Justus Moser and the German Enlightenment.* New York, NY: Cambridge University Press.

Kornfield, J. (2001). *After the ecstasy the laundry: How the heart grows wise on the spiritual path.* New York, NY: Bantam.

Loy, D. (2003). *The great awakening: A Buddhist social theory.* Somerville, MA: Wisdom Books.

MacDonald, E., & Shirley, D. (2009). *The Mindful Teacher*. New York, NY: Teachers College Press.

Mahajan, R. (2003). *Full spectrum dominance: U.S. power in Iraq and beyond*. New York, NY: Seven Stories Press.

Marcuse, H. (1964). *One-Dimensional Man: Studies in the ideology of advanced industrial culture*. Boston, MA: Basic Books.

McMurtry, J. (2002). *Value wars: The global market versus the life economy*. London, England: Pluto Press.

Merton, T. (1975). *The Asian journal of Thomas Merton*. New York, NY: New Directions.

Miller, J. (2006). *Educating for wisdom and compassion: Creating conditions for timeless learning*. Thousand Oaks, CA: Corwin.

Morck, R. (2009, Nov. 24). *Why markets fail*. Keynote address at a SSHRC panel event exploring why markets fail, University of Alberta, Edmonton.

Muller, J. (2003). *Mind and the market: Capitalism in western thought*. New York, NY: Anchor Books.

Nandy, A. (1987). Reconstructing childhood. In *Traditions, tyranny and utopia: Essays in the politics of awareness* (pp. 67–80). Oxford University Press.

PBS Frontline. (2001, February 27). *Merchants of Cool* [TV]. Available from http://www.pbs.org/wgbh/pages/frontline/shows/cool/

Peters, M. (2007). *Knowledge economy, development and the future of higher education*. Rotterdam, Netherlands: SensePublishers.

Petras, J., & Veltmeyer, H. (2001). *Globalization unmasked: Imperialism in the 21st century*. New York, NY: Zed Books.

Polanyi, K. (2001). *The great transformation: The political and economic origins of our time*. Boston, MA: Beacon Press.

Scaff, L. (1989). *Fleeing the Iron Cage: Culture, politics and modernity in the thought of Max Weber*. University of California Press.

Schumpeter, J. (2008). *Capitalism, socialism and democracy*. New York, NY: Harper.

Seidel, J. (2006, September). Some thoughts on teaching as contemplative practice. *Teachers College Record, 108*(9), 1901–1914.

Smith, A. (1776/1976). *An inquiry into the nature and causes of the wealth of nations* (R. Campbell, A. Skinner, & W. Todd, Eds.). Oxford: Clarendon Press.

Smith, A. (1780/1982). *The theory of moral sentiments* (A. Macfie & D. Raphael, Eds.). Indianapolis, IN: Liberty Classics.

SSHRC. (2009, Spring). Enhancing prosperity and innovation through research: Canada's competitive edge. *Dialogue*, n.p. Retrieved from http://www.sshrc-crsh.gc.ca/newsletter-bulletin/spring-printemps/2009/mbf-eng.aspx

Trungpa, C. (1990). *Meditation and the myth of freedom.* Boston, MA: Shambhala.

Von Hayek, F. (2007). *The road to serfdom.* University of Chicago Press.

Voltaire (1734/1980). *Letters on England* (L. Tancock, Trans.). New York, NY: Penguin Classics.

Voltaire et. al. (1901). *The works of Voltaire: A contemporary version* (Vol. 36). Paris: E. R. Dumont.

Waley, A. (1992). *Confucianism: The Analects of Confucius.* New York, NY: Book of the Month Club.

Weber, M. (1978). *Economy and Society: An outline of interpretive sociology* (G. Roth & C. Wittich, Trans. & Eds.). University of California Press.

Whitaker, R. (2010). *Anatomy of an epidemic: Magic bullets, psychiatric drugs and the astonishing rise of mental illness in America.* New York, NY: Crown Publications.

Wilde, S. (2007). *The pedagogy of no-separate-self* (Unpublished doctoral dissertation). University of Alberta, Edmonton.

Wolff, K (Trans. & Ed.). (1965). *The sociology of Georg Simmel.* New York, NY: Free Press.

A COMPLICATED FREEDOM: POLITICS AND THE CULTURE OF TEACHING

Anne M. Phelan, University of British Columbia

This work was made possible by a grant from the Social Sciences and Humanities Research Council of Canada.

Understanding Autonomy: Freedom From or Freedom To?

TEACHERS REQUIRE AUTONOMY in order to speak and act in schools. As a useful starting point, I define autonomy as thinking for oneself in situations that require judgment rather than routine. The nature of teachers' work and its social context complicates teacher autonomy, however, for teaching involves placing one's autonomy at the service of the best interests of children and their communities (Pitt & Phelan, 2008). A range of recent policies in North America and Europe have sought to define and protect those interests by the establishment of teaching standards, the introduction of licensed and certified teacher schemes, the creation of prescriptive, outcome-based curricula, and systems of accountability through standardized testing constrain the autonomy of teachers (Furlong, J., Barton, L., Miles, S., Whiting, C., & Whitty, G., 2000; Phelan 1996; Smyth & Shacklock 1998). As a result, teachers seem inevitably caught between their own judgments and external constraints of policy, professional culture.

The experience of being "caught" is particularly acute for beginning professionals who enter a world – a professional culture – that precedes them and yet holds them responsible for understanding, deferring to, and ultimately embracing that world (Phelan, Sawa, Barlow, Hurlock, Myrick, Rogers, & Irvine, 2006). As Natasha Levinson (2001) has elegantly explained, "This puts [them] in the difficult position of being simultaneously heirs to a particular history and new to it, with the peculiar result that [they] experience themselves as 'belated' even though [they] are newcomers" (p. 14). Or in the words of early career teacher Moira:[1]

> It's hard to want to try something new because . . . I already know there's an idea of what [it] looks like. . . . That kind of information is valuable but I think you want the freedom to feel like . . . maybe we're going to . . . [do something other than what is usually done] . . . and if there's the feeling of there's already kind of an end result that's already there, why would you try?

Not unlike "every child born into the continuity of Roman history," every new teacher must learn "the glories of the heroes and the deeds of the fathers [and mothers]" so as to be able to do what all teachers are supposed to do – help "rule the world" that their predecessors (policy-makers and colleagues) have made (Arendt, 1978, p. 213). The Romans were sure that salvation always comes from the past, that the ancestors were "greater ones" by definition and as such represented greatness for each successive generation (Arendt).

A study of autonomy in professional life suggests teachers' reactions to practices and policies are not always so straightforward (Phelan, 2009; Pitt & Phelan, 2008). The response of early career teachers to what has preceded them takes several forms including: a complete rejection of responsibility, an insistence on teachers' complete freedom of choice, and the creation of teacher groups which meet to discuss educational matters outside of school. As such, an examination of new teachers provides a stark portrayal of the possibilities and impossibilities of creating a political culture in teaching.

Some early career teachers embrace a negative freedom (Greene, 1988) as they take up long-term teacher-on-call or substitute teacher positions. Jill, another early career teacher, explains her motivation for doing so in terms of the avoidance of responsibility: "['C]ause you're just there for the day, and they know that, and they treat you like they know you're not going to be there tomorrow. It's nice that there's no responsibility, no work after work. You just leave. I love the freedom." The "lightness" of the wandering life of the teacher-on-call suggests a resistance to constraint of any kind. Freedom from encounters with others is hardly the ground upon which one might construct a strongly articulated and convincing sense of shared professional and social-political purpose (Pitt & Phelan, 2008). Yet, reflected in the teacher's pursuit of quiet and order is, perhaps, an appreciation of the difficulty of living with others in schools. One of the irreducible conditions of human action, Hannah Arendt (1958/1998) tells us, is that others take up our action in ways we can neither predict nor control. Sovereignty (individual autonomy) represents the human attempt to control or determine the world in the face of radical and absolute contingency (Martel, 2008). Seeking solace and solitude, teachers may turn away from colleagues to preserve the fantasy of sovereignty and a subject-centered notion of freedom.

Another response to the perceived imposition of policy or practice is the assertion of *free will*. As one teacher, Liz, expressed it, "the power to do what I want, when I want, how I want . . . more control . . . power to chose." Here freedom is defined in terms of the individual "faculty of choice between objects and goals" (Arendt, 1978, p. 158). The association of freedom with "free will" began with the apostle Paul, and we almost automatically equate freedom with free will, a faculty almost unknown to classical antiquity (Arendt, 1968, p. 158). Known as *liberum arbitrium*, the notion of free will or free choice or free decision is, for Arendt, a false notion of freedom. As simply "a choice between options predetermined by the will itself" (Martel, 2008, p. 290), free will pays little regard to history or authority. In the modern view, when the past returns, it does so in the guise of tradition – the way we've always done it – or as reprimand – the way things should be done. In the attitude of modernity, free will involves placing a high value on the present, often positing it as heroic. The modern teaching subject expresses an eagerness to focus on the here and now, often in the attempt to re-imagine what has been otherwise. The teaching self and the teaching world are viewed as the objects of the individual's own invention and reinvention (Zerilli, 2005).

A third response to external constraint is evident when early career teachers speak and act openly, thereby creating a public sphere. Some participants in the autonomy study hosted informal gatherings in their homes on a monthly basis. Many of those attending were practicing teachers who had graduated from the same university but who worked in a range of schools and school districts. Participants seemed to derive both support and challenge from these gatherings. When school cultures offer such opportunities in-house for teachers, professional discourse is animated by educational (non-materialistic, non-economic) concerns and "a joy in argument" (Villa, 2008, p. 101). Action research is just one example. Through the exchange of arguments, where the latter can be received and have an impact, teachers begin to feel a shared world that makes a meaningful life together possible. This is what Arendt (1958/1998) termed *political freedom*, and it requires a kind of relation to others in a space defined by plurality – a common world. The will, in this instance, is the autonomous mental faculty that makes speech and action possible. The will is spontaneous, the "spring of action" (Honig, 1988, p. 79). It is what propels teachers into speech and action.

> No willing is ever done for its own sake or finds its fulfilment in the act itself. Every volition . . . looks forward to its own end, when willing something will have changed into doing it. In other words, the normal mood of the willing ego is impatience, disquiet and worry (Sorge) because the will's project presupposes an I-can that is by no means guaranteed. The will's worrying disquiet can be stilled only by the I-can-and-I-do, that is, by a cessation of its own activity and release of the mind from its dominance. (Arendt, 1978, pp. 37–38)

The will frees us from what Arendt believed to be the trivial preoccupations of the private realm – concerns about biological needs and psychological well-being – that prevent us from speaking and acting as we might. Instead of prioritizing the relative comfort and safety of our private worlds – job security, for example – we are eager to act in the public realm and to engage with different others no matter the inconvenience or cost. Such "liberation from the private self, won by the will's coup d'etat, sets the condition for the appearance of the acting self whose action makes freedom manifest in the world" (Honig, 1988, p. 80). It is difficult for early career teachers to leave their private concerns about job security and livelihood aside in order to participate in dialogue and debate with colleagues about things that matter. This may be one reason why they seek political communities outside of the school workplace. As one teacher explained her own reluctance to argue with colleagues at school, "I don't know very *safe* ways, I guess, of saying, no, you're wrong."

It is the challenges associated with argumentation in schools, and concomitantly with political freedom, that I explore further in what follows. I couch my exploration in the Arendtian understanding that to experience political freedom, that is to build a culture of speaking and acting, teachers at all stages of their careers must exercise their individual will but not so much that it overrides or excludes the possibility of the other's power to speak and be heard. The other can be represented in policy, the words and actions of an authority figure, or other colleagues' expressed (and unexpressed) understandings of how things ought to be done. Hannah Arendt recognized that the reconciliation staged between the individual will and political freedom is a fragile one because of the challenges posed by the will's insistence on its own power to the detriment of plurality. Put simply, the will is what makes teacher speech and action possible, but it is also that which can inhibit the speech and action of others.

"More Than Advice, Less Than Command":
An Encounter of Wills

Early career teacher Laoise's narration[2] of interactions with the school pastor provides an interesting opportunity to examine the question of the individual will's insistence on its own power in the face of an Other.

Laoise is a teacher in an independent Catholic school in a large urban area in Canada. She explains that she is often at odds with the school pastor and what he represents. "There's the official church's stance . . ., and then there's mine. And then there's what the priest would tell me to say and then there's [my own beliefs]. So, I find myself being in a position of not truly being able to express what I truly believe." Part of Laoise's responsibility as the Grade 2 teacher is to prepare the children for the sacraments of Reconciliation (First Confession) and Eucharist (First Holy Communion). When she includes a child from the Greek Orthodox faith to participate in the ceremonies and receive the communion bread with the other children, she says that she was "chewed out publicly" by the parish priest. He tells her that the child and other non-Catholics in the classroom should not be actively involved in the mass; they must not bring the gifts to the altar or take communion bread. He explains that in 1504 the then-Christian church split into the two related but distinct traditions of Roman Catholicism and Greek Orthodox, each of which regards the communion in its own way. While respecting the priest's "depth of knowledge" and his reasoned criticism (the Greek Orthodox children have access to their own church where they are able to receive communion), Laoise opines that his response is "too rule bound" and that the "human aspect gets lost."

> I don't want any child to feel different, and if this is a religion of love and welcoming and acceptance, then why should somebody not be included and made to feel different or infe-

rior . . . I object, I really object to that but those are things that are non-negotiable and that I find really hard.

Catholicism for Laoise is about belonging and tolerance in present relationships; but her attitude to the past may unknowingly amount to a sentimentalizing of church history and the erasure of the memory of its foundation. Laoise grounds her authority as teacher in a consoling relation to the helplessness of the child (Arendt, 1968, p. 92).

> And I do, I do believe I have an impact within my classroom, if, if not within the larger scheme of things, and, yeah I truly do, I think I've been very successful in you know the community building and the empathy building and the social skills and those sorts of things, um, you know certain kids I can see, you know, Matthew, when I see Matthew I know he was that kid on the brink, you know, and Grade 2 was a good year for him. Not that that solved all his problems but you know I could see an increase in self-esteem in him, and that, so I do, I do believe, yeah, that I have made a difference that way, yeah. But I guess it's a question of what I do in the context of the institution.

Within the confines of her classroom, she can live her value of particular children in the present, "ma[k]e a difference," and bolster her sense of agency that again removes her from the company of other adults in the school. Yet, Laoise's assertion of responsibility for the well-being of the child is significant. The teacher's authority rests on the assumption of responsibility for the world, yet it also turns, as Arendt (1968) would have it, "in a certain sense against the world" (p. 186).

> The child requires special protection and care so that nothing destructive may happen to him from the world. But the world, too, needs protection to keep it from being overrun

and destroyed by the onslaught of the new that bursts upon it with each new generation. (p. 186)

Laoise concludes that "looking at what's in the best interests of the kids, and not just their future academically but their emotional and social well-being," is "more important," than Church history and tradition, and she sees in her position a "sort of higher purpose, a higher goal" of pedagogical watchfulness.

The authority of the pastor arises in part from his association with the Catholic church. Church authority rests on a foundation in the past as its unshaken cornerstone and as such, the institution has the semblance of permanence and durability (Arendt, 1968). Endowed with power, obtained by descent and transmission (tradition), Catholic schools and their associated pastors are dedicated to the continuity of their variant of Christianity: things can not be otherwise (a blow to modernity). As a result, Laoise confronts the "deep sense of necessity" (Zerilli, 2005, p. 137) that pervades her institution, and she feels that "there is no negotiation" possible. The realm of obedience and the realm of reason are distinguishable in this case (Kant, 1784/1991). The parish priest might attest, for example, that while the matter is a question of past (church history), it is not simply a question of tradition. Without a memory of the past, quite apart from forgetting its contents, the modern teaching subject is in danger of depriving herself from "the dimension of depth in human existence . . . for memory and depth are the same" (Arendt, 1968, p. 93–94). Laoise posits knowledge of the past as an admirable attribute of the priest; it becomes a matter of his personal distinction and as such insufficient to contest or overturn her present concerns about the child. And so she is in danger of erasing history.

While Laoise is not being asked to practise in a blindly obedient manner (she appreciates the reasons proffered by the priest), her location in an independent Catholic school means that her obligation to the authority of the church is established as prior to the "natural necessity of teacher authority in relation to the helplessness of the child" (Arendt, 1968, p. 92). Judgments are risk laden when those judging are held to external standard – in this case, Roman Catholicism. Laoise recalls the story of the music teacher whom she witnessed crying alone in the hallway and who "is on the transfer list for next year."

> I know the music teacher got in big trouble for her choice of the Christmas play. It was too, sort of, secular. It was just kind of a funny, family Christmas where everything went wrong . . . a Christmas comedy of errors. For the most part parents don't care. They like seeing their kids, and they're cute, which was fine. But there was a small minority that were very vocal in their complaints, that it wasn't in the spirit of a Catholic school, and it wasn't in the spirit of Christmas, the true meaning of Christmas. And all – so there was that, and there was the priest, um, charged in on the music teacher and went up one side of her and down the other.

The introduction of external standards creates a strong link between curriculum aims and consequences and hence introduces responsibility in a way that seeks to eliminate contingency. In this instance, the music teacher, as vehicle of the church, failed to meet her responsibility. The greater the degree of control assumed (by wilful self or wilful church), the more responsible one becomes for the consequences of actions. In a school climate where the external standard is clear, Laoise and the music teacher become increasingly concerned with their own security and sense of self. Laoise describes a "culture of . . . toeing the line and not sort of saying anything." In light of what she describes as a "very religious" and "very strict" "camp" of teachers at the school, she feels unable "to truly be myself with colleagues . . . there's things I just wouldn't talk about or can't mention and everybody knows." She believes that the childless state of her Catholic marriage raises potentially dangerous questions about her standing as "Roman Catholic." Concerned with her individual well-being, Laoise becomes private and inner directed; open dialogue with colleagues becomes impossible. Within the relative privacy of the classroom, however, Laoise continues to assert her will – what she calls "my own flavour," or "a different angle." The result is that the school can continue to represent itself publicly as a "harmony of interests" and "one opinion" (Arendt, 1958/1998, p. 46) – a "communistic fiction" of sameness (Arendt, p. 44. fn. 36). The possibility of argument across difference and political freedom among teachers is seriously undermined.

The Necessity of Distinctiveness and Distance
for Political Freedom

One could argue that the example of a religious school is hardly a good one when thinking about a culture of politics and political freedom among teachers. In schools like Laoise's where a single mentality dictates policy and practice, it is as if "a band of iron" holds the school faculty so tightly together that their difference (their plurality) has disappeared into "One Man of gigantic dimensions" (Arendt, 1968, p. 164). I would argue, however, that the One Man of Roman Catholicism is little different in its impact on school culture from the One Man of excellent test scores or standardized curriculum outcomes; in all cases there seems little room for "breaking with sameness" (Gambetti, 2005, p. 435; Phelan, 2009). It is here that teachers become entirely private, that is, they are deprived, and deprive themselves, of seeing and hearing others, of being seen and being heard by them (Arendt, 1958/1998).

New teachers in the autonomy study, working in both independent (religious and non-religious) and public schools, often represent their experience of themselves as interchangeable and lacking in any specificity or singularity. Some speak of the absence of "belief conversations" wherein they would have the opportunity to express (or Arendt would say "impress") "what I believe and what I think." Their short-term or beginning status haunts them. Despite being "fairly young and just brand new," they "want to be consulted" and not "dismissed" with others assuming "that [they] wouldn't care . . . that [they] wouldn't be that invested." Even in the context of teaching evaluations carried out by school administrators, descriptive comments are read as something "that could be sent to anyone." Without having their specificity acknowledged, they describe themselves in terms of "just being there [at school] as a worker and less as part of it." The early career teacher's distinctiveness is defined only in terms of years of experience or terms of employment; they are at once differentiated from their more experienced colleagues and at the same time, rendered forgettable.

What kind of distinctiveness is necessary for teachers' political freedom? And isn't there a danger that an emphasis on distinctiveness can lead to the problem of self-referential wilfulness on the part of the teacher?

The point may be to preserve the teacher's will as "a crucial element in making action and politics possible" *while* ensuring that the will is rescued from an exclusive self-referentiality (Martel, 2008, p. 298). This is the Arendtian compromise, perhaps, that humans require both sovereignty and non-sovereignty. Teachers need autonomy but they also need to be able to yield or defer to the will of others. How might the latter be accomplished so as to allow other perspectives into the will's solipsistic character? A return to Laoise may be instructive here.

While Laoise names the pastor's inclination to rule "with an iron fist" as the source of her problem, she also voices a concern with herself.

> Um, I guess, I guess I tend to take things to heart. And so I feel, I feel that pull. That somehow I'm not being genuine or true to one thing or the other. It would be easier to be black and white. It would be easier to [pause] totally, to either fully toe the official church line, or to say, I can't work here and get out, but I see, I see the good parts of where I'm at also. And I

see my role as being important in teaching tolerance and empathy and understanding. And I feel that I can make a difference that way. You know, and in some way, I am the new face and the new voice of the new church.

The aggrandizement of self in modernity as integrated, non-contradictory, and distinct – "the new face, the new voice" – is evident and yet called into question. "It would be easier to be black and white," but she cannot chose between them. Laoise's will to shape the world and religion by "teaching tolerance and empathy and understanding" (her version of Catholicism) is in conflict with the very institution that allows her "to make a difference." The pastor is symbolic of the possibility and impossibility of fulfilling her wilful desire. While the laws of the church constitute her as a particular kind of teaching subject, and in doing so constrain her will, they may also "open up some space of freedom for action that actually sets the constituted bodies . . . in motion" (Arendt, 1978, p. 199). One could say that Laoise wants to want the church to continue on its own terms because it enables her to "make a difference," but at the same time she wants the church to reflect her beliefs and values more closely: "Amo: Volu Ut Sis," meaning "I love; I want you to be" or "I wish to want you to be" (Martel, 2008, p. 298). The very term "volo" ("I want" or "I will") preserves the centrality of the teacher's will which is both obstacle to be overcome *and* the source of (the desire for) that overcoming (Martel). It is Laoise's wilful sense of and dream for power that enables her to speak back to dominant policy and practice *but* it is also her will that wishes the church and her school to be rescued from her (Laoise's) own desires – she wants more for them than what *she* wants for them. In acknowledging others and in recognizing the alternative positions they represent, Laoise achieves distance from her own will.

The achievement of distance from the will itself requires a particular relation with others. It is a relation based on distance, a secularized caritas: in a word, respect. Caritas does not merely redeem, it transforms the human will, making it available for politics without recourse to sovereign phantasms of control (Martel, 2008).

> Respect, not unlike the Aristotelian philia politike, is a kind of "friendship" without intimacy and without closeness; it is a regard between us, and this regard is independent of qualities which we may admire or of achievements which we may highly esteem. (Arendt, 1958/1998, p. 243)

Such regard is necessary if teachers are to reveal their unique personal identities through speech and action and thus make their appearance in the professional world. Without respect from and for colleagues and school leaders, teachers are condemned to "whatness" – qualities, gifts, talents, and shortcomings (Arendt, 1958/1998, p. 179): experience, qualifications, competence in the case of the teaching profession. For Arendt, the modern loss of respect, or the belief that respect is due only to those whom we admire or with whom we agree, is symptomatic of the increasing depersonalization of public and social life (Arendt).

There is an important distinction, for Arendt, between love, which we can experience only privately, and respect, which we experience in and for our public lives. Respect speaks to a necessary distance or separation that creates the "inter-space" for public engagement, what Jonathan Lear (2007) refers to as the space of necessary misunderstanding. Anything that threatens the in-between space is dangerous. The One Man of test scores or religion being a case in point, as we have seen. What preserves the distance is the pride of equals that is exemplified in the political realm, the public space. Distance between teachers is the basis of an Arendtian community.

In Closing: A Modest Political Freedom

The challenges of creating a political culture in the profession are indisputable, and they point to a fundamental paradox: that teachers need autonomy to act yet they need to forego autonomy to be free (to act in concert with others). Perhaps what conversations with early career teachers gesture toward is a more limited, contingent, less free vision of politics in the profession. Teachers' reflections in this study of professional autonomy keep alive a memory of what one might term the modesty of political freedom, enabling us to see as significant small moments of engagement that might otherwise be overlooked. Laoise's conversation with the music teacher and with the school pastor become potential sites for spontaneous, original action. In such moments, teachers like Laoise become a little less private, no longer deprived of being seen and heard or of seeing and hearing others, and a little less interchangeable. They have a chance to appear, in the Arendtian sense, and as such their words and actions can be witnessed and narrated by others; in such moments, they experience political freedom and as such what it means to be human.

Notes

1   The research study (Pitt & Phelan, 2005; Pitt & Phelan, 2008), from which I draw this and subsequent quotes from early career teachers, is entitled, "Paradoxes of Autonomy in Professional Life." The purpose of the study is to investigate the qualities, conditions, and difficulties of autonomy in professional life. Guided by discussions of autonomy in the humanities, the social sciences, and the human service literature, the inquiry involves in-depth phenomenological interviews with thirty-six practicing teachers at different junctures in their teaching careers – early career, mid-course, and nearing retirement. Interviews were two to three hours in duration and conducted one-on-one. Teacher participants are drawn from Ontario and British Columbia, Canada. The inquiry into professional autonomy asks the following questions:
 • How do teachers experience, construct and negotiate autonomy as a problem of judgment and constraint? How are teachers constituted as subjects of their own knowledge and judgment?
 • What are the dilemmas of autonomy for becoming and being a member of the teaching profession? What are the dilemmas of autonomy during periods of significant social change? How do teachers notice and fail to notice dilemmas concerning autonomy?

- Have any discourses of autonomy emerged as normative, while others have been eclipsed or silenced, and how do processes of privileging and silencing affect professional identity?

2   The main narrative in this chapter concerns Laoise (pseudonym); it is drawn from a conversation with one of the early career participants in the project entitled "Paradoxes of Autonomy in Professional Life" (Pitt & Phelan, 2008). Laoise, the teacher featured in this chapter, had four years of teaching experience.

References

Arendt, H. (1958/1998). *The Human Condition.* University of Chicago Press.

Arendt, H. (1968). *The Origins of Totalitarianism.* New York, NY: Harcourt.

Arendt, H. (1978). *The Life of the Mind.* New York, NY: Harcourt Brace Jovanovich.

Furlong, J., Barton, L., Miles, S., Whiting, C, & Whitty, G. (2000). *Teacher Education in Transition: Re-forming Professionalism?* Buckingham, England: Open University Press.

Gambetti, Z. (2005). The agent is the void! From the subjected subject to the subject of action. *Rethinking Marxism, 17*(3), 425–436.

Greene, M. (1988). *The Dialectic of Freedom.* New York, NY: Teachers College Press.

Honig, B. (1988, February). Arendt, identity and difference. *Political Theory, 6*(1), 77–98.

Kant, I. (1991). An Answer to the Question, What is Enlightenment? In H. Reiss (Ed.), *Kant: Political Writings* (pp. 54–60). New York, NY: Cambridge University Press.

Lear, J. (2007). *Radical Hope: Ethics in the Face of Cultural Devastation.* Cambridge, MA: Harvard University Press.

Levinson, N. (2001). The paradox of natality. In M. Gordon (Ed.), *Hannah Arendt and Education: Renewing Our Common World* (pp. 11–36). Boulder, CO: Westview Press.

Martel, J. (2008). Amo: Volu ut sis: Love, willing and Arendt's reluctant embrace of sovereignty. *Philosophy and Social Criticism, 34*(3), 287–313.

Phelan, A. (1996). "Strange Pilgrims": Nostalgia and Disillusionment in Teacher Education Reform. *Interchange, 27*(3–4), 331–348.

Phelan, A. (2009). Between judgment and constraint: Understanding autonomy in the professional lives of teachers. In Alice Pitt (Ed.), *Key Notes in Teacher Education: CATE Invited Addresses 2004-2008* (Vol. 1, pp. 83–102). Canadian Association for Teacher Education (CATE). Available from http://www.csse-scee.ca/cate/PBS.htm

Phelan, A., Sawa, R., Barlow, C., Hurlock, D., Myrick, F., Rogers, G. & Irvine, K. (2006). Violence and subjectivity in teacher education. *Asia-Pacific Journal of Teacher Education, 34*(2), 161 179

Pitt, A., & Phelan, A. (2008). Paradoxes of autonomy in professional life: A Research Problem. *Changing English: An International Journal of English Teaching, 15*(2), 189–197.

Smyth, J., & Shacklock, G. (1998). *Re-making Teaching: Ideology, Policy and Practice.* London, England: Routledge.

Villa, D. (2008). *Public Freedom.* Princeton University Press.

Zerilli, L. M. G. (2005). *Feminism and the Abyss of Freedom.* University of Chicago Press.

8

COLONIZING THE DESIRE OF CULTURALLY AND LINGUISTICALLY DIVERSE (CLD) CHILDREN IN EARLY CHILDHOOD EDUCATION: CURRICULUM AND THE CREATION OF CONSUMERS

Luigi Iannacci, Trent University

THE RAMIFICATIONS OF INTERNATIONAL economic restructuring have had a direct impact on the ESL field and CLD children.[1] Globally it has increased mobility of labour markets and cross-cultural contact (Burbules & Torres, 2000; Cummins, 2005), resulting in 375 million people currently learning English as a second language worldwide (British Council: Learning, n.d.). Locally, students in North American elementary schools are more culturally and linguistically diverse than they have ever been (Obiakor, 2001). Within the Canadian context, a significant number of children in elementary schools located in urban centers speak a first language (L1) other than English or French (Citizenship & Immigration Canada, 2003; Roberts-Fiati, 1997). The province of Ontario has experienced a 29% increase of what it once referred to as "ESL students" (now ELL, English Language Learners) within elementary schools since 2000 (People for Education, 2007). The province is expected to grow from roughly 12 million in 2001 to 16 million in 2028, with 75% of this growth coming from immigration (Glaze, 2007). Ideologically, globalization has driven and is being driven by intensified consumerism and consumerist polices and practices (Dunn, 2008, p. 9). "Domestically and globally, the push for greater economic affluence is supported by frequent appeals to the notion of 'consumer sovereignty', an ideological slogan announcing a shift to a worldwide consumerist agenda" (p. 9). This shift has had a direct impact on culture and identity (Dunn, 2008) and the construction of children as a vital new market to be exploited (Steinburg & Kincheloe, 2004).[2] This construction has defined children in relation to their consumer habits (Media Awareness

Network, 2009), while colonizing their desires toward further con-sumption (Giroux, 2009). Bezaire and Cameron (2009) note that children have become recognized "as both primary and future mar-kets, expanding well beyond the traditional limits of marketed candy and breakfast cereals" (p. 274).

Despite these demographics and phenomena, educational researchers have noted a dearth of research about CLD students in early childhood education (ECE) and disparity in providing for these students (Bernhard, Lefebvre, Chud, & Lange, 1995; Falconer & Byrnes, 2003; Suárez-Orozco, 2001; Toohey, 2000). Further, the limited scholarship about young children learning English as second language has traditionally been methods-focused, with very little produced from socio-cultural and critical perspectives (Toohey, 2000), and lesser still from eco-justice standpoints that can specifi-cally explore the ways in which school curricula and literacy practices further develop consumer identities among children in ways that contribute to the current "ecological crisis" (Martusewicz, Lupinacci, & Edmundson, 2011). This exploration is essential as long-standing and limited questions concerning curriculum have focused on what to teach and how to teach, yet Heydon and Iannacci (2008) point out that these questions cannot be discussed unless there has been an open discussion of who the students are.

In contrast, this study adds to the growing body of work in early years literacy research grounded in socio-cultural theory and recon-ceptualist curriculum theories relating to early literacy (Bourne, 2001; Boyd & Brock, 2004; Gee, 2001, Iannacci & Whitty, 2009). This study therefore draws on eco-justice perspectives to develop analytical methods and curricular principles to address these issues. What is specifically examined is how consumer culture is present within ritualized early years literacy curricula and how this curricula can serve to colonize children's desires and forward their consumer identities, as well as various principles that may destabilize this "lived" curricula (Marsh & Willis, 2007).

Theoretical Framing

Two basic tenets of socio-cultural theory highlight its relevance and applicability to this research. The first tenet is that "the mind is social in nature" (Wertsch, in Boyd & Brock, 2004, p. 4). The second tenet is that "language in use plays a central role in mediating our actions as humans. Consequently, the uses of language in the context of interactions, and the various analytical ways of looking at that language become central when considering human learning" (p. 4). Literacy is conceptualized as a social practice and is socially mediated. As such, coming to literacy is not exclusively about the acquisition of a code, but also, and more importantly, a culture. Classroom literacy practices can therefore be understood as a particular set of cultural events that need to be critically examined in order to understand what students appropriate as they encounter school literacy as well as the impact this appropriation has on their identities. Eco-justice theory supports this view of language as inextricably linked to culture (Bowers, 2001) and informs an analysis of literacy curricula encountered by the CLD students discussed in this study. Drawing on these perspectives allows for a critical examination of what CLD students culturally appropriate as well as how this appropriation effects identity development and the environment. The theoretical pastiche created by this approach to re-examining curricula is commensurate with reconceptualist theorizing, as is the focus on the social transformation and reconstruction of curricula (Iannacci & Whitty, 2009).

As the body of work forwarding eco-justice perspectives is vast and expansive, it may be difficult to provide an all encompassing definition of the term/field. However for the purposes of this chapter, eco-justice education involves the linguistic and cultural analysis of the ecological crisis and therefore a critical awareness of destruction of the world's diverse ecosystems, languages, and cultures by consumer culture. One of the many prevailing concerns within the field is therefore the impact of commodification: "a process by which market values overwhelm the world and nature, people and even ideas into commodities for sale on the market" (Martusewicz, Lupinacci, & Edmundson, 2011). Specifically, eco-justice theory sheds light on the ways in which commodification has shaped every aspect of modern culture and subsequently contributed to "a cycle of degrading ecosystems by extracting the 'resources' necessary for the production of consumer items which are shortly returned to Nature as waste" (Bowers, 2001, p. 161). In line with these concerns is the "global spread of the monoculture of consumerism" (p. 149) and how this culture has commodified various aspects of living, including relationships, health care, leisure activities, death, etc. (Bowers). The consequences of commodification such as "an emphasis on consumption of purchased items, thus exacerbating the ecological crisis" (Martusewicz, Lupinacci, & Edmundson, in press) are also addressed in a great deal of eco-justice-focused research. Eco-justice perspectives have specifically recognized how market-oriented relationships have effected the social construction of childhood and how consumer culture has altered conceptualizations of and provisions for early learning (Bowers). Pedagogy is therefore understood as a cultural practice that produces rather than merely transmits knowledge (Sleeter and Bernal, 2004). These cultural practices can be deconstructed in order to reveal how they contribute to commodification and ecological degradation. It is imperative to cultivate and consider knowledge produced in this way, as theoretical links grounded in ecological perspectives have traditionally been absent from discussions about and conceptualizations of a variety of critical frames (Bowers).

Data and Methods

The aforementioned framing informs the year long ethnography (Iannacci, 2005) this paper reports on. The study examined literacy curricula provided to CLD children in two kindergarten and two Grade 1 classrooms. Data collection consisted of two phases of observation in four early years classrooms in two schools throughout a school year. During both phases of the research, the researcher engaged in "overt participant observation" (Wallen & Fraenkel, 2001, p. 436) and ensured that research subjects knew that they were being observed. Once approval and permission to conduct research were granted and secured from the university, school board, principals, and teachers, preliminary briefing sessions with students took place. The briefing introduced and made explicit the researcher's role within the classroom and clarified the information and permission letter students took home to their parent(s) or guardian(s). The letter clearly stated the nature of the research as well as the role of the researcher. Letters and permission forms were written in the CLD students' first language to ensure that their parents fully understood the study. The languages included Albanian, Arabic, Serbo-Croatian, Spanish, and Turkish.

During fieldwork, school documents, field notes, photographs, and children's work were collected. Interviews with teachers, parents, school board personnel, and students were also conducted throughout the year. These multiple forms of data were used to construct narratives that were then deconstructed through reflection about and a distancing from what was observed in order to develop principles and curricular possibilities, a process grounded in reconceptualist curriculum theory realized through text construction, deconstruction, and reconstruction (Iannacci & Whitty, 2009). Literacy events and practices that comprised curricula and themes and salient issues that emerged from the narratives were therefore analyzed after they had been contextualized and interrogated for inconsistencies and contradictions. Reconceptualized understandings about the data were subsequently developed as a result of this threefold mimesis (Ricoeur, 1992). This analytic-interpretive process that began with the archiving, sorting, development, and rereading of field texts (Clandinin & Connelly, 2000) allowed for the juxtaposition and identification of similarities and contrasts within data which subsequently revealed patterns, themes, narrative threads, and tensions. Data from the larger study that are relevant to key findings being examined in this paper are presented as a way of demonstrating and exploring specific issues and offering alternatives.

One of the specific issues that emerged as a result of data analysis informed by eco-justice perspectives concerns the ways consumer identities were fostered among early years CLD children through early years literacy curricula. This is significant in light of the growing body of work mentioned earlier that is beginning to explore how children are increasingly and purposefully positioned as consumers (Barbaro and Earp, 2008; Hughes, 2005; Kapur, 2005; Steinburg & Kincheloe, 1997). The contextual specifics that link globalization, increased consumerism, and commodified childhood are mirrored, reinforced, and demonstrated through data about literacy curricula provided to CLD students. The examination and discussion of this data is specifically concerned with how schools and schooling foster consumer identities which contribute to commodification and "planetary ecological breakdown" (Bowers, 2006, p.71). Focusing the analysis on these issues is intended to shed light on problematic practices within schools, and to then to further develop eco-justice-informed curricula that provide teachers and teacher educators ways of developing pedagogies and curricula that resist furthering consumer rituals and identities. The following narratives constructed from field data and transcripts from interviews with Sarah[3] (a Grade 1 teacher) and some of her CLD students who participated in this study demonstrate the current context and facilitate follow up discussion intended to conceptualize this curricula. Parts of these narratives have been published previously (Iannacci, 2007) and have been edited and excerpted to serve the focus of this paper.

"Multicultural" Santa Visit

I enter Sarah's Grade 1 classroom and, as usual, she informs me about the plans for the day. She seems a bit anxious as she explains that it will probably be "broken up," and we will not get much done. She says that a couple of her colleagues have organized a visit from someone they refer to as "Multicultural Santa." That morning, Sarah and I have a scheduled interview. She is skeptical about the visit, but has a "wait and see" attitude about it.

> So we have Santa coming today. . . . It was kind of imposed as sort of a multicultural Santa, that he's going to acknowledge other religions and stuff like that. . . . I want to acknowledge all the different religions, but speaking as someone who doesn't celebrate Christmas, I'd rather learn about Christmas and teach my kids about Christmas independently just like any other holiday. . . . In public school I had more of a problem with it when they combined the Christian holidays and sort of said, "Well, this is your Christmas. That's why we do Eid or Hanukkah - it's your Christmas." It's not your Christmas. It's a different holiday. That's the problem when you get a Santa sort of saying . . . even though Santa is commercial, and it has nothing to do with Christmas in sort of a religious sense. You know what I mean?

When we eventually are called to see Santa, we are the first class to enter the open door of the music room. The room is dimly lit, and the children carefully sit in front of a human tableau made by Mr. and Mrs. Claus (two senior citizens who volunteer their time each year to do this). They pretend to sleep in front of a Norman Rockwell Christmas backdrop complete with a Christmas tree and presents in front of a fireplace. Once all of the primary classes are seated, Mr. and Mrs. Claus slowly awaken, greet the children, and let them know that they have a candy cane for all of the "good" children. Santa addresses the large crowd and asks who has been "good" or "bad" and what they want for Christmas.

The teachers call each of their students up to the front to sit on Santa's knee to receive their candy cane. Sarah begins, "Farah. . .Tom. . .Halim. . .etc". Each child has a moment with Santa in front of all of their peers. Santa loudly asks them what they want for Christmas. Eleven of the twenty-four children in Sarah's class are Muslim and have just had Eid. This is similar to the other classes in attendance. When a child who Santa assumes is Muslim approaches, he asks in a deep voice, "Ho! Ho! Ho! Do you celebrate Eid or Christmas?" as if they are synonymous. At one point a Muslim child is greeted with a rambunctious "Olla!" before being asked what he wants for Christmas. When Santa asks the children if they celebrate Eid and they respond affirmatively, he asks what presents they got on Eid. He then whispers quietly enough so everyone can hear, "Well, maybe we can sneak something in for Christmas too. Don't tell anyone, ok?" The children nod in agreement and whisper what they want for Christmas into his ear. They receive a candy cane, have their picture taken on Santa's knee, and head back to their seat to watch their classmates experience the same ritual. I notice Sarah giving me a stare that seems dismayed and disappointed. I flash a stare back at her very quickly so Mr. and Mrs. Claus do not catch our glance. He knows if you've been naughty or nice.

After each child has had a turn, the teachers leave with their students. Sarah's class is the last to go, having been seated in the front. Sarah leads the line; I mind the back for stragglers. As I wait for the long line of students to leave the room, I can feel Mr. and Mrs. Claus' eyes on me. I am wearing a tie. I know this territory all too well. I am expected to have a chat with them. I know they assume I am a teacher at the school and to do any less would compromise their view of the school. Mrs. Claus extends her hand to me as I approach and say, "Thank you for coming." Mrs. Claus replies, "Wow, there's a lot of Arabic kids here." I respond, "Yeah, there are" with a hint of edge in my voice. She says, "Well, you know, it's nice that they're getting used to Christmas too."

I return to the class to find the students busy with their journals. Halim, Farah, Akil and Sanela draw pictures or write about Santa's visit. During an interview I have with Akil, we talk about his entry. He states:

'Member we came back from the music place [inaudible] and Santa was sleeping, pretending to sleeping and then he called everybody up to get a candy cane and said, "What do you want for Christmas"? And then when we came back to the classroom we had to do a journal about Santa.

Although Sarah asked the students to write in their journals, I am not sure whether she actually told them to write about Santa's visit since I was still speaking with Mr. and Mrs. Claus when the task was explained. Sarah occasionally assigned journal topics but also allowed and encouraged students to choose their own.

Later that day, my interview with Sarah continues. It is clear that she has a few things to say about "Multicultural" Santa's visit.

I was horrified [nervous laughter]. I just thought . . . first of all we went into the room and Santa and his wife were sleeping, or pretended to be sleeping. I don't know. Maybe I should have looked into it a little bit more, but I didn't know he was going to call them up. He called them up one by one and asked them what they wanted for Christmas, how they were and how much they had grown because he saw them last year, which he might have [it's Sarah's first year at the school]. That was the impression I got. I, I was blown . . . first of all I was thinking a couple of things. First of all, I was glad you were here to see that, it was a good opportunity for you to see that for your study, to see some of the reactions of the kids and Santa Claus. I didn't feel that it was multicultural at all. The way he incorporated Eid was . . . well, first of all he only asked the children that were sort of dark skinned or had sort of "odd" names. I was looking at that. He didn't ask any of the kids that were fair skinned. . . . I think he was asking the kids who were more, more black . . . and he would say, "Do you celebrate Eid or do you celebrate Christmas?" And if they would say, "I celebrate Eid", he would say, "He celebrates Eid, oh, well, did you get a lot of things for Eid? Yeah, well, I will get you something for Christmas." He gave them a candy cane for Christmas . . . and then said, "Shhh, don't tell anybody, let's just sneak a little something, don't tell anybody". I have a big problem with that because they're not . . . what you do is not to belittle Eid, and to sort of dismiss the holiday, "Oh, well you know, you'll still celebrate Christmas". I think they get that, they get that too much everywhere. They get it at the mall, they get it at the . . . you know, it's just . . . no, Eid is their holiday, they don't celebrate Christmas.

Sarah's own approach to religious celebrations and holidays attempted to counter the dominance of Christmas. Throughout the year she read books and shared artifacts about various religious celebrations. She also organized activities that were responsive to and helped inform her students about world religions, particularly those followed by her students.

Sarah: In September, if something comes up then do that in September. Just don't do it when it's Christmas time. If it's Christmas time, then we'll do Christmas stuff and there's no reason not to in a public school 'cause we do have a lot of kids that celebrate Christmas. . . . I just think you can add it all year long. If a holiday comes up then you do that holiday. I don't think you need try to fit everything into Christmas cause you're sort of buying into the . . . I keep on calling it commercialized but the only reason I keep calling it that is because you just see it everywhere.

. . .

I just felt that Ramadan, right now, was more important to talk about in this classroom this year. We have eleven kids that are celebrating this out of twenty-four and that's, you can't just ignore that. So, I think whenever it's personal, you need to talk about it. It needs to be in the forefront. So, that's why Ramadan got a lot of attention. But, I think it's still important to mention other things.

Two weeks prior to Santa's visit, Sarah's sensitivity to these issues was already evident. She had planned a letter-writing activity intended to capitalize on the diversity within her classroom. Rather than simply organizing students to write a letter to Santa (a common activity in elementary schools), Sarah intended to have a discussion to highlight the notion of performing good deeds towards friends and relatives and provide a writing frame for Muslim students to express their thanks to their parents or anyone in their lives they viewed as special during Ramadan. The writing frame would have been available to all students; however, a "Dear Santa" frame was also provided for students who wanted to write a traditional letter to Santa where they could list what they wanted for Christmas. Unfortunately, Sarah was absent the day of the lesson and activity. Although she had left plans for the supply teacher outlining her intentions, they were not carried out since the supply teacher lacked knowledge of the context of Sarah's classroom and the school.

Letters to Santa

Since Sarah is away, I introduce myself to the supply teacher. Right after the morning announcements, the "ESL" students line up and wait for Paula (the ESL teacher) to pick them up. I attend the ESL session with them, then escort them back to their classroom. Just before I enter the room, Sarah's grade partner stops me to ask about the bilingual and multicultural books I have been using in Sarah's classroom. We have a discussion about them, and she requests a bibliography of the books since she hopes the school parent association will purchase them. After our conversation, I walk into the Grade 1 classroom and find students already assigned to a writing task. Akil immediately signals me over to his desk.

Akil, the youngest of two children in his Arabic speaking family, was extremely proud of and generous about sharing his cultural and linguistic background with me. Akil's family had visited Lebanon before he began junior kindergarten. He remembered this time with great fondness and talked about friends and relatives. Akil even insisted that he was born in Lebanon, although his father and documents in his Ontario Student Record (OSR) attested to the fact that he was born in Canada. In November, Akil completed a frame sentence Sarah had assigned that began, "When I wish upon a star I wish . . ." by writing "I wish I was in Lebanon." On one of my first visits to the Grade 1 class, Sarah asked Akil to let me see me what he was wearing. Underneath his white turtleneck with a Canadian maple leaf was an olive t-shirt that read "I Love Lebanon." He smiled from ear to ear as he proudly showed it to me.

Akil and Farah sit beside each other and are in the same group. Both of them are busy copying the "Dear Santa" writing frame as is everyone else in the group who began the activity while Akil and Farah attended ESL class. The supply teacher, busy with another group, has not visited yet. Akil seems tentative about what he's doing. He looks at the piece of paper in which he has written "Dear Santa, My name is Akil I ha . . .", then looks at me, then to the charts where Sarah has prepared two different writing frames (a "Dear Santa" frame, and a letter to parents, family, or friends frame). He does this very quickly several times before he stops and asks, "Do I copy that?" as he points to the "Dear Santa" frame. I reply, "Well, you don't have to. There are different letters you can write" Akil asks, "Well, which one do I copy? What do they say?" I read both frames and explain that there are different types of letters so that anyone who celebrates Ramadan can write a letter to anyone they choose, as can everybody else. He tells me about Ramadan and how he is looking forward to

Eid as he puts the letter he has started aside and begins a new one. "I think I wanna write a letter to my mom and dad." Just before beginning his new letter, Akil turns to Farah who thus far has written "Dear Santa" and says, "Farah, we don't celebrate this. We celebrate Ramadan. We're Muslim". Farah looks at him and quietly asks, "Which letter is ours then?" He informs her, "That other one . . . only says 'Dear,' and then you can write it all down and put whatever you want."

Before Farah begins her new letter, she turns around and leans forward toward the next group where Halim is seated. Halim has also begun to write a "Dear Santa" letter. Farah says, "Halim, you have to write the other letter. We're Muslim." Halim briefly stops what he's doing and then continues. Farah leaves her chair and attempts to tell her other Muslim classmates the same thing and then rushes back to her group to begin her new letter.

Unfortunately, the alternative frame is much longer than the "Dear Santa" frame, and although Akil and Farah are eager to begin personalizing their letters, the rather laborious task of copying the frame takes the remainder of the time left to work on the task. I exclusively work with Farah and Akil and their group since the supply teacher seems to have unofficially assigned me governance over them. I'm not sure if she has made Sarah's plans clear to everyone.

As they prepare to go outside for first recess, my doubts are confirmed. I notice that all of the Muslim students except Akil and Farah have written "Dear Santa" letters. I couldn't help but wish the supply teacher had made Sarah's plans explicit to students who had come back from the ESL session rather than having them mirror what everyone else was doing. I was however, glad that Akil had questions and asked for help.

Discussion

Literacy researchers and theorists operating from socio-cultural perspectives have highlighted the importance of accessing prior knowledge and experience in order to forge links between school literacy curricula and students' lives. Guillaume (1998) reveals that of the ten "big ideas" found in a synthesis of the literature on reading and learning, accessing and building on prior knowledge was number one. Such practices hold that accessing children's background knowledge and experiences can help foster meaningful and purposeful literacy activity, positively affecting transactions with texts. By extension, such practices can draw on students' current interests and therefore help teachers find the literacy "hook" needed to motivate them to engage in literacy activity. The "Multicultural Santa" visit followed by journal writing in Sarah's classroom and the "Dear Santa" letters capitalized on experiences students were assumed to have had or be interested in. Dominant understandings of what constitutes the holiday season were the hook used to prompt students towards literacy.

It is of course pedagogically sound to capitalize on and access children's background knowledge, experiences, and interests while planning for and organizing literacy curricula. However, the limited ways in which this practice was applied in relation to CLD students proved problematic. The socio-cultural backgrounds, experiences, and interests of CLD students were by no means monolithic. However, the assumptions that informed most of the Christmas related school and literacy events suggested that Christmas was of importance and interest to all, thus reinforcing universal constructions of a "normal" childhood.

Although accessing and capitalizing on children's background knowledge and personal experiences instantiated the practices and events described and discussed thus far, other notions and discourses also undergirded configurations of practice related to the ways in which Christmas was dealt with. How public schools should address holidays with significant religious overtones has been described as a "major problem" (Menendez, 1994). Historically, school curricula has reflected local religious conditions, usually protestant in tone, and therefore celebrating Christmas in schools with the full panoply of activity that included strong religious content was viewed as acceptable and "tended to follow the increasing legal, commercial and religious acceptability of the holiday" (p. 4). Although successful and necessary boycotts and legal action have curtailed this approach to Christmas in schools, sensitivities toward the issue have not necessarily resulted in comprehensible and consistent alternatives. In fact, the discussion has become further bifurcated and dominated by two perspectives.

According to Haynes and Thomas (2001) and al-Hibri, Elshtain, and Haynes (2001), those who advocate for the "sacred public school" argue for the imposition of *their* faith on all students, while others believe that a "naked public school" devoid of all references to religion is an appropriate response to increasingly diverse public schools. Haynes and Thomas argue that neither model makes sense in a multicultural society. When we consider that "religion is a fundamental part of most cultures" (Fraser, 1999, p. 5) and therefore essential to consider when organizing responsive and engaging literacy curricula, the "naked public school" argument does nothing to assist students in negotiating their identities as they navigate literacy curricula. The "sacred public school" position is of course problematic since it reinscribes a majority-conformity form of assimilation.

Other notions that inform school contexts in which teachers and students work and learn are equally limiting. Specifically, "cultural congruence" (Banks in Asimeng-Boahene & Klein, 2004), which attempts to import diversity through topics such as Christmas, informed the rationale for and events during the "Multicultural" Santa Visit. Cultural congruence reinforces the idea that "everyone needs to learn how other religions celebrate Christmas" (Miller, 1999/2000, p. 316). World religions and their celebrations or observances are presented and positioned as the equivalent to another version of Christianity and Christmas. Sarah was very aware of the problems associated with cultural congruence and pointed out the ways in which this approach to holidays in schools reinforced the idea that Hanukah or Ramadan are other peoples' Christmas. Her views regarding "Multicultural" Santa and her insistence that various celebrations and religious observances be taught when they actually occur reinforced the ways in which cultural congruence reaffirmed the dominance of one culture over another through a veneer of multiculturalism.

Although a full-fledged subscription to the "naked public school" model was not evident in interviews with teachers, it was present within some of the practices the teachers were faced with having to reconcile. The justification Sarah was given by her colleagues regarding "Multicultural" Santa's visit, for example, de-emphasized and distanced it from overt religious devotion and celebration. This might suggest that the "naked public school" argument also informed the rationale for Santa's visit and the letters to Santa that took place in each of the classrooms I observed. However, what was also evident in Sarah's interviews and dominant in the *"Multicultural" Santa Visit* narrative and the letter writing to Santa was the idea that replacing an overtly religious celebration of Christmas with a commercial focus was appropriate and addressed debates and sensitivities about this issue. In other words, although the religious acceptability of the holiday was somewhat questioned (albeit inadequately), what remained unquestioned and even endorsed was a commercialized approach to Christmas understood to be politically correct and innocuous. Such a view is consistent with and further reinforces an increasingly commodified and consumerist view of education and childhood, views that are imperative to examine in order to forward eco-justice-informed curricula.

Although "Christmas in the classroom" is a dominant feature in the data presented, the analysis needs to extend well and beyond the ways religious observances and celebrations are recognized and occur within schools. This analysis needs to consider the ecological consequences of adults colonizing children's desires as a result of their anxiety about responding to increased student diversity. Cannella and Viruru (2004) state:

> The more obvious tie between education and colonization is the physical control of the bodies of those who are younger; the bodies of "childhood" are only permitted to engage in sanctioned forms of pleasure, while spaces, times, and distances around them are compartmentalized, centered, scheduled, and separated. (p. 115)

What is especially significant is the link between "sanctioned forms of pleasure" and colonization, a link that Kincheloe and Steinburg (1997) have also noted in tracing the ways in which "power is 'written' on the mind and body via colonization of desire and pleasure" (p. 29). The colonization CLD children experienced was not limited to how they were constructed and provided for, but also through the ways in which they were inculcated toward normalized experiences of pleasure associated with and constructed as ideal for all children to experience in fostering desirable childhoods. What these sanctioned forms of pleasure had in common were the commercial and consumptive frameworks they invoked. Events such as the visit from and letters to Santa as well as a great deal of the Christmas-focused activity that occurred in the classrooms reflected a consumerist focused curriculum that both reinforced universal constructions of childhood and positioned children as instruments of hypercapitalism. Canella and Viruru (2004) note that "hypercapitalism can be characterized by (1) interpretations of the world that are entirely based on capital, resources, and markets, (2) a fear of losing material commodities, and (3) a belief that capital . . . is now the solution to human problems" (p. 117). The shift towards hypercapitalism has ensured that "globalization [has] become the everyday work of parents, teachers, and administrators within and across the institutions of social reproduction" (Griffith, 2001, p. 83). The social relations that occur outside of the school and the nexus of power that informs these relations have direct influence on the micro dynamics of school curricula. For example, asking and allowing students to consider what it means to be Muslim was less significant and evident than the accoutrements of a consumer culture complete with shopping mall rituals (e.g., visits to Santa, wish lists in letter form, etc). Within this context, presentations and interpretations of the world focused on capital, resources, and markets rather than a plurality of religious and other forms of experience, thus corroborating the ways in which "corporate consumptive and profit agendas are manifested in attempts to construct 'child' through pedagogies of representation and consumption" (Cannella, 2002, p.12). The hypercapitalist orientation evident within the lived literacy curriculum can be understood as a new "religion" that promised to address the increasing diversity of the student body through, ironically, corporate cultural dominance. Just as children have been constructed as future *producers* in the global labour market via standardized assessment and curriculum, this corporate religion required its worshippers to be understood and constructed as future *consumers*. Burbules and Torres (2000) point out that "schools are not only concerned with preparing students as producers; increasingly, schools help shape consumer attitudes and practices as well" (p. 20). This focus on children as producers and consumers is reflective of macro discourses influenced and shaped by economic international restructuring.

The shift positions children as a market to be exploited in order to sustain and further the economic goals and conditions in which first world countries, now commonly referred to as "minority world" countries (Dahlberg, Moss, & Pence, 1999, p. 6) (i.e., "developed world") have become accustomed. The targeting and indoctrination of this market group mirrors curriculum downloading and has similarly meant a "hurrying" in marketing directed at children also known as "age compression," a practice of marketing messages and products originally designed and reserved for older children and targeting them to younger ones in order to accelerate their entrance into consumer culture (Schor, 2004). Just as concentrated efforts to ensure accelerated preparation into the global market have affected assessment and pedagogy practices in schools, so too has the largely unquestioned corporatization of childhood. The "hostile takeover over childhood" was named one of the "big ideas" of 2005 in the January/February issue of *Adbusters* and can be understood as coinciding with and parallel to the hostile take over of curriculum within schools. Schor points out that reasons for this takeover are largely economically driven since comprehensive branding strategies and intense levels of consumer immersion directed at children ultimately ensure profits (p. 56). Although the forms of consumer immersion children experienced during events such as "Multicultural" Santa's Visit and writing letters to Santa could be deemed "age appropriate," what is similar to and at the heart of these strategies is a focus on ensuring that children participate in consumer culture. Within the data that describes these events, "a pedagogy of consumption is revealed that uses constructions of child 'needs' and 'experiences' as necessary for the universal 'ideal' child" (Cannella, 2002, p. 12).

Research has demonstrated that minority parents are concerned about the ways in which celebrations such as Christmas and Halloween occur within Canadian early years classrooms (Berhard et al., 1995; Zine, 2001). Although this was corroborated in interviews I conducted with a few of the parents, other parents of the children in this study described their child's participation within these rituals of consumer culture as acceptable, even using words such as "normal," "joyful," and "fun" to rationalize their curricular presence. Schor (2004) has commented on the pervasiveness of an unquestioned and dominant corporate habitus. "Corporations have infiltrated the core activities and institutions of childhood, with virtually no resistance from government or parents" (p. 13). Fjellman offers further insights that explicate the hegemonic impact of consumer culture.

Building on the model of the human being as consumer, corporations and all those who benefit from the prevailing polit-

ical and economic structure of the market have been so successful that the consumer model and the personal entitle-
ments attached to it have been accepted as true, beautiful and
universal. Thus personal identity, place in society, and even
self-worth are commoditized, with consumption and commodities standing as symbols of this identity. Our ontological
acceptance of the model of consumer as the new human
being leads us to new natural rights of enlightenment and to
new evidence of fulfillment. (in Kasturi, 2002, p. 50)

Perhaps an unquestioned ontological acceptance of consumerism
furthered the idea that practices and events featured in the Christmas
related narratives were unobjectionable. The lack of power CLD parents demonstrated during an interview I conducted with Farah's parents, for example, illustrates this point. They asserted that it was not
their "business" to complain about what the school was doing, which
may help to explain the acceptance of practices that were often at
odds with their own religious and cultural beliefs.

Schor (2004) has argued that children have suffered under the
regime of a largely unquestioned corporate cultural habitus.
"Involvement in consumer culture causes dysfunction in the forms of
depression, anxiety, low self-esteem, and psychosomatic complaints"
(p. 17). This claim has been recently corroborated by a study conducted by The Children's Society which found consumerism to be a
contributing factor in the increase of depression and anxiety among
children over the past two decades (Bennet, 2008). Linn (2004)
adds that "children are multifaceted beings whose physical, psychological, social, emotional, and spiritual development are all threat-
ened when their value as consumers trumps their value as people" (p.
10). Another study has demonstrated that assimilation into consumer culture has been equally problematic for many people regardless of their age.

When Mexican immigrants arrive in the US, they are not as

well-off as Americans, but their rates of mental dysfunction are considerably lower. Within a decade's time, however, their problems with depression, anxiety and addiction nearly double, to the same levels as the general American population (about 32 percent). (Adbusters, 2005)

Although Suzuki (2004) corroborates the psychological effects of consumerism, he additionally questions why people willingly participate in a commercialized version of Christmas that is a "monument to excess" and the "pinnacle of our hyper consumptive lifestyles" (p. 5). Suzuki argues that this participation is sparked by a need to fill a void created by a world of increasing uniformity devoid of rituals that reflect natural, cultural, and geographic diversity.

> In the absence of God or spirituality, in the absence of a capacity to respond to seasonal patterns and natural rhythms and in the absence of meaningful social rituals, people are grasping onto whatever they can to help ground them in their communities. If that means spending days at a time in a crowded mall, then that's what we do. That becomes the ritual. That becomes Christmas. (p. 5)

Suzuki additionally argues that although many people find rituals of consumption unsatisfactory and are desperate for more meaningful cultural ceremony, they are ultimately "trapped" by the trappings of consumerism. I argue that schools should actively resist rather than reinforce and encourage "traps" that assimilate students into becoming compliant consumers. This resistance is not just essential to children's mental health, but to the fate of the earth.

It must be pointed out that the teachers I worked with were by no means simply CEOs of their classrooms, nor did they intentionally colonize their students' desires in order to ensure their active participation in consume culture. It is important to be sensitive to and aware of the fact that teachers can be conflicted by the relations in which they find themselves and "resent being stereotyped as bearers of middle-class culture or agents of social control" (Livingstone, 1987, p. 251). Interviews I conducted with Sarah demonstrated this dilemma and further stressed how important it is to emphasize taken-for-granted understandings that instantiate assimilative practices and events as well as challenge what early years educators do in the name of pleasure since it is often understood as harmless and done without malice and certainly not considered in relation to it's effect on the environment. It is therefore essential for teacher educators to explore the historical legacy of these practices and the current configurations of what this past has meant for early years curricula, students, and the ecology. This revelation is not intended to blame teachers for "indoctrinating" students, but rather to make explicit the ways in which dominant economic discourses shape schools and relationships between teachers, students, parents, and the environment. Ultimately, this interrogation of what has seemingly been constructed as innocent and even desirable is intended to forward a decolonizing agenda that challenges and rejects the normalization of a consumptive lifestyle and an assimilationist agenda that has traditionally plagued elementary schools, and reinscribed neglectful attitudes towards mental and ecological health.

My professional experiences in elementary schools during a conservative party regime render me sympathetic to a teacher's desire to organize pleasurable experiences for their students. The last thing I want to argue for is less pleasure in early years classrooms since the current standardized educational context has done much damage to the idea and nurturing of pleasure within schools. This ambivalence toward and critical concern about pleasure in early years classrooms was evident during data collection and meant that I gave way to pressure to accede to dominant ways of constructing desire. During a session that took place at Norman Bethune one week before Halloween, a participating teacher very pointedly told me, "I expect you to be in costume next week." Rather than "forgetting" my costume or having a discussion about how I felt about Halloween, I complied and showed up as a Crayola crayon, giving credence to and reinforcing dominant notions of pleasure and how it can be derived by participating rather than resisting the commercial forms it has taken. Therefore, despite the practices and events I advocate, I am aware of and acknowledge that I am implicated in the same relations I critique. I have also come to recognize how the power of dominant cultural consumer habitus is reinforced and reproduced as a result of "expected" pleasurable and ritualized experiences passed on as rights of passage and thereafter normalized within early years classrooms. Clearly, what is done in the name of pleasure and how these rituals impact CLD students is of concern. Further, the ways these experiences are understood as innocuous, innocent, and expected are problematic and need to be both recognized as reinforcing an assimilationist orientation and actively resisted by educators who work with children. There is great need to re-think and re-define the ways in which children's pleasure is organized and presented so that it is not inextricably linked to consumerism and consumer practices. At the same time, adults need to be cognizant of colonizing children's desires and as such be respectful of their agency and autonomy. Principles and practices described later on in this paper attempt to offer specific ways for teacher educators and teachers to develop curricula that meets these goals.

Children's agency and autonomy are especially important to consider, as they are not just passive recipients of culture, they also create hybrid "third spaces" or "borderland" territories which are a "physical and metaphorical space ... where children negotiate culturally-appropriate ways of operating" (Gee in Wilson, 2003, p. 296). This space is often formed in order to (re)construct a sense of individuality and community and is "generated from necessity, at sites of struggle, or when existing spaces do not provide the necessary feeling of belonging" (p. 296). The space can resist and even subvert the commodified and consumerist identities and ways of being in the world that they are exposed to. This is essential to recognize, as consumers are both systemic agents and human actors who have:

multiple identities that originate from a variety of sources. Theorists and researchers [and teachers] need to be wary of overestimating the significance of consumption and consumerism for identity formation relative to other, often enduring forms of identification, such as occupation, kinship, gender, and ethnicity. Identification with one's material possessions and lifestyle intermingle in complicated ways with other, sometimes stronger identifications, which consumption only serves to materialize, elaborate, and certify. The intrusions of consumer culture have [however] arguably weakened the hold of traditional and conventional affiliations, strengthening the role of consumption in definitions of self and other. (Dunn, 2008, pp. 188–189)

The impact of some of Sarah's practices demonstrated and allowed for this intermingling. The way she organized letter writing allowed Akil and Farah's religious identities to inform their interactions with the event, thus reinforcing the importance of drawing on students' backgrounds while recognizing the multiplicity of experience. Sarah's ability to draw on and extend this literacy practice opened up a space for Akil and Farah to negotiate through the event in ways that allowed their religious identities to become an integral rather than a subjugated and repressed resource that to some degree allowed them to resist the consumer identity and rituals they were immersed in. This corroborates Zine's (2001) assertion that Muslim students' strong engagement with Islamic religious practices provides them with strategies for negotiating resistance to assimilation within schools (p. 419). In this regard, Sarah's practice reflected an additive orientation since it recognized the importance of maintaining and validating CLD students' first culture while fostering interactional conditions of empowerment that combat subtractive orientations which seek to assimilate students to the dominant culture (Cummins, 2001). In this sense, the students managed to subvert practices reflective of and shaped by dominant economic discourses

that privileged consumer practices and positioned them as consumers. Subsequently, students were able to establish moments
when they attempted to negotiate their identities, desires, and the
consumption-oriented literacy curriculum. Had Sarah been present
during the lesson, I imagine that this would have been more pronounced, and that other CLD students in her class would have benefited from this configuration of practice. Without this instructional
provision, all of the Muslim students in Sarah's class resorted to
drawing pictures or writing about Santa after his visit and, in essence,
did what everybody else was doing. Consequently, the
"Multicultural" Santa visit and the journal writing experiences that
followed mostly enforced the normality of consumption.
Constructions of childhood experiences and interests reflective of
consumer culture were reinforced and limited the potential for a culturally relevant, responsive and eco-justice-informed literacy curriculum. Additionally, alternative conceptualizations of "children" and
"childhood" were not questioned or developed during these specific
events since mainstream cultural celebrations indicative of commodified notions of childhood were taken for granted and reproduced. A
potentially rich incorporation of culture that tapped into the multifaceted identities of CLD students was excluded from a literacy curriculum that sustained and furthered the consumer-laden cultural
values of the dominant group.

Although Sarah's modification created the potential for culturally
responsive literacy curricula where students could exert their identities and disengage from dominant consumer practice and culture, I
harbour no illusions that this or any practice will rectify or address
some of the dominant understandings that shape the ways unrespon-
sive and environmentally problematic literacy curricula are constructed. Practices are not in and of themselves transformative; they
alone cannot reconceptualize schools and schooling in ways that are
relevant and environmentally educative for all students. The material presented in this paper thus far indicates that an entire shift in our
thinking, being, and the way we construct desire needs to occur in

order for transformation to burgeon. Some overarching principles and general practices can, however, help educators develop ways of combating and destabilizing the dominance of economically driven discourses shaping consumer oriented student identities, school events, rituals, and literacy curricula. These principles and practices are necessary in stimulating, fostering, and accompanying transformation and are vital to offer and pedagogically consider. Although some of these principles and practices are implicit within the data and discussion, other concrete examples include:

- Redirecting students who celebrate Christmas to retell "a story about a traditional cultural practice to Santa about hand-made gifts and why they are important. These discussions and investigations will reveal how commodified practices reinforced through dominant cultural narratives that 'celebrate progress' are taken-for-granted" (Young, 2009).
- Asking students to have group discussions about how they demonstrate care or love to people in ways that do not involve purchasing anything. Students can make a list that is posted in the classroom, word processed, and used as choral or independent reading material.
- Approaching celebrations from a "civil public school" model (Haynes, 2001, p. 101) which means neither inculcating nor inhibiting religion. Schools must be places where religion and religious conviction are treated with fairness and respect and as such curriculum includes study about religion and religious celebrations (Haynes, 2001) as opposed to consumer practices and rituals that hide and dismiss diversity.
- Accessing parents' "funds of knowledge" (Moll, 1992) by asking them to come into the classroom to share religious practices and artifacts with the students that demonstrate the meaning behind their celebrations and observances and how these meanings are non-commodifed or based on consumption.
- Asking students to collect and bring wrapping paper discarded in their homes to class as a way of demonstrating the sheer vol-

ume of waste produced as a result of commodifying how we honour one another. Further, students can think about the various ways the wrapping paper can be used in the class (art projects, writing material, etc).

- Reading various books during shared reading sessions that contain strong anti-consumerist messages as well as language and situations that are meaningful, interesting, and pleasurable in order to demonstrate how desire can be felt for and toward events, people, practices, and relationships without relying on consumption. These books include:
  - *The Gift of Nothing* by Patrick McDonnell, a narrative that demonstrates how a friend celebrates his friend's birthday by buying him "nothing" which turns out to be an empty box, his company, and the gift of nature.
  - *Three Cheers for Catherine the Great* by Cari Best and Giselle Potter. The main character's grandmother asks that guests of her party do not bring presents. Guests give the grandmother a dance, a song, and the main character offers to teach her grandmother to read and write in English.
  - *The Sneetches* by Dr. Seuss demonstrates the power, impact, problems, and silliness that result when we ascribe to commodified desires.
  - *Something From Nothing* by Phoebe Gilman. The main character observes how a gift given to him by his grandfather takes on various useful forms rather than being thrown out.

Conclusion

Environmentally, we are at a dangerous precipice. What we decide to do (or not do) about the current environmental crisis will significantly impact the fate of the earth and its people. We have become more aware of various activities that have been heralded in the wake of the crisis (e.g., recycling); however, the necessary shift in thinking and being that will alter discourses and practices that undergird, instantiate, and forward our consumption-obsessed way of life has not yet been fully understood or acted upon. Without this shift, we continue to foster limited, limiting, and violative "identity options" (Cummins, 2005) and desires for all human beings including children. If we are committed to improving mental and ecological health, we must think critically about the ways in which current constructions of desire and pleasure have significantly contributed to "planetary ecological breakdown" (Bowers, 2006, p.71), and subsequently act in ways that destabilize and discard the destructive culture our children are colonized into receiving and reproducing.

Notes

1   I use the term culturally and linguistically diverse (CLD) (Herrera & Murry, 2005) to refer to children who elsewhere are designated as English as a Second Language (ESL), English Language Learners (ELL), or English as an Additional Language learners (EAL). At the time of the research for this study, ESL was the official designation in Ontario of children for whom English was not their first language. It has subsequently changed to ELL. However, ESL, EAL, and ELL are problematic since they focus on the language the child is acquiring rather than their existing "funds of knowledge" (Moll, 1992). Consequently, these labels are deficit oriented. While CLD is not without its problems as it uses the dominant language and culture as the referent, it is a preferred option as it makes explicit children's resources (Heydon & Iannacci, 2008).

2   The shift has resulted in a host of other issues as well. The loss of linguistic diversity, for example, is yet another consequence of globalization. This has also been a concern for forerunners within the field of eco-justice (Bowers, 2006, Skutnabb-Kangas, 2000). I have spoken about the "monolingual habitus" (Bourne, 2001) that existed within the classrooms observed in this research elsewhere (Iannacci, 2005, 2007, 2008).

3   All names in the study are pseudonyms.

References

Adbusters. (2005, January/February). The hostile takeover of childhood. *Adbusters: Journal of the Mental Environment, 57*(13), n.p.

al-Hibri, A. Y., Elshtain, J. B., & Haynes, C. C. (2001). *Religion in American public life: Living with our deepest differences.* New York, NY: W. W. Norton & Company.

Asimeng-Boahene, L., & Klein, A. M. (2004). Is the diversity issue a non-issue in mainstream academia? *Multicultural Education, 12*(1), 47–52.

Barbaro, A. (Producer), & Earp, J. (Director). (2008). *Consuming kids: The commercialization of childhood* [Motion picture]. USA: Media Education Foundation.

Bennet, R. (2008, February 26). Pressures of consumerism make children depressed. *The Times Online.* Retrieved from http://women.timesonline.co.uk/tol/life_and_style/women/families/article3434233.ece

Bernhard, J. K., Lefebvre, M. L., Chud, G., & Lange, R. (1995). *Paths to equity: Cultural, linguistic and racial diversity in Canadian early childhood education.* Toronto, ON: York Lanes Press.

Bezaire, K., & Cameron, L. (2009). Toys as text: Critically reading children's playthings. In L. Iannacci & P. Whitty (Eds.), *Early childhood curricula: Reconceptualist perspectives* (pp. 271–298). Calgary, AB: Detselig Enterprises.

Bourne, J. (2001). Discourses and identities in a multi-lingual primary classroom. *Oxford Review of Education, 27*(1), 103–114.

Bowers, C. A. (2001). *Educating for eco-justice and community.* Athens: University of Georgia Press.

Bowers, C. A. (2006). Silences and double binds: Why the theories of John Dewey and Paulo Freire cannot contribute to revitalizing the commons. *Capitalism Nature Socialism, 17*(3), 71–87.

Boyd, F. B., & Brock, C. H. (2004). Constructing pedagogies of empowerment in multicultural and multilingual classrooms:

Implications for theory and practice. In F. B. Boyd, C. H. Brock, & M. S. Rozendal (Eds.), *Multicultural and multilingual literacy and language* (pp. 1–11). New York, NY: Guilford Press.

British Council: Learning. (n.d.). *How many people are learning English?* Retrieved from http://www.britishcouncil.org/learning-faq-the-english-language.htm

Burbules, N. C., & Torres, C. A. (2000). Globalization and education: An introduction. In N. C. Burbules, & C. A. Torres (Eds.), *Globalization and education: Critical perspectives* (pp. 1–26). New York, NY: Routledge.

Cannella, G. S. (2002). Global perspectives, cultural studies, and the construction of a postmodern childhood studies. In G. S. Canella & J. L. Kincheloe (Eds.), *Kidworld: Childhood studies, global perspectives, and education* (pp. 3–20). New York, NY: Peter Lang.

Cannella, G. S., & Viruru, R. (2004). *Childhood and postcolonization: Power, education, and contemporary practice.* New York, NY: Routledge-Falmer.

Citizenship & Immigration Canada. (2003). *Facts and Figures: Immigration Overview.* Available from http://publications.gc.ca/pub?id=367095&sl=0

Clandinin, J. & Connelly, M. (2000) *Narrative inquiry: Experience and story in qualitative research.* San Francisco, CA: Jossey-Bass.

Cummins, J. (2001). *Negotiating identities: Education for empowerment in a diverse society* (2nd ed.). Los Angeles: California Association for Bilingual Education.

Cummins, J. (2005, April). *Diverse futures: Rethinking the image of the child in Canadian schools.* Lecture presented at the Joan Pederson Distinguished Lecture Series, University of Western Ontario.

Dahlberg, G., Moss, P., & Pence, A. R. (1999). *Beyond quality in early childhood education and care: Postmodern perspectives.* London, England: Falmer Press.

Dunn, G. D. (2008). *Identifying consumption: Subject and objects in consumer society.* Philadelphia, PA: Temple University Press.

Falconer, R. C., & Byrnes. D. A. (2003). When good intentions are not enough: A Response to increasing diversity in an early childhood setting. *Journal of Research in Childhood Education, 17*(2), 188–200.

Fraser, J. W. (1999). *Between church and state: Religion and public education in a multicultural America.* New York, NY: St. Martin's Press.

Gee, J. P. (2001). A sociocultural perspective on early literacy development. In S. B. Newman, D. K. Dickinson (Eds.), *Handbook of Early literacy research* (pp. 30–42). New York, NY: Guilford Press.

Giroux, H. (2009). Commodifying kids: The forgotten crisis. *Truthout.* Retrieved from http://www.truthout.org/040309J

Glaze, A. (2007, December). English language learners: Will we deliver? In *From the roots up: Supporting English Language Learners in Every Classroom.* Provincial symposium of the Ontario Ministry of Education, Toronto.

Griffith, A. (2001). Texts, tyranny, and transformation: Educational restructuring in Ontario. In J. P Portelli, & R. P. Solomon (Eds.), *The Erosion of democracy in education: Critique to possibilities* (pp. 83–98). Calgary, AB: Detselig Enterprises.

Guillaume, A. (1998). Learning with text in the primary grades. *The Reading Teacher, 51,* 476–485.

Haynes, C. C. (2001). From battleground to common ground: Religion in the public square of 21st century America. In A. Y. al-Hibri, J. B. Elshtain, & C. C Haynes (Eds), *Religion in American public life: Living with our deepest differences* (pp. 96–136). New York, NY: W.W. Norton & Company.

Haynes, C. C., & Thomas, O. (2001). *Finding common ground.* Available from http://www.freedomforum.org

Herrera, S. G., & Murry, K. G. (2005). *Mastering ESL and bilingual methods: Differentiated instruction for culturally and linguistically (CLD) students.* Boston, MA: Pearson Allyn and Bacon.

Heydon, R., & Iannacci, L. (2008). *Early childhood curricula and the de-pathologizing of childhood.* University of Toronto Press.

Hughes, P. (2005). Baby, it's you: International capital discovers the under threes. *Contemporary Issues in Early Childhood, 6*(1), 30–40.

Iannacci, L. (2005). *Othered among others: A critical narrative of culturally and linguistically diverse (CLD) children's literacy and identity in early childhood education (ECE)* (Doctoral dissertation). University of Western Ontario, London.

Iannacci, L. (2007). Learning to "do" school: Procedural display and culturally and linguistically diverse (CLD) students in Canadian early childhood education (ECE). *Journal of the Canadian Association for Curriculum Studies, 4*(2), 55–76.

Iannacci, L. (2008). Beyond the pragmatic and the liminal: Culturally and linguistically diverse (CLD) students code switching (CS) in early years classrooms. *TESL Canada Journal, 25*(2), 103–123.

Iannacci, L. & Whitty, P. (Eds.). (2009). *Early childhood curricula: Reconceptualist perspectives.* Calgary, AB: Detselig Enterprises.

Kapur, J. (2005). *Coining for capital: Movies, marketing, and the transformation of childhood.* Piscataway, NJ: Rutgers University Press.

Kasturi, S. (2002). Constructing childhood in a corporate world: Cultural studies, childhood, and Disney. In G. S. Canella, & J. L. Kincheloe (Eds.), *Kidworld: Childhood studies, global perspectives, and education* (pp. 39–58). New York, NY: Peter Lang.

Kincheloe, J. & Steinburg, S. (1997). *Changing multiculturalism.* Philadelphia, PA: Open University Press.

Linn, S. (2004). *Consuming kids: The hostile takeover of childhood.* New York, NY: New Press.

Livingstone, D. (1987). *Critical pedagogy and cultural power.* Toronto, ON: Garamond Press.

Martusewicz, R., Lupinacci, J., & Edmundson, J. (2011). *Ecojustice education: Toward diverse, democratic, and sustainable communities.* New York, NY: Routledge.

Media Awareness Network. *Marketing and consumerism: Special issues for young children.* Retrieved from: http://www.media-awareness.ca/english/parents/marketing/ issues_kids_marketing.cfm

Marsh, C. J., & Willis, W. (2007). *Curriculum: Alternative approaches, ongoing issues* (4th ed.). Upper Saddle River, NJ: Prentice Hall.

Menendez, A. J. (1994). Christmas in school: December dilemma. *The Educational Digest, 60*(4), 4–7.

Miller, H. M. (2000). Teaching and learning about cultural diversity: Without a prayer. *The Reading Teacher, 53*(4), 316–317.

Moll, L. (1992). Funds of knowledge for teaching: Using a qualitative approach to connect homes and classrooms. *Theory into Practice, 31*(2), 132–141.

Obiakor, F. E. (2001). Research on culturally and linguistically diverse populations. *Multicultural Perspectives, 3*(4), 5–10.

People for Education. (2007). *The annual report on Ontario's public schools.* Available from: http://www.peopleforeducation.com/reportsbytopic

Ricoeur, P. (1992). *Oneself as another.* University of Chicago Press.

Roberts-Fiati, G. (1997). Observing and assessing young children. In K. M Kilbride (Ed.), *Include me too! Human diversity in early childhood* (pp. 122–140). Toronto, ON: Harcourt Brace & Company.

Schor, J. B. (2004). *Born to buy: The commercialized child and the new consumer culture.* New York, NY: Scribner.

Skutnabb-Kangas, T. (2000). *Linguistic genocide in education or worldwide diversity and human rights?* Mahwah, NJ: Lawrence Erlbaum.

Sleeter, C. E., & Bernal, D. D. (2004). Critical pedagogy, critical race theory, and antiracist education. In J. Banks, & C. Banks (Eds.), *Handbook of research on multicultural education* (2nd ed.) (pp. 240–258). San Francisco: Jossey-Bass.

Steinberg, S. R., & Kincheloe. J. L. (Eds.). (2004). *Kinder-Culture. The corporate construction of childhood.* Boulder, CO: HarperCollins.

Suárez-Orozco, C. (2001). Afterword: Understanding and serving the children of immigrants. *Harvard Educational Review, 71*(3), 579–589.

Suzuki, D. (2004, December 8). Christmas complaints miss the point. *London Free Press*, p. 5.

Toohey, K. (2000). *Learning English at school: Identity, social relations and classroom practice.* Clevedon, England: Multilingual Matters Ltd.

Wallen, N. E., & Fraenkel, J. R. (2001). *Educational research: A guide to the process.* San Francisco, CA: Lea Publications.

Wilson, A. (2003). Researching in the third space: Locating, claiming and valuing the research domain. In S. Goodman, T. Lillis, J. Maybin, & N. Mercer (Eds.), *Language, literacy and education: A reader* (pp. 293–308). Staffordshire, England: Trentham Books.

Young, K. (2009). Reconceptualizing early childhood literacy curriculum: An ecojustice approach. In L. Iannacci, & P. Whitty (Eds.), *Early childhood curricula: Reconceptualist perspectives.* Calgary, AB: Detselig Enterprises.

Zine, J. (2001). Muslim youth in Canadian schools: Education and the politics of religious identity. *Anthropology and Education Quarterly, 32*(4), 399–423.

9

QUEER NOTES ON SEX EDUCATION IN ONTARIO

Sheila L. Cavanagh, York University

> What can be the purpose of withholding from children – or, let
> us say, from young people – enlightenment of this kind about
> the sexual life of human beings? Is it from a fear of arousing their
> interest in these matters prematurely, before it awakens in them
> spontaneously? (Freud, 1977b, p. 174).

> To be clear, the new curriculum is not a how-to sex manual
> ("Sex ed belongs," 2010).

I BEGIN THIS CHAPTER BY NOTING that sex education is an epistemological problem saturated by linguistic tropes conjuring up
images of bodily disorientation. Much like sex, our relationship
to objects of study is pivotal, and orientation is a matter of perspective. In *Symposium* (1999), Plato passionately argues that Eros
evokes the desire to pursue knowledge and truth; one cannot exist
without the other and yet, in the present day, it seems as though we
cannot easily think about sex and education as mutually constitutive.
The relation between sex and education is disorienting to those who
prefer to divorce the two because the curriculum has traditionally
functioned as, what Sara Ahmed (2006) calls, an "orientation device"
(p. 26). This orientation device tends to anchor straight forward
"lifelines" (p. 17) – that is, normative and sequential developmental
life stages leading to adulthood (one must "grow up," not sideways
[Stockton, 2009] or down) – and it pulls anyone who ventures off
course and into queer terrain back onto the straight and narrow.

If sexuality is conceived of as a tension between distance and
proximity, an effect of one's relation and orientation to others – we
are always turning away and toward others depending upon who we
imagine those others to be – as opposed to a knowable sexual practice that can be taught and tested, it may be easier to understand why

those favouring and opposing sex education never see eye to eye or appear in the same place. Take, for example, the recent debate about the proposed changes to the 2010 Health and Physical Education curriculum in Ontario. Even a cursory glance at the mainstream media coverage reveals reliance upon body positions and movements in space, along with feelings of disoriented desire and intentionality, to connote anxious responses to sex education. Tory leader Tim Hudak said the proposed "changes [to sex education] 'don't sit right' with the vast majority of Ontario parents and [Premier Dalton] McGuinty should hold off on the changes until he gets more feedback" (Babbage, 2010). After cancelling the new curriculum, McGuinty said that most parents are "obviously not comfortable with the proposal we put forward" (Howlett & Hammer, 2010, April 22), and that it was not in keeping with the "sensitivities and desires of parents" (Howlett & Hammer, 2010, April 27). The premier was accused of doing a "spectacular flip-flop" (Howlett, 2010, April 26) in his decision to bury the curriculum he defended only days before; others complained that he "pulled the plug on the document" (Howlett, 2010, April 28), "Premier Dalton McGuinty's lightning retreat from a controversial education ministry document caught even his own caucus with its pants down Thursday" (Artuso, 2010, April 24). Speaking about what we might call the ultimate bodily anchoring device, Tabatha Southey (2010) of *The Globe and Mail*, who endorsed the new sex education proposal, wrote that she wished "someone had taught Mr. McGuinty [in his own school days] that he had a spine."

Multiple references are made to bodily plumbing and to correct positions and approaches to talk, quiet, or censorship about sex in education. If learning is relational and subject to peculiar reversals and negations as queer and psychoanalytic theory so convincingly argues, there must be a way to think productively about the images of bodily contortions designed to mirror psychically invested anxiety about an unauthorized pairing. I wonder how to conceive of inappropriate topics like sex and gender when education has been like antibacterial soap (Steinberg, 1998, p. 194), sanitizing unauthorized pleasures taken in others socially coded as un-familial and abject.[1]

For those following debates in education it is obvious that what is most likely to be foreclosed or eclipsed in the formal curriculum is explicit talk about sex. In the face of adult anxieties about what Sigmund Freud called the sexual enlightenment of children, it is helpful to call upon queer theory to better understand why sex and education do not seem to get along. They don't mix well or make good academic bedfellows – at least not without public controversy leaving people in emotional knots. I wonder why education can't know about sex and why childhood curiosities about the body, its gender, and sexuality are deemed out of educable bounds? How can an institution founded upon knowledge acquisition embrace such passion for ignorance?

Before I say more about the sex education debates in Ontario, a word or two is in order with respect to queer theory and queer pedagogy. While we are right to be suspicious of origin-stories, it is perhaps fair to say that queer theory made its debut in academe with the publication of Judith Butler's (1990) *Gender Trouble*, Eve Kosofsky Sedgwick's (1990) *Epistemology of the Closet*, Diana Fuss's edited collection *Inside/Out: Lesbian Theories, Gay Theories* (1991), and *The Lesbian and Gay Studies Reader* edited by Henry Abelove, Michéle Aina Barale, and David Halperin in 1993. But queer theory, as one might suppose, has been in gestation for quite some time. Its coming out in the late twentieth century reveals multiple academic bedfellows and improper (cross-disciplinary) pollinations. It is influenced by postmodernism and notably the work of Michel Foucault (1978) in his three volumes on the history of sexuality, the work Jacques Derrida published in *Of Grammatology* in 1967 on deconstruction, the early psychoanalytic writings of Sigmund Freud (1960) on child psycho-sexual development and later works by French psychoanalyst Jacques Lacan (1975/1999) on desire and the impossibility of a sexual relationship, and postcolonial theory and criticism (Bhabha, 1994; Muñoz, 2007; Said, 1979; Stoler, 1995).[2]

Queer pedagogy made its most well-cited debut in 1998 with the publication of William F. Pinar's edited collection *Queer Theory in Education*. But like all coming-outs, it was a little bit late, and so its impact is felt in retrospect or, as Lee Edelman (1991) might say, from behind. "(Be)hindsight" is not only about the "supposition or imagining of the sodomitical scene" (Edelman, p. 101), but a positional logic from which one may begin to think queerly about the education of bodies. As I argued in *Sexing the Teacher: School Sex Scandals and Queer Pedagogies* (Cavanagh, 2007), queer pedagogy is founded upon a wish to think outside the straightjackets of conventional logic and a desire to disorient what we take to be true about the body and its sexuality. It is not excited by the reproduction of the family in the image of the white Christian nation or in what Jasbir Puar (2007) calls homonationalism, or even in what Lisa Duggan (2003) calls "homonormativity." Queer pedagogy maintains a healthy skepticism of that which is "normal" or status quo. It is perhaps most committed to challenging the conventional wisdom of childhood sexual innocence. Queer pedagogues refuse to imagine their students as innocent because they are well positioned to see the harm that gets done by refusing to acknowledge, or to validate, the myriad of ways children are stirred to intrigue by others. By dispensing with the mythology of child sexual innocence, defined by Christopher Bollas (1992) as an aggressive non-relation (or incapacity to desire) along with fantasies of rescue and salvation (which only ever work in the movies), queer pedagogy embarks on the difficult job of teaching one to grapple with what happens in school without callously disregarding those socially coded as different or non-normative.

The point is to conceive of a new relation or pedagogical position from which something new can be thought. In order to facilitate unconventional thinking and student curiosities about life, queer theorists are concerned with the removal of what we might call learning blocks – that which halts or stifles queer imaginings. If the most frightening thing in education is to "not to know" or, conversely, to

"forget," then a queer pedagogy inspired by psychoanalysis is compelled to address what interferes with learning difficult life lessons
and the associated passion for ignorance (Britzman, 1998; Felman,
1987; Sedgwick, 1990). As Shoshana Felman and Eve Kosofsky
Sedgwick have so eloquently argued, ignorance is not the absence of
knowledge. By maintaining the pretence of childhood sexual innocence in class, for example, the room ironically becomes preoccupied
with sex – a queer optic zone ripe for the production of improper
objects and relations. There are no blank sexual slates in class. In the
case of refusing sex education in the formal curriculum, ignorance
can be seen as a passionate refusal to know or, rather, to acknowledge
what is already happening in class and in young minds. Ignorance is
best understood as a passionate refusal to know what one already
suspects to be true.

Learning can upset the "ego's strategies of self-perception"
(Britzman, 1998, p. 7) and disorient the subject. Adult refusal to
enlighten children about sex or gender may be, as Deborah Britzman
(2006) suggests, echoing Freud (1977b), symptomatic of the limitations placed on their own sex education. Adults may worry about the
formal education of sex in school because it seems to have things on
offer denied to the parent and (wrongly) thought to be impossible.
My son may grow up to be a woman or to love another man. My
daughter may grow up to be a man or to love another woman.
Biology may not be destiny in the case of gender identity or human
reproduction – the rise of assisted reproduction in LGBTQI (lesbian, gay, bisexual, trans, queer and/or intersex) communities is but
one example of the latter – and fantasy (who I imagine myself to be
and desire) may not need to be quashed by the weight of the so-
called facts of life (the science of sex), or by what Michel Foucault
(1978) calls *scientia sexualis*.

Queer theorists recommend that sex education not be reducible
to the bio-scientific study of health and physical education. It must
be something more than a bio-politic designed to govern the subject
in the service of healthy nations. Building upon queer writings about

pedagogy (Britzman, 1998; Felman, 1987; Patton, 1996; Pinar, 1998; Sedgwick, 2003), I venture to think about how sex education might disorient or trouble a straight-forward positional logic authorizing a truth about sexual difference and heteronormativity.

Sex Education in the Ontario Curriculum

Sex education in Ontario is part of the health and physical education curriculum. The most recently proposed changes to the curriculum were posted on the Ministry of Education website in January 2010. The posting didn't receive a lot of public attention until Charles McVety, president of Canada Christian College and leader of the "Family-focused Coalition", raised moral objections to it in the spring.[3] A handful of Christian conservative activists, including Brian Rushfeldt and Ekron Malcolm, following McVety, made wild allegations suggesting the curriculum was "absurd," "bordering on criminal," "corrupt," "dirty," "evil," "ideological," the product of a "militant gay agenda," driven by "mind control," improperly focused on the "perils of promiscuity," "sinister," "traumatic," "unconscionable," "unwholesome," etc. A few Muslim groups also opposed the sex education proposal.[4] Ministry spokespeople acknowledged that the criticism was not widespread but limited to a few people heading up socially conservative religious groups. Despite pleas by the Elementary Teachers Federation of Ontario, Queer Ontario, Egale Canada, Planned Parenthood Ottawa, the LGBTQ Parenting Network, the AIDS Committee of Toronto, the AIDS Committee of London, and the Sex Information and Education Council of Canada (among other community groups and publicly funded organizations), McGuinty scrapped the new curriculum which would have given kids technical information about gender identity, sexual orientation, human reproduction, safer sex practices, and contraception. The decision caught even McGuinty's own government by surprise. After initially defending the curricular changes, he retracted the proposal after less than three days of public controversy. The proposal subsequently vanished from the ministry website and this author's attempt to get a copy of the now-debunked curriculum was thwarted by a telephone receptionist refusing to re-issue the document.

The 211 page document was the result of more than two years of public consultation with 2400 parents, teachers, professors of education, community workers, activists, psychologists, and doctors; 700 students; and 70 organizations, including the Ontario Physical and Health Education Association.[5] The Ontario sex education curriculum hadn't been updated since 1998, the time of the Mike Harris government. The most significant changes involved an expanded definition of sex to include oral and anal sex (in Grade 8) along with a discussion about the importance of vaginal lubrication, sexually transmitted infections (STIs) including HIV, safer sex practices, and condoms (in Grade 6 and 7); puberty (in Grade 4); masturbation, gender identity[6] and sexual orientation with a focus on "visible" and "invisible" differences (in Grade 3); and the teaching of "proper" names for male and female genitals including penis, testicles, and vagina (in Grade 1). The curriculum was heavily weighed in favour of sexual abstinence, the prevention of pregnancy and STIs, healthy lifestyles (not a pseudonym for gay folks), tolerance, and respect for differences.

The proposed curriculum was by no means exceptional or unique in comparison to other provinces across Canada. It was not more explicit in its attention to human anatomy, puberty, sex, and sexual orientation than, for example, the British Columbia curriculum but is more comprehensive in its attention to gender and sexual diversity than the New Brunswick curriculum introduced in 2005 (revised when parents complained that the first version of the 2005 curriculum was too explicit in its focus on homosexuality, orgasm, and masturbation). The Alberta curriculum doesn't mention homosexuality at all, and the Prince Edward Island curriculum is rather narrowly focused on puberty and human reproduction in a heterosexual context. Most provinces and territories have clearly written provisions whereby parents can request to have their children opt out of sex education classes, including Ontario.

It is parents, and not students, who get to make the ultimate decision about what will and won't be learned. The problem is proffered as one of knowledge and imposition. For example, reverend Ekron Malcolm, director of the Institute for Canadian Values, affiliated with the "Family focused Coalition," said "I think it's a sort of infringement on parents, because you're talking about a very personal and sensitive area and dealing with kids so young I believe what it will end up infringing on their thought processes and their desires and ability to make correct choices" (Hammer & Howlett, 2010, April 20). The "correct choice" for students, as conservative opponents and many liberal-minded advocates of sex education both make abundantly clear, is to delay sexual experimentation. Christian conservatives in particular argue that talk about sex will prompt kids to have sex while liberal advocates frequently quote studies showing a positive correlation between sex education in schools and the postponement of sexual experimentation along with a decrease in "unsafe" or "high-risk" activities.[7]

No one in my survey of the mainstream provincial and national news media is endorsing what French philosopher Michel Foucault (1978) calls an *ars erotica*, an erotic art for those under the age to consent to sex narrowly defined in adult terms.[8] How might teachers talk about desire in age-appropriate ways, and must this be framed as a hazard to child development? What would it mean to think about sex as healthy and fun as opposed to un-healthy and inevitably dangerous? What if sex was for pleasure as opposed to a larger nationalist agenda involving the reproduction of normative adult heterosexual body politics? As Michelle Fine first observed in 1988, sex education is, curiously, devoid of carnal desire and heterosexist in its imagining of sex and gender differences. It is about abstinence and protection. Few players in the sex education debate balk at talk about sex as dangerous and at curricular materials that reinforce the "natural" differences between "men" and "women" while extolling the virtues of sex after marriage. Sex is, allegedly, a fundamental concern to the sanctity of the family and its future: a serious topic.

But the funny thing about sex is that we cannot agree on what it is. As is evident in debates about the proposed changes to the Ontario sex education curriculum, people can't even agree on its merit let alone its proper object of investigation. Is it about the body or gender identity? Is it about human reproduction or contraception? Should teachers focus on safer sex practices or lubrication? Desire or sexual abstinence? Fact or fantasy? Are the sexual habits of the individual or the population at large a greater concern? Is it about public hygiene or pleasure? Even when provisional agreements about what sex might mean are made it continues to signify in excess of any given curricular objective.

Moreover students seem to read teacher anxieties about sex. Our lessons are spliced by slips of the tongue (unintended word substitutions), jokes (remember what Freud wrote about their relation to the unconscious and I will leave you alone to ponder jokes made about the tight asses of teachers), discomfort (how often do students squirm in their seats), embarrassment (who doesn't go red in the face), and bewilderment. Sex education sometimes becomes an occasion for laughter and about the negotiation of discomfort. It is, ironically, a productive foreclosure. Students sense that there is always something left unsaid or, rather, something that defies representation in even the most technical and open instructional methods. Youth exploit and make fun of adult omissions while seeming to ignore teacher intention. Sex appears where it is not supposed to be and is curiously absent in teachings meant to evoke it. Sexuality is in excess of the subject insofar as it defies capture and narration. There is an unconscious mooring to our desires that are never in the place we expect to find them. In other words, desire is always on the move, closeted or found in retrospect.

This brings us to the problem of developmental time in school. Those opposing sex education in schools sometimes characterize pre-adolescence as time interrupted. The sexual clock stops. The official name for this phenomenon is the latency period (Bernstein, 2001; Erikson, 1963; Hunt & Kraus, 2009). In an editorial entitled "Sex ed requires prudence and parents" (2010, April 22) published in the *National Post*, the author evokes latency period research. Referring to the "settled" science surrounding latency, the author writes:

> In this schema, the second sexual phase in children following infancy and early childhood, from the age of six to 12, is a period in which direct sexual energies fall dormant. During this phase, the child gathers his inner resources and develops mental and physical strength for entry to young adulthood. Only at adolescence do hormonal changes create the appropriate psychological context for absorbing ideas about "gender identity" and sexual ethics in a meaningful light. Until that time schools should butt out of sex education.

The essential idea is that children don't think about sex until they reach adolescence unless, of course, they are prematurely exposed to sexual imagery. Children are allegedly asexual and innocent. McVety writes: "they're innocent, they're clean, they're beautiful" (Quoted in Artuso, 2010, April 20) and proceeds to argue against corrupting them with premature talk about sex and gender identity.

It is interesting to note that the scholarly literature McVety references to back up his argument does not confirm but in fact disconfirms his interpretation of latency. In the early 1960s, Peter Blos (1962) wrote in his discussion of adolescence and psychoanalysis:

> The literal interpretation of the term latency period to mean that these years are devoid of sexual urges – that is, that sexuality is latent – has long ago been superseded by an acknowledgement of clinical evidence that sexual feelings expressed in masturbatory, voyeuristic, exhibtitionistic, and sadomasochistic activities do not cease to exist during the latency

period. . . . What does change in the latency period is the growing control of the ego and superego over the instinctual life."[9] (p. 54)

In other words, the child is, during this phase, increasingly *able* to separate fact and fantasy. He or she is also able to make separations between what Blos (1962) refers to as the "public-world and private-world behavior" (p. 55), and can more easily recognize sexual and gender-based differences between people. The focus upon "visible" and "invisible" differences in the domain of gender identity and sexual orientation, as first proposed in the now retracted Ontario sex education plan, would seem to be *especially* age appropriate in this model of adolescent development.

It is also noteworthy that the idea of latency derives from the writings of Sigmund Freud on childhood psychosexual development. Freud (1977b) not only endorsed sex education but wrote that it is the "duty of schools not to evade the mention of sexual matters" (p. 180). Pointing to the absurdity of concealing knowledge about sex from children Freud also says that the "concealment leads a boy or girl to suspect the truth more than ever. Curiosity leads us to pry into things which, if they had been told us without any great to do, would have aroused little or no interest in us" (p. 174).[10] The Freudian concept of latency has been misconstrued by conservatives, like McVety, to legitimize their opposition to sex education when Freud was one of the first and most influential advocates for such an education in school.

I venture to guess that students are growing tired of adult projections and fantasia about sexual innocence. I also suspect that kids are queerer than adults might think (or remember) and less committed to normative body politics than those who have aged. While the Ontario sex education curriculum originally proposed was not wholeheartedly queer in its theoretical underpinnings, it did seem to upset developmental time lines routed in biology, and non trans[11] or cisgendered (Serano, 2007) fantasies about the essential relation between sexed embodiment and gender identity. It had other imaginings of the future on offer. It should not be forgotten that the proposal was the first to mention gender identity, and by Grade 8, students are to demonstrate an understanding of those who are two-spirited, transgendered, transsexual, and intersex (p. 202). After distinguishing between gender identity and sexual orientation, the proposed document emphasizes that both are key to

> the way we see ourselves and to our interactions with others. Understanding and accepting our gender identity and our sexual orientation can have a strong impact – positive or negative – on the development of our self-concept. A person's self-concept can develop positively if the person understands and accepts his or her gender identity and sexual orientation and is accepted by family and community. It is harder to develop a positive self-concept, however, if the way a person feels or identifies does not meet perceived or real societal norms and expectations or is not what they want, or if they do not feel supported by their family, friends, school, or community. A person's self-concept can be harmed if a person is questioning his or her gender identity or sexual orientation and does not have support in dealing with his or her uncertainties. (p. 202)

Based on the principles of mutual respect for social differences and healthy physical and emotional development, the document made significant strides in validating the needs of LGBTQI youth.

Those opposed to introducing gay, trans and/or intersex folks into the curriculum often cite the developmental needs of students as a uniform group who are almost always imagined to be straight and non trans or cisgendered. This tendency is especially evident in the public debates in Canada about the rights of trans students to use a school bathroom consistent with their gender identity (Cavanagh, 2003, 2010).[12] Parents resistant to trans-positive policies in schools often refer to their worries about the rights to privacy of non trans girl students. The well-publicized case involving a Grade 12 trans girl enrolled at Cedar Community Secondary School in Nanaimo, British Columbia in 2002 is a case in point. Carola Lane, Ladysmith School District Superintendent, acting on legal advice received from the B.C. Human Rights Commission, granted the student access to the "girl's" bathroom. But the parent advisory council chairwoman, Vicki Podetz, insisted that the student use a gender neutral washroom (the toilet designated for students with disabilities) instead of the "girl's" washroom because the decision supposedly did not take into consideration the "comfort level of the [non-transgender] female students" (Middleton, 2002). Podetz argued that the "privacy of other female students at the school" would be compromised (Rud, 2002). She stressed that some students were only thirteen years of age. By referencing age of consent laws, Podetz evoked the phantom of the pedophile lurking in the toilet.[13]

Not coincidentally, the toilet also figures into the Ontario sex education debate as a pivotal trope. It is a place where we are hyper attuned to gender and it is culturally marked in school as a place of danger. For example, Ted Temertzoglou, the Ontario board representative for PHE in Canada, noted that by censoring sex education, students will relapse to the age-old fallacy that people "could pick up STDs (sexually transmitted disease) from a door knob or off of a toilet seat" (Lajoie, 2010).[14] Professor Elizabeth Saewyc of the University of British Columbia was quoted as saying that in order to prepare children for puberty it is necessary to talk "about more than just plumbing: Children must also understand the fundamentals of healthy relationships, how to avoid the pressure to have sex and the dangers of sexual assault and exploitation" (Agrell & Picard, 2010). But despite the attempts to legitimize sex education as a means to protect kids, the proposal was – to extend the metaphor – flushed down the toilet. Educational theorist Michelle Fine (1988) even found evidence of student sexual desire in bathroom graffiti in her search for the missing discourse of desire in sex education.

When driven underground, talk about sex appears in unexpected places, and the water closet is a repository for what I would like to call the educational unconscious, to be distinguished from the hidden curriculum. Hidden curricula operate just below a conscious pedagogical register or censor. We are almost always aware of what critical pedagogues (Giroux & Penna, 1983) refer to as the inadvertent teachings in school leading to what sociologists call social stratification and to the reproduction of societal institutions (like the family, the factory, the nation, etc.). The hidden curriculum is a by-product or after-effect of formalized curriculum and instruction. The educational unconscious is another thing entirely. It is a product of disavowal and negation and operates in a psychic underground. "In Freud's work, the unconscious is another scene, a parallel process which works by its own logic; it uses its own language, signs and symbols, makes its own connections; it is born out of prohibitions, repressions and taboos – all of which are nested in the psycho-social-spatial field of everyday life" (Pile, 1996, p. 76). In other words, the educational unconscious, like the toilet, is a dumping ground for unacceptable impulses, practices, identifications, and desires that are unknowable in class. The educational unconscious is shaped by what the formal curriculum negates and excludes.

It is therefore productive to consider the school bathroom as a site in which that which is disavowed or driven underground in the formal curriculum comes to an architectural surface. The trope and iconography of the toilet stands in for that which has been eclipsed or censored in school. "Plumbing, so often aligned with bodily trauma, is a volatile signifier of that which cannot directly be acknowledged in the symbolic order – a toilet, a plunger, a shower stall to take the place of the unspeakable – and to make it all the more charged" (Morgan, 2002, p. 178). Queers know all too well that the toilet – closet par excellence – is a storehouse for desirous and aggressive impulses. Students have sex and get beaten up in toilets. Illicit messages are etched onto partition walls that span from the lascivious to the hate ridden. It is a recess or cavity in the otherwise seamless fold of the school. Most teachers will not walk into student washrooms, as the news media reports of bullying in high schools make abundantly clear, and wilfully ignore what happens behind its closed doors.

By focusing on taboo zones in school we can better understand how learning is a matter of positioning the self in relation to others and to unauthorized spaces in the built environment. One's epistemological orientation grounds identity and desire. Gender orients what Butler (1990) calls the heterosexual matrix, and so it should not be surprising that bathrooms, as gendered architectures of exclusion, consolidate, as they also undo, the oppositional logic of masculinity and femininity deployed to produce a naturalized heterosexual effect. The psychic life of gender identity and sexuality banned in the formal curriculum is acted out in the toilet. "Boys" stand side-by-backside in full-frontal view before the urinal (assuming an upright and straight-forward stance), while "girls" back into cloistered stalls (assuming a sitting or squatting position). Urinary positions keep gender intact, but the obsessive gendering of elimination – a hallmark of modernity in the west – is curiously homoerotic as the literature on gay male public sex cultures, tearooms, cottages, and bathhouses amply notes.[15] Homoerotic desire in the water closet does and doesn't escape notice by sexually conservative administrators, parents, and teachers.

For example, trans students, staff, and faculty in universities across Canada and the United States, in pursuit of gender-neutral toilets or access to a room befitting their new gender identities, are often met by an administrative or managerial refusal to develop trans-positive bathroom policies. Again, the problem becomes one of assuming unauthorized positions. We are dealing with an obsessive interest in the "proper" objects of scholastic attention which do not include LGBTQI folks. Take, for example, the discussion emerging from a round-table dialogue on transpedagogies published in the trans- issue of *Women's Studies Quarterly* in 2008 (edited by Paisley Currah, Lisa Jean Moore, and Susan Stryker). Transpedagogies, as theorized in the special issue, are often concerned about how to theorize female and trans-masculinities in women's studies classrooms (and not coincidentally in bathrooms) when the proper object of investigation is supposed to be "women." What Anne Enke refers to as a "gender-disciplinary perspective" (2008, p. 298) which negates a trans-, inter-, or cross-disciplinary mode of inquiry is a central focus and preoccupation. "What happens to the capacity to create knowledge – new, unexpected, transformative – when the 'inter' and the 'trans' are contained within the already established categories of discipline" (Garrison, 2008, p. 297)?[16] Building upon Ahmed's (2006) writing on orientations, objects, and others, Susan Stryker (2008) makes the claim that trans studies compels us to reorient our thinking about bodies by invoking non-linear "spatio-temporal metaphors" (p. 13). She recommends that we also think about transing as involving movement "along a vertical axis, one that moves between the concrete biomateriality of individual living bodies and the biopolitical realm of aggregate populations that serve as resource for sovereign power" (p. 14). Stryker encourages the reader to think about vertical movement so as to upset conventional constructions of gender as a fixed territory. This enticement to move vertically is not about a will to grow up straight or, alternatively, to identify within a given spatial regime but rather to think about practices and points of connection as they operate within and against a dominant spatial and directional nexus.

Now if we have trouble thinking queerly about time and body-space along with the new trans-politics of sex and gender identity, we may return to the example of the pre-Oedipal child theorized by Freud. Despite the insistence by those lobbying for sex education in Ontario that kids don't get sex education at home, the claim is misleading. While many might not get sex education at home in the way educators and those writing curriculum documents envision it, it does happen. But it is in disguise and quickly forgotten. Most adults don't remember being toilet trained. Sex education on the throne is closeted or, as Freud might say, subject to adult amnesia.[17] What we today call gender identity is, for Freud, consolidated on the potty. In fact, the Freudian Oedipal complex begins with the onset of toilet-training. Referring to anal eroticism in children he wrote that the "concepts of faeces, baby and penis are ill-distinguished from one another and are easily interchangeable" (1960, p. 296).[18] The gender identity of the pre-Oedipal toddler has not yet been anatomized along a sexual and eliminatory corporeal grid. By separating the orifices and genital zones meant for elimination from those meant for sexual pleasure, the child forges a sexed embodiment in relation to normative hetero-reproductive body-politics.

A hidden curriculum of toilet training is to sort out the body's substratum. The vagina, not the anus, the penis, not the fecal stick (coded as baby, money, or gift in the Freudian unconscious) are to be dominant centers of pleasure. Freud hypothesizes that "The faecal mass . . . represents as it were the first penis, and the stimulated mucous membrane of the rectum represents that of the vagina. . . . During the pregenital phase . . . penis and vagina were represented by the faecal stick and the rectum" (Freud, 1960, p. 300). The boy learns that the fecal stick (coded as penis) is detachable, and the association may instil a fear of castration. The girl may learn that she does and does not have a penis if the making of a fecal stick feels like an erection and if it is detachable (ejected into a toilet-bowl as part-object or floater). I would venture to suggest that this is an early incarnation of Judith Butler's (1993) lesbian phallus in the morphological imagination.[19]

Of course, one need not accept the chains of association made by Freud to recognize the relevance of toilet-training to gender and sexual identity construction. In the normative landscape, the penis is to be seen before the urinal while vaginas are to be cloistered in stalls. The urinal, as a larger or more publicly visible receptacle, amplifies and exaggerates the presence of masculine organs while the mirror – more prominently displayed and less likely to be broken in the "women's" room – positions women in a visual field where her so-called genital or phallic lack will be intercepted. Public bathrooms are at once segregated (insisting upon an absolute difference between the sexes) and strangely the same (urinals and amplified glass mirrors not withstanding). There is an uncanny likeness to the two rooms. Most people have, at one time or another, walked into the "wrong" bathroom and not known it right away. There is a pregnant moment in which we are uncertain about sexual difference and where we fit in relation to it.[20]

While most children master the art of elimination – a prerequisite for entry into kindergarten in many Ontario school districts – the toddler is inevitably left with some queer ideas. This child becomes (as Freud himself suggests) a little sex researcher in disguise. Because questioning on the pot is often subject to interdiction by parents, and talk about excretion is considered to be crude and impolite in almost all other jurisdictions (accept perhaps the doctor's office), the child is left with a lot to ponder on his or her own. Like a detective searching for clues, the child busily pieces together the fragments of his or her own unfinished sex education in the home. Sex education in school is similarly unfinished. It feels suspiciously censorial and de-sexed (void of desire).

It is no surprise that the sex education proposal died under suspicious circumstances and that the assassin's intentions were questionable. Curiously, there is no public space afforded to mourn let alone recognize the loss. Some lives matter more than others, and LGBTQI youth are, in this epistemological crime scene, not supposed to be. If it is true that queer and trans youth don't exist for those opposing even their very mention in curriculum documents, it is, I suggest, fruitful to trouble the place of innocence marked as the "healthy" child's future living space. If it is also true that queerness or trans-ness are not discrete identities so much as they are orientations and identifications foreclosed in heterosexist and cissexist (non trans) cultures, let us revisit the criminal motive with an eye to exposing the childhood sexual innocence defence as a ruse.

In *The Queer Child*, Kathryn Bond Stockton (2009) notices that children are queered by innocence. They are not yet sexual and to-be (future) heterosexual(s) at the same time – a queer predicament if ever there was one. Their alleged asexuality is a misnomer because they are also supposed to be heterosexuals in waiting. The proposed latency period that so interests McVety is not devoid of desire. Latency is not a defence that is convincing to a queer jury. It is recognized as a covert attempt to conceal the non-normative desires and imaginings had by those deemed underage. I would even go so far as to suggest that the best queer theorists have always been children. They have not yet made identity-based and marital commitments that act as barriers to thought. If parents are honest, they will tell you that their kids have great difficulty thinking straight. It just doesn't seem to come naturally. Not only do children come up with strange stories about sex, but they disturb reproductive logic as we adults know it. Take for example the temporal and spatial challenge to conventional developmental logic in what Stockton (2009) calls the backward-birthing process. Gay and lesbian and trans kids are born in retrospect or after-death. As in a motive surmised by detectives investigating a crime, the "protogay child can only publicly appear retrospectively, after a death. Only after one's straight life has died can the tag 'homosexual child' be applied. This is a purely retrospective application . . . because all children are first presumed to be straight and are only allowed to come out as gay, or queer, or homosexual when it is thought they could know their sexuality – in their late teens or after, presumptively" (p. 158). The same backward birthing process may also be seen in the student who transitions from male to female or female to male (or, conversely, adopts a genderqueer identification) now requesting access to a gender-appropriate bathroom. The image of the child had by parents and educators must die before an LGBTQI student (or adult – depending upon the play of chronological time) can be born. "For this reason, the phrase 'gay child' acts as a gravestone marking a death: the point at which one's future as a straight adult expired, along with parental plans for one's future" (Stockton, 2009, p. 158). The gay coming-out literature written for parents even posits a term for this: "the Bereavement Effect"

(Stockton, 2004, p. 285). This is an effect resembling the one incited by an actual death. The beloved child dies only to be replaced by a "sinister version of the same person" (p. 285). It is not a child per se, but a parental image of a son or daughter that dies.

This psychic death may not be a surprise to those familiar with Butler's (1997) notes on gender-melancholia (in which she conceptualizes gender identification as melancholic attempt to incorporate the gender identity of the same-sex parent on to the body of the self in order to preserve that parent fantasmatically as lost object).[21] But the death may be a surprise to those who do not imagine the life of the child as having anything to do with love and loss, desire and prohibition. It is here where education fails us. Insofar as education negates talk about sex, it refuses to engage with what William Haver (1998) calls extremities: the "extremities of suffering and the extremity of pleasure" (p. 351). The failing is well illustrated by Cindy Patton (1996) in her discussion of how the American (and I would add Canadian) government failed to develop a national pedagogy of AIDs in the face of a world-wide pandemic. Silence equals death, and the pretence of innocence will not save us.

If we, as educators, wonder what happened to sex education, I suggest that we revisit the toilet. As adults we forget the formative losses incurred by the self. But we are, like the Freudian hysteric, troubled by reminiscences – recollections of the past and disavowed desires. The water closet acts as a storehouse for disavowed desires and gender identifications, the non-subjects of formal education. It also stands as a museum or relic of the subject's past. José Esteban Muñoz writes: "*The Toilet* represents a violent and tragic past that, when seen through the optic of queer utopia, becomes a source for a critique of a limited and problematic straight time" (2007, p. 353). The time of the present is not the time of the past, and as educators we may forget that psychic time can queer or obfuscate the place of the self in the normative landscape. Identities are bound up with the problem of time and memory in space along with psychically invested desires and epistemic positions. Insofar as sex education is closeted in Ontario schools, it will turn up in unauthorized and unexpected places that eclipse adult censors and overturn conventional positional logic.

Notes

1   In his discussion of Michel Foucault, Leo Bersani (2001) says: "Nothing, it would seem, is more difficult than to conceive, to elaborate, and to put into practice 'new ways of being together'" (p. 351). And this, Foucault tells us, is our most urgent ethical project, one in which we queers are destined to play a pivotal role.

2   It should be remembered that Lacan (2006) thought of men and women as borderlands that would never meet and evoked the curious phenomenon of "urinary segregation" to denote the primacy of the signifier writ large on the bathroom door to evoke man and woman.

3   McVety also objected to the Charles Darwin exhibit at the Royal Ontario Museum in Toronto.

4   See an otherwise inflammatory article entitled "Canadian Tradition Matters" (2010) published in the *National Post* about how McGuinty evokes Ontario's multicultural population to legitimize his decision to pull the plug on the sex education curriculum. The premier is quoted as saying "We have a very diverse province in so many different ways and I think it is really important as a government we listen carefully.... Especially when it comes to sex education." ("Canadian Tradition Matters," 2010). While there were south Asian religious groups opposing the curriculum change, it is misleading and unfair to frame the decision as an attempt to respect cultural differences because the folks protesting most vehemently were white Christians (not Muslims), and all parents are given the right to have their children opt out of the sex education classes.

5   In 2009 the United Nations Educational, Scientific and Cultural Organization (UNESCO) even advocated for early sex education beginning at the age of 5.

6   This would have been the first Ontario curriculum to explicitly mention transgender and two-spirited folks.

7   For example, Lyba Spring, who works with Toronto Public Health, insists that the World Health Organization is very clear about how sex education leads to a delay in sexual experimentation: "When children get compre-

hensive sexual-health education from an early age, they are more likely to postpone the higher-risk activities" (Agrell & Picard, 2010).

8　See Curtis and Hunt (2007) for a relevant discussion of the "fellatio epidemic" among Canadian teens and their access to what Foucault (1978) calls the *ars erotica*.

9　The Latency period is no longer characterized as a period of sexual disinterest and nor is it a developmental stage had by all pre-adolescent children (Bernstein, 2001; Erikson, 1963; Hunt & Kraus, 2009).

10　Sigmund Freud's preliminary notes on the mythology of childhood sexual innocence (which he, incidentally, regards as a problem of adult memory), and upon the intricate relation between sexuality and aggression in children, has been pivotal to more recent writing on what Stockton (2009) calls the queer child in her book by the same name. See also the landmark collection edited by Steven Bruhm and Natasha Hurley (2004) entitled *Curiouser: On the Queerness of Children*, the psychoanalytically inspired notes on the child in Lee Edelman's (2004) book *No Future: Queer Theory and the Death Drive*, and the controversial works of James Kincaid (1998, 1992) in his books *Erotic Innocence: The Culture of Child Molesting* and *Child-loving: The Erotic Child and Victorian Culture*. Shadows of Freud and psychoanalysis more generally are also evident in Susan Talburt and Shirley R. Steinberg's (2000) collection *Thinking Queer: Sexuality, Culture, and Education*, in William J. Letts IV and James T. Sears (1999) collection *Queering Elementary Education: Advancing the Dialogue about Sexualities and Schooling*, and in a long-line of theorizing on power and pleasure in pedagogical encounters (Britzman, 1998; Cavanagh, 2007; Gallop, 1995; Jagodzinski, 2002).

11　See Stryker (2008); Stryker, Currah, & Moore (2008); and Stryker & Whittle (2006) for a discussion of trans subjectivities. As Stephen Whittle puts it, the category trans is "accessible almost anywhere, to anyone who does not feel comfortable in the gender role they were attributed with at birth, or who has a gender identity at odds with the labels 'man' or 'woman' credited to them by formal authorities" (Stryker & Whittle, 2006, ix).

12　School administrators, parents, students and community members throughout the United States and Canada are debating the rights of trans teachers and students to use bathrooms consistent with their gender identities. Consider the following American examples: in Eagleswood Township near Atlantic City, parents were concerned about a trans substitute teacher, Miss McBeth. At a "school board meeting last winter, some decr[ied] what they termed an experiment, with their young children as guinea pigs" (Parry, 2006). Carla Cruzan, a teacher at Southwest High School (who is not transgender) "filed a complaint with the Minnesota Department of Human Rights ... alleging that her rights to privacy [were] being violated" because a transgender colleague was permitted to use the same restroom (O'Connor, 1999). Cruzan refused to recognize her colleague as a woman and believed that her privacy and safety were compromised by the trans-positive School Board policy.

There is now a gender neutral bathroom for students at Park Day School in Oakland, San Francisco. "Park Day's gender-neutral metamorphosis happened over the past few years, as applications trickled in for kindergartners who didn't fit on either side of the gender line. One girl enrolled as a boy, and there were other children who didn't dress or act in gender-typical ways" (Lelchuk, 2006). The California Student Safety and Violence Prevention Act of 2000 prohibits discrimination on the basis of gender identity. This legislation is being used to make bathroom and change-room provisions for gender non-normative children.

A New York organization called Advocates for Children interviewed 75 lesbian, gay, bisexual, and transgender students and learned that many students had to fight to use a school bathroom consistent with their gender identity (Yan, 2005). Numerous other cases in the United States and Canada of student difficulty accessing appropriate washrooms without harassment by students and teachers appear in the news media (Meadows, 2006).

13 We can observe what James T. Sears (1998) identifies as the culturally specific pairing of the homosexual (and I would add the transsexual) with the child molester.

14 See Sacco (2002) for a fascinating discussion of how public toilets came to be thought of as breeding grounds for sexually transmitted diseases.

15 For a discussion of gay male public sex cultures, tearooms, and cottages See: Aldrich, 2004; Bapst, 2001; Berlant & Warner, 1998; Delph, 1978; Desroches, 1990; Edelman, 1994a; Edelman, 1994b; Flowers, Marriott, & Hart, 2000; Hollister, 2004; Houlbrook, 2000; Humphreys, 1975; van Lieshout, 1995; Leap, 1999; Magni & Reddy, 2007; Merrick, 2002; Nardi, 1995; Potvin, 2005; and Tewksbury, 1996, 2004.

16 Putting the objective of transpedagogy in slightly different terms, Muñoz and Garrison (2008) write: "To expose gender as transitional within a changing cultural, political, geographic, and historical matrix creates feel-

    ings of confusion that dislodge fixed notions of identity, whether these be racial, ethnic, economic, or sexual" (p. 301).

17   It should give us pause to wonder how even the psychoanalytically mind-ed – with their penchant for abject thoughts – side-step the toilet. While psychoanalytic theorists engage Freudian ideas about psycho-sexual development, they often omit his notes on toilet training. The elimination function is an area of bio-political regulation that is often designated "out of scholarly bounds" (not to mention crude and subject to interdiction in polite discourse), yet, curiously, central to an over-emphasis upon an absolute and unchanging sexual difference. Robyn Longhurst, in her study of bodies, fluids, and excremental space, notes that toilets are "one of geography's abject and illegitimate sites that have been deemed (perhaps unconsciously) inappropriate and improper by the hegemons in the disci-pline" (2001, p. 131). Yet ideas about what is a "proper," "worthy," and "respectable" topic of inquiry operate to censor, repress, and prohibit but also, as Foucault (1978) tells us, to map the terrain of the thinkable, the analyzable.

18   In "Fragments of an Analysis of a Case of Hysteria ('Dora')," Freud (1977a) writes in a footnote that "It is scarcely possible to exaggerate the pathogenic significance of the comprehensive tie uniting the sexual and the excremental, a tie which is at the basis of a very large number of hys-terical phobias" (Footnote 1, 63). While we may question Freud's under-standing of hysteria and female psycho-sexual development, there is an important association between sex and feces given voice in the early twen-tieth century.

19   The "lesbian phallus" is, of course, Butler's (1993) key example of an internalized bodily image that doesn't correspond to a visible anatomy, though somatized through what we might call a transmasculine, butch, and/or lesbian identification.

20   Defecation (not unlike the vaginal recess not to be seen) is also closeted because it draws sensory attention to an orifice that is less susceptible to sexual difference. As Guy Hocquenghem (1993) famously notes "from behind we are all women" (p. 87). Because we all have assholes, attention to the posterior (or backside) confounds the "stability or determinacy of linguistic or erotic positioning" (Edelman, 1991, p. 105). As William Pinar suggests in his reflections upon the anus and its capacity to instruct us in the art of queer relationality: "Anal eroticism draws libido from its overin-vestment in the phallus and diversifies it throughout the rest of the body, deterritorializing not only sexuality but power as well. The anus does not

lend itself to comparison and competition, and from the anal point of view, what criteria could be employed to judge them? Sexuality is equalized as it is diversified, not only within the male sex, but between the sexes" (1998, p. 240). It is an equal opportunity orifice. To libidinize the anal region is to de-center the master phallic signifier. The anus is, consequently, gendered female (hidden from view and privatized), racialized as "dark" (see David Eng [2001] on the feminization of Asian men in America), and over-determined by the specter of sodomy. Unlawful attention to the anus in public threatens to reverse hetero and homosexual positions. One is disoriented by the back-side because heterosexuality demands attention to the front. "To refuse to maintain the schizoid distinction between public and private, and to excrete in public what commodification requires we save for our wives, lovers, or psychiatrists, soils the social fabric" (Pinar, 1998, p. 241). It should thus not be surprising that the renunciation of the anus as centre of pleasure inducts the child into the genital stage, a prerequisite for adult hetero-normative sex.

21 According to Butler the injunction against homosexuality and incest makes it difficult to overtly love and desire the same-sex parent, and so the pre-Oedipal toddler agrees to forgo a prohibited love so long as he or she may incorporate the "attachment as identification, where identification becomes . . . a psychic form of preserving the object" (Butler, 1997, p. 134).

References

Abelove, H., Barale, M. A., & Halprin, D. M. (Eds.). (1993). *The lesbian and gay studies reader*. New York, NY: Routledge.

Agrell, S., & Picard, A. (2010, April 23)."When it comes to sex ed, the kids aren't all right. *The Globe and Mail*.

Ahmed, S. (2006). *Queer phenomenology: Orientations, objects, others*. Durham, NC: Duke University Press.

Aldrich, R. (2004). Homosexuality and the city: An historical overview. *Urban Studies, 41*(9), 1719–1737.

Artuso, A. (2010, April 20). Sex education program sparks outcry. *Toronto Sun*.

Artuso, A. (2010, April 24). How Dalton failed sex ed. *Toronto Sun*.

Babbage, M. (2010, April 21). Catholic Schools must follow new sex ed curriculum: McGuinty. *The Globe and Mail*.

Bapst, D. (2001). Glory holes and the men who use them. *Journal of Homosexuality, 41*(1), 89–102.

Berlant, L., & Warner, M. (1998). Sex in public. *Critical Inquiry, 24*(2), 547–566.

Bernstein, A. (2001). A note on the passing of the latency period. *Modern Psychoanalysis, 26*(2), 283–287.

Bersani, L. (2001). Genital chastity. In T. Dean & C. Lane (Eds.), *Homosexuality & Psychoanalysis* (pp. 351–366). University of Chicago Press.

Bhabha, H. K. (1994). *The location of culture.* New York, NY: Routledge.

Blos, P. (1962). *On adolescence: A psychoanalytic interpretation.* New York, NY: Free Press.

Bollas, C. (1992). *Being a character: Psychoanalysis and self experience.* New York, NY: Hill and Wang.

Britzman, D. P. (1998). *Lost subjects, contested objects: Toward a psychoanalytic inquiry of learning.* State University of New York Press.

Britzman, D. P. (2006). Little Hans, Fritz, and Ludo: On the curious history of gender in the psychoanalytic archive. *Studies in Gender and Sexuality, 7*(2), 113–140.

Bruhm, S., & Hurley, N. (Eds.). (2004). *Curioser: On the queerness of children.* University of Minnesota Press.

Butler, J. (1990). *Gender trouble: Feminism and the subversion of identity.* New York, NY: Routledge.

Butler, J. (1993). *Bodies that matter: On the discursive limits of "sex."* New York, NY: Routledge.

Butler, J. (1997). *The psychic life of power: Theories in subjection.* Palo Alto, CA: Stanford University Press.

Canadian traditions matter [Editorial]. (2010, April 24). *The National Post,* p. A24.

Cavanagh, S. L. (2003). Teacher transsexuality: The illusion of sexual difference and the idea of adolescent trauma. *Sexualities: Studies in Culture and Society, 6*(3–4), 365–388.

Cavanagh, S. L. (2007). *Sexing the teacher: School sex scandals and queer pedagogies*. University of British Columbia Press.

Cavanagh, S. L. (2010). *Queering bathrooms: Gender, sexuality, and the hygienic imagination*. University of Toronto Press.

Curtis, B., & Hunt, A. (2007). The fellatio "epidemic": Age relations and access to the erotic arts. *Sexualities, 10*(1), 5–28.

Delph, E. W. (1978). *The silent community: Public homosexual encounters*. London, England: Sage Publications.

Derrida, J. (1967). *Of Grammatology* (G. C. Spivak, Trans.). Baltimore, MD: John Hopkins Press.

Desroches, F. J. (1990). Tearoom trade: A research update. *Qualitative Sociology, 13*(1), 39–61.

Duggan, L. (2003). *The twilight of equality? Neoliberalism, cultural politics and the attack on democracy*. Boston, MA: Beacon Books.

Edelman, L. (1991). Seeing things: Representation, the scene of surveillance, and the spectacle of gay male sex. In D. Fuss (Ed.), *Inside/out: Lesbian Theories, Gay Theories* (pp. 93–116). New York, NY: Routledge.

Edelman, L. (1994a). Capital offenses: Sodomy in the seat of American government. In L. Edelman, *Homographesis: Essays in Gay Literary and Cultural Theory* (pp. 129–188). New York, NY: Routledge.

Edelman, L. (1994b). Tearoom and sympathy; or, the epistemology of the water closet. In L. Edelman (Ed.), *Homographesis: Essays in Gay Literary and Cultural Theory* (pp. 148–170). New York, NY: Routledge.

Edelman, L. (2004). *No future: Queer theory and the death drive*. Durham, NC: Duke University Press.

Eng, D. L. (2001). *Racial castration: Managing masculinity in Asian America*. Durham, NC: Duke University Press.

Enke, A. (2008). Enke responds to Freedman, Jones, and VanHooser. *Women's Studies Quarterly, 36*(3–4), 297–298.

Erikson, E. H. (1963). Eight ages of man. In E. H. Erikson, *Childhood & Society* (pp. 247–274). New York, NY: W.W. Norton.

Felman, S. (1987). *Jacques Lacan and the adventure of insight: Psychoanalysis in contemporary culture.* Cambridge, MA: Harvard University Press.

Fine, M. (1988). Sexuality, schooling, and adolescent females: The missing discourse of desire. *Harvard Educational Review, 3*(2), 29–53.

Flowers, P., Marriott, C., & Hart, G. (2000). The bars, the bogs, and the bushes: The impact of locale on sexual cultures. *Culture, Health & Sexuality, 2*(1), 69–86.

Foucault, M. (1978). *The history of sexuality: An introduction* (Vol. 1). New York, NY: Vintage.

Freud, S. (1960). On transformations of instinct as exemplified in anal eroticism. In J. Strachey (Ed.), *The Standard Edition of the Complete Works of Sigmund Freud* (Vol. 7, pp. 130–243). London, England: Penguin Books.

Freud, S. (1977a). Fragments of an analysis of a case of hysteria ('Dora'). In J. Strachey (Ed.), *The Standard Edition of the Complete Works of Sigmund Freud* (Vol. 8, pp. 31–43). London, England: Penguin Books.

Freud, S. (1977b). The sexual enlightenment of children. In J. Strachey (Ed.), *The Standard Edition of the Complete Works of Sigmund Freud* (Vol. 7, pp. 171–181). London, England: Penguin Books.

Fuss, D. (Ed.). (1991). *Inside/out: Lesbian theories, gay theories.* New York, NY: Routledge.

Gallop, J. (1995). *Pedagogy: The question of impersonation.* Indiana University Press.

Garrison, E. (2008). Garrison Responds to Freedman, Jones, and VanHooser. *Women's Studies Quarterly, 36*(3–4), 296–297.

Giroux, H., & Penna, A. (1983). Social education in the classroom: The dynamics of the hidden curriculum. In H. Giroux and D.

Purpel (Ed.), *The Hidden Curriculum and Moral Education* (pp. 100–121). Berkeley, CA: McCutchan Publishing.

Hammer, K., & Howlett, K. (2010, April 20). Ontario to introduce more explicit sex education in schools. *The Globe and Mail.*

Haver, W. (1998). Of mad men who practice invention to the brink of intelligibility. In W. F. Pinar (Ed.), *Queer theory in education* (pp. 349–364). Mahwah, NJ: Lawrence Erlbaum.

Hocquenghem, G. (1993). *Homosexual desire* (D. Dangoor, Trans.). Durham, NC: Duke University Press.

Hollister, J. (2004). Beyond the interaction membrane: Laud Humphrey's tearoom tradeoff. *The International Journal of Sociology and Social Policy, 24*(3–5), 72–94.

Houlbrook, M. (2000). The private world of public urinals: London 1918–57. *London Journal, 25*(1), 52–70.

Howlett, K. (2010, April 26). Ontario offered funding to help Catholic Schools develop their own sex-ed course. *The Globe and Mail.*

Howlett, K. (2010, April 28). Catholic groups say they'll work with Ontario's Education Ministry on sex ed. *The Globe and Mail.*

Howlett, K., & Hammer, K. (2010, April 22). McGuinty backs down on frank sex ed. *The Globe and Mail.*

Howlett, K., & Hammer, K. (2010, April 27). Ontario salvages reworked curriculum, minus the sex part. *The Globe and Mail.*

Humphreys, L. (1975). *Tearoom trade: Impersonal sex in public places.* New York, NY: Aldine de Gruyter.

Hunt, S. A., & Kraus, S. W. (2009). Exploring the relationship between erotic disruption during the latency period and the use of sexually explicit material, online sexual behaviors, and sexual dysfunctions in young adulthood. *Sexual Addiction & Compulsivity, 16*(1), 79–100.

Jagodzinski, J. (2002). *Pedagogical desire: Authority, seduction, transference, and the question of ethics.* Westport, CT: Bergin and Garvey.

Kincaid, J. R. (1992). *Child-loving: The erotic child and Victorian culture*. New York, NY: Routledge.

Kincaid, J. R. (1998). *Erotic innocence: The culture of child molesting*. Durham, NC: Duke University Press.

Lacan, J. (1975/1999). *The seminar of Jacques Lacan: Book XX; On feminine sexuality, the limits of love and knowledge, 1972–1973* (J.-A. Miller, Ed. & B. Fink, Trans.). New York, NY: W.W. Norton & Company.

Lacan, J. (2006). The instance of the letter in the unconscious, or reason since Freud (B. Fink, Trans.). In J. Lacan, *Écrites* (pp. 138–168). New York, NY: W.W. Norton & Company.

Lajoie, D. (2010, April 26). Ontario backtracking on sex ed program puts children at risk: group. *The National Post*.

Leap, W. L. (1999). *Public sex/gay space*. New York, NY: Columbia University Press.

Lelchuk, I. (2006, August 27). When is it okay for boys to be girls, and girls to be boys? *San Francisco Chronicle*.

Letts, W. J., IV, & Sears, J. T. (1999). *Queering elementary education: Advancing the dialogue about sexualities and schooling*. New York, NY: Rowman & Littlefield.

Longhurst, R. (2001). *Bodies: Exploring fluid boundaries*. New York, NY: Routledge.

Magni, S., & Reddy, V. (2007). Performative queer identities: Masculine and public bathroom usage. *Sexualities, 10*(2), 229–242.

Meadows, B. (2006, October 30). From girl to boy. *People Magazine*.

Merrick, J. (2002). Sodomites and police in Paris, 1715. *Journal of Homosexuality, 42*(3), 103–128.

Middleton, G. (2002, March 5). Transsexual teen's use of girl's toilets raises fears: Parents fight B.C. school's decision. *The Ottawa Citizen*, p. A3.

Morgan, M. (2002). The plumbing of modern life. *Postcolonial Studies, 5*(2), 171–195.

Muñoz, J. E. (2007). Cruising the toilet: LeRoi Jones/Amiri Baraka, radical Black traditions and queer futurity. *GLQ, 13*(2–3), 353–367.

Muñoz, V., & Garrison, E. K. (Eds.). (2008). Transpedagogies: A Roundtable Dialogue. *Women's Studies Quarterly, 36*(3–4), 288–308.

Nardi, P. M. (1995). The breastplate of righteousness: Twenty-five years after Laud Humphrey's "Tearoom trade: Impersonal sex in public places." *Journal of Homosexuality, 30*(2), 1–10.

O'Connor, A. (1999, August 24), Law firm takes on case against transgendered librarian: A Minneapolis high school teacher says her privacy rights have been violated by having to share restroom. *Star Tribune*, Minneapolis, MN.

Parry, W. (2006, November 26). Transgender teachers face touch transition: While some schools embrace them, others struggle with change. *The Dallas Morning News.* Available from http://www.dallasnews.com

Patton, C. (1996). *Fatal advice: How safe-sex education went wrong.* Durham, NC: Duke University Press.

Pile, S. (1996). *The body and the city: Psychoanalysis, space and subjectivity.* New York, NY: Routledge.

Pinar, W. F. (Ed.). (1998). *Queer theory in education.* Mahwah, NJ: Lawrence Erlbaum.

Plato. (1999). *The Symposium* (C. Gill, Trans.). New York, NY: Penguin Books.

Potvin, J. (2005). Vapour and Steam: The Victorian Turkish bath, homosexual health, and male bodies on display. *Journal of Design History, 18*(4), 319–333.

Puar, J. K. (2007). *Terrorist assemblages: Homonationalism in queer time.* Durham, NC: Duke University Press.

Rud, J. (2002, March 5). Boy can use girl's washroom before sex change. *National Post*, p. A5.

Sacco, L. (2002). Sanitized for your protection: Medical discourse and the denial of incest in the United States, 1890–1940. *Journal of Women's History, 14*(3), 80–101.

Said, E. (1979). *Orientalism.* New York, NY: Vintage Books.

Sears, J. (1998). A generational and theoretical analysis of culture and male (homo)sexuality. In W. F. Pinar (Ed.), *Queer theory in education* (pp. 73–105). Mahwah, NJ: Lawrence Erlbaum.

Sedgwick, E. K. (1990). *Epistemology of the closet.* University of California Press.

Sedgwick, E. K. (2003). *Touching feeling: Affect, pedagogy, performativity.* Durham, NC: Duke University Press.

Serano, J. (2007). *Whipping girl: A transsexual woman on sexism and the scapegoating of femininity.* Emeryville, CA: Seal Press.

Sex ed belongs in curriculum [Editorial]. (2010, April 22). *The Toronto Star,* p. A30.

Sex ed requires prudence and parents [Editorial] (2010, April 22). *The National Post,* p. A16.

Southey, T. (2010, May 1). Go ahead, teach my kid about sex. Please. *The Globe and Mail,* p. F2.

Steinberg, S. R. (1998). Appropriating queerness: Hollywood sanitation. In W. F. Pinar (Ed.). *Queer theory in education* (pp. 187–195). Mahwah, NJ: Lawrence Erlbaum.

Stockton, K. B. (2004). Growing sideways, or versions of the queer child: The ghost, the homosexual, the Freudian, the innocent, and the interval of animal. In S. Bruhm, & N. Hurley (Eds), *Curiouser: On the queerness of children* (pp. 277–315). University of Minnesota Press.

Stockton, K. B. (2009). *The queer child, or growing sideways in the twentieth century.* Durham, NC: Duke University Press.

Stoler, A. L. (1995). *Race and the education of desire: Foucault's history of sexuality and the colonial order of things.* Durham, NC: Duke University Press.

Stryker, S. (2008). *Transgender history.* Berkeley, CA: Seal Press.

Stryker, S., Currah, P., & Moore, L. J. (2008). Introduction: Trans-, Trans, or Transgender. *Women's Studies Quarterly, 36*(3–4), 11–22.

Stryker, S., & Whittle, S. (Eds.). (2006). *The transgender studies reader*. New York, NY: Routledge.

Talburt, S., & Steinberg, S. R. (2000). *Thinking queer: Sexuality, culture, and education*. New York, NY: Peter Lang.

Tewksbury, R. (1996). Cruising for sex in public places: The structure and language of men's hidden, erotic worlds. *Deviant Behavior: An Interdisciplinary Journal, 17*, 1–19.

Tewksbury, R. (2004). The intellectual legacy of Laud Humphreys: His impact on research and thinking about men's public sexual encounters. *The International Journal of Sociology and Social Policy, 24*(3–5), 32–57.

van Lieshout, M. (1995). Leather nights in the woods: Homosexual encounters in a Dutch highway rest area. *Journal of Homosexuality, 29*(1), 19–39.

Yan, E. (2005, October 28). Gay students face hostile environment, report says. *New York Newsday*.

10

Complexity and Transdisciplinarity: Conceptualizing Curriculum as Learning Landscapes

Darren Stanley, University of Windsor

I like walking because it is slow, and I suspect that the mind, like the feet, works at about three miles an hour. If this is so, then modern life is moving faster than the speed of thought, or thoughtfulness. (Solnit, 2000, p. 10)

Most often I would meander down the path by the market garden to the mouth of the brook. Here, fresh water from a spring-fed wetland at the back of the farm mingled with the incoming tide and its salt waters. This was the meeting place for Earth's two great biomes: the land and the sea. It is this handshake, this biological reciprocity, that accounts for the riches of salt marshes, which are among the most productive habitats on the planet. (Thurston, 2004, p. 5)

That which we term "language" remains as much a property of the animate landscape as of the humans who dwell and speak within that terrain. (Abram, 1996, p. 139)

On the Complexities of One Marshy Landscape in Early Spring

IT IS LATE-MARCH, AND I DECIDE, on one brilliant sun-drenched Sunday morning, that I want to go out for a walk in the country. Not too far from where I live – certainly within driving distance – is a wonderful conservation area known as Hillman Marsh. I have gone for walks there many times before, although not at this time of year. A quick check of the weather reveals a rainstorm swirling around the lower end of Michigan and making its way – slowly – across Lake Erie, where it is bound to strike the southern-most tip of Southwestern Ontario and Hillman Marsh. Still, I head out in hopes that I can make it to the marsh and enjoy a walk in the sunshine before the rains hit.

As I walk around the marshy ponds and wooded areas, five kilometres of trails through the wetland and birdland areas and Hillman Creek itself, I notice just how different the area is in spring than in summer – the colors, the smells, the sounds. This is not the same place that I recall having visited last summer in the overbearing heat and heavy air that makes breathing rather difficult. Today, the air is relatively still and, yet, activity abounds. Today, one of the last days of March, the activity of this place is seemingly quite different from past visits. Today, the marsh is speaking to me and it is speaking to me in a particular way.

I notice that I am forcing myself to pay attention to the landscape around me, something I don't think I necessarily did on previous walks. The walls of grasses – the non-indigenous Phragmites – mark off the path around the marsh and sound like the wings of gigantic flies hidden in the grasses themselves, a sound which I hear when the off-shore breeze blows, brushing against my face ever so slightly with a certain touch of coldness. In the openings of the grasses, I see a few birds – some early Canada geese are getting ready to settle in, to raise some young most likely. A number of red-winged Cardinals fly by and then disappear amongst the taller, dry, golden sun-bleached grasses further out in the wetland. Other birds, unidentifiable to me, flock from one tree to another, and then I notice the smell of dry, musty air.

Most of the time when I walk, it is an "unconsidered locomotive means between two sites" (Solnit, 2000). But not today. I'm not rushed, and yet, I do not seem to dilly-dally. The time for walking, also a time for contemplation and thought, which Solnit notes is hardly something that could be described as "doing nothing" in this production-oriented culture, is the closest thing to *just* breathing or the beating of one's heart. But, just as importantly, I recall, only afterwards, my mind moving and wandering around, like my footsteps along the trail, from thoughts of planning to particular recollections to my own observations of the marsh – of me observing me observing the marsh.

And, so, in this particular landscape, I wonder about other kinds of landscapes – landscapes of learning.

Landscapes as a Complex of Diversely Connected and Nested Bodies

> Many people nowadays live in a series of interiors – home, car, gym, office, shops – disconnected from each other. On foot everything stays connected, for while walking one occupies the spaces between those interiors in the same way one occupies those interiors. One lives in the whole world rather than in the interiors built up against it. (Solnit, 2000, p. 9)

For many people, the world seems to unfold in a rather linear fashion. Even more, in moving from one box to another, as reflected in the growing "carchitecture" structure of the world and the increasing move towards urbanization, the world appears as a place of disconnections, a world falling apart (Kunstler, 1996). This is not, many might say, a particularly new thought or belief. Of course, the world is not so disconnected – certainly not in some absolute manner. Even more, in fact, saying that the world is "connected" is no more true or meaningful. That said, it is important to note that the degree and manner in which the world is connected does tell us something of importance – especially in concerns of health and well-being, sustainability, and democracy (Stanley, 2005).

Often, I find myself walking through a variety of fields – literally and figuratively. The fields within and that surround Hillman Marsh, for instance, come to mind as do the fields of study that I engage in as an academic and scholar. My walk through Hillman Marsh, on that one particular day, reminds me that I have walked through *other* fields and other *kinds* of fields, sometimes hardly stopping by for any great period of time, where I am prompted and reminded of other reified organizations – references to anatomy and physiology, collections of social insects, the rise and fall of neighbourhoods, cities, and local industries, cultural and political happenings, and other kinds of smaller and larger bodies of ecology. I think about the playful possibility of thinking about the world as a collection of nested bodies – bodies of knowledge even.

While I think about a particular day, a particular marsh, a particular season, and so on, I am reminded about how necessary and yet how not-so-necessary it is to study other kinds of landscapes. Naturally, there are various kinds of languages and ways of speaking about places, similar to and different from Hillman Marsh. A particular landscape shows us something about a particular scale of life, which may make it a different kind of "thing" from other landscapes – different in substance, but not so particularly different in terms of the principles of dynamics that underlie that landscape. And so, when I study, with some curiosity, the plants alongside a country road, an attempt to discern the difference between a chicory plant and a fringed aster, say, I cannot help but note how these plants are already in some context of living relationships. So it must be when I look at the marsh as a whole or the edge of a holding pond and slough, carefully restored by children from local schools, where a muskrat and family of beavers have made new homes, a chorus of frogs or knot of toads (I can't tell one from the other) announce their presence, and the bull rushes wave and rustle, having been given a new lease on life from the thoroughly suffocating chokehold of the phragmites, to say nothing of the many other chirps, buzzes, and hums of other animals.

This is complexity, and, especially in healthy local ecologies, it is something recognizable and comparable when looking at other healthy local ecologies (Stanley, 2005). As such we might consider, by our own already-given complicity, our own relationships to and with one another as our own families, classrooms, schools, and workplaces. If we were so concerned about living and working in healthy local ecologies, we would do well to think like a healthy marsh – any healthy, vibrant, diversely-informed ecology, in fact, will do just as well. To do so in the classroom, however, would require many things, including transcending our own narrowly-defined disciplinary silos.

Perception, Language, and the Indefinite Plurality of Connections

If, as Vaclav Havel (2000) once noted, "education is the ability to perceive the hidden connections between phenomena," then we ought to be able to say how and if some success has been had. These "hidden connections" (conceptual and perceptual) speak to the importance of (inter-)connections and matters of relationships. That we might find ourselves, in the twenty-first century, in places of academic learning that still enforce, embrace, and hold up models of learning that continue to privilege or give priority to narrowly defined silos of thought and modes of thinking does not bode well for our understanding and ability to perceive hidden connections. And yet, in many particular ways, we remain deeply connected.

Beginning with the notion of "knowledge," it should not be lost that people generally speak of "things" – things in isolation – and in fact, one might say that although courses taught in classrooms, on whatever topic presented, present a great deal about "things" or "knowledge," very little is actually discussed in terms of "knowing" – a verb, an action. To avoid such trappings of isolating knowledge into silos and such, we might do well to be a bit more attentive to our vocabulary and webs of association (Davis, Sumara, & Luce-Kapler, 2008). That the language of schooling, classrooms, and places of higher learning sounds more like machines, factories, businesses, quality control structures, and things to be managed will not be surprising to many. There is, most assuredly, nothing in such places that resonates with natural ecosystems. Do we treat such matters organically or as if they were machines? As such, it should be clear that how we speak and what we say cannot, and is not, separable from our own actions (Maturana & Varela, 1992). Moreover, silos of activity are hardly benign and harmless, mere conceptual disciplinary artifacts. We are deeply connected to the world in particular ways – ways that are not necessarily healthy and sustainable.

Unlike monolithic silos of disciplinary thought, however, "humans are not self-contained, insulated, or isolated beings, but are situated in grander social, cultural, and ecological systems" (Davis et al., 2008, p. 7). In education, when we do not recognize or otherwise ignore such connections, we do so to our peril. In such fashion, certain cultural beliefs and practices continue to be carried on. But is this, in and of itself, the or even a problem at all? This is, in fact, a matter of perception and constitutes the very act of knowing itself, which is always partial, incomplete, and biased. As Davis and his colleagues remind us, "knowing consists of enacted partialities" (2008, p. 8). Failing to notice and understand how our own perceptual limitations give shape to what is and can be known means that we run the risk of believing certain things as if we know enough, that prevailing ideologies are acceptable, other worldviews need not be considered or respected, and that the impact of our own actions are not important.

To be sure, places of higher learning are obviously diverse in their academic silos – perhaps even too diverse, if that could be the case – and yet, we do see attempts to "build bridges" between and across academic disciplines; they take the form of departments like biochemistry and art history and of programmes like biotechnology and environmental studies. Do such departments actually serve to "bridge" several disciplines? If it is in our best interests, collectively, to be much more attentive to those hidden connections, in spite of our limited and limiting perceptual abilities, what are we to do? Does such a tack announce more of a multidisciplinary approach to knowing? Should we aim for and seek something more or different?

Transdisciplinarity: Complexifying Learning

The field of complexity has enjoyed some rather important successes over the past couple decades, not only as scholars in the field have moved towards a different understanding of phenomenon in their own fields of study as self-organizing, emergent phenomena, but also in terms of the connectivity between different scales and kinds of complex, dynamics phenomena. Capra's (2002) work, for instance, speaks to the kinds of connections, that individuals like him are describing, that "integrate life's biological, cognitive and social dimensions" (p. xv). In his work, as with many other texts on "complexity theory," "the nature of life, the nature of mind and consciousness and the nature of social reality" cohere together as diversely nested bodies of knowledge and knowing. That complexity theory may be a most useful theoretical framework to understand such a diversity of nature, the concept of learning systems bodes well for a transdisciplinary framework that aims to understand the life and learning inherent in all landscapes.

Complexity, one of the newest members in the "intellectual tradition of systems thinking" (Capra, 2002), speaks to a systems view of life and, for right or wrong, organizational practitioners and theorists have asked how it might apply to human organizations. For the remaining section of this paper, I shall refer to the classroom and schools as my examples of "human organizations." With a focus upon schools and the classroom, then, with sufficient preamble on ecological settings and the nature of life and learning therein, we might ask how and if such organizational structures and settings and their underlying principles, portraits, and practices could be described as healthy and announce the need for *transdisicplinarity* as a way to understand and act in such settings.

In matters that arise in the study of educational issues, in fact, a number of "vital simultaneities" (Davis & Sumara, 2006) arise, expressed as different "levels of phenomena, intersections of disciplines, and interlacings of discourses" (p. 159). Following Davis and Sumara, in thinking about learning, personal understandings are rooted in genetic structure, framed by bodily activity, elaborated in social interactions, enabled by cultural tools, and are a part of local and globally coherent "conversations" in and with the world. These "levels" or "layers," in turn, suggest a need to focus on particular relevant disciplines: such as, neurology, psychology, sociology, anthropology, and ecology. These disciplines likewise invoke discourses of analytic science, phenomenology, post-structuralism, cultural studies, and ecological philosophy. The need to attend to the nestedness of these vital simultaneities is clear, if not compelling.

And, while the nestedness of such complex entities and the processes that give rise to them may be a given, other aspects of complex dynamic systems also present themselves, suggesting the appropriateness of a transdisciplinary framework, like complexity theory, with and from which to view learning most generally, and the life of classrooms and schools more specifically. In particular, the presence of diversity, redundancy, local interactions, and self-organization as important principles of emergent living systems can be found and identified across every scale, and the degree to which such principles of organizational life can be found tell us much in terms of how healthy and sustainable an organization is.

Principles, Portraits, and Practices of Complexity

Naturally, places like Hillman Marsh are abundant in diverse biological forms and processes that give rise to a myriad of living creatures and phenomena, but to what extent could it be said that our classrooms are similarly diverse. Rather than embraced or encouraged, in a truly inclusive sense, diversity is often seen as something to be managed, controlled, or eliminated. How is it that diversity would or could be encouraged and "used" in the classroom to support learning? Surely, as some measure of intelligence within any learning system, there should be some reasonable level of diversity present amongst and between the many interacting learners.

But just as diversity is an important principle for any healthy, sustainable learning system or organizational entity, redundancy is, like the opposite side of a coin, just as important, albeit for different reasons. While diversity may be important for the group's overall "intelligence quotient," redundancy is what helps sustain networks and systems in times of crisis and disaster. As its etymological roots might suggest, "redundancy" is an "overflow," an excess of the kinds of features that might be necessary for a particular phenomenon to happen. They serve as a guarantee that some aspect of a system can continue to exist and function even if some crucial element is lost. In a relatively redundant system, mistakes and errors can happen, and the system can still continue as many other existing possibilities will still be available to and for the system (Luhmann, 1995). Put differently, redundancy is characterized by more than simple excesses: the concept of redundancy points to the innumerable possibilities for fulfilling some given function of interest.

Redundancy is also not simply about the "replicative" nature of an organization. There is also a "generative" quality that redundancy brings to an organization (Kelly & Stark, 2002). That is, instead of a replication of parts or people, the redundancy lies in the complex patterns of organizational ties or relations. Where there is redundancy of relations in an organization, if a particular tie becomes broken, other relations can be enacted to get around problems or blockages. It is in this manner that an organization is generative: the organization re-generates itself around damaged relations, becoming more innovative and adaptable to change.

All of these remarks about diversity and redundancy are meaningless without some consideration for relationships, connections, and interactions. Local interactions are, in fact, a necessary condition for the possibility of self-organization to happen where a system can bring itself into being with little assistance from "external" sources. Connections, therefore, help create coherence. Where self-organizing patterns are visible, the descriptions of the phenomenon cannot be deduced from the individual interacting parts of the systems to account for features that can only be observed at the level of the self-organized whole. In other words, the behavioural complexity of self-organizing systems depends on interactions, and not its individuals or parts (Solé & Goodwin, 2000). Moreover, the type and variety of interactions have a great deal to do with the behaviour of the emergent system.

Of course, not all processes or approaches to carrying out some task are self-organizing in nature. Templates, recipes, and lesson plans, for instance, are sometimes understood to be prescriptive approaches to carrying out some required task; that is, there is no self-organization present. To be clear, there is not always the need for self-organization. It is the situation that would seem to matter. In the context of education, for example in classrooms and school settings, people have often experienced school life as if it were a machine, functioning in rather prescriptive ways. Lesson plans are presented as templates to be filled in. Curricula are written as isolated and isolatable chapters of topics and concepts intended to be presented as sequentially explored matters. Learning is normalized with classroom averages calculated, and schools compared by subject at the end of each school year. Subjects are treated as if they were as insular as the classroom walls of each group of students. These matters would seem to suggest that self-organization does not play much of a role in such a setting – a setting that treats learning and teaching as already known phenomena. As part of the normative discourses of schooling, many of the complexities of schooling are often reduced to functionalist and instrumentalist forms of socialization where teaching and learning are sometimes presented as prescriptive activities (Britzman, 1991).

On the Need to Re-Imagine a More Transdisciplinary Educational Landscape

What are we to do to create a more transdisciplinary landscape of learning? This paper has argued for the importance of a more complexified understanding of the world, drawing upon a systemic view and framework of the world. The language that we use is important in this instance; it is a language that most natural healthy ecosystems, large and small, speak – if only we were more attentive. It is the language of landscapes, diverse as landscapes are, that remind us that the poet and writer, the scientist and mathematician, the artist, the historian, and cultural studies scholar, can find themselves at home. These settings, transdisciplinary spaces, are the kinds of places that bring us all, in a more than human world, together. So how does his happen?

To be sure, there could not be just one answer to this question. Our responses to this question must be multiple, diverse, and redundant, too. It is more than fair to say that not much has changed in terms of education and schooling over the past century, no matter what the grade or institutional level. By and large, we still get into cars and buses (although some do walk) and go to these "boxes," large and small, where we sit at desks (usually) and do what someone else – the teacher – tells or asks or invites us to do.

I sit at my office desk as I work towards "wrapping up" the draft of this paper. I am fortunate, I suppose, as I get the opportunity to look out a window, not at some salt water marsh, but some green space with a Chalk or Whitebarked Maple almost fully within the frame of my window. That the windows in my building don't open is not lost on me or others. No fresh air – just recycled air pushed through duct systems throughout this and other buildings on campus. Many office doors are closed either because few are around or they, like me, are working in the relative silence of staid, boxy offices filled with books and stuff. The "landscape" of my office and building is hard, linear, flat, boxy, diminished of anything remotely "natural." And as I look across the open space outside my window, I see another building, admittedly newer and nicer, but a building just like this one.

During the school day I notice students, professors, staff, and administrators walking to and fro between these buildings, from one box to another. Just how connected are we all really? Just as this window separates me from the world "outside," we are just as disconnected from one another, not just in terms of what we study but with one another and the more-than-human world. We could start there. Let's take a walk while we are at it.

References

Abram, D. (1996). *The spell of the sensuous: Perception and language in a more-than-human world.* Toronto, ON: Random House of Canada.

Britzman, D. P. (1991). *Practice makes practice: A critical study of learning to teach.* State University of New York Press.

Capra, F. (2002). *The hidden connections: Integrating the hidden connections among the biological, cognitive, and social dimensions of life.* New York, NY: Doubleday.

Davis, B., & Sumara, D. J. (2006). *Complexity and education: Inquiries into learning, teaching, and research.* Mahwah, NJ: Lawrence Erlbaum.

Davis, B., Sumara, D. J., & Luce-Kapler, R. (2008). *Engaging minds: Changing teaching in complex times* (2nd ed.). New York, NY: Routledge.

Havel, V. (2000, October 15). Opening speech. In *Education, Culture and Spiritual Values in the Age of Globalisation.* Forum2000 Foundation symposium conducted in Prague, Czech Republic.

Kelly, J., & Stark, D. (2002). *Crisis, recovery, innovation: Responsive organizations after September 11.* New York, NY: Center on Organizational Innovation, Columbia University.

Kunstler, J. H. (1996). *Home from nowhere: Remaking our everyday world for the twenty-first Century.* New York, NY: Simon & Schuster.

Luhmann, N. (1995). *Social systems.* Palo Alto, CA: Stanford University Press.

Maturana, H. R., & Varela, F. J. (1992). *The tree of knowledge: The biological roots of human understanding.* Boston, MA: Shambhala.

Solé, R. V., & Goodwin, B. C. (2000). *Signs of life: How complexity pervades biology.* New York, NY: Basic Books.

Solnit, R. (2000). *Wanderlust: A history of walking.* New York: Viking.

Stanley, D. (2005). *On the importance of connectivity in health learning organizations: A comparative dynamics perspective.* Paper presented at the Third Annual Complexity Science and Educational Research Conference, Louisiana State University.

Thurston, H. (2004). *A place between the tides: A naturalist's reflections on the salt marsh.* Vancouver, BC: Greystone Books.

PART THREE

CANADIAN CURRICULUM & INDIGENOUS AND ENVIRONMENTAL PERSPECTIVES

Curriculum Reform through Constitutional Reconciliation of Indigenous Knowledge

11

Marie Battiste, University of Saskatchewan

P RIOR TO FORMAL SCHOOLING, Indigenous learning was responsive to the needs of the ecology and the communities, cultivated in holistic lifelong learning processes that were the foundations of Indigenous knowledge (IK). These processes created vast learning civilizations based on multiple skills and competencies that have been transmitted to succeeding generations through Aboriginal languages, oral traditions, and community socialization, cultural, and spiritual ceremonies and traditions, and extended relationships with large Aboriginal confederacies and alliances. The success of these holistic processes for lifelong learning created a collective, sustainable lifestyle that contributed sufficiently to the needs of the present and took into consideration the needs of the future seven generations (Battiste & Semeganis, 2002).

Aboriginal peoples' enthusiasm for learning is revealed in their many treaties with European Crowns. Continued learning of First Nations students was a prime concern of their ancestors in the treaties, as they transferred jurisdictions of vast territories to fund these educational rights. Treaty education in schools, overseen by the chiefs, provided both a shared vision of their future and an enriched livelihood of First Nations, as they anticipated that the transmission of European knowledge would effectively give their families additional competencies to negotiate the enriched livelihoods of the new relationships (Henderson, 1995). Under the written terms of the treaties, parental choice would continue to control the learning in the families and in the communities. Although treaty rights gave the Crown different levels of discretion in the funding and establishing of schools and educational programs that would benefit their families, parents did not give up their rights to control the language and cultural socialization of their families in what they perceived would be a continuing, lifelong, holistic learning process.

The original First Nations vision of education in the treaty commitments has not been implemented yet, as they have had to submit to an educational curriculum, whether federal or provincial, that has diminished their livelihood and capacities and ignored their prior knowledge and experiences to enable them to move from the bottom of Canada's educational achievement statistics. Early Eurocentric education was based on the assumed inferiority of Aboriginal languages, cultures, and livelihood that has generated a legacy of systemic racism in residential and provincial schools. Curriculum was assimilative, degrading, and punitive, leaving Aboriginal students traumatized and their families damaged from cycles of internalized colonization, which continue in multiple ways as evidenced by the high rates of suicide and incarceration and low graduation and achievement rates in schools (Royal Commission on Aboriginal Peoples [RCAP], 1996). These are the legacies of educational curricula that this generation of educators is challenged to address as the provinces and territories across Canada target new priorities in Aboriginal education (Council of Ministers of Education [CMEC], 2008). Aboriginal youth are Canada's largest growing demographic, but indicators point to the continuing losses among Aboriginal peoples in their language, culture, and livelihood, as well as in their lack of employment and low performance in formal education (Battiste, 2005; Canadian Council on Learning [CCL], 2009).

This chapter, then, is aimed at providing a background, context, and perspective that may inform current decision makers in revising curriculum, beginning with an overview of the obligations and commitments made to First Nations in the treaties, and more recently as Aboriginal rights to education have been affirmed by the United Nations in their *Declaration on the Rights of Indigenous Peoples* (2007) and finally affirmed in Canada in 2010. Federal and provincial school systems have not translated these constitutionally protected rights into current models of education, but rather the discursive modes of analysis have led to various models of education that focus on students' perceived deficits and ignore systemic racism and structural failures of the educational systems. A Eurocentric approach to curricula reform in most educational systems continue to have a conceptual bias that ignores the system and structure and relies on the dispositional self of individual children as central to understanding their educational failure and tragic circumstances. This approach overestimates the influence of individual dispositions of the children (or victims) in explaining people's behaviour and underestimates the role of situational or contextual (i.e., systemic) influences within the educational curricula or system. This dispositional bias runs very deep. To understand the failure of these approaches, I address how many educators focusing on retention and access of Aboriginal students have utilized an Aboriginal-content-and-stir model of inclusion that is based on a Eurocentric dispositional analysis of education, rather than focusing on a systemic analysis of the curriculum in which federal and provincial schools are positioned. This provides, then, a prelude to a decolonizing perspective about what provinces and territories need to reform in the educational systems to begin to effectively address the achievement gaps among Aboriginal and non-Aboriginal students. Reconciling Aboriginal and treaty rights with the core competencies of IK and its variants in the Indigenous humanities is illustrated as a way to reconcile the assimilative and acculturative approach of education to generate a curricula that is ameliorative, restorative, nurturing, respectful, and accountable.

Eurocentric Curricula and the Failure of Educating Aboriginal Peoples

The horrific legacy of education of Aboriginal children began with the federal Indian residential school (IRS) system and forced assimilative curricula for First Nations children, operated during the nineteenth and twentieth centuries by churches of various denominations (about sixty per cent by Roman Catholics, and thirty per cent by the Protestants) and funded by treaty transfer funds administered under the *Indian Act* by Indian and Northern Affairs Canada, a branch of the federal government. The schools' purpose and curricula was, according to the *Indian Act*, to "civilize" First Nation children, teach them English or French, convert them to Christianity, and end their traditional ways of life. Its legacy is now understood as a systemic and human tragedy that has denied First Nations, Inuit, and Métis viable tools for their future and dignity. This human experiment in the cultural destruction of young children's minds, posing as education, denied them the opportunities for a promised transformative and responsive education in the treaties. It made federal education policy a distrusted and dysfunctional concept, whose legacy remains in the public provincial and territorial schools as well.

In 2008, Prime Minister Stephen Harper aptly summarized the goal of that IRS education in his apology to residential school survivors and their families:

> Two primary objectives of the residential school system were to remove and isolate children from the influence of their homes, families, traditions and cultures, and to assimilate them into the dominant culture. These objectives were based on the assumption that Aboriginal cultures and spiritual beliefs were inferior and unequal. Indeed, some sought, as was infamously said, "to kill the Indian in the child." Today, we recognize that this policy of assimilation was wrong, has caused great harm, and has no place in our country.

An apology and financial atonement for the past biases cannot erase the damage suffered. However, a new consciousness of what that past has wrought among Aboriginal peoples and among non-Aboriginal society in terms of the false presumptions held in crafting out the educational curricula and the systemic outcomes of that tragic history is needed. The reconciliation requires a two-way healing process not just among Aboriginal peoples but also among Canadian society at large. Education is one of the critical sites for this reconciliation work, particularly because modern systems of education and economics have been crafted out of Eurocentric colonial borrowings from European systems. Thus, historically, the purposes and structures of education are not politically neutral (Bartolome, 1994, 2008). Nor are they devoid of politics in the present, as they are sustained by public funds. The current step is for Canadian society, and its structures and systems, to conduct their own forms of reconciliation, beginning with the recognition of this socio-historic reality: presumptions and assumptions based in Eurocentric superiority have led to this damage. On the part of the schools and education, this requires a decolonizing of the education system, most notably through curricula reform and teacher education.

In Canada, most political decisions about education have been addressed without the input and direction of Aboriginal people. Aboriginal people were not invited to be voting citizens in provincial or federal elections until the mid-1960s. Control of the education of their children on reserve was partially restored in the mid-70s, with the policy heralding Indian control of Indian education (National Indian Brotherhood [NIB]/Assembly of First Nations [AFN], 1972). By this time most of Canada's educational structures and curriculum policies had already been shaped, and the federal government sought to create parity with provincial systems by imposing provincial curricula on all First Nations–administered schools. The provincial educational systems have ignored the treaty provisions for education, which since 1982 have been constitutionally protected, and they have ignored Aboriginal choice, thus creating systemic discrimination against Aboriginal knowledge and heritage (Henderson, 1995).

Curricula can be a site to maintain domination or to decolonize. It is a site of reproduction or it is a site of transformation. Curricula in schools, then, present a challenge and an opportunity. Reclaiming, recovering, restoring, and celebrating IK are all part of a revisionist project of great magnitude. Today, the critically important decolonizing quest for Indigenous peoples around the world is to integrate fully IK into their children's lives. It is a project that many Indigenous peoples have taken to all their sites of work, research, and study, including blockades, protests, and the courts. This is what is understood as the Indigenous renaissance, and Indigenous scholars throughout the Commonwealth world are challenging Eurocentrism and its outcomes to activate new forms of ethical dialogue with Indigenous peoples that will generate an inclusive curriculum (Henderson, 2008). The challenge and opportunity for educators are found within the Canadian constitutional framework that has diffused authority of educational jurisdiction, creating a complex intersection of interrelated educational issues to be addressed in transforming the current and future educational outcomes.

Constitutional Reconciliation of Education of Aboriginal Peoples

Constitutional law of Canada creates education authorities and systems. Under section 91(24) of the *Constitution Act, 1867*, the federal Crown has constitutional responsibility for "Indians and lands reserved for Indians." Education, or schooling, is a specific constitutional commitment and obligation in the treaties and federal legislation and an Aboriginal right, creating a unique fiduciary responsibility for the education of First Nations students in Canada and activates the honour of the Crown. In 1982, Canada passed in the *Constitution Act* their independence from the British Crown. In that historic document, Canada affirmed its commitment to Aboriginal and treaty rights of Aboriginal peoples, among them First Nations, Inuit, and Métis peoples. Section 35 of the *Constitution Act* recognizes and affirms Aboriginal and treaty rights, and specifically the education rights of First Nations. It continues to empower Indigenous education and protects their knowledge systems and culture. For example, the Supreme Court of Canada has determined in *R. v. Coté* (1996) that every substantive constitutional right will normally include the incidental constitutional right to teach such a practice, custom, and tradition to a younger generation.

The provincial counterpart to the imperial treaties and federal jurisdiction over Indians is section 93(1) of the *Constitution Act, 1867*, which provides the constitutional authority of the provincial Crown over education to students in public schools, both secular and Catholic. When First Nations students who are residents of federal reserves go into provincial schools, the federal government pays for their tuition based on transfer agreements with the provincial governments. First Nations students who are residents off reserves and who attend the public school system are treated like all other students within the municipalities with regard to school tuition being paid by local property taxes. Education (elementary, secondary, and post-secondary) is thus within the provincial Crown's jurisdiction for those attending public schools and institutions, and the ten provincial legislatures and educational departments oversee their curriculum. Territorial education in the North is under the jurisdiction of Indian and Northern Affairs Canada (INAC) that funds education for Inuit and First Nations students.

The theme of constitutional reconciliation of various constitutional rights and powers pervades the contemporary judicial decisions about Aboriginal and treaty right relations to executive and legislative constitutional powers. This discourse is permeated with constitutional respect for rights and searching for a positive and durable constitutional relationship. As Madame Justice McLachlin explained in *R. v. Van der Peet* (1996), "The desire for reconciliation, in many cases long overdue, lay behind the adoption of section 35 of the *Constitution Act, 1982*" (para. 310). The concept of reconciliation characterizes the contemporary relationship between rights of Aboriginal peoples and the various manifestations of the divided jurisdiction of the Crown. The courts have declared that the rights of Aboriginal peoples exist within a matrix of other powers and rights of the constitution. They use reconciliation as a process to expand the

Crown's duties to consult and accommodate, in good faith (*Haida Nation v. B.C.*, 2004) and to implement treaties.

The Court has stated that the basic purpose of section 35 of the *Constitution Act, 1982*, is the reconciliation of the pre-existence of Aboriginal societies with the assumption of the sovereignty of the Crown (*Haida Nation v. B.C.*, 2004). This is a cornerstone reconciliation of the educational provisions. The Royal Commission on Aboriginal Peoples (1996) further adopted reconciliation as the key theme for renewing relationships with Aboriginal peoples within the Canadian federation. It articulated the relationship principles of mutual recognition, mutual respect, mutual benefit (sharing), and mutual responsibility as the basis for renewed relationships with Aboriginal peoples. These relationship principles have been endorsed by most Aboriginal groups and have become central framework for constitutional reconciliation.

The constitutional reconciliation of educational rights and privileges involves the federal Crown (s. 91(24)), the provincial Crown (s. 93), and Aboriginal peoples (s. 35) and is central to a responsive education and curricula reform (Battiste, 2009). Reconciliation of educational rights of Aboriginal peoples with the federal and provincial crowns is established in Aboriginal holistic lifelong learning and in the educational choice of First Nations parents. The transfer of jurisdiction of Aboriginal land to the Crown provides the means and framework for implementing these educational rights for their benefit of First Nations, Inuit, and Métis peoples. While constitutional reconciliation is becoming a critical educational necessity, it also generates a reorientation of the dialogue needed between First Nations and those seeking to build relations in what has been theorized by Ermine (2007) as ethical space. Ethical space is one where positive relations between Indigenous and Western systems can be nurtured, where two cultures agree to engage in a neutral zone where two cultures can meet with respect for one another, and where the "notions of universality are replaced by concepts such as the equality of nations . . . [and] triggers a dialogue that begins to set the parameters for an agreement to interact modeled on appropriate, ethical and human principles" (p. 202).

The Supreme Court of Canada has said that what section 35 constitutionally protects is what is "integral to the Aboriginal community's distinctive culture" (*R. v. Van der Peet*, 1996, para. 53) or their pre-contact way of life (*R. v. Sappier-Gray*, 2006, para. 37). The Court declared that section 35 is a constitutional commitment to protecting practices that were historically important features of particular Aboriginal communities. Further, it stated "Aboriginal rights are communal rights: These Aboriginal models are grounded in the existence of a historic and present community, and they may only be exercised by virtue of an individual's ancestrally based membership" (*R. v. Sappier-Gray*, 2006, para. 24). While the nature of Aboriginal practice upon which a constitutional right is founded must be considered in the context of pre-contact Aboriginal activities, the "nature of the right must be determined in light of present day circumstances" (*R. v. Powley*, 2003, para. 48). The Supreme Court noted that "a certain margin of flexibility might be required to ensure that Aboriginal practices can evolve and develop over time" (para. 45). The constitutional acknowledgement and affirmation of these constitutional rights require that the Crown "recognize and protect those customs and traditions that were historically important features of Métis (a.k.a Aboriginal) communities prior to the time of effective European control, and that persist in the present day" (para. 18). This distinguishes Aboriginal peoples from other groups in Canada or a province or territory. Both Aboriginal knowledge systems and cultural rights are constitutionally protected and must be eventually reconciled with existing curricula, learning, and educational models in Canadian education.

The constitutional framework and court decisions generate an emerging need for reconciliation of IK in learning and pedagogy that impacts all public forms of education. It creates the innovative context for systemic curricular reform to include the various models of the holistic, lifelong learning paradigm in existing constitutional rights. This includes: Indigenous science, humanities, visual arts, and languages as well as existing education philosophy, pedagogy, teacher education, and practice.

Decolonizing Education:
Situated Learning in Indigenous Knowledge

Indigenous knowledge is part of the collective genius of Aboriginal peoples, and their knowledge system is an Aboriginal and treaty right under the Constitution of Canada. IK is the foundation and Aboriginal framework of a honourable education. IK is not a singular concept that dominates other perspectives, no single knowledge system or heritage informs it, and no two heritages produce the same knowledge (Battiste & Henderson, 2000). These interconnected forms of IK have the capacity for a total systems understanding and management. IK has a resourceful capacity for creating the context and texture of a good life in the core principles of its teachings with the potential for a life-giving and lifelong process to be absorbed and pondered and shared. The UN Special Rapporteur on protecting Indigenous heritage affirmed that

> the heritage of an Indigenous people is a complete knowledge system with its own concepts of epistemology, philosophy, and scientific and logical validity. The diverse elements of an indigenous people's heritage can only be fully learned or understood by means of the pedagogy traditionally employed by these peoples themselves. (Daes, 1993, para. 8)

A global consensus for the change in education was integral to the UN *Declaration of the Right of Indigenous Peoples* (2007). The Declaration affirms that all peoples contribute to the diversity and richness of civilizations and cultures, which constitute the common heritage of humankind. It declares "Indigenous peoples and individuals have the right not to be subjected to forced assimilation or destruction of their culture" (article 8). It declares that "Indigenous peoples have the right to the dignity and diversity of their cultures, traditions, histories, and aspirations, which shall be appropriately reflected in education and public information" (article 15). It affirms that "Indigenous peoples have the right to establish and control their educational systems and institutions providing education in their own languages, in a manner appropriate to their cultural methods of teaching and learning" (article 14). It declares that "Indigenous peoples have the right to maintain, control, protect, and develop their cultural heritage, traditional knowledge, and traditional cultural expressions, as well as the manifestations of their sciences, technologies, and cultures, including human and genetic resources, seeds, medicines, knowledge of the properties of fauna and flora, oral traditions, literatures, designs, sports and traditional games, and visual and performing arts. They also have the right to maintain, control, protect, and develop their intellectual property over such cultural heritage, traditional knowledge, and traditional cultural expressions" (article 31).

The Declaration affirms the urgent need to respect and promote the inherent rights of Indigenous peoples which derive from their political, economic, and social structures and from their cultures, spiritual traditions, histories, and philosophies, especially their rights to their lands, territories, and resources (articles 33–35). It affirms the right of Indigenous peoples to the "recognition, observance, and enforcement of treaties, agreements, and other constructive arrangements concluded with States or their successors and to have States honour and respect such treaties, agreements and other constructive arrangements" (article 37).

Curricula Reform of Eurocentrism

The fundamental question in constitutional reconciliation of education is whether Aboriginal peoples can represent their constitutionally protected values in the design of education programs. Aboriginal people have operated from a position of weakness with respect to federal and provincial governments and their educational institutions. Education and its curricula has never been a neutral enterprise (Bartolome, 2008; Carnoy, 1974). It has always been embedded with meanings constructed from the economic, political, social, and cultural ideologies related to race, class, and gender (Calliste & Dei, 2000; Dei, Hall, & Goldin Rosenberg, 2000; St. Denis, 2002). Developed within a colonial system of Anglo-Christian patriarchy, Canadian education has systematically excluded the rich diversity of peoples of Canada, more specifically women, minorities, and First Nations perspectives, experiences, beliefs, and diverse knowledge (Minnich, 1990; Suzack, Huhndorf, Perreault, & Barman, 2010). Canadian educational curricula have been and continue to be built on the foundation of Eurocentrism (Quinn, 1999). It was socially constructed and designed for a colonial society that left its original communities and knowledge to achieve a newly constructed vision of society built on an education that would carve out their new conceptions of hierarchy and power and benefit. Such a society has not served all peoples equally, as certain sectors of Canadian society have not gained or benefited from the de facto culturally exclusive educational systems. It has largely developed into a Eurocentric, learned consciousness in which all of us have been marinated. Perhaps one of the greater challenges to bringing IK to the educational systems will be that fact that IK does not mirror classic Eurocentric knowledge systems (EK). Rather it is a knowledge system in its own right with its own internal consistency and ways of knowing, and therefore, there are limits to how far it can be comprehended from a Eurocentric point of view and from within European languages, theories, and research processes. As well, one of IK will have to remain in Aboriginal languages, families, and communities as forms of collective knowledge and consciousness.

In Eurocentric thought, a person's behaviour is generally understood to manifest not simply his or her disposition, but a particular dispositionist's causal schema (people's dispositions, such as personalities, preferences, identities, and the like) that presumes that behaviour reflects freely willed (often consciously made) "choices," which in turn reflect a stable set of "preferences" (Quinn, 1999, pp. 146–152; Hanson & Yosifon, 2004). This theory of human behaviour is central and vital to virtually all of Eurocentric educational system. It places far too much unreflective emphasis on an individual's perceived motivations, preferences, choices, as well as on their perceived weaknesses and character in analyzing and accounting for their education achievement. Dispositionalism or dispositional knowledge defines tendencies or creates biases about what Eurocentric researchers see and how they construe what they see: i.e., incarcerated youth is strongly presumed to reflect their freely willed, preference-satisfying individual choice without a context such as cycles of residential school abuse, systemic violence, racism, and poverty being considered strongly for how those "choices" are made.

In the Indian residential schools, a false, distorted, Eurocentric disposition of First Nations children systemically infected most of the educational system and curricula. The reason for Aboriginal children's non-progress in education and life was attributed to their lack of certain Eurocentric traits or factors, which had to be supplied by the educational system or integrated cultural foundation, which was conceived as universal and neutral. The internalization of Eurocentric dispositionalism in the Indian residential school created and sustained for several generations the collective soul wound of Aboriginal peoples, evidenced by persistent and acute colonization disorder, a form of post traumatic stress disorder (Duran & Duran, 1995). It has damaged not only the residential school students, but also their families and communities, eroded or destroyed their language systems, and driven their continuing teachings and ceremonies underground.

Many generations of students continue to feel violated, abused, and shattered from their past and from an education that still operates from these Eurocentric biases, and this lies at the heart of their negative self-concepts and subsequent intergenerational harm that is evidenced in the tragic statistics of high drop out rates, alcohol and drug abuse, intergenerational violence, and suicide. The situation in which Aboriginal peoples have been placed has not sufficiently been acknowledged as creating the operating factors that contribute to their current situation. The Eurocentric dispositional bias still exists in the Aboriginal deficit theory played out in contemporary efforts for dealing with Aboriginal modes of learning. By focusing on the perceived problems of Aboriginal people, including their lack of English, math, socialization in schools, and focusing on counselling, access, and transition programs, schools apply a deficit theory or always seeing the problem residing in the Aboriginal people, not in the Eurocentric educational curricula, teachers, or system.

The artificial structure and curricula of the IRS and its variants in the current educational systems remain an unseen and unexplored force in constructing a responsive educational system. These systemic forces made up of ideologies, perspectives, and methodologies implicit to Eurocentrism continue to shape, transform, sometimes determine, and almost always influence the education of Aboriginal youth in provincial, territorial, and First Nations schools. To properly understand the IRS and conventional educational systems, administrators, curriculum researchers, scholars and policy makers need to ascertain how the place or situation of the curricula was set, who had the power to set it, and what the purpose of the staging was and where the Aboriginal students were positioned. In the last few decades, a *real* meaningful divide between the traditional dispositional schema and the new situationist approach has been emerging, originating in mind science, which bases attributions of systems, context, and place, and views causation and responsibility on unseen or unappreciated systemic influences that generate learning and consciousness (Hanson & Yosifon, 2004). These different methods of understanding human nature define the boundaries of the broader liberal-conservative crevasse in Eurocentrism.

For more than thirty-five years, Aboriginal peoples and educators in Canada have been articulating their goals for Aboriginal education

(NIB/AFN, 1972; AFN, 2010; Inuit Tapirit Kanatami [ITK], 2008). Since Aboriginal children are regarded as a precious and sacred gift, the objective of Aboriginal peoples is to take control over the constitutional right and jurisdiction over the education of their children. They want to create educational systems and curricula based on Indigenous knowledge, language, and culture that will prepare them to participate fully in their communities and in Canadian society (RCAP, 1996). They expect education to be lifelong and holistic and to serve as a vehicle for cultural and economic renewal. This educational system must develop the whole child, intellectually, spiritually, emotionally and physically. In 1996, the Commissioners of the Final Report of the Royal Commission on Aboriginal Peoples (RCAP) stated,

> We believe that Aboriginal parents and Aboriginal communities must have the opportunity to implement their vision of education. Aboriginal children are entitled to learn and achieve in an environment that supports their development as whole individuals. They need to value their heritage and identity in planning for the future. Education programs, carefully designed and implemented with parental involvement, can prepare Aboriginal children to participate in two worlds with a choice of futures. Aboriginal people should expect equity of results from education in Canada. (RCAP, 1996, volume 3, chapter 5, section 1.5)

This will not happen if the education system continues unchanged. For significant change to occur, Aboriginal people must have the authority to organize their own education and to influence how their children are educated (RCAP, 1996, volume 3, p. 442).

The Commissioners noted that current education curricula and policies fail to realize these Aboriginal visions of education and the immense human costs due to this failure (volume 3, pp. 433–434). They noted that while 70% of the Aboriginal students beginning at

the age of six are under provincial and territorial authorities and curricula, Aboriginal people have been restricted in their efforts to
implement curricula that would transmit their cultural or linguistic
heritage to the next generation. (volume 3, p. 441). They were aware
that modest improvements have been made to school curricula over
the last fifteen years, but these improvement have been far too slow
and inconsistent. In Canada, although Aboriginal and treaty rights
are entrenched in section 35 of the 1982 *Constitution Act,* there is
currently no federally legislated protection for Aboriginal languages
(Canadian Heritage, 2003, p. 29). And according to Canadian
Heritage (2003), "Only five of the thirteen provincial and territorial
governments have developed policies and programs in support of
Aboriginal languages" (p. 29). While more Aboriginal visual and textual content has appeared, and fewer textbooks portray Aboriginal
people in blatant negative terms, and while some provinces have initiated Aboriginal language programs and curriculum, the
Commission stresses that the revisions often gloss over or avoid tack-
ling the fundamental changes that are necessary to create curriculum
that is rooted in Aboriginal knowledge systems and understanding of
the world, in subjects such as history, art, health, mathematics, and
sciences (RCAP, 1996, pp. 456–63).

The Commission recommends that Aboriginal, provincial, and
territorial governments act promptly to reach agreements for mutual
recognition of programs provided by their respective educational
institutions so as to facilitate the transfer of students between educational systems while protecting the integrity of cultural dimensions
of Aboriginal education (recommendation 3.5.4, p. 463). It also recommends that Federal, provincial, and territorial governments collaborate with Aboriginal governments, organizations, and educators
to develop or continue developing innovative curricula that reflect
Aboriginal cultures and community realities, for delivery (a) at all
grade levels of elementary and secondary schools; (b) in schools
operating under Aboriginal control; and (c) in schools under provincial or territorial jurisdiction (p. 463). It also recommended that

Aboriginal language education be assigned priority in all educational systems (p. 468). It also urged Aboriginal control and parental involvement in the education system and curriculum development (pp. 468–472).

In 1997, Canada's statement of reconciliation with Aboriginal peoples acknowledged:

> Sadly, our history with respect to the treatment of Aboriginal people is not something in which we can take pride. Attitudes of racial and cultural superiority led to a suppression of Aboriginal culture and values. As a country, we are burdened by past actions that resulted in weakening the identity of Aboriginal peoples, suppressing their languages and cultures, and outlawing spiritual practices. . . . In renewing our partnership, we must ensure that the mistakes, which marked our past relationship, are not repeated. The Government of Canada recognizes that policies that sought to assimilate Aboriginal people, women and men, were not the way to build a strong country. We must instead continue to find ways in which Aboriginal people can participate fully in the economic, political, cultural and social life of Canada in a manner that preserves and enhances the collective identities of Aboriginal communities, and allows them to evolve and flourish in the future. (Indian and Northern Affairs Canada [INAC], 1997, para. 4)

Dr. Erica Irene Daes, United Nations Working Group on Indigenous Peoples at the UNESCO Conference on Education, in July 1999 noted:

> Displacing systemic discrimination against Indigenous peoples created and legitimized by the cognitive frameworks of imperialism and colonialism remains the single most crucial cultural challenge facing humanity. Meeting this responsibil-

ity is not just a problem for the colonized and the oppressed, but also rather the defining challenge for all peoples. It is the path to a shared and sustainable future for all peoples.

What is becoming clear to educators is that any attempt to decolonize the curricula is a complex and daunting political and educational task. Yet that is the role of constitutional reconciliation in education. The colonial model that offers students a fragmented and distorted picture of Aboriginal peoples in curricula must be rejected; as well, students must be offered a critical perspective of the historical context that has created that fragmentation. Understanding Eurocentric assumptions of superiority and understanding how these assumptions continue to dominate in the curricula is necessary to change this situation and improve the education of Aboriginal children; it is necessary to focus on some of the systemic obstacles that continue to block the attainment of Aboriginal visions of educating their children.

Educators have begun the constitutional reconciliation with negotiated principles for working with Indigenous peoples, new protocols for engaging respectful relationships (Ermine, Sinclair, & Browne, 2005), new foundations for curriculum change (Government of Alberta et al., 2000), and new lifelong holistic models for identifying success and collective well-being (CCL, 2007). In 2004, the Council of Ministers of Education, a provincial body of all the provincial ministers of education, made Indigenous education its highest priority. In its foundational document, the Council of Ministers made several recommendations: recognize early childhood education as a key to improved literacy; provide clear objectives and a commitment to report results, including working closer with the Government of Canada and Aboriginal communities; institute strong teacher development and recruitment; improve accountability arrangements with Aboriginal parents and communities; share learning resources; support the elimination of inequitable funding levels for First Nations Schools; and create a National

Forum on Aboriginal Education (Avison, 2004). The Council's work has just begun, but more important to their objectives needs to be a focus on curricula reform by examining Indigenous knowledge and humanities as the foundation.

If we are to create a new, more equally blended curriculum that respects the constitutionally protected knowledge system, languages, and cultures of the Aboriginal people, curriculum experts need to understand IK and Aboriginal learning. We need to know the epistemologies that Aboriginal peoples provide in a foundation for learning, how they are transmitted in formal learning systems (i.e., K–12 schools, post-secondary institutions, alternative schools, in health and wellness, in the workplace, and in reformative and restorative justice), and how they continue through lifelong learning. We also need to examine current knowledge of learning and bring the most promising of these innovations together with the knowledge of Aboriginal learning so as to inform institutions and training programs. Ball and Pence (2006), speaking of their partnership work with Canadian First Nations communities in the delivery of professional training programs in child and youth care, refer to

> the words of a representative of one of British Columbia's inter-tribal health authorities: "Yes, we need training. But what do we want to train our people to do and to become? The transition to Aboriginal control should not mean simply Aboriginal people taking over white jobs, doing things in white ways. We want to do things in Aboriginal ways. We need training that will support our members in remembering their cultures and creating Aboriginal services that are really Aboriginal." (p. 111)

Conclusions

The key in designing meaningful educational curricula in Canada is to confront the hidden standards of racism, colonialism, and cultural and linguistic imperialism in the modern curriculum and see the theoretical incoherence with modern theories of society. Under the biases of Eurocentric dispositionalism, Aboriginal peoples (and other minorities) have been led to believe that their poverty and impotence is a result of their cultural and racial origins and characteristics. The modern solution to their despair has been described in reports with the overriding burden being placed upon their being a member of a racial or cultural minority. The gift of modern education has been the ideologies of oppression, which negates the process of IK as a process of inquiry, and seeks to change the consciousness of the oppressed, not change the situation that oppressed them.

Most Canadians, both Aboriginal and non-Aboriginal, have long accepted some of the fundamental assumptions underlying modern public school education. We have assumed that knowledge, like education, is a kind and necessary form of mind liberation that opens to the individual options and possibilities that ultimately have value for society as a whole. On the face of it, knowledge and education appear beneficial to all people and intrinsic to the progress and development of modern technological society. But public schooling has not been benign (Carnoy, 1974; Freire, 1973). It has been used as a means to perpetuate damaging myths about Aboriginal cultures, languages, beliefs, and ways of life. It has also established Western knowledge and science as dominant modes of thought and inquiry that homogenizes diversity and jeopardizes us all as we move into the next century. After nearly a century of public schooling for tribal peoples in Canada, the most serious problem with the current system of education does not lie not in its failure to liberate the human potential among Aboriginal peoples, but rather in its quest to limit thought to cognitive imperialistic policies and practices. This quest denies Aboriginal people access to and participation in the formulation of government policy, constrains the use and development of Aboriginal cultures in schools, and confines education to a narrow scientific view of the world that threatens the global future.

Cognitive imperialism is a form of cognitive manipulation used to disclaim other knowledge bases and values. Validated through one's knowledge base and empowered through public education, it has been the means by which whole groups of people have been denied existence and have had their wealth confiscated. Cognitive imperialism denies people their language and cultural integrity by maintaining the legitimacy of only colonial languages and cultures and their frame of reference. As a result of cognitive imperialism, the Canadian public has been led to believe that Aboriginal peoples' poverty and powerlessness is a result of the construction of their race rather than of the systemic barriers facing them. Part of this analysis is achieved by the focus on statistics about Aboriginal peoples. The Canadian Council on Learning has noted:

> Although current data and indicators on Aboriginal learning provide useful information, they are limited for a number of reasons: Most research on Aboriginal learning is oriented toward the educational deficits of Aboriginal people, overlooks positive learning outcomes and does not account for the unique political, social and economic realities of First Nations, Inuit and Métis. (CCL, 2007, p. 2)

What is apparent to Indigenous peoples is the need for a serious and far-reaching examination of the assumptions inherent in Eurocentricsm and modern educational theory. How these assumptions create the moral and intellectual foundations of modern society and culture have to be unpacked and deconstructed in order to allow space for Aboriginal consciousness, language, and identity to flourish without ethnocentric or racist interpretation. The current educational shortcomings may or may not be in the curriculum, or in finance, or in testing, or in community involvement, but no one will ever know this – or the changes necessary for improvement – without a deeper philosophical analysis of modern thought and educational practices.

In practical terms, the *Declaration of the Rights of Indigenous Peoples* presents a decolonizing framework of Eurocentric curricula that requires a trans-systemic approach to Eurocentric and Indigenous knowledge. Indigenous peoples must be involved at all stages and in all phases of education planning and future governing. The current challenge is not so much finding receptivity to inclusion of the synthesis among curriculum specialists, but the challenge of ensuring that receptivity to inclusive, diverse education is appropriately and ethically achieved and that the educators become aware of the difficult systemic challenges for overcoming Eurocentrism, culturalism, racism, and intolerance. The "add and stir" model of bringing Aboriginal education into the curricula, environment, and teaching practices has not achieved the needed change (RCAP, 1996) but rather continues to sustain difference and superiority of Eurocentric knowledge and processes. The challenge thus continues for educators to be able to reflect critically on the current educational system in terms of whose knowledge is offered, who decides what is offered, what outcomes are rewarded and who benefits, and more importantly how those are achieved in an ethically appropriate process. Curriculum change and student outcomes are every educator's responsibility and need not be addressed for only First Nations, Métis, and Inuit learners but for all students in the context of inclusion, diversity, and respect.

References

Assembly of First Nations (2010). *First Nations control of First Nations education: It's our vision, it's our time.* Retrieved from http://www.afn.ca/calltoaction/Documents/FNCFNE.pdf

Avison, D. (2004, May). *A challenge worth meeting: Opportunities for improving Aboriginal education outcomes.* Prepared for the Council of Ministers in Education, Canada.

Ball, J., & Pence, A. (2006). *Supporting Indigenous children's development.* University of British Columbia Press.

Bartolome, L. I. (1994). Beyond the methods fetish: Toward a humanizing pedagogy. *Harvard Educational Review, 64*(2), 173–194.

Bartolome. L. I. (2008). *Ideologies in education: Unmasking the trap of teacher neutrality.* New York, NY: Peter Lang.

Battiste, M. (2005). *State of Aboriginal learning.* Ottawa, ON: Canadian Council on Learning.

Battiste, M. (2009). Constitutional reconciliation of education for Aboriginal peoples. *Directions, 5*(1), 81–84.

Battiste, M., & Henderson, J. (Sa'ke'j) Y. (2000). *Protecting Indigenous knowledge and heritage: A global challenge.* Saskatoon, SK: Purich Publishing.

Battiste, M., & Semeganis, H. (2002). First thoughts on First Nations citizenship: Issues in education. In Y. Hébert (Ed.), *Citizenship in transformation in Canada* (pp. 93–111). University of Toronto Press.

Calliste, A., & Dei, G. J. S. (Eds.). (2000). *Anti-racist feminism: Critical race and gender studies.* Halifax, NS: Fernwood Press.

Canadian Council on Learning. (2007). *Redefining how success is measured in First Nations, Inuit and Métis learning: Report on learning in Canada 2007.* Retrieved from http://www.ccl-cca.ca/CCL/Reports/RedefiningSuccessInAboriginalLearning/index.html

Canadian Council on Learning. (2009). *The state of Aboriginal learning in Canada: A holistic approach to measuring success.* Retrieved from http://www.ccl-cca.ca/CCL/Reports/StateofAboriginalLearning.html

Canadian Heritage (2003). *Aboriginal languages initiative (ALI) evaluation.* Available from http://www.pch.gc.ca/pgm/em-cr/evaltn/2003/index-eng.cfm

Carnoy, M. (1974). *Education as cultural imperialism.* New York, NY: David McKay Company.

Council of Ministers of Education. (2008). *Learn Canada 2020: Joint declaration provincial and territorial ministers of education.* Retrieved from http://www.cmec.ca/Publications/Lists/Publications/Attachments/187/CMEC-2020-DECLARATION.en.pdf

Daes, E.-I. (1993). *Study on the Protection of the Cultural and Intellectual Property Rights of Indigenous Peoples.* United Nations document E/CN.4/Sub.2/1993/28. Available from http://www.un.org/en/documents/index.shtml

Daes, E.-I. (1999). *Cultural challenges in the decade of Indigenous peoples.* Unpublished paper presented at the UNESCO Conference on Education, Paris, France.

Dei, G. J. S., Hall, B. L., & Goldin Rosenberg, D. (Eds.). (2000). *Removing the margins: The challenges and possibilities of inclusive schooling.* Toronto, ON: Canadian Scholars' Press.

Duran, E., & Duran, B. (1995). *Native American postcolonial psychology.* State University of New York.

Ermine, W. (2007). The ethical space of engagement. *Indigenous Law Journal, 6*(1), 193–203.

Ermine, W., Sinclair, R., & Browne, M. (2005). *Kwayask itôtamowin: Indigenous research ethics.* Report of the Indigenous Peoples' Health Research Centre to the Institute of Aboriginal Peoples' Health and the Canadian Institutes of Health Research. Retrieved from http://www.iphrc.ca/Upload/IPHRC_ACADRE_Ethics_Report_final.pdf

Freire, P. (1973). *Pedagogy of the oppressed*. New York, NY: Seabury Press.

Governments of Alberta, British Columbia, Manitoba, Yukon Territory, Northwest Territories and Saskatchewan as represented by the respective ministers of education/learning. (2000). *Western Canadian protocol for collaboration in basic education: The common curriculum framework for aboriginal language and culture programs; Kindergarten to grade 12*. Retrieved from http://education.alberta.ca/media/929730/abor.pdf

Haida Nation v. British Columbia (Minster of Forests), Supreme Court Reports 511 (2004).

Hanson, J. D., & Yosifon, D. G. (2004). The situational character: A critical realist perspective on the human animal. *Georgetown Law Journal, 93*(1), 1–179.

Harper, Stephen. (2008). Prime Minister Harper offers full apology on behalf of Canadians for the Indian Residential Schools system. Retrieved from http://pm.gc.ca/eng/media.asp?id=2149

Henderson, J. (1995). Treaties and education. In M. Battiste & J. Barman (Eds.), *First Nations education in Canada: The circle unfolds* (pp. 245–261). University of British Columbia Press.

Henderson, J. [Sa'ke'j] Y. (2008). *Indigenous diplomacy and the rights of peoples: Achieving United Nations recognition*. Saskatoon, SK: Purich Publishing.

Indian and Northern Affairs Canada. (1997). Statement of reconciliation: Learning from the past. In *Gathering Strength – Canada's Aboriginal Action Plan*. Retrieved from http://www.ahf.ca/downloads/gathering-strength.pdf

Inuit Tapirit Kanatami. (2008). *Report on the Inuit Tapiriit Kanatami education initiative: Summary of ITK summit on Inuit education and background research*. Retrieved from http://www.itk.ca/sites/default/files/2008FinalEducationSummitReport.pdf

Minnich, E. (1990). *Transforming knowledge*. Philadelphia, PA: Temple University Press.

National Indian Brotherhood/Assembly of First Nations. (1972). *Indian control of Indian education*. Policy Paper presented to the Minister of Indian Affairs and Northern Development. Retrieved from http://www.afn.ca/calltoaction/Documents/ICOIE.pdf

Quinn, B. (1999). *Counterpoint: An analysis of Canadian native educational academic discourse* (Doctoral dissertation). University of Alberta, Edmonton.

R. v. Côté, Supreme Court Reports 139 (1996).

R. v. Powley, Supreme Court Reports 207 (2003).

R. v. Sappier - R. v. Gray, Supreme Court Reports 2, 686 (2006).

R. v. Van der Peet, Supreme Court Reports 2, 310 (1996).

Royal Commission on Aboriginal Peoples (1996). *Report of the Royal Commission on Aboriginal peoples*. Available from http://www.ainc-inac.gc.ca/ap/rrc-eng.asp

St. Denis, V. (2002). *Exploring the socio-cultural production of Aboriginal identities: Implications for education* (Doctoral dissertation). Stanford University, Palo Alto, CA.

Suzack, S., Huhndorf, S. M., Perreault, J., & Barman, J. (2010). *Indigenous women and feminism: Politics, activism, culture*. University of British Columbia Press.

United Nations. (2007). *Declaration on the Rights of Indigenous Peoples*. United Nations document A/61/L.67. Available from http://www.un.org/en/documents/index.shtml

12

Decolonizing Narrative Strands of our Eco-civic Responsibilities: Curriculum, Social Action, and Indigenous Communities

Nicholas Ng-A-Fook, University of Ottawa

The provincial curricula continue to disinherit Aboriginal languages and knowledge by ignoring their value. (Battiste, 1998, p. 17)

Far from being merely an inert and lifeless natural resource, rock is an acute manifestation of wakonda and the living source of all life. Rock is our grandparent. (Tinker, 2004, p. 122)

BLACK CROWS GAGGLING TOGETHER, "caw," "caw," "caw" . . . from an old solitary white pine tree. Standing a hundred feet high, it is one of the last of its kind. From its historic hollows, the wind ripples colonial narratives across the shores of, what is called by the Algonquin who continue travel or live by it, the *Kichi Sibi*. It is autumn here in the Ottawa valley. The foreshadowing of winter darkness casts its presence across the landscape. Standing on the south shores of the riverbank, hiding silently within a cluster of sumac trees, my two sons and I watch migratory geese glide above the treetops of Duck Island, navigating their bodies, wings expanded, feet still dangling, entering the water, and coming to a momentary pause, before proceeding to feed within the weeds on what is now called by settler colonies . . . the Ottawa River.

Meanwhile, my two sons play among the rocks strewn along the sandy shoreline reading the historical traces of what *wakonda* has left behind. We listen to the rocks, to their teachings about *Wisakedjàk*, a spirit being sent to teach the first Anishinàbeg of how the Creator made the universe, the stars, the sun, the moon, and all wonders of the Earth (McGregor, 2004). My sons and I learn through reading these historical teachings scarred into the bedrock of this ecological narrative valley that for the Anishinàbeg, "the Creator exists in all things, both living and non-living" (McGregor, 2004, p. 7). And, within the educational crevices of the non-living, of the rocks, in their hidden curriculum, we can reread colonial settler narratives of fur trade wars, deforestation, pollution of watersheds, and destruction of what was once an abundant ecosystem vibrant with a biodiversity that included thousands of beavers and white pine trees.

Our family now resides a few hundred meters from the Ottawa River. However due to the effluents released from lumber mills and sewage plants upstream, my sons and I cannot catch or eat the fish that inhabit the depths of its watery shallows. We can only imagine as we play among the rocks what once was, and what might still, or never be. This is a sad narrative imagining of the land . . . indeed. Nonetheless, this is the place we have chosen to inhabit as a settler family now living within the urban territorial boundaries of our colonial capital city. And sometimes during our walks along the river, we have been lucky enough to catch a glimpse of an elusive beaver. Yes, remnants of the destructive forces of colonization, like the ecological industriousness of beavers within these waters, are still in the process of recovering from the trade wars among the first Dutch, French, and British "multinational" corporations. Yet as Canadians we don't think of ourselves this way, "because the myth-makers of the late nineteenth century were busy writing out Canada's past and writing in the glory of the British Empire and British" (Ralston Saul, 2008, p. 12). Still, glimpses of such colonial remnants remind our children who play amongst the red earth and narrative white lies that the land remains the best teacher our settler families can ever have (Chambers, 2006; Deloria, 1997; Haig-Brown & Dannenmann, 2002).

Each summer, like many seasonal nomadic travelers before us, our family migrates from the shores of the Kichi Sibi south to visit our families who reside within the Nottawasaga watershed, where its tributaries flow out into Georgian Bay. At the height of the fur trade, the Algonquin retreated with their birch-bark canoes from the vast tributary system of the Kichi Sibi into the woodlands of the Ottawa Valley due to the ravages of our colonial trade wars and ensuing epidemics brought on by contact with Jesuit priests and the first European settlers.

McGregor (2004) tells us that during their absence,

> the Ottawa nation from Georgian Bay, a sub-group of the Anishinàbeg, . . . became the middlemen to the French on the St. Lawrence. The Ottawa were fortunate enough to be spared the ravages of war and epidemics. This put them in a position of power and between the years 1655 and 1680, they were the only visible nation of any consequential number on the Kichi Sibi. Someone, a "coureur de bois" or maybe a Jesuit priest, with no consideration of Anishinàbeg history, coined the name "rivière des outaouais" and the Kichi Sibi became the "river of the Ottawas," the Ottawa River. (p. 61)

"This historical slight," McGregor continues, "is perhaps more tragic than the wars and epidemics combined because it signifies not only an insult, but also the loss of a traditional identity" which eventually resulted in their being denied access to traditional territories in what would later be called Canada (p. 61). The ways in which we as curriculum theorists, educators, and teacher-candidates reread the Ontario curriculum often continue to narrate historical slights and insults that disinherit indigenous knowledge and language by ignoring the potential pedagogical value they might have within contemporary educational contexts to help us fulfil our eco-civic relational responsibilities to the land.

Mbembe (2001) calls such narratives of settler ignorance and disavowal a colonial curriculum of "zombification" (p. 104). How might we then awaken from our settler sleepwalking and, as Haig-Brown (2008) suggests, take indigenous thought seriously in our future curriculum theorizing and designs? Here indigenous thought, as Haig-Brown stresses, is founded first and foremost, "on a deep understanding that we all live in relation to land" (p. 12). Indigenous teachings can help us to recursively question the banality of our national narrative visions and respective limit-situations of living a postcolony curriculum (Donald, 2009a, 2009b; Mbembe, 2001; Stanley, 2009). Therefore, taking indigenous thought seriously as a form of curriculum theorizing asks us to consider intergenerational teachings of place. Nonetheless, weaving together the narrative "limit-situations" of such historical teachings remains a vexed and unsettling decolonizing curricular process. Yet here, I am referring to limit-situations not as the impassable boundaries where our possibilities end, but rather as the curricular boundaries where our pedagogical possibilities begin (Freire, 1970/1990). In response to such educational possibilities, this chapter provides examples of teacher-candidates taking up indigenous thought seriously through engaging social action curriculum projects with international and local indigenous communities as an aesthetic form of braiding our historical, present, and future narrative strands – what we might also now refer to as narrative métissageing (Donald, Hasebe-Ludt, & Chambers, 2002; Hasebe-Ludt, Chambers, & Leggo, 2009).

As curriculum scholars, pre-service teachers, settlers, and indigenous communities, we come from different walks of life, are at different stages of our educational careers, and work (or will work) at public institutions located across the diversified narrative landscape of Canada. Some of us are first-, second-, or third-generation (or later) immigrants to the different territories of this landscape we now call home; whereas others were born here and can trace their genealogical narrative histories to the indigenous peoples who inhabited, migrated, and traded with other communities across this land. As such, we strategically walk across the crevices of our national narrative bedrock, métissageing and lingering, intermingling our differing lived experiences, deconstructing and braiding our curricular texts to generate autobiographical anti-colonial stories of our migratory inhabitations of a Canadian landscape. "Carefully crafted autobiographical texts," Hasebe-Ludt et al. (2009) suggest, "open apertures for understanding and questioning the social conditions in which those experiences are embedded, and the particular languages, memories, stories, and places in which these experiences are located and created" (p. 35). Furthermore, at the opening of such apertures, métissageing provides a place for the creative interplay of life writing texts, "a contact zone where dialogue among multiple and mixed socio-cultural, racial, transnational, and gendered groups can occur" (Ibid.). During our social actions projects in class, we take up course readings that walk across physical and intellectual interdisciplinary territories of colonial narrative artifacts scarred into the very material fabric of the land, as an aesthetic form of métissageing.

Moreover, this curricular space, "where discourse includes action and where action is formed by discourse," provides a narrative praxis for connecting indigenous epistemologies to our understandings of the "vertical" and "horizontal" narrative dynamics of a contemporary Canadian topos (Donald, 2004, 2009a; Hasebe-Ludt et al., 2009, p. 37). Chambers (1999) and Pinar (2007) call such narrative dynamics the vertical and horizontal topographies of the particular places and regions we both live and work within. Verticality is the historical and intellectual narrative topography of a discipline, like curriculum studies; whereas horizontality refers to analyses of present circumstances, both in terms of internal intellectual trends as well as the external social and political milieus influencing the field of curriculum studies. Studying the verticality and horizontality of our interdisciplinary narrative locations, as Pinar makes clear, affords us opportunities to understand a series of (anti-colonial) scholarly moves both outside and within what Chambers (1999, 2003) calls the topos of contemporary Canadian Curriculum Studies.

In order to interrogate our disciplinary inhabitations of the diverse interdisciplinary territories, I invite teacher-candidates to strategically reread this Canadian Curriculum Studies landscape and its respective intellectual, physical, and cultural topographies from what Hingangaroa Smith (2000) calls a proactive, deconstructive, anti-colonial position that in turn challenges interpretations of the past and present formations of neo-colonization. "I do not think for an instant," Hingangaroa Smith (2000) stresses, "that we are in a postcolonial world" (p. 215). Or, that we have seen the last of neo-colonial formations. "Many of these new formations," as Hingangaroa Smith reminds us, "are insidious, and many of them have yet to be fully exposed" (p. 215). Nonetheless, through our narrative métissageing of such rereadings, we might also move beyond binary strategies and categories for deconstructing colonizer/colonized, resistance/passivity, hegemony/counter-hegemony, for example (Mbembe, 2001).

Instead, we might take up a social action curriculum and work autobiographically with the hyphen, and finesse the fallibility of the historical and emergent narrative relations between anti (-) colonial, and métissage(-)ing the postcolony (Butler & Spivak, 2007). Furthermore, our narrative navigations and assemblages might play with what Wah (2000) calls the contradictions, paradoxes, and theoretical assumptions active at the edges of the hyphen. "This constant pressure that the hyphen brings to bear against the master narratives of duality, multiculturalism, and apartheid," Wah tells us, "creates a volatile space that is inhabited by a wide range of voices" (p. 74). Here narrative métissageing in relation to curriculum theorizing involves the geopolitical, cultural, and psychic play with the "poetics of the 'trans,' methods of translation, transference, transposition, or poetics that speaks of the awareness and use of any means of occupying" the narrative locations of our eco-civic responsibilities (p. 90). At the crossroads of these narrative locations, we can then perform the aesthetic dynamics of métissageing the narrative character of our hyph-e-nated relocations within the vertical and horizontal topographies of Canadian Curriculum Studies. Before we do so, let us turn toward decolonizing an immigrant settler's doubly hyph-e-nated historical narrative curricular strands.

Decolonizing An Immigrant Settler's Curriculum

> We struggle to talk and listen to one another while never losing sight that no matter what the story, no matter how many generations of people of immigrant or diasporic ancestry have been here, beneath all our feet is land which has existed and does exist first of all in relation to Indigenous people. (Haig-Brown, 2009, p. 15)

> It is a call to develop an awareness of our own historical conditioned self-formative processes as well as an awareness of those socially unnecessary modes of domination that shape the larger society. (Giroux, 1980/1999, p. 16)

I am a foreign-born Canadian with dual citizenships (British and Canadian). However, my father's family traces their oral histories to the Hakka people. We are indigenous nomads originally from a northern part of what is now known as the Republic of China. Some of us were displaced due to natural disasters and civil wars. Consequently they migrated to the southern shores of Guangdong province and eventually overseas to places like Taiwan, Malaysia, Hong Kong, and Jamaica. In 1833, Britain passed the *Slavery Abolition Act*, which in turn necessitated the establishment of a new workforce for their colonies in the Caribbean. In 1853, the first three ships carrying 637 indentured labourers from China arrived at the ports of Guyana, who would all for the most part work as cane reapers on colonial plantations (Sue-A-Quan, 1999). Once Fook Ng (or John Cyril) finished fulfilling his indentured contract as a cane reaper, he opened up a small business as a shopkeeper.

During the 1960s, his grandson (my grandfather) received a grant from the government which was attempting to nationalize its industries as part of the process of decolonizing itself from British and American private corporate ownership. Consequently, my grandfather travelled to Chattanooga Tennessee to purchase an industrial ice-cream cone machine. He established a prosperous ice-cream cone factory, taxi business, and auto shop despite living within the economic and civic confines of Burnham's dictatorship. The economic capital produced from those businesses, the Chinese community's appropriation of the colonial English language, and let us not forget the violent usurpation of the local indigenous populations whether physical or psychological, directly or indirectly, afforded his children an opportunity to attend universities in the United Kingdom. As a result, my father studied medicine at Glasgow University where he eventually met my mother, who was a psychiatric nurse at that time.

My mother's life narrative can be traced back to Ireland, where her grandfather, a Kenny and a member of the original Irish Republican Army, fought against British colonization during the War of Independence, between 1919 and 1921. Her family, who were Celtic, and who historically spoke Gaelic, migrated both voluntarily and involuntarily from Ireland to Scotland, where they later survived the ration lines and German bombing raids of WWII. During the early 1970s my parents met and fell in love. Soon thereafter they married, even though miscegenation was, and to some extent still is, taboo. Although my brother and I were born in Glasgow, my mother was a British citizen, and my father was a qualified physician, the United Kingdom denied granting him the privileges procured under the title of British citizen.

In 1975 our family landed as immigrants here in Canada. The narrative setting that would play a major role in my self-formation as a child and adolescent before leaving for university was Kapuskasing, a small rural logging town in Northern Ontario. Even though the name Kapuskasing is Anishinàbeg (meaning "bend in the river"), the local indigenous communities, their historical narratives, and their accounts of post-colonial contact were absent from the school textbooks we studied in class. Nonetheless, original inhabitants' ancestral relationships with the land were ever-present in Kapuskasing, in the curriculum of conquests taught at school, and the derogatory conversations of ignorance that took place outside.

This narrative landscape of settler disinheritance – physical, geopolitical, architectural, institutional, historical, psychic, etc. – represents the banality of colonial inscriptions hidden in plain sight within the bedrock of our publicly instituted provincial curriculum. However the banality of colonial power, Mbembe (2001) writes, "does not simply refer to the way bureaucratic formalities or arbitrary rules, implicit or explicit, have been multiplied," nor are they simply concerned with a colonial curriculum that has become routine (p. 102). Instead, the curriculum of banality refers to the colonial aesthetics of vulgarity located in "non-official" sites "intrinsic to all systems of domination and to the means by which those systems are confirmed or deconstructed" (p. 102). Here in Canada, we are surrounded "by artefacts of the histories of colonialism, but these artefacts are rendered invisible, common sense, and a part of taken-for-granted discursive formations, that in some instances are quite literally set in concrete" (Stanley, 2009, p. 158). Moreover, the historical discursive formations that inscribe themselves both physically and psychically into the concrete narrative character of our Canadian narration of settler landscapes work in turn to reproduce the socio-cultural formations of what Mbembe calls a curriculum of the "postcolony."

A curriculum of the "postcolony" identifies a given historical trajectory of societies recently emerging, as Mbembe (2001) maintains,

> from the experience of colonization and violence which the colonial relationship involves. To be sure, the postcolony is chaotically pluralistic; it has nonetheless an internal coherence. It is a specific system of signs, a particular way of fabricating simulacra or re-forming stereotypes. . . . The postcolony is characterized by a distinctive style of improvisation, by a tendency to excess and lack of proportion, as well as by

distinctive ways identities are multiplied, transformed, and put into circulation. (p. 102)

Consequently, settlers of what is now known as Canada, as Stanley (2009) stresses, "remade the cultural landscape of the territory imposing their disciplinary practices and ways of knowing on the territory and its inhabitants, effectively steamrolling the systems and ways of cultural representation and the meanings already in place" (p. 158). And as an immigrant child it is within this narrative vision of national banality where I first learned how to become a Canadian citizen.

Not until being asked to decolonize narratives of my settler relationship to the land during my graduate studies, and more importantly to the original people who live on it, did I start to question how I narrated the "limit-situations" of my "successful" integration into the dominant settler culture and its respective capitalistic economy (Ng-A-Fook, 2001, 2007; Haig-Brown, 2009). Moreover, I did not question the ways in which such educational assimilation works as a process of narrative zombification for forgetting our inheritance of a colonial past. How might we then begin to advocate for a curriculum of decolonization that asks teachers and students to remember colonialism's narratives of forgetting?

Such acts of colonial remembrance, like our historical implications with residential schooling and appropriation of indigenous territories, entail a pedagogical openness to the possibilities of experiencing a certain amount of epistemic violence with students in the classroom. Despite the pedagogical risks, I remain committed to living a curriculum that redresses our historical relationships with indigenous communities. Clearly there is no pedagogical recipe for preparing teacher-candidates to engage their psychic encounters with the violence of colonialism's histories as learners. However, I suggest that engaging a social action curriculum as an aesthetic form of narrative métissageing provides a generative opportunity for students and indigenous communities to work through their curricular and pedagogical encounters with the remnants of colonialism's historic violence. Let us turn toward such narrative action.

Engaging A Social Action Curriculum with Indigenous Communities

> Global education is a tapestry in the making: it weaves together separate threads, such as economy, environment, society and technology, by which we currently makes sense of the world. (Pike, 2000, p. 218)

> We say that our education must respect our values and customs, yet we encourage competition rather than cooperation, the individual over the group, saving instead of sharing. We are uncomfortable when too much time is spent outdoors learning from the land, because we have been conditioned to believe that education occurs in the classroom. (Kirkness, 1998, p. 13)

In 2008 the Faculty of Education at the University of Ottawa incepted its first global education cohort. Its initial organizational inception emerged out of a larger extracurricular program called *Developing A Global Perspective for Educators*. Through their Global Classroom Initiative, the Canadian International Development Agency (CIDA) has funded our program for the past eight years. The primary curricular and pedagogical goal of this unique program is to establish collaborative partnerships with local schools, community leaders, and NGOs. In turn, our curriculum is designed toward encouraging the development of critically reflective teaching professionals who personify an ethic of caring, knowledge, and commitment to their eco-civic responsibilities through public education.

The primary/junior teacher-candidates who are accepted into this global cohort seek to understand, among other things, how they can imagine educational issues in terms of international development, social justice, peace education, and environmental sustainabil-

ity, as well as how to articulate their eco-civic responsibilities in relation to narrative visions of the existing Ontario curricula (Mclean,
Cook, & Crowe, 2006; Ng-A-Fook, 2010). Moreover, these students
are invited to participate in various social action projects that move
beyond the "prorogation" of armchair activism (Westheimer, 2005).
And although we work to weave these various narrative visions in
terms of international development and environmental sustainability, for example, we often fail to consider how we might do so as a curriculum of decolonization with local indigenous communities.

Nonetheless, our partnership with the Community Service
Learning program at the University of Ottawa has provided an
invaluable opportunity to design, advocate, and model a social action
curriculum within the courses I teach at our Faculty of Education.
Students who participate in this larger university program are
required to complete thirty hours of community service learning.
Upon completion students receive a co-curricular certificate from
the university. For the past three years I have attempted to incorporate a social action project component into the curriculum of the
courses I teach within the Bachelor of Education program. Much like
William Heard Kilpatrick's "Project method" (1918), I ask students
to create social action projects that they can implement wholeheartedly within the local, national, and international communities outside the institutional walls of our university.

In 2007, as part of a Schooling and Society course, I travelled with
Bachelor of Education students to Raceland, Louisiana in two mini-
vans to work with the Houma people who continue to suffer the devastating effects of recurring hurricanes like Katrina and the recent
Gulf of Mexico oil spill. As part of this international community service learning project, students worked with elders at a New Orleans
Jazz Festival non-profit food booth, attended eco-justice workshops
with indigenous community activists, and created podcasts to share
their stories. During these workshops, students learned to take
indigenous thought seriously in relation to their understanding of
this southern territory – no monolithic place to be sure.

Currently, the United States government refuses to act on the United Houma Nation's forty-year petition for federal recognition. Such colonial recognition by the settler government would afford the Houma rights to claim land that has been historically appropriated by land agents and large oil companies. Consequently, the United Houma Nation do not receive the federal funding promised through treaties negotiated prior to the Louisiana Purchase, which would provide much-needed social services. Therefore the funds raised by their "non-profit" booth are put toward financing the administrative costs of running their government building (property taxes, electricity, water, rent, maintenance, etc.). Consider the following student's narrative strand about our community service-learning project with the Houma in Louisiana:

> In working with the Houma community, narratives emerged that have been formerly suppressed, such as their contentious relationships with the Louisiana schooling system and historical struggle to maintain access to their traditional lands. As these accounts are negated from American history texts, verbal pronouncements serve as a primary source of legitimization, validated through our reciprocal sharing of stories. As a result, experiential learning transpired through a participatory engagement with their crucial community services such as the operation of the food booth at the Jazz festival, which in turn funds part of the Houma government, its elders' and children's yearly means of sustaining their social services. As an education student, community service-learning has exposed me to a potent pedagogical tool. As a future teacher, I now hope to open our classroom learning in a way that is significant to students' lived experiences. Working within future multicultural classrooms, this international community service-learning project has broadened my epistemological worldview, and thus helped me to disrupt previously

ingrained curricular and pedagogical assumptions, both within socio-cultural and international contexts.

Our trip to the former Golden Meadow Settlement School was a historic moment both for Houma elders and these future Canadian teachers. For the first time in Houma history, teachers travelled down to what is now the UHN Tribal Centre to learn rather than teach. For most students it was their first crossing of international and cultural borders to learn from an indigenous community. Consider another student's narrative strand:

> After meeting with the elders at the community center, a small group of us took a walk outside to the adjacent cemetery. Lucas accompanied us. Lucas was a young Houma man in his early twenties. We first met Lucas in the community center where he shared a demonstration of men's traditional straight dancing and answered all of our questions.
>
> As we were guided through the cemetery and Professor Ng-A-Fook shared some of the history of the Houma, we navigated around large red-ant nests and some other strange looking piles of mud. When asked about the piles of mud, Lucas told us that a small crab called a Tootaloo created them. For the same reasons the Houma bury the dead above the surface, the Tootaloo digs into the dirt to reach the water a couple of feet under the ground. It was in the water that the Tootaloo would nest.
>
> Later in the afternoon, everyone walked down the road to Whitney's house. Whitney's father was a "traiteur," what we now call a doctor. Once there he gave us a tour of his gardens and taught us about his traditional ecological knowledge. Again we navigated around red-ant nests and these strange-looking little towers of mud. I then asked Whitney about the mounds. Adding to Lucas's story, he explained that it was instead a special kind of crawfish that made them. "Different in

size and color to other crawfish," Whitney told us, "it digs into the mud to access the water and lay its eggs until they hatch, or the water returns." "It does so," he continued, "by bringing to the surface one grain of mud at a time."

Our conversations with the Houma elders often led to their largest concern, which is their ongoing petition for federal recognition. Nonetheless, like these special crawfish, the Houma people continue to work one day at a time toward federal recognition. In turn, they have moved us all individually to perhaps be part of this daily civic movement. During this trip I met a group of people so hospitable, caring, and eager to share their stories. As a result, I believe the greatest community service we can offer is sharing their story with others.

As a curriculum theory professor, I often ask students to engage with the curricular processes of imagining a different world, a hopeful world, a world in which, as future teachers, they have the potential to make a difference through the power of sharing stories. Our trip to Louisiana afforded students a unique opportunity to conduct a social action curriculum first hand with an international indigenous community, and thus develop a global perspective relevant to the United Houma Nation government and their rural Louisiana communities.

Since 2008, many of the students enrolled within the global cohort continue to take up the pedagogical call for action today in order to shape responsible eco-citizens of tomorrow. In 2009, these students designed various community service-learning social action projects, which in turn continued to address local, national, and international concerns. For example, committed groups of students raised funds for the Guatemalan Stove Project, Pennies for Pencils, and clothing and food for homeless people in Ottawa. Other students developed educational resources that provided curricular opportunities for teachers and students to question how we are implicated in the root causes of local and global social and economic inequities due to the continued enclosure of what is often referred to as the Commons.

In *An Ecological and Postcolonial Study of Literature* (2007), Marzec maintains, "two historical developments parallel the coming to presence of the English novel: the rise of the British Empire, and the land-reformation phenomenon known as the Enclosure Movement" (p. 1). And while many still "associate the commons with a public space and with the enclosure movement in England that followed the introduction of new crops, farm technologies, and the beginning of the Industrial Revolution," as Bowers (2010b) reminds us, "the cultural and environmental commons still exist around the world – including in rural and urban areas of the West" ("The cultural and environmental commons", para. 3). Here Bowers (2010a) situates cultural commons as "the local traditions of knowledge and patterns of mutual support that enabled communities to be relatively self-sufficient . . . which are, in turn, dependent upon the environmental commons" (p. 88). Such commons represent, as Bowers makes clear, diverse cultures and bioregions, which have yet to be monetized and assimilated into corporatized industrialized capitalistic markets. And yet the continued exploitation of both cultural and environmental commons can often only be heard from the cawing of a solitary black crow sitting on the branches of an old dying white pine tree.

That year-one group of primary/junior teacher-candidates perhaps heard such colonial cawing and created a resource document called *Where do you get your Coltan?* In this document, the students tell us that the existence and ecological impact of Coltan is relatively unknown to the average person living outside of the Democratic Republic of Congo (DRC). Nonetheless, the choices we make here in Canada, these socially concerned students remind us, have global impacts on local indigenous communities in terms of their access and sovereign utilities of the commons. These students, therefore, call us to make eco-civic informed decisions about the narrative visions we choose to teach. Yet they warn us that we cannot do this without access to information. "As teachers, we may wish to encourage our students to think critically about global issues, but we cannot do this without information. As students we may wish to be agents of positive change; but we cannot do this without information" (Bellissimo et al., 2009, p. 2). In response to the narrative absence of information within the elementary public school system, these students designed and articulated their eco-civic responsibilities across the transdisciplinary terrains of our provincial curricula.

Students created lessons that laboured to politically deconstruct the ecological impact of our consumption practices and the respective social, cultural, and economic complexities entailed with mining for Coltan (Colombo-tantalite) in the Democratic Republic of Congo. When refined, this mineral is then referred to by many NGOs as blood tantalum, utilized in the production of capacitors for computers, cell phones, and various other electronics. The students' lessons examined the violent impacts of exploiting and consuming this resource in relation to the displacement and systematic genocide of indigenous communities, the impact of deforestation on eastern lowland gorilla habitats, and the recruitment of child soldiers.

During the winter term of 2010, a few students from the global cohort asked if we could collaborate on a social action project with a local indigenous community. This cohort of students wanted to take on an indigenous community service-learning project wholeheartedly. However, unlike the prior project with students and the United Houma Nation, I had yet to develop any kind of collaborative partnership with a local indigenous community (Ng-A-Fook, 2007). Prior to taking students down to work with the United Houma Nation, I had lived within and worked for over fours years with their community. So let us rewind to four years earlier.

It is the fall of 2006. I had developed an initial contact with the Kitigan Zibi, a local Algonquin First Nation community who had been displaced by the processes of settler colonization to their present location. Their community is located ninety minutes north of our university, across the provincial border in Quebec near the township limits of Maniwaki. As a burgeoning tenure-track professor, I wanted to continue the kind of educational research I did as a doctoral student with the United Houma Nation in Louisiana. Consequently, I attempted to establish a collaborative research partnership with the head of Kitigan Zibi's Department of Education.

I initially met with her to discuss some potential collaborative projects we could work on together. She and some elders were interested in establishing a teaching and learning research centre to develop curriculum for their Algonquin language program. Elders who fluently speak the language teach within the program. She expressed that due to experiences in residential schooling, some elders taught their language program through rote learning. Consequently, the director was interested in collaborating with elders to develop indigenous-centered pedagogical and curricular strategies to teach their children enrolled in the language program. Although I was keen to work with her and the community, I was unable to secure funding at the time to support this potential collaborative curriculum development project. Nor did I feel that I could commit as a new professor the necessary amount of time needed to fulfill my participatory responsibilities to the proposed project. Fast-forward to four years later.

In November 2009, after the students had approached me, I applied for a small community service-learning grant to help facilitate our social action project with a local indigenous community. Once we were awarded the grant that December, I contacted the director and asked her if she was still interested in working on a curriculum development project. She said yes. In turn, I had to revise my Schooling and Society syllabus in terms of the chosen readings in order to support the scope and sequence of our proposed community service-learning social action project. Both the director and the principal of Kitigan Zibi Kikinamadinan elementary and secondary school invited the global cohort to work on an Algonquin language curriculum development project. Students made three field trips to the Kitigan Zibi community in order to work with the director of education, the school principal, and elders. In turn, our Bachelor of Education students collaborated with elders to develop a place-based, culturally responsive curriculum that took up social, political, cultural, and historical issues that remain important to the larger Kitigan Zibi community.

Prior to making our first field trip to the Kitigan Zibi community, students engaged readings on how we might develop a global perspective as critical reflective educators (like Freire, 1970/1990; Pike, 2000; Westheimer, 2005). We viewed documentary films like *Refugee of the Deep Blue Planet*, where teachers and students can deconstruct our current global and local consumptive relationships with the earth and its respective natural resources. The film examines the ecological impacts of rising sea levels on the Maldives, planting green deserts in Brazil, and drilling sour gas wells in Alberta. We attempted to understand these texts' curricular complexities and how our pedagogical consumptions of toilet paper, oil, and natural gas work to displace indigenous communities both here and abroad. We challenged ourselves to act against our current consumptive practices, practices that facilitate multinational corporations and their respective colonial curriculum to enclose and expropriate the biodiversity of traditional indigenous territories.

We studied the historical colonial politics of residential schooling from an indigenous perspective (Battiste, 1998; Kirkness, 1998). We utilized such readings as a methodological prism to discuss the various historical narratives put forth in the film *Where the Spirit Lives*. Moreover, we discussed the violent colonial legacy of residential schooling (Brody, 2000; Johnston, 1988). During the week leading up to our first field trip to the Kitigan Zibi community we studied research about non-indigenous teachers working with indigenous communities as well as the mediated narrative representations of indigenous identities through popular culture (King, 2003; Taylor, 1995). I also made *Since Time Immemorial "Our Story"*, a history textbook written and published by the Kitigan Zibi, a required reading. As part of our course requirements I also asked students to develop a sixty-minute lesson plan that addressed a specific chapter of the book.

Taking indigenous thought seriously through such articles, text-books, and pedagogical activities challenged many students to question the limit-situations of their narrative visions of indigenous communities living within (or at the borders of) the territorial boundaries of what we call now Canada. For many, such readings evoked a certain amount of epistemic violence, incidents of white guilt, and/or narrative performances of missionary rescue fantasies. Whereas some students expressed that readings like Taylor's (1995) discouraged them from making future plans to teach for a year or two in northern indigenous communities. Regardless of the pedagogical effects of such readings, my hope was that students would be prepared to work respectfully with the elders of the Kitigan Zibi community. Consider the following student's narrative strand:

I remember when I was in grade 6 (which isn't all that long ago) we did an entire language unit on Lynne Banks' novel "Indian In The Cupboard". There is one scene in the book (and subsequent movie) that has stuck with me over the years. Little Bull (the plastic Indian toy that comes to life) comes screaming out of the cupboard on his horse firing arrows dressed in full ceremony wear. Up until quite recently in my life, this was what I knew about Aboriginal culture in North America. Together we need to "cut the shackles" (Kirkness, 1998) of the past and step forward so that future students can "come to see the world not as a static reality, but as a reality in process" (Freire, 1970/1990). Aboriginal culture is very alive in Canada, and we need their help to bring it into our classrooms.

As teachers, together we need to figure out how to "decolonize Canadian education" (Battiste, 1998) and really start to take steps in the right direction. While beginning my journey to decolonize my future classroom, I was lucky enough to learn about the education system of the Kitigan Zibi people. They have been able to start to take steps in the right direction and write their own textbooks, as they realized that "it was time for the Algonquin to share their story with [us]" (McGregor, 2004). We need to follow in their footsteps to ensure that "Canadian curriculum theorists can [begin to] write from this place, of this place, and for this place" (Chambers, 2006). The lack of Native content in the Ontario curriculum is evident and we must work together to change this.

I ask, as my Eurocentric ancestors did so long ago, that you help us. Work with us to find the Native artists and writers that speak as Stephen McGregor does, telling the past through your eyes. Allow us to explore the conflicts and issues from both sides and ensure that the raw history of this great country doesn't get lost in the melting pot of Eurocentric textbooks.

During our first trip to the Kitigan Zibi community cultural centre, Anita Tenasco provided an orientation to the educational infrastructure of the community and provided some cultural background information about the students who attend the Kitigan Zibi Kikinamadinan elementary and secondary schools. The principal, Shirley Whiteduck, also spoke to the global cohort about the various school programs at the school. While eating moose steak pie during lunch, students had an opportunity to discuss their questions about Kitigan Zibi history with Stephen McGregor, who authored *Since Time Immemorial "Our Stories."*

Before heading back to Ottawa, the director expressed that she would send me an email outlining a potential social action project we could work on together. In that e-mail, she asked us if we could create lesson plans that utilized emergent technologies like Smart Boards, writing activities, art activities, games or quizzes, and take up specific Algonquin thematic curricular strands like hunting, dancing, art, government, spirituality, etc. Prior to our second fieldtrip, students organized themselves into small groups and tentatively developed thirty-minute workshops that they could facilitate for students at Kitigan Zibi Kikinamadinan elementary school.

We were then invited to present our proposed workshops to elders at the Kitigan Zibi community centre during our second field trip. Prior to beginning our presentations, an elder, the appointed Sacred Fire Keeper, conducted the opening prayer and smudge ceremony in order to welcome us and bless our work that day. After listening to students' presentations, elders were invited to join different groups to counsel students on how they could improve their proposed workshops. Elders advised students how they might further incorporate an Algonquin conceptual framework in terms of the cultural and narrative dynamics of their proposed teaching and learning activities. Consider the following student's narrative strand:

On our second visit to the Kitigan Zibi reserve, we were introduced to some of the elders in the community. Before we could discuss what was on the agenda, we participated in a circle spiritual cleansing ceremony. The tribal Elder began the procession by lighting a smudging bowl filled with herbs. The smell of burning sage permeated the room. The spiritual leader used a feather to waft the fragrant sage towards us as we received the billow of smoke. We continued in our circle formation and began to share our workshop ideas with the elders of the community.

The old adage of age implying wisdom has been bandied around for ages. However, in First Nations culture, age does not merely imply wisdom. Kirkness (1998) espouses the importance of elders, "Elders possess the wisdom and knowledge that must be the focus of all our learning. It is through them that we can understand our unique relationship to the Creator, our connection with nature, the order of things and the values that enhance the identity of our people" (p. 13). In speaking with our Elder, I was comforted by her calm and pleasant demeanor. We had asked her opinion regarding our sacred spaces project and her take on how children and youth connect with nature. She expressed that modernity has taken its toll and Algonquin youth are more interested in video games and hockey rather than exploring the landscape. She waxed nostalgic of camping trips and canoe rides when her children were young in age. She talked about pockets of rivers that were the most turbulent, specific moose sightings and other anecdotal information of years before her time.

Listening to her speak, I became sidetracked from the initial task of lesson plan feedback. Her stories were interesting and candid accounts of life in and around the reserve. It is her candid accounts and experiences with nature that can give me a glimpse of her historical journey, which is steeped in oral tradition. Deloria (1997) describes it as the "distilled memory of the People describing the events they had experienced and the lands that they live in" (p. 36). This knowledge does not present itself by way of textbooks and academic journals. This knowledge, this lived experience, is obtained by speaking to an elder.

Working collaboratively with elders provided a unique opportunity, as this student expressed, to gain glimpses into historical narrative journeys that remain absent from textbooks and academic journals. Moreover, this specific community service-learning social action project afforded students a pedagogical opportunity to experience an indigenous conceptual framework that informs elders' teachings.

We then returned to the University of Ottawa and attempted to incorporate the elders' teachings to improve their workshops before returning to implement them at Kitigan Zibi Kikinamadinan elementary school. As a whole, the global cohort developed the following six workshops: Animal Tracking, Writing Monsters, Birch Bark Canoe Making, Hot Seat and Algonquin Jeopardy, Talking Circle, and Sacred Places. The students implemented these workshops as part of a rotating schedule with students from Grades 3, 4, 5, and 6. The workshops had to be focused enough to be completed during a sixty-minute period, but flexible enough to work with different grade levels over that period of time. Although students worked hard in terms of integrating Algonquin thematic strands, they also were able to integrate themes related to developing a global perspective such as, but not limited to, peace education, international development, and environmental sustainability. Consider this final student narrative:

> The point of the workshop was to teach kids how to track an animal, or how to discover which animal had been lurking in your backyard, by looking at their scat. Although this activity does fit into the Ontario Curriculum for Science and Technology (2007, p. 86), the purpose was not to teach the curriculum defined by the government, but to allow the students to experience a knowledge of the land, a knowledge once used daily by their ancestors for survival (Chambers, 1999, p. 141–142). The original Aboriginal education did not consist of reading or writing a printed language or figuring out obscure mathematical problems, but "was geared to knowledge necessary for daily living" (Kirkness, 1998, p. 10).
>
> Traditionally, education served as a preparation for everyday life. Now, the majority of education seems to aim for the highest point, or to prepare students for the highest sense of achievement according to society's ranking of success, and often forgets the necessary lessons needed for everyday living. In fact, the complaint I hear most from students, the complaint I made as an elementary student, is "Why do I have to learn this? How is this going to help me?" And in some way, this complaint is valid. Through this workshop, we attempted to bridge this gap, teaching through experimentation a knowledge which could be put to use on a regular basis.

The Aboriginal people have a long and unfortunate history of a loss of culture and traditional education. For the most part, this problem stemmed from a misunderstanding of the Aboriginal culture by the European communities. They assumed Aboriginals were unintelligent since they did not possess the same knowledge as they did. They failed to recognize that the "hunter-gatherers [of the Aboriginal communities] read and write. They did not have the alphabetical or pictorial scripts that agricultural societies developed in relatively recent times. They did not use letters to represent sounds. But all hunter-gatherers read tracks; everyone who lives by hunting or gathering must notice, read, interpret, and share the meanings of signs in the natural world. . . . [This] is also a form of literacy" (Brody, 2000, p. 183). In this sense, the study of scat can be seen as literacy. Just like words, scat can tell you something, or direct you to something. It can tell you the animal's eating habits, its identity, its proximity to you, and can direct you towards or away from the animal. Scat, although often smelly and full of germs, is educational.

During our final fieldtrip, the global cohort was able to successfully live their curriculum-as-planned with Kitigan Zibi Kikinamadinan elementary students and, more importantly, learn to address their limit-situations in terms of their narrative curricular visions of indigenous communities. Moreover, some students were able to engage the dynamic recursive processes of developing a curriculum of decolonization as an aesthetic form of narrative métissageing to retrace the colonial remnants of the post colony.

Whether it is in Curriculum Design and Evaluation or Schooling and Society courses, I continue to ask teacher-candidates to engage with the limitless possibilities of trying to develop social action projects that embrace civic public action and connect to the local, national, and international needs of various communities, and to listen for black crows cawing from an old pine tree. I invite students to experience the world outside schools, to play among the rocks, and work toward developing global and local perspectives on various social justice issues, such as poverty, environmental sustainability, and human rights within the contexts of métissageing their narrative strands of engaging a community service-learning social action project collaboratively with both local and international indigenous communities.

References

Battiste, M. (1998). Enabling the autumn seed: Toward a decolonized approach to Aboriginal knowledge, language, and education. *Canadian Journal of Native Education, 22*(1), 16–24.

Bellissimo, A., Bender, S., Coghlin, D., Dao, K., Pretty, O., & Trick, A. (2008). *Where do you get your Coltan?* Retrieved from http://www.developingaglobalperspective.ca/wp-content/assets/thematicpackages/coltan_resource_booklet.pdf

Bowers, C. (2010a). *Essays on ecologically sustainable educational reforms.* Retrieved from http://www.cabowers.net/pdf/Book-Essays-Eco.pdf

Bowers, C. (2010b). Understanding the connections between double bind thinking and the ecological crises: Implications for educational reform. *Journal of the American Association for the Advancement of Curriculum Studies, 6*(1). Retrieved from http://www2.uwstout.edu/content/jaaacs/vol6/Bowers.pdf

Brody, H. (2000). *The other side of Eden.* New York, NY: North Point Press.

Butler, J., & Spivak, G. C. (2007). *Who sings the nation-state?* New York, NY: Seagull Press.

Chambers, C. (1999). A Topography for Canadian Curriculum Theory. *Canadian Journal of Education, 24*(2), 137–150.

Chambers, C. (2003). "As Canadian as Possible Under the Circumstances": A View Of Contemporary Curriculum Discourses in Canada. In W. F. Pinar (Ed.), *International*

Handbook of Curriculum Research (pp. 221–252). Mahwah, NJ: Lawrence Erlbaum.

Chambers, C. (2006). "The land is the best teacher I ever had": Places as pedagogy for precarious times. *Journal of Curriculum Theorizing, 22*(3), 27–37.

Deloria, V. Jr. (1997). *Read Earth white lies*. Golden, CO: Fulcrum Publishing.

Donald, D. (2004). Edmonton pentimento: Rereading history in the case of the Papaschase Cree. *Journal of the Canadian Association for Curriculum Studies, 2*(1), 21–54.

Donald, D. (2009a). The curricular problem of indigenousness: Colonial frontier logics, teacher resistances, and the acknowledgement of ethical space. In J. Nhachewsky & I. Johnston (Eds.), *Beyond "presentism": Re-imagining the historical, personal, and social places of curriculum* (pp. 23–39). Rotterdam, Netherlands: Sense Publishers.

Donald, D. (2009b). Forts, curriculum, and indigenous métissage: Imagining decolonization of Aboriginal-Canadian relations in educational contexts. *First Nations Perspectives: The Journal of the Manitoba First Nations Education Resource Centre, 2*(1), 1–24.

Donald, D., Hasebe-Ludt, E., & Chambers, C. (2002). Creating a curriculum of métissage. *Educational Insights, 7*(2). Available from http://www.educationalinsights.ca/

Freire, P. (1970/1990). *Pedagogy of the oppressed*. New York, NY: Continuum Press.

Giroux, H. (1980/1999). Dialectics and the development of curriculum theory. In William F. Pinar (Ed.), *Contemporary curriculum discourses: Twenty years of JCT* (pp. 7–23). New York, NY: Peter Lang.

Haig-Brown, C. (2008). Taking indigenous thought seriously: A rant on globalization with some cautionary notes. *Journal of the Canadian Association of Curriculum Studies, 6*(2), 8–24.

Haig-Brown, C. (2009). Decolonizing diaspora: Whose traditional land are we on? *Cultural and Pedagogical Inquiry, 1*(1), 4–21.

Haig-Brown, C., & Dannenmann, K. (2002). A pedagogy of the land: Dreams of respectful relations. *McGill Journal of Education, 3*(3), 452–468.

Hasebe-Ludt, E., Chambers, C., & Leggo, C. (2009). *Life writing and literary métissage as an ethos for our times.* New York, NY: Peter Lang.

Hingangaroa Smith, G. (2000). Protecting and respecting indigenous knowledge. In Marie Battiste (Ed.), *Reclaiming indigenous voice and vision* (pp. 209–224). Vancouver: University of British Columbia Press.

Johnston, B. (1988). *Indian school days.* Toronto, ON: Key Porter Books.

Kilpatrick, W. H. (1918). The project method. *Teachers College Record, 19,* 319–334.

King, T. (2003). *The truth about stories.* Toronto, ON: House of Anansi Press.

Kirkness, V. J. (1998). Our peoples' education: Cut the shackles; cut the crap; cut the mustard. *Canadian Journal of Education, 2*(1), 10–15.

Marzec, R. (2007). *An ecological and postcolonial study of literature.* New York, NY: Palgrave Macmillan.

Mbembe, A. (2001). *On the postcolony.* Los Angeles: University of California Press.

McGregor, S. (2004). *Since time immemorial: "Our story".* Maniwaki, QC: Anishinabe Printing.

McLean, L., Cook, S., & Crowe, T. (2006). Educating the next generation of global citizens through teacher education one teacher at a time. *Canadian Social Studies, 40*(1). Retrieved from http://www.quasar.ualberta.ca/css

Ng-A-Fook, N. (2001). *Beginning re-search: Towards an understanding of vulnerable education* (Master's thesis). York University, Toronto, ON.

Ng-A-Fook, N. (2007). *An indigenous curriculum of place: The United Houma Nation's contentious relationship with Louisiana's educational institutions.* New York, NY: Peter Lang.

Ng-A-Fook, N. (2010). Another bell ringing in the empty sky: Greenwashing, curriculum, and ecojustice. *Journal of the Canadian Association for Curriculum Studies*, 8(1), 41–67.

Ontario Ministry of Education. (2007). *Science and Technology Grades 1–8. Toronto.* Queen's Printer for Ontario.

Pike, G. (2000). A tapestry in the making: The stands of global education. In Tara Goldstein & David Selby (Eds.), *Weaving connections: Educating for peace, social and environmental Justice* (pp. 218–241). Toronto, ON: Sumach Press.

Pinar, W. (2007). *Intellectual advancement through disciplinarity: Verticality and horizontality in curriculum studies.* Rotterdam, Netherlands: Sense Publishers.

Ralston Saul, J. (2008). *A fair country: Telling truths about Canada.* Toronto, ON: Viking Canada.

Stanley, T. (2009). The banality of colonialism: Encountering artifacts of genocide and white supremacy in Vancouver today. In Shirley Steinberg (Ed.), *Diversity and multiculturalism* (pp. 143–159). New York, NY: Peter Lang.

Sue-A-Quan, T. (1999). *Cane reapers: Chinese indentured immigrants in Guyana.* Vancouver, BC: Riftswood Publishing.

Taylor, J. (1995/1999). Non-native teachers teaching in native communities. In Marie Battiste (Ed.), *First nations education: The circle unfolds* (pp. 224–242). University of British Columbia Press.

Tinker, G. (2004). The stones shall cry out: Consciousness, rocks, and Indians. *Wicazo Sa Review*, 19(2), 105–125.

Wah, F. (2000). *Faking it: Poetics and hybridity.* Edmonton, AB: NeWest Press.

Westheimer, J. (2005). Schooling for democracy. Our Schools, Our Selves: *The Canadian Centre for Policy Alternatives*, 15(1), 25–39.

Birding Lessons and the Teachings of Cicadas

13

David W. Jardine, University of Calgary

Reproduced with permission from *Canadian Journal of Environmental Education*, 3 (1998): 92–99.

I WENT BIRDING LAST SUMMER with some old friends through the Southern Ontario summer forests where I was raised, crackling full of songbirds and head-high ferns and steamy heat. It was, as always, a great relief to return to this place from the clear airs of Alberta where I have lived for eleven years – academic, Faculty of Education, curriculum courses, practicum supervision in the often stuffy, unearthly confines of some elementary school.

As with every time I return here, it was once again a surprise to find how familiar it was, and to find how deeply I experience my new home in the foothills of the Rocky Mountains through these deeply buried bodily templates of my raising. It is as if I bear a sort of hidden ecological memory of the sensuous spells (Abram, 1996) of the place on Earth into which I was born. How things smell, the racket of leaves turning on their stems, how my breath pulls this humid air, how birds' songs combine, the familiar directions of sudden thundery winds, the rising insect drills of cicada tree buzzes that I remember so intimately, so immediately, that when they sound, it feels as if this place itself has remembered what I have forgotten, as if my own memory, my own raising, some of my own life, is stored up in these trees for safe keeping.

Cicadas become archaic storytellers, telling me, like all good storytellers, of the life I'd forgotten I'd lived, of deep, fleshy, familial relations that worm their way out of my belly and breath into these soils, these smells, this air. And I'm left shocked that they know so much, that they remember so well, and that they can be so perfectly articulate.

I became enamoured, during our walk, with listening to my friends' conversations about the different birds that they had been spotting. They spoke of their previous ventures here, of what had been gathered and lost, of moments of surprise and relief, of expectation and frustration. Their conversations were full of a type of discipline, attention, and rich interpretive joy, a pleasure taken in a way of knowing that cultivated and deepened our being just here, in this marsh, up beside these hot, late-afternoon sun-yellowy limestone cliffs.

Updraughts had pulled a hawk high up above our heads. We spotted a red-winged blackbird circling him, pestering, diving.

Sudden blackbird disappearance.

Hawk remained, over a hundred feet overhead, backlit shadowy wing penumbras making it hard to accurately spot.

Where had that blackbird gone?

"There. Coming down the cliff face."

Sudden distinctive complaint around our heads. He had spotted us as worse and more proximate dangers to this marsh than the hawk that'd been chased far enough away for comfort.

My friends' conversations were, in an ecologically important sense, of a kind with the abundance of bird songs and flights that surrounded us – careful, measured, like speaking to like, up out of the hot and heady, mosquitoed air. And, standing alongside them there, sometimes silent, certainly unpractised in this art, involved a type of learning that I had once known but, like cicadas, long-since forgotten.

I had forgotten the pleasure to be had in simply standing in the presence of people who are practised in what they know and listening, feeling, watching them work.

I had forgotten the learning to be had from standing alongside and imitating, practising, repeating, refining the bodily gestures of knowing.

I had forgotten how they could show me things, not just about this place, but about how you might carry yourself, what might become of you, when you know this place well.

Part of such carrying, such bearing, is to realize how the creatures of this place can become like great teachers (Jardine, 1997a) with great patience. Such a realization makes it possible to be at a certain ease with what you know. It is no longer necessary to contain or hoard or become overly consumptive in knowing. One can take confidence and comfort in the fact that this place itself will patiently hold some of the remembrances required: like the cicadas, patiently repeating the calls to attention required to know well of this place and its ways.

So we stood together in the bodily presence of this place. Listening, watching, waiting for knowing to be formed through happenstance arrivals and chance noticings. Seeking out expectant, near-secret places that they knew from having been here before, often evoking slow words of fondness, remembrance and familiarity – intimate little tales of other times. Repeating to each other, with low and measured tones, what is seen or suspected. Reciting tales from well-thumbed-through books that showed their age and importance. Belly-laughing over the wonderful, silly, sometimes near-perfect verbal descriptions of bird songs: "a liquid gurgling *konk-la-ree* or *o-ka-lay*" for Peterson's (1980, p. 252) version of the red-winged blackbird.

Then settling, slowing, returning, listening, and looking anew. Meticulousness: "at the edge, below the canopy of the oak, there, no, left, there, yes!"

These are, in part, great fading arts of taxonomic attention, and the deep childly pleasures to be had in sorting and gathering and collecting (Shepard, 1996). There is something about such gathering that is deeply personal, deeply formative, deeply pedagogical. As I slowly gathered something of this place, it became clear that I was also somehow "gathering myself." And as I gathered something of the compositions of this place, I, too, had to become composed in and by such gathering. And, with the help of cicadas, I did not simply remember this place. Of necessity, I remembered, too, something of what has become of me.

A birding lesson: I *become* someone through what I know.

This little lesson may be the great gift that environmental education can offer to education as a whole. Coming to know, whatever the discipline, whatever the topic or topography, is never just a matter of learning the ways of a place but learning about how to carry oneself in such a way that the ways of this place might show themselves. Education, perhaps, involves the invitation of children into such living ways.

This idea of a knowledge of the "ways" (Berry, 1983) of things and the immediacy, patience, repetition, persistence and intimacy – the "attention and devotion" (Berry, 1977, p. 34) – that such knowledge requires, is ecologically, pedagogically, and spiritually vital. It suggests that a knowledge of the ways of red-winged blackbirds is not found nestled in the detailed and careful descriptions of birding guides. Rather, such knowledge lives in the living, ongoing work of coming to a place, learning its ways, and living with the unforeseeable consequence that you inevitably become someone in such efforts, someone full of tales to tell, tales of intimacy, full of proper names, particular ventures, bodily memories that are entangled in and indebted to the very flesh of the Earth they want to tell.

It was clear that my friends loved what they had come to know and what such knowing had required them to become. They took great pleasure in working (Berry, 1989), in showing, in listening, in responding to the simplest, most obvious of questions. There is a telling, disturbing, ecopedagogical (Jardine, 1994) insight buried here. Because a knowledge of the ways of a place is, of necessity, a knowledge webbed into the living character of a place and webbed into the life of the one who bears such knowledge, such knowledge is inevitably fragile, participating in the mortality and passing of the places it knows. A knowledge of ways, then, must, of necessity, include the passing on of what is known as an essential, not-accidental part of its knowing. It is always and already deeply pedagogical, concerned, not only with the living character of places, but with what is required of us if that living and our living there is to go on.

Another birding lesson: if this place is fouled by the (seeming) inevitabilities of "progress," the cost of that progress is always going to be part of my life that is lost.

Some days, it makes perfect sense to say that all knowledge, like all life, is suffering, undergoing, learning to bear and forbear. Because of this fearsome morality that is part of a knowledge of ways, we are obliged, in such knowledge, to cultivate a good, rich, earthy understanding of "enough" (Berry, 1987). We are obliged, too, to then suffer again the certain knowledge that in our schools, in our lives, in our hallucinations of progress, and all the little panics these induce (Jardine, 1996), there never seems to be enough.

Sometimes, in bearing such knowing, I feel my age. I feel my own passing.

At one point we stood on a raised wooden platform in the middle of a marsh just as the sun was setting, and the vocal interplays of red-winged blackbirds' songs, the curves of their flights and the patterning of both of these around nests cupped in the yellow-and-black-garden-spidery bulrushes – audible but invisible sites bubbling full of the pink, wet warbling smallness of chicks – were clearly, in their own way, acts of spotting *us*.

"Ways" bespeaks a thread of kindredness with what one knows, a sense of deep relatedness and intimate, fleshy obligation (Caputo, 1993). But it betrays another little birding lesson: that we are their relations as much as they are ours, that we are thus caught in whatever regard this place places on us:

> The whole ensemble of sentient life cannot be deployed except from the site of a being which is itself visible, audible, sensible. The visible world and the eye share a common flesh; the flesh is their common being and belonging together. (Caputo, 1993, p. 201)

Or, if you like, a more drastic mosquito lesson about living relations: "flesh is . . . a reversible, just insofar as what eats is always edible, what is carnivorous is always carnality" (p. 200). So just as these mosquitoes eat up my sweet, sweaty blood skinslicked under the lures of CO_2 that drew them near, I get their lives in return, gobbled up into liquid gurgling *konk-la-rees*. This is the meaty, trembly level of mutuality and interdependence that crawls beneath all our tall tales of relations. This common flesh is the fearsome limit of our narrativity.

In a knowledge of ways, I do not simply know. I am also *known*. These cicadas and I turn around each other, each forming the other in kind, "both sensible and sensitive, reversible aspects of a common animate element" (Abram, 1996, p. 66). Even more unsettling than this, as we know this place, so are we known by it (Palmer, 1989). That is, the character of our knowing and how gracefully and generously we carry what we know reflects on our character.

One final birding lesson for now. Catching a glimpse of a blue heron pair over past the edge of the marsh, tucked up under the willowy overhangs.

Shore edge log long deep bluey sunset shadow fingers.

Sudden rush of a type of recognition almost too intimate to bear, an event of birding never quite lodged in any birding guides:

"It's *that* pair!"

What a strange and incommensurate piece of knowledge (Jardine, 1997b). How profoundly, how deeply, how wonderfully *useless* it is, knowing that it is *them*, seemingly calling for names more intimate, more proper than "heron," descriptions richer and more giddy than "**Voice**: deep harsh croaks: *frahnk, frahnk, frahnk*" (Peterson, 1980, p. 100). Such knowing doesn't lead anywhere. It is, by itself, already always full, already always enough.

Perhaps this irreplaceable, unavoidable intimacy is why our tales of the Earth always seem to include proper names ("obligations require proper names" [Caputo, 1993, p. 201]), always seem to be full of love and heart, always seem to require narrations of particular times and places, particular faces, particular winds, always seem to invite facing and listening and remembering.

It is squarely here that a great deal of my own work has come to rest: how to carry these birding lessons home, back into the often stuffy confines of elementary schools (Jardine, 1990a), back into the often even stuffier confines, for example, of elementary school mathematics (Jardine, 1990b, 1995), back, too, into the archaic, often literal-minded narrows of academic work and the forms of speaking and writing and research it allows (Jardine, 1992).

Just imagine: mathematics conceived as a living discipline, a living topography, a living place, full of ancestors (Jardine, 1997a) and kin and living relations (Friesen, Clifford, & Jardine, in press), full of tales told and tales to tell. And imagine, too, mathematics education conceived as an open, generous invitation of our children into the intimate ways of this old, mysterious, wondrous place.

References

Abram, D. (1996). *The spell of the sensuous: Language in a more-than-human world*. New York, NY: Pantheon Books.

Berry, W. (1977). *The unsettling of America*. San Francisco, CA: Sierra Club Books.

Berry, W. (1983). *Standing by words*. San Francisco, CA: North Point Press.

Berry, W. (1987). *Home economics*. San Francisco, CA: North Point Press.

Berry, W. (1989, March). The profit in work's pleasure. *Harper's Magazine*, pp. 19–24.

Caputo, J. (1993). *Against ethics: Contributions to a poetics of obligation with constant reference to deconstruction*. Indiana State University Press.

Friesen, S., Clifford, P., & Jardine, D. (in press). On the intergenerational character of mathematical truth. *JCT: An Interdisciplinary Journal of Curriculum Studies*.

Jardine, D. (1990a). To dwell with a boundless heart: On the inte-
grated curriculum and the recovery of the Earth. *Journal of Curriculum and Supervision, 5*(2), 107–119.

Jardine, D. (1990b). On the humility of mathematical language. *Educational Theory, 40*(2), 181–192.

Jardine, D. (1992). The fecundity of the individual case: Considerations of the pedagogic heart of interpretive work. *Journal of Philosophy of Education, 26*(1), 51–61.

Jardine, D. (1994). Littered with literacy: An ecopedagogical reflec-
tion on whole language, pedocentrism and the necessity of refusal. *Journal of Curriculum Studies, 26*(5), 509–524.

Jardine, D. (1995). The stubborn particulars of grace. In B. Horwood (Ed.), *Experience and the Curriculum: Principles and Programs* (pp. 261–275). Dubuque, Iowa: Kendall/Hunt.

Jardine, D. (1996). Under the tough old stars: Pedagogical hyperac-
tivity and the mood of environmental education. *Canadian Journal of Environmental Education, 1*, 48–55.

Jardine, D. (1997a) All beings are your ancestors: A bear Sutra on ecology, Buddhism and pedagogy. *The Trumpeter: A Journal of Ecosophy, 14*(3), 122–23.

Jardine, D. (1997b). The surroundings. *JCT: The Journal of Curriculum Theorizing, 13*(3), 18–21.

Palmer, P. (1989). *To know as we are known: Education as a spiritual discipline.* New York, NY: Harper Collins.

Peterson, R. T. (1980). *A field guide to the birds east of the Rockies* (4th ed.). Boston, MA: Houghton Mifflin Company.

Shepard, P. (1996). *The others: How animals made us human.* Washington, DC: Island Press.

INDIGENIZING CURRICULUM:
THE TRANSFORMATION OF ENVIRONMENTAL DUCATION 14

Andrejs Kulnieks, Nipissing University
Dan Roronhiakewen Longboat, Trent University
Kelly Young, Trent University

IN 1992, DAVID ORR ASSERTED that "all is education is environmental education" (p. 81). While we believe that Orr is correct, we assert that all education *needs* to be environmental education, and we have fallen short of this goal. In the Canadian context, whether considering curriculum from the K–12 level or at the post-secondary level, not all education is currently environmental education. We believe that all education needs to become environmental education. To this end, the key issue that all humans are facing is that the environmental crisis impacts food security, climate change, water and natural resource exploitation, and unimpeded development and industrialization at all levels. Our own experience as educators in Canada leads us to assert that the core of curricula is dislocated from natural landscapes through a reductionist approach to education that we are still perpetuating and that continues to enable a consciousness of human disconnection from natural environments. Nabhan and Trimble (1994) write:

> There are still many children in the this world who live where they have primary contact with wild nature; who still hear the old stories; and who have uncles and grandfathers or grandmothers and aunts to guide them through their gender's rites of passage. Yet the percentage of children who have frequent exposure to wildlands and to other, undomesticated species is smaller than ever before in human history. (p. 85)

Curriculum needs to rectify the separation of humans and the natural world. There is urgency and necessity for learners to understand that disconnected human activity has caused and continues to cause the environmental crisis. Therefore, public systems of education need to address the present situation if we are to impact future relationships with the Earth by incorporating ecological theories, many of which have been based upon Indigenous knowledge perspectives. Davis, Sumara, and Luce-Kapler (2008) write, "Ecological theories tend to regard humanity as one species among many in a grand web of relations – that is, as part of a grander body whose cognitive processes are seen by humans as ongoing co-evolutions of species and habitats" (p. 107).

Ecological theories view all education as holistic in nature without placing an emphasis on expertise and the separation of disciplines. Educational discourses that perpetuate notions that humans are at the top of a hierarchy of relations rather than part of a grand web of relations need to be analyzed as to their overall environmental and social impacts, as we believe that these discourses continue to dominate Canadian curricula. Since we believe that systems of education are not currently addressing the ways in which language perpetuates a human hyper-separation from the natural world, we conceptualize core principles of curriculum that help (re)connect people to the land on which they live. Our research demonstrates how a scientific model has dominated environmental education curricula in Canada. Our curriculum theorizing considers the ways in which both a scientific model and Indigenous Knowledge(s) (IK) model are needed for all education to become environmental education. IK refers to Earth-based peoples, for example in the places where we live in eastern North America, the Anishinaabeg and Haudenosaunee peoples maintain their traditional knowledge in the form of sustainable environmental knowledge and practices that have been sought across the world in order to inform environmental issues and environmental education (Kulnieks, Longboat, & Young, 2010; Longboat, Kulnieks, & Young, 2009; Young, 2009). While we believe that we need to infuse Indigenous knowledge into the curriculum, our assertions are not about Indigenous culture per se; they are about focusing that knowledge upon building and sustaining a connection to place and valuing a place where people live by enhancing, restoring, cultivating, and sustaining relationships with environments in which they live. Canadian systems of education overall teach very little about a sustainable approach to the environment. Therefore, in this chapter: (a) we consider how conceptions of curriculum have historically been theorized through a scientific model since the early twentieth century in relation to the environment, (b) we examine recent environmental educational policies developed by the Ontario Ministry of Education that are embedded in a scientific inquiry model in relation to our belief that all education should lead toward environmental learning, and (c) we provide a cultural and linguistic analysis of the environmental crisis vis-à-vis an eco-justice approach to education as we turn our attention to successful examples of models of Indigenous curriculum that can inform all aspects of environmental education in order to move toward a holistic approach toward education. We have chosen the field of eco-justice in this context as it is a transdisciplinary framework informed through deep ecology, socio-linguistic theories, feminist perspectives, and IK in order to include a cultural and linguistic analysis of the environmental crisis as part of a healthy, environmentally infused curriculum (Bowers, 2002). In particular, we outline educational curricula that include eco-hermeneutic Indigenous focal practices that involve cultivating relationships between humans and the natural world. In doing so, we show that while scientific inquiry is an important part of environmental education, Indigenous perspectives need to be a crucial part of the underlying core principles that prompt and give shape to integral, holistic, sustainable, environmental education in Canada. In the following section we provide a brief historical overview of conceptions of curriculum in North America that have influenced current curricula before turning to successful models of sustainable environmental education in the final section.

Conceptions of Curriculum

In Western educational practices, modern conceptions of curriculum generally assert a particular way of organizing curriculum experience with a focus on "curriculum development," whereby teachers are to facilitate students' apprehension of knowledge that already exists. In North America, modern conceptions of curriculum began with Dewey's (1908, 1922) approach to curriculum as a complex set of relations among students, teachers, subjects, and society, followed by Bobbit's (1918, 1924) "simple method" approach to curriculum that later became known as Tyler's (1949) *Basic Principles of Curriculum and Instruction* as a "commonsense" approach to curriculum that fell in line with scientific method. Schwab (1969, 1971, 1973) added to this approach by asserting a need for curriculum inquiry and paying attention to "commonplaces of schooling" in order to better understand the relationship among teachers, students, subjects, and context. This method was followed by Kliebard (1986) and Schubert (1986) well into the late twentieth century. These theorists for the most part aligned their thinking with a scientific approach to curriculum theorizing as there was an assumption that outcomes of curriculum and learning could be planned and predicted in a classroom (Pinar, 1975, 1981, 2004; Pinar, Reynolds, Slattery, & Taubman, 1995). This is evidenced by North American curriculum documents set out by governments for teachers to follow.

In contrast, postmodern conceptions of curriculum have emerged suggesting that teachers do not only point to existing knowledge for learners to acquire, but that both teachers and learners also participate in a process of inquiry through Pinar's (1975) notion of *currere*. He writes:

> Thus currere refers to an existential experience of institutional structures. The method of currere is a strategy devised to disclose experience, so that we may see more of it and see more clearly. With such seeing can come deepened under-

standing of the running, and with this, can come deepened agency. (p. 518)

For Pinar, learning is viewed as a path laid while walking, as he announced the idea of "curriculum theorizing" in contrast with thinking about curriculum in terms of "conceptual empirical." In the following year, Pinar and Grumet collaborated by further developing the conception of currere through various essays published in *Toward a Poor Curriculum* (1976). Curriculum was then conceptualized as creating interpretive possibilities toward the production of knowledge. Currere gradually led to a shift away from a modernist view of theorizing curriculum development toward a postmodern view of understanding curriculum. Pinar et al. (1995) named the group of curricularists who pioneered this shift the Reconceptualists. In order to escape the history that has structured curriculum conceptualization, theorists such as Pinar et al. (1995), Sumara (1996), and Greene (1995) assert that part of the process of curriculum is to bring both familiar and unfamiliar things together. Davis et al. (2008) write:

> Learning refers to a system's ongoing adaptations that enable it to maintain both its internal coherence and its external coherence. That is, an agent's learning is simultaneously about its memory (i.e., internal co-activities of subagents) and its knowing (i.e., the ways its actions are entangled with others' actions in grander systems). (p. 107)

To develop deeper relationships with learning and knowing, familiar knowledge should be juxtaposed with new and interesting active learning situations. Pinar (1975) and Pinar and Grumet (1976) changed the way curriculum is theorized by paying particular attention to the lived experience of curriculum. Their notion of currere encouraged a shift from *conceptual empirical* thinking toward *curriculum theorizing*. According to Sumara (1996), currere acknowledges that "there can be no fixed and clearly defined boundary between schooling and other lived experiences; events of schooling become inextricable from the path of life" (p. 174). This suggests that the modern conception of curriculum has ignored historical, environmental, and cultural human experiences resulting in the severing of curriculum from lived experiences. Pinar et al. (1995) write:

> Curriculum understood as a symbolic representation refers to those institutional and discursive practices, structures, images, and experiences that can be identified and analyzed in various ways, i.e. politically, racially, autobiographically, phenomenologically, theologically, internationally, and in terms of gender and deconstruction. We can say that the effort to understand curriculum as symbolic representation defines, to a considerable extent, the contemporary field. (p. 16)

Accordingly, the hermeneutical interest in postmodern curriculum theorizing is to locate "haplike" moments amid planned structures, in order to initiate interpretations and invite uncertainty and ambiguity. Embracing Pinar's "currere" approach to curriculum opens the door to possibilities. If curriculum is conceptualized without fixed boundaries between lived experiences and events of school, then teachers can begin to think about how the imagination can play an important part in the experience of curriculum. Pinar et al. (1995) write: "Curriculum is a moving form . . . conceived as an aspiration, the object and hope of our intentionality, it comes to form and slips, at the moment of its actualization, into the ground of our action. It is this movement which Merleau-Ponty and Ricoeur recover for language and reading" (p. 435).

It is difficult to separate modern and postmodern conceptions of curriculum. This is due to the fact that modernist assumptions continue to be embedded in current discourse involving conceptions of curriculum through a predominantly scientific method – one that is set out with predetermined outcomes steeped in a particular Western hierarchical discourse. North American curriculum discourse is historically informed by Eurocentric ideologies with underlying root metaphors of mechanism and scientism (Bowers, 2002). Curriculum entirely in this vein, then, involves a model that is outcome based.

Davis et al. (2008) assert that language is a tool of consciousness and a technology of the self. They follow in the footsteps of Bowers (2002, 2006) and Merchant (1980) who recognize the ways in which modernist metaphors that equate humans to machines continue to dominate postmodern discourse. Subsequently, twenty-first-century conceptions of curriculum have come to include ecological postmodern theory, whereby knowledge is viewed not only as socially constructed but also biologically and ecologically influenced (Davis et al., 2008). Since North American curriculum theories that have guided education have been driven by scientific inquiry, industry, and consumerism, it is important to move towards an ecological postmodern understanding of curriculum that by necessity involves indigenizing it. By indigenizing curriculum we mean including both a cultural and linguistic analysis of language using an eco-justice framework and by an infusion of "focal practices" into curricula. In so doing, we acknowledge a need for curriculum reform that includes both a scientific approach and IK perspectives that are outlined in the following section.

Canadian Curriculum Reform in the Twenty-First Century

The origins of environmental education in North America can be traced to both an early direct scientific approach and of a later indirect influence from Indigenous knowledge in the early twentieth century (Sheridan, 1994; Young, 2006). At the turn of the twenty-first century, with the burgeoning of the environmental crisis rising to catastrophic levels, sustainability has become an important topic for all educational settings. Unfortunately, in the midst of this, all traces of environmental curricula were removed in their entirety from the Ontario curriculum by the Ministry of Education in the mid-1990s. As the environmental crisis became prominent in the news across Canada and around the world, it became more and more difficult for the education system to ignore it. By 2006, the Ontario Ministry of Education decided to re-infuse the curriculum with environmental education through its report that was published the following year entitled *Shaping Our Schools, Shaping Our Future* (Ontario Ministry of Education, 2007). The report states that "responsible environmental citizenship incorporates problem solving, hands-on learning, action projects, scientific inquiry, higher order thinking, and cooperative learning" (p. 6). Environmental education is once again aligned with scientific inquiry as a model without considering an indigenous focus.

In addition, in the June 2009 edition of "Professionally Speaking: The Magazine of the Ontario College of Teachers," the cover story on "The Greening of Ontario's Curriculum" hailed the Ontario Ministry of Education's new policy framework for environmental education as "radical, ambitious and transformative" (Benedict, 2009, p. 36). We closely examined the "radical" policy framework and found that it fails to address IK, as it embraces a scientific inquiry model that falls in line with the twentieth-century modern curriculum theories of Dewey, Tyler, Schwab, etc. We believe that the report reproduced an approach to environmental education based solely on a scientific model. Young (2009) writes:

> The report reproduced the illusion of an ecologically sound method of environmental education as it replicates the very Eurocentric language steeped in scientific root metaphors that espouse Enlightenment principles that ultimately (re)inscribe an anthropocentric and individualistic approach to environmental education curriculum. (pp. 300–301)

We believe that the policy also fails to address the cultural and linguistic roots of the environmental crisis in addition to omitting indigenous environmental knowledge and perspectives despite the comments in the magazine of the Ontario College of Teachers:

> The policy framework seeks to move beyond a focus on symptoms – air and water pollution, for example – to encompass the underlying causes of environmental stresses, which are rooted in personal and social values and in organizational structures," says Acting Today, Shaping Tomorrow. (Benedict, 2009, p. 36)

With the 2007 policy clearly not addressing core issues of sustainability and the cultural and linguistic roots continuing to perpetuate the environmental crisis, we turn our hope to the most recent efforts of the Deans of Education across Canada to move toward a national agreement that recognizes the necessity of including indigenous knowledge. On June 1st, 2010, in Montreal, the Association of Canadian Deans of Education (ACDE) Accord on Indigenous Education was signed, which hailed a Canada-wide agreement on behalf of all faculties of education to uphold a vision "that Indigenous identities, cultures, languages, values, ways of knowing, and knowledge systems will flourish in all Canadian learning settings" (ACDE, 2010, p. 4). The Accord suggests that there is a need for:

> transformative educational change and acknowledging the unique leadership responsibilities of deans, directors, and chairs of education within the Canadian university context, ACDE supports, endorses, and fosters the following goals: Respectful and Welcoming Learning Environments, Respectful and Inclusive Curricula, Culturally Responsive Pedagogies, Mechanisms for Valuing and Promoting Indigeneity in Education, Culturally Responsive Assessment, Affirming and Revitalizing Indigenous Languages,

Indigenous Education Leadership, Non-Indigenous Learners and Indigeneity, Culturally Respectful Indigenous Research. (pp. 5–8)

In order to meet the vision and goals of the accord that were not addressed in the Ministry of Ontario's policy on environmental education, we believe that a cultural and linguistic analysis of curricula vis-à-vis an eco-justice pedagogical framework is needed in addition to an infusion of IK through focal practices. An outline of eco-justice and eco-hermeneutic Indigenous focal practices are offered in the next section.

Eco-Justice Pedagogy and Focal Practices

Eco-justice is defined by the Oxford English Dictionary as "the condition or principle of being just or equitable with respect to ecological sustainability and protection of the environment, as well as social and economic issues." Eco-justice thinking is inherently an interdisciplinary framework and field. The field of eco-justice education has grown considerably in the past couple of decades. An eco-justice education framework involves, among other things, clarifying the ways in which language and, more specifically, root metaphors are linked to the development of anti-ecological ways of knowing and being that often exclude human relations with the natural world (Bowers, 2001, 2006). Examples of root metaphors include a privileging of patriarchy, anthropocentrism, ethnocentrism, individualism, progress and development, etc. whereby hierarchies are reproduced in language that become taken-for-granted ways of knowing, being, and acting. Specifically, for the most part, it has become a "given" that humans dominate over the natural world; progress and development are hailed while notions of cultural traditions are deemed primitive or anti-progressive, and individual achievement is celebrated over collective endeavours. Forests become commodities; animals become live stock; minerals become aggregates to be owned through mining rights. By naming the root metaphors in the language that we use in everyday life that reproduce hierarchies, we are addressing human hyper-separation from the natural world. We use this framing to (re)conceptualize environmental curriculum in order to facilitate a greater understanding of the ways in which sustainable relationships with the earth are important parts of the educational process. We understand the ways in which root metaphors play a major role in informing dominant cultural narratives that mediate human relationships and disconnections from the natural which then serve to create re-constructed, unsustainable environments.

By including an eco-justice framework in environmental curricula, we are addressing the fact that a deep analysis of language is often overlooked in environmental education curriculum decision-making processes. Tracing both the etymology of a word and its contemporary interpretation often helps to reveal its historical associations and its present-day meaning and application. For example, the word language can be traced to the Latin *lingua* and French *langue*. Several associations are linked to the word language. First, language is related to a body of words as an expression of thoughts and feelings. Second, the word language also refers to the tongue as a part of the body that produces various applications of speech. Finally, language can also depict the phraseology of terms such as law, science, art, or of a profession. Although words are expressive, they require thoughts (the mind), feelings (the senses), and the human body (the tongue). We believe that through this kind of hermeneutic inquiry, a new theory of language will unfold that embraces the existence and importance of the mind-heart-body relationship found in eco-hermeneutic, Indigenous theories of learning. Abram (1996) writes:

> In order to read phonetically, we must disengage the synaesthetic participation between our senses and the encompassing earth. The letters of the alphabet, each referring to a particular sound or sound-gesture of the human mouth, begin to

361

function as mirrors reflecting us back upon ourselves. They
thus establish a new reflexivity between the human organism
and its own signs, short-circuiting the sensory reciprocity
between that organism and the land. (p. 187)

As Abram suggests language is an integral part of human learning
about natural landscapes. However, current educational discourses
that perpetuate unhealthy, disconnected relationships with a sense of
place and the natural environment continue to dominate curricula.

There are many discrepancies between the different kinds of education that public systems of school should provide for students.
Often, it is difficult to find common ground between students, teachers, principals, and curriculum writers. Clearly, having a curriculum
that is written down inspires the belief that the best way to make sure
learners can demonstrate an understanding of that curriculum is in a
written form. The reality of this type of system is that in its sole
dependence it serves only to further distance learners from the natural places and intact ecosystems that we depend upon for life. Public
systems of education should also provide students with opportunities to move within natural places as part of the process of developing a broader understanding of and a deeper relationship with these.
It is our understanding that written forms of curriculum are only part
of a much older and richer oral tradition. It would appear that the dis-
orders that many children face may at least be influenced by ways in
which schools inspire and demand a sedentary learning lifestyle. To
be able to demonstrate epistemologies (ways of knowing) may not
be as cost effective as written forms of evaluation, but we need to recognize that this written style of learning does not serve the students
as well as curriculum writers would have us believe. Ecological orality, the state preceding what Orr (1992) defines as ecoliteracy, is a
way of connecting personal experience and stories with environmental learning. Eco-orality and eco-linguistics are recognized conditions of biocultural consciousness in North America and as such
should involve learning ancestral stories that involve a deep under-

standing about local habitats (Longboat, 2008). Retelling stories that share intergenerational knowledge as well as communicate and interact with local places that Abram (1996) defines as the more-than-human world is a way of fostering the realization that people have a responsibility to the Earth because "She" sustains "Life" upon which continued human existence depends.

Following the work of Borgmann (1992) and Sumara (1995) regarding focal practices, we suggest that curricula that are based upon focal practices can help diminish and resolve differences between literacy and orality because they set the stage for knowledge interaction and the equitable sharing of information. Sumara (1995) writes:

> I include this definition here although we take in up in greater detail in the chapter on focal practices: "Inspired by both Borgmann and Franklin, we have combined the phrases "focal reality" and "holistic practice" into the term "focal practice." For us, a focal practice is a particular activity which functions to render visible usually-invisible interpersonal and intertextual relations. As well, a focal practice announces a location of inquiry into personal and cultural histories that have preceded our involvement in any focal practice. As Rebecca Luce-Kapler (1995) suggests, "poets must read poetry to become better readers of poetry." (p. 23)

Indigenous focal practices are ecologically-minded practices that require participants to engage with a series of tasks from a beginning point to a state of completion throughout a course of time and place. These practices are a gateway towards reconceptualizing the inter-connectedness of natural places and spaces because they involve learning about the relationship of human language as expressed in engagement with local places, adding to Sumara's thoughts the necessity of these being founded within a "holistic reality." Examples of ecologically relevant focal practices range from being part of eco-poetic processes commonly associated with oral and literary tradition to growing, harvesting, gathering, and preparing foods that one has contributed to or engaged with in some way, shape, or form, specific to a place.

Focal practices, becoming part of a process of growing or knowing how to collect the food that one consumes, for example, is an integral part of developing a deep understanding of how the places in which people live allow them to survive and thrive, as well as the developing a connective relationship to that place which fosters appropriate actions that will enable life to be sustained. A curriculum that helps students to become part of the process of breaking soil and/or planting seeds in the earth, distributing appropriate amounts of water, tending to, connecting with, and collecting the bounty that the Earth gives us, learning how to make those gifts palatable and consuming them and expressing gratitude for this age-old cycle, are practices that all students used to be part of. In today's society, it is because those students do not have the opportunity for social, economic, and cultural ways of living that necessitates these life skills or ways of knowing be infused back in to the curriculum in multiple ways of learning. Similarly, learning the stories that are indigenous to particular places, learning how to identify specific plants that are edible, medicinal, as well as those that are poisonous, are skills that should be experienced. Knowing about wild berries, mushrooms, and roots, as well as cultivated fruits and vegetables should be part of new "radical" changes in how students understand their relationship with North America, as well as their connections to the rest of the world. Understanding the difference between forests and tree farms and the history of medicine older than pharmaceuticals from the drug store is important in becoming aware of our dependence upon, and connection with, how we engage with what Abram calls the more-than-human world.

Asking students to engage with focal practices brings together multiple ways of learning and what Gardner refers to as multiple intelligences. A focal practice like, for example, developing a deepened understanding of the food we eat involves understanding both scientific and indigenous knowledge perspectives regarding seasonal changes, weather patterns, geography, soil nutrients, water, manual dexterity through tool usage, as well as the age-old expressions of gratitude, all of which will impact our day-to-day lives. In addition, understanding the impact that cultural or lifestyle practices have on the earth is important due to the devastating effects industrialization in particular, oil companies, and other resource-extractive industries are currently unleashing on our world. The ways in which we engage with the earth are also clearly evident in the way in which students behave towards one another. Eco-justice pedagogical practices like gardening on school property, as illustrated by Sachs (2001), would make a clear improvement to paving schoolyard landscapes and change the student perspective from being individualistic to learning how to co-operate and work together.

In this sense, the principal research is in the determination of the cultural apparatus of landscape representation whose success exists in the authority, legitimacy, and validity of its eco-poetic fit within the locales of its presence, while maintaining the importance of remembering the pedagogical nature of ancestral homelands and the recognition and inclusion of the Indigenous knowledge that resides in that place. As Bringhurst (2006) explains, "All literature is oral. Writers are simply that unusual or deviant class of storytellers and singers who take their own dictation" (p. 178). That is to say that the cultural craft of meaning-making is symmetrical with the stewardship of ecosystems. Health in one domain must equal health in another. Ecosystems create knowledge in their image and it is the task of the storyteller to embody and express that knowledge in all of its numinous and practical forms. Understanding this enables one's learning to change from its current focus of learning *about* nature to learning *from* nature. The compelling dimension of this research is in the correspondence between intact ecosystems and cultures that embody those traditional territories, embedded within the concept of the biocultural, for if one was to make a comparison between the health of ecosystems and the health of cultures, one would find that those that embody one another have the most bio-diverse and sustainable presence on land and through time.

Our contention is that making a sustainable culture requires a very large component for understanding orality as the best apparatus for articulating human belonging to natural systems, because storytelling and focal practice are the most natural bio-cultural meaning-making system for articulating one's place in the natural world. Oral tradition and focal practice can be used as a model for understanding how undertaking an engagement with the numinous qualities of unfamiliar landscapes can create a spiritual tradition in keeping with Indigenous pedagogies of intact, integral, life-giving ecosystems. In so doing, language and storytelling naturalizes oral traditions and connections to those landscapes. Learning the story of the plants and more-than-human beings that live within a particular place can foster a condition for inhabiting these unfamiliar lands that is consistent with their care and so develops an environmental ethic predicated upon Indigenous reality. Berry (1987) describes what takes place when curriculum fails to address future ways for humans to cultivate relationships with natural places:

> Obviously, the more artificial a human environment becomes, the more the word "natural" becomes a term of value. It can be argued, indeed, that the conservation movement, as we know it today, is largely a product of the industrial revolution. The people who want clean air, clear streams, and wild forests, prairies, and deserts are the people who no longer have them. (p. 7)

In keeping with ancestral practice, the health of ecosystems is in part an expression of the health of cultures. Canadian curriculum should reflect these healthy ways of living. To illustrate this symmetrical relationship, we make reference to North Americas' first Treaties – The Kaswentha or "Two Row" Wampum Belt and the subsequent "Silver Covenant Chain" or Friendship Treaty Belt between the early Europeans and the Haudenosaunee – as a way of understanding and eventually measuring or describing settler progress toward the making of an eco-poetic belief system adapted to the landscapes of their belonging and beginnings. These depict two vessels, a canoe and a sailing ship, traveling down the river of Life. The essence of which provides for how the Peoples will live and interact together; as well it focuses on our well-being as dependent upon the River of Life. Eco-poetics may be constructed as the cultural fulfillment of settler obligations and so represent a manifestation of compliance and resonance at a populist level. As human beings living in North America, indigenous or non-indigenous, we have a responsibility to uphold these ancient obligations and have a responsibility to care for each other and for the land we all depend upon for life. It then becomes incumbent upon us all to understand that our actions have consequences. The present reality of unbridled development for the sake of "progress" should be critically examined to understand the full cost of progress for both this society and the world. "But for two-thirds of the people on earth, this positive meaning of the word "development" – profoundly rooted after two centuries of its social construction – is a reminder of *what they are not*. It is a reminder of an undesirable, undignified condition" (Esteva, 2007, p. 10).

Our investigation of Canadian curriculum documents follows in the footsteps of eco-theorists who question etymological ramifications of language expectations of what students will accomplish. For example, when the 1999 Ontario Curriculum documents were released initially, teacher candidates were expected to implement all expectations throughout the course of the teaching year. Ten years later, it has become more reasonable to understand that these documents are a guide to where the students should be moving toward throughout the course of the year. One of the primary questions we have in terms of the language of Canadian curriculum documents is an etymological inquiry and its impact upon both pedagogy and the continuation of hegemony. We are interested whether language was purposefully used to separate humans from the natural world in order to facilitate the continuation of the loss of connection to the nature, as then it no longer becomes important or vital to our existence, enabling unbridled development and its ensuing environmental and ecological devastation to continue. Lakoff and Johnson (1980) allude to how we often forget that the metaphors that we use in our day to day mediation become a substitute for imagining that those metaphors define the reality from the way things are written: "Expressions like *wasting time, attacking positions, going our separate ways,* etc., are reflections of systematic metaphorical concepts that structure our thought and enable our actions. They are 'alive' in the most fundamental sense: they are metaphors we live by" (p. 55). Thus, language continuously interferes with the understanding that Earth is a living being. For example, the use of mechanized sayings like flushing water "down the drain" certainly evokes a different meaning that pouring dangerous chemicals into a river or stream, but often the effects are the same.

Schools of knowledge have been built around the language of industrialization. Words like waste versus compost, lumber versus trees, or dirt versus soil demonstrate certain ways of thinking. We need to question how many schools of knowledge have been built around water, forest, earth, etc. As we can find very few schools that fit this way of knowing the world, we question the role of public education in terms of its ability to influence environmental values and behaviours in society in general. If you want to make societal change, education must be at the core. We believe in using language to foster "embeddedness" rather than continuing the disconnection. Embeddedness expands our world view to include all living systems. Beyond Al Gore's "political" problem, education must assume responsibility for helping make the changes to address global climate change.

There are many Indigenous theorists and thinkers who have long ago explained that the Earth is alive; we need but to search the literature or listen to traditional teachings. Even within western knowledge traditions this reality is becoming more evident. Lovelock (1988) outlines this theory in scientific terms: "There is no clear distinction anywhere on the earth's surface between living and non-living matter. There is merely a hierarchy of intensity going from the 'material environment' of the rocks and the atmosphere to the living cells" (p. 40).

In the Anishinaabe sweat lodge, for example, the stones used in the lodge, are referred to and respected as "Grandfathers" because they are of the oldest substances on Earth. Landscapes are the intellectual and spiritual legacy of these elemental Elders. For Haudenosaunee, this familial relationship to the world around them is reconfirmed within the language, the Earth is our Mother, the Sun our Elder Brother, the Moon our Grandmother, the Thunders our Grandfathers, etc. There is a connection to and a relationship with everything that exists. Of course, in Western tradition there is very little engagement of the relationships with ancestors or landscapes, and this may be why the concept of text and textual analysis is of limited cache among Indigenous traditionalists. As a way of addressing this limitation, the eco-hermeneutic lens goes beyond an interpretation of text to include Indigenous oral narratives that stretch back to time immemorial. The issue of privileging literacies and written texts over oral tradition in Western educational settings is an underlying factor of creating continuing limitations in learning and furthering a disconnection from place. Western culture has a deep history of tracing texts that serve as the basis of what is construed as the beginnings of knowledge, back to Greek philosophy, therefore enabling it to overlook Indigenous ontologies (ways of being) and epistemologies (ways of knowing). Interpretation of ancestral understandings of scientific knowledge is an eco-hermeneutic aspect of this multi-dimensional research methodology, enabling multiple learning strategies and a fostering of multiple intelligences.

From a Western perspective, historically readers were considered intellectually superior to those who could not read. Hermeneutic interpretation of the law was also recognized in the same way. This power relationship that has its ancient roots in the reading and interpretation of the Bible has also been applied to textualized legal statutes. The stories in the Bible were translated and interpreted by people who held positions of power as intermediaries between God and the people. These interpretive practices were later adopted by those who translated and decoded legal texts exteriorly to landscapes, also in a position of power over the people.

In contrast, textual investigations reveal how the words on a page are lifeless. Without the vibrancy of interaction and interpretation, they are without voice or power; they are not alive. Rosenblatt explained that the reader or interpreter is an integral part of the text. Another way of looking at the contradictions of oral and literary tradition is that whereas orality provides a space for active and interactive dialogue, processes of reading and writing are singular and passive.

Whereas the privileging of written texts over oral tradition in educational settings separates humans and the natural world, an oral perspective brings them together in storytelling and focal practice. The basis of Western culture traces itself through texts of what is construed as the beginnings of knowledge back to Greek philosophy. For example, when Socrates told a story, everybody had the opportunity to engage with the storyteller, to ask questions, and to discuss the meaning with other listeners. Later, Plato wrote his stories down, allowing only those in a position of privilege, wealth, or power to have access. This system worked to ensure that only those in possession of the text were able to be part of this process of knowledge making and interpretative practices. Kings were divined by God while priests became God's chosen representatives. They formally entrenched themselves economically, politically, and socially above and separate from place and the people they ruled. Written texts ultimately isolated humans from themselves as well as from the natural world. Today we are seeking to use text along with other learning approaches to reverse its impact and to help re-make the connection to the natural world.

For Longboat (2008), language necessitates understanding of respect as it is language that creates an appropriate world view. Whether this is right or wrong is not as important as understanding that language provides a framework for seeing the world. Speaking about this in reference to the Anishinaabeg or Ojibwe "Good Life Teaching" – implicit within the Seven Grandfather Teachings is the concept of Pimaadiziwin, "The Art of Living Well" which serves to provide a framework for living a good life. A good life means a life of happiness and fulfillment through understanding the necessity of creating and maintaining quality relationships to one another and to the world around us. Education for all students, within a non-aboriginal academic context, creates the opportunity for these principles to be shared, but they have not been talked about in relation to education as a whole, especially in relation to environment until the emergence of Indigenous Environmental Studies. Ultimately, we must seek to offer an integrated, meta-disciplinary educational framework with practical application for environmental curriculum by outlining eco-hermeneutics, science and technology, and indigenous focal practices that can be incorporated into Canadian classrooms at all levels. Imagine the possibilities and think of their impact upon future generations!

References

Abram, D. (1996). *The spell of the sensuous: Perception in a more-than-human world.* New York, NY: Pantheon Books.
ACDE. (2010). *Accord on indigenous education.* Retrieved from http://experience.congress2010.ca/wp-content/uploads/2010/05/Congress-Indigenous-Accord.pdf
Benedict, M. (2009, June). Environmental education. *Professionally Speaking: The Magazine of the Ontario College of Teachers.*

Retrieved from http://professionallyspeaking.oct.ca/ june_2009/enviro_ed.asp

Berry, W. (1987). *Home economics*. San Fransisco, CA: North Point Press.

Bobbitt, F. (1918). *The curriculum*. Boston, MA: Mifflin.

Bobbitt, F. (1924). *How to make curriculum*. Boston, MA: Mifflin.

Borgmann, A. (1992). *Crossing the postmodern divide*. University of Chicago Press.

Bowers, C. A. (2001). *Educating for eco-justice and community*. University of Georgia Press.

Bowers, C. A. (2002). Cultural and ecological consequences of globalizing computers. In K. S. Tong & S.-W. Chan (Eds.), *Culture and humanity in the new millennium: The future of human values* (pp. 93–108). Hong Kong: Chinese University Press.

Bowers, C. A. (2006). *Revitalizing the commons: Cultural and educational sites of resistance and affirmation*. Langham, MA: Lexington Books.

Bringhurst, R. (2006). *The tree of meaning: Thirteen talks*. Kentville, NS: Gaspereau Press.

Davis, B., Sumara, D., & Luce-Kapler, R. (2008). *Engaging minds: Changing teaching in complex times* (2nd ed.). New York, NY: Routledge.

Dewey, J. (1908). *The child and the curriculum*. University of Chicago Press.

Dewey, J. (1922). *Democracy and education*. New York: MacMillan.

Esteva, G. (2007). Development. In W. Sachs (Ed.), *The development dictionary: A guide to knowledge as power* (pp. 6–25). New York, NY: Zed Books.

Greene, M. (1995). *Releasing the imagination: Essays on education, the arts, and social change*. San Francisco, CA: Jossey-Bass Publishers.

Kliebard, H. (1986). *The struggle for the American curriculum, 1893–1958*. New York: Routledge.

Kulnieks, A., Longboat, D., & Young, K. (2010). Re-indigenizing curriculum: An ecohermenutic approach to learning. *AlterNative: An International Journal of Indigenous Scholarship*, 6(1), 16–24.

Lakoff, G., & Johnson, M. (1980). *Metaphors we live by*. University of Chicago Press.

Longboat, D. R. (2008). *Owehna'shon: A (the islands) kawenoke the haudenosaunee archipelago; The nature and necessity of biocultural restoration and revitalization* (Unpublished doctoral dissertation). York University, Toronto, ON.

Longboat, D. R., Kulnieks, A., & Young, K. (2009). Beyond dualism: Toward a transdisciplinary indigenous environmental studies model of environmental education curricula. *The EcoJustice Review: Educating for the Commons*, 1(1), 1–18.

Lovelock, J. (1988). *The ages of gaia: A biography of our living earth*. New York, NY: WW Norton & Co.

Merchant, C. (1980). *The death of nature: Women, ecology, and the scientific revolution*. San Francisco, CA: Harper & Row.

Nabhan, P., & Trimble, S. (1994). *The geography of childhood: Why children need wild places*. Boston, MA: Beacon Press.

Ontario Ministry of Education. (2007, June). *Shaping our schools, shaping out future*.

Orr, D. (1992). *Ecological literacy: Education and the transition to a postmodern world*. State University of New York Press.

Pinar, W. (Ed.). (1975). *Curriculum theorizing: The reconceptualists*. Berkley, CA: McCutchan.

Pinar, W. (1981). The reconceptualization of curriculum studies. In H. Giroux, A. Penna, & W. Pinar (Eds.), *Curriculum and instruction* (pp. 87–89). Berkley, CA: McCutchan Publishing.

Pinar, W. (Ed.). (2004). *Contemporary curriculum discourses: Twenty years of JCT*. New York, NY: Peter Lang.

Pinar, W., & Grumet, M. (1976). *Toward a poor curriculum*. Dubuque, IA: Kendall/Hunt.

Pinar, W., Reynolds, W., Slattery, P., & Taubman, P. (1995). *Understanding curriculum: An introduction to the study of historical and contemporary discourses*. New York, NY: Peter Lang.

Sachs, W. (Ed.). (2001). *The development dictionary: A guide to knowledge as power*. London, England: Zed Books.

Schubert, W. (1986). *Curriculum: Perspective, paradigm, and possibility*. New York: Macmillan Publishing Company.

Schwab, J. (1969). The practical: A language for curriculum. *School Review, 78*, 1–23.

Schwab, J. (1971). The practical: Arts of the eclectic. *School Review, 79*(4), 493–542.

Schwab, J. (1973). The practical 3: Translation into curriculum. *School Review, 81*(4), 501–522.

Sheridan, J. (1994). *Alienation and integration: Environmental education in turtle island* (Unpublished doctoral dissertation). University of Alberta, Edmonton.

Sumara, D. (1995). Response to reading as a focal practice. *English Quarterly, 28*(1), 18–26.

Sumara, D. (1996). *Private readings in public: Schooling the literary imagination*. New York, NY: Peter Lang.

Tyler, R. W. (1949). *Basic Principles of Curriculum and Instruction*. University of Chicago Press.

Young, K. (2006). *Girls of the empire: The origins of environmental education and the contest for brownies and girl guides* (Unpublished doctoral dissertation). York University, Toronto, ON.

Young, K. (2009). Reconceptualizing elementary language arts curriculum: An ecojustice approach. In L. Iannacci & P. Whitty (Eds.), *Early childhood currricula: Reconceptualist perspectives* (pp. 299–325). Calgary, AB: Detselig Enterprises.

15

CREATING SHARED UNDERSTANDINGS: MEETING INDIGENOUS EDUCATION NEEDS

Nicole M. Bell, Trent University

A SIX-YEAR OLD, GRADE ONE *Indigenous student completes his "fall" title page with the words "mother earth puts on her most beautiful dress and dances." He sees the world through his Indigenous eyes and world view from which he has learned about the seasonal cycles of the earth and his people's cultural teachings from his parents and community Elders. His mother has told him numerous times that he was born at the time when "mother earth puts on her most beautiful dress and dances before going to sleep under her white blanket," and so the boy eagerly anticipates his birthday once he sees the leaves starting to change colour. The mother has heard an Elder speak many times about the teachings of the seasons and what the earth is doing at those times, resulting in the cultural knowledge transmission to her son. The title page is returned to the boy with a check mark beside the picture of the squirrel gathering nuts, another check mark beside the picture of the tree with its coloured leaves, and yet another check mark beside the picture of leaves that have fallen. There is no check mark beside the words "mother earth puts on her most beautiful dress and dances." What does this say to the Indigenous child, to his parents and community, who taught him about what it means to be an Indigenous person?*

The transmission of culture and world view to First Nation, Métis, and Inuit children and youth is essential to the spiritual survival of Indigenous[1] people in Canada. Education is therefore a high priority for the Indigenous community toward instilling Indigenous knowledge such as language, history, traditions, behaviour, and spiritual beliefs. Additionally, cross-cultural understanding is imperative to realize the cultural needs of Canada's First Peoples and foster a sense of respect for their beliefs and practices. These understandings have been recently adopted as a priority for the Ontario Ministry of

Education (OME) (2007) as it strives to ensure all students have knowledge and an appreciation of contemporary and traditional Indigenous traditions, cultures, and perspectives. As a result, *The Ontario First Nation, Métis, and Inuit Education Policy Framework* was launched in 2007.

This chapter articulates the importance of cultural identity development for First Nation, Métis, and Inuit students while presenting the role of the education system in the identity process. Suggestions are then provided to create Indigenous culturally inclusive educational spaces. Medicine Wheels are presented as an Indigenous educational framework accompanied by their teachings and pedagogical applications. In conclusion, the journey of articulating and implementing Indigenous education in Ontario schools is infused with hope as another story of the Indigenous boy is shared. The cultural knowledge shared in this chapter represent universal principles found across Indigenous nations in Ontario. Specific teachings are reflective of an Anishinaabe[2] cultural world view.

The Need for Cultural Identity Development

Many First Nation, Métis, and Inuit culture groups have a foundational teaching that states people must know who they are and where they come from. This awareness enables them to develop a strong cultural identity[3] so that they may know where they are going in order to create a positive future for themselves, their community, and their nation. The question "Who am I?" and the ensuing search is an imperative quest for Indigenous children and youth (Anderson, 2002), one that the publicly funded educational system in Ontario must assist First Nation, Métis, and Inuit students in answering (Battiste, 2000) toward meeting their cultural identity needs. Research (Antone, 2000; Bell, 2004, 2005; Schissel & Wotherspoon, 2003) confirms that a positive cultural identity among Indigenous students contributes to happiness in school and academic success.

It is important to note that some Indigenous people, including children, do not wish to identify themselves as an Indigenous person. Suffice it to say that there are many reasons for this, as identity is a complex concept. However, there are many Indigenous children who yearn, either consciously or subconsciously, for an understanding of what it means to be an Indigenous person. Healing research provided by the Aboriginal Healing Foundation (Castellano, 2004) states the most effective mode of healing for Indigenous people is learning about their culture, as this fills the void and satisfies their yearning for a cultural self-identity with pride and understanding. It is equally important that educators do not assume there are no Indigenous students in their classroom. Surnames and physical appearances are not accurate indicators of an Indigenous student's ancestry.

The urgency and importance of reclaiming one's identity is understandable when considering that North America is the homeland of its Indigenous peoples. Essentially there is no other land to which First Nation, Métis, and Inuit people may return to reclaim and maintain their identity as a culture-based people. While First Nation, Métis, and Inuit peoples will continue to physically exist in Canada,[4] their spirituality is at risk of extinction.

Traditional Indigenous education was implemented in a holistic manner. "Holistic" education is the positive development of the whole child in relation to his/her world. "Positive development" is the ongoing progression of the child's mind, body, spirit, and emotion in a good way. Because it is an ongoing progression, it is never complete. Therefore, this growth or development is a life-long process which is only started as a child and then fostered in a positive way through the school, home, and community.

The word "good" holds a lot of weight in Indigenous culture where in English it is somewhat neutral to other terms that are used such as "great," "fantastic," and "amazing." "Living a good life" or "following the good red road" or "doing things in a good way" requires a great deal of energy from a person and results in many rewards. The word "good" should not be taken lightly when spoken by an Indigenous person. "The good way" means fostering the child's development using the seven sacred values of honesty, wisdom, love, respect, bravery, humility, and truth, which results in great things for the person receiving. For many people it takes a whole lifetime to learn how to live according to these values. This is why Elders are often respected for their wisdom; they have come to know sharing, humility, kindness, caring, strength, and respect. Again, these words cannot be taken lightly. Each one involves a great deal of work on the part of the person to come to a true understanding of what these words really mean.

The "whole child" is a child who is a person with emotions, a body, a spirit, and a mind. This idea was recently supported by the Royal Commission on Aboriginal Peoples (1996) when a framework was presented to address "lifelong, holistic education from an Aboriginal perspective. Each of these aspects must be addressed in the learning process" (pp. 445–446). Each aspect should not only be addressed, but should be addressed in balance. The child must grow in a balanced way in order to be a healthy person and contribute to his/her life in a healthy way. For instance, a person who knows mentally everything there is to know to create a nuclear weapon and can physically create one, yet has not connected emotionally and spiritually to the creation of a nuclear weapon, may very well destroy every living thing, including themself.

The child's "world" begins from the inside and then extends to the family, community, nation, and his/her multi-verse which includes the world/place that cannot be physically seen. The child must have a strong sense of positive identity in order for him/her to develop into a healthy person who will contribute to a society (Antone, 2000). Healthy individuals will create healthy families, communities, and ultimately nations and world. Spirituality has a lot to do with the "inner world" of the child. There must be a spiritual connection at an internal level with the self but also at an external level with the cosmos. For traditional Indigenous people, spirituality (the interconnectedness and interrelatedness between the self and external world) is in everything they do; it is a part of them; it is a lifeway. Spirituality can therefore exist in every aspect in the education of their children since the ultimate goal of education is to help prepare children for a satisfying adult life and a satisfying childhood in the process.

All of the characteristics of "holistic education" that have been described are interdependent and all must be developed in balance. This means that there is an ongoing interconnected relationship that exists among the child and his/her world. These relationships must be fostered in the education system to develop whole and healthy children and ultimately adults.

This concept of "holistic" education is not new. Traditional Indigenous education is based on a premise of holism. The theory and practice of holistic education discussed by Miller (1993) is not that different from the Indigenous understanding of "education." Miller speaks of an ecological interdependent perspective within a social context, the body and mind connection, and the connections between the self and the community. The common theme is connection and inter-relationship rather than setting up binaries such as the mind/body split. All students need to be able to put the "whole" together with the "bits." They therefore need the methodology to be able to put the bits together. Stating that students need to learn on a physical, mental, emotional, and spiritual level, is speaking of interconnectedness. Holistic education teaches a child that they do not exist without the trees. The scaffolding of holistic education is therefore the teaching of interconnections.

In an education system that does not plan, design, or deliver from a place of balance between all aspects of a person (physical, emotional, mental, spiritual) or a place of balance between that individual and all of Creation, fragmentation is ultimately the result – fragmentation of the person and their relationship to Creation. This is why so many Indigenous people believe that "the public school system is limiting the knowledge base of [their] children, [that] they are being denied access to knowledge bases that they need to sustain themselves and the planet in the future" (Battiste, 2000, p. 202). Therefore the requirement is to provide culturally inclusive educational spaces for First Nation, Métis, and Inuit student learning to realize the instructions of their Elders:

> We, as educators, must realize that Anishinaabe [Indigenous] children don't fit into the moulds that are made for non-Indigenous children. We are a spiritually-based, natural people of the earth, and in order for our children to know where they are going, they must know who they are as Indigenous people. (Elder Edna Manitowabi in OME, 1975, p. 74)

Intercultural contact between Indigenous and non-Indigenous peoples in Canada (both historically and at the present time) has initiated a process of acculturation that has resulted in cultural disruption for First Nation, Métis, and Inuit peoples, leading to reduced well-being, identity confusion and loss, and academic challenges (Royal Commission on Aboriginal Peoples [RCAP], 1996). The effects of historical acculturation can be seen in contemporary statistics which state that while Indigenous people in Canada comprise 3.8% of the population, they represent 18% of the prison population (Statistics Canada, 2001). Indigenous people aged 20–24 years who do not have a secondary school diploma are three times the national average (Statistics Canada, 2006). Additionally, the suicide rates among Indigenous youths aged 15–24 is six times higher than any other group in Canada (Statistics Canada, 2001). Clearly the current needs of Canada's First Peoples are not being met.

Since the acculturation process has resulted from interactions between Indigenous and non-Indigenous peoples, the key to re-establishing a sense of well-being, a secure cultural identity, and academic success resides in restructuring the relationships between these two communities (RCAP, 1996), and the public school provides the awesome opportunity to build these positive relationships. First Nation, Métis, and Inuit students, whose presence in public schools is increasing dramatically[5] (Statistics Canada, 2006), need to see themselves reflected in the curriculum in an accurate and authentic way. This is an important step toward developing a positive sense of self-esteem and identity and fosters their success as learners. Additionally, non-Indigenous students need to learn about the history, experiences, and world view of Canada's First Peoples to help them better understand the current struggle of First Nation, Métis, and Inuit peoples to maintain identity and cultures. This cross-cultural awareness allows non-Indigenous students to understand how the past led to the current reality of First Nation, Métis, and Inuit peoples and the issues that need to be addressed (Toronto District School Board, 2006). Both Indigenous and non-Indigenous peoples, through the public school system, have a mutual interest in developing new, equitable, and mutually respectful relationships. (Toronto District School Board).

Indigenous people around the world are engaging in a process of identity development, creating a collective voice and struggling to combat the acculturation of all Indigenous peoples. Today's First Nation, Métis, and Inuit children and youth have been denied their culture because of oppressive institutions established by colonization. As a result, many Indigenous people do not necessarily have the teachings or knowledge to ensure the cultural survival of their people because they were denied the culture themselves. This "cultural loss" created the break in the chain regarding the transference of cultural knowledge from one generation to the next. The public education system therefore has an important role in assisting Indigenous children in securing their culture so that they may identify positively with themselves and "imagine" their own future free from the hegemony that is so prevalent.

Creating Indigenous Culturally Inclusive Educational Spaces

The public education system must always recognize and acknowledge its limitations in teaching to, for, and about First Nation, Métis, and Inuit people. Mainstream schools are certainly challenged with providing intensive cultural-based education such as life-stage ceremonies to its Indigenous students. The cross-cultural sharing of Indigenous knowledge is also limited by the depth of cultural knowledge a non-Indigenous teacher can respectfully share. However, the public education system must embrace that which it can do by implementing culturally responsive teaching and learning strategies.

A fundamental method to learning about one's Indigenous culture, world view, and identity is securing a connection to the land by engaging in land-based activities and opportunities (Cajete, 1994). Indigenous students report the incredible benefit to their sense of self by understanding themselves in relation to Creation through land-based cultural activities (Bell, 2004, 2005; Haig-Brown, Hodgson-Smith, Regnier, & Archibald, 1997). Generally, exposure to all traditional activities (such as storytelling, traditional teachings, ceremonies, language, survival skills) reinforce the value of the Indigenous student's culture, and therefore opportunities for these activities are essential to re-establish strong cultural identities (Bell, , 2005; Berry, 1999; Haig-Brown et al., 1997).

Indigenous Elders, as the holders of cultural knowledge, provide a direct connection to an understanding of the land and traditional activities. Indigenous students value opportunities to learn from Indigenous Elders. This relationship also fosters an intergenerational understanding important to Indigenous cultural survival (Kulchyski, McCaskill, & Newhouse, 1999).

Indigenous students report (Bell, 2004, 2005; Berry, 1999; Haig-Brown et al., 1997; Schissel & Wotherspoon, 2003) that acts of racism, prejudice, and discrimination against them as individuals, and collectively as a people, have extremely negative effects on their cultural identity. Students share the extreme stress they encounter having to face racism on a daily basis resulting in a lack of desire to attend school, leading to many dropping out of school to save their sense of self (Bell, 2005; Schissel & Wotherspoon, 2003).

Indigenous students report that formal education has not recog-

nized their cultural needs and has subsequently impacted very nega-
tively on their cultural identity. Specifically lacking is a culturally relevant curriculum (Battise, 2000), including traditional activities, historically accurate information as part of the curriculum, acts of discrimination, and a lack of Indigenous teachers and Elders (Schissel &
Wotherspoon, 2003).

Envisioning the future for Indigenous students requires the need
to address the values of the particular Indigenous culture group for
which the education system is striving to include (Medicine, 1993).
To this end, teachers need to present learning about Indigenous people that addresses "real" (not idealized or contrived) culture and thus
become less involved with the accoutrements such as craft making
(Medicine, 1993). Unless Indigenous and non-Indigenous students
understand Indigenous world view and values, they will never be
effective change agents toward healthy cross-cultural relations.
Imperative in this process is the need to honour the sacredness of
certain aspects of Indigenous cultures and traditions. Additionally,
teachers are required to acknowledge the distinct and unique differences among Indigenous nations while also acknowledging the
diversity within all culture groups. Culture needs to be addressed as
dynamic and not static, thus ensuring that the history of Indigenous
peoples reflects change over time and does not simply assign
Indigenous peoples to a place "frozen in time" in the distant past
(Toronto District School Board, 2006).

An acknowledgement of a local Indigenous culture group is a
great way to begin establishing learning climates that are culturally
friendly to Indigenous culture and tradition. Toward supporting
Indigenous students in their classroom, teachers should search out
opportunities to learn first-hand about the Indigenous peoples living
in the area of their school. Strong community ownership and partnership in school programs can be fostered by "prominent displays of
culturally relevant items, and by inviting local Elders and community people to share their knowledge in classes" (Toronto District
School Board, 2006, p. 12).

Teachers need to refrain from teaching only historical information about Indigenous peoples (Toronto District School Board, 2006). This needs to be balanced with current issues and perspectives by bringing authentic voices into the classroom through invited Elders, storytellers, artists, community leaders, and traditional peoples. Additionally, teaching resources (Indigenous authored and produced works or videos, Indigenous concepts of math and science, exploration of Indigenous artists) can be utilized that represent an authentic Indigenous voice and thus an acknowledgement of a rich Indigenous knowledge base and world view (Toronto District School Board, 2006). Hearing voices of people whose lives are affected by the history and the daily lived experience challenges the everyday condition of appropriation of voice, both within and surrounding the public school setting.

Using content that is biased or inaccurate serves to further marginalize the experiences of Indigenous peoples. Stereotypical beliefs about Indigenous peoples need to be deconstructed in the classroom to allow a firm foundation upon which to build understanding and knowledge (Toronto District School Board, 2006). Teachers need to assess teaching resources for bias and teach students to critically analyze and assess bias in their learning materials. Teachers need to ensure that the information being presented is authentic and accurate.

Schools need to be creative at providing cultural experiences for the benefit of all students. These activities could include language or culture programs and special events or celebrations. Additionally, cross-cultural experiences for non-Indigenous teachers and students are essential toward fostering healthy cross-cultural relationships and eradicating racism.

School boards need to recognize the importance of employing teachers and school leaders with the expertise and personal qualities that have been shown to be most effective with Indigenous learners and providing the appropriate support and community liaison personnel to ensure holistic programming (Bell, 2004).

Indigenous ontology and epistemology needs to be honoured and reflected in educational practice. Specific cultural constructs such as Medicine Wheels reflect deep cultural understandings that can inform a paradigm shift in contemporary public education. Some of the teachings of Medicine Wheels is shared below in an effort to create Indigenous culturally responsive learning environments.

Medicine Wheels as an Indigenous Educational Framework

In many Indigenous cultures, the Medicine Wheel[6] metaphor contains all of the traditional teachings and can therefore be used as a guide on any journey, including the educational process. While there is some variation in its teachings and representations, the underlying thread of meaning to the web of uses and significance of Medicine Wheels remain the same: the importance of appreciating and respecting the ongoing interconnectedness and interrelationships of all things. Therefore, there is no "right" or "wrong" way of representing or using Medicine Wheels. All forms hold particular meaning to the various culture groups while all transmit a common understanding of the interconnectedness and interrelationship of all things.

The wheel drawing simply begins by making a circle. Superimposed on the circle are four equidistant points. These points symbolically identify the power/medicine of the four directions using four different colors. The final drawing resembles a compass for human understanding. Around the spirit world of the four directions is the Creator above and Mother Earth below whereby "a three dimensional sphere is created which mysteriously contains, reflects, and possesses within itself the perimeters and powers of the entire universe, indeed of reality itself" (Sanderson, 1991, p. 51).

According to Anishinaabe Elder Edna Manitowabi, the number four is considered significant among Indigenous peoples, but with some differences. For example, Hampton (1995), who is Chicksaw, uses six directions in his Medicine Wheel to develop a foundation model for Indigenous education across North America. The additional two directions in his model are above and below to symbolize Sky Father and Earth Mother. Many prefer to address the Medicine Wheel in a basic way using only the four directions, or a more complex way using seven directions – the six that Hampton uses with the addition of the center, the point at which we are.

There are many different ways that Elders and traditional teachers have expressed the four directions: the four teachings, the four winds, the four cardinal directions, and many other relationships that can be expressed in sets of four. "Just like a mirror can be used to see things not normally visible (e.g. behind us or around a corner), Medicine Wheels can be used to help us see or understand things we can't quite see or understand because they are ideas and not physical objects" (J. Bopp, M. Bopp, Brown, Lane, 1984. p. 9).

Medicine Wheels have been used by many Indigenous groups to address the complex issues they face such as racism (Calliou, 1995), the impact of residential schools (Assembly of First Nations, 1994), healing (Coggins, 1990; Hart, 2002; Regnier, 1994), sexual abuse (Hollow Water Community Holistic Circle Healing, 1993), education (Odjig-White, 1996) and research (Graveline, 1998; Young, 1999). "Medicine Wheels can be pedagogical tools for teaching, learning, contemplating, and understanding our human journeys at individual, band/community, nation, global, and even cosmic levels" (Calliou, 1995, p. 51). However, one should keep in mind Black Elk's caution that the "relationality of the universe is a spiritual proposition, a force so complex and so powerful that it creates a sense of wonder and impotence in any sane human who truly considers it" (Black Elk, 1982, p. 148).

Within Medicine Wheels there are many, many "rings" of teachings (see Figure 1) that exist with significant meaning independently but are all the more powerful when understood as a collective of interdependent knowledge, teachings, and practices. Some of those teachings are outlined below.

Using Medicine Wheel Pedagogy

According to Absolon (1994), in following the path of Medicine Wheels, "the fourth direction involves creating a healing movement towards change – this is possible only when the other components have been acknowledged" (p. 18).The following Medicine Wheel diagram (see Figure 2) reviews the gifts of each of the directions as informed by Cree Elder Michael Thrasher. In the east, the gift of "vision" is found where one is able to "see." In the south, one spends "time" in which to "relate to" the vision. In the west, one uses the gift of "reason" to "figure it out." In the north, one uses the gift of "movement" in which to "do" the vision.

Moving into the "doing" phase of the north requires that one take the knowledge gained from all the directions and enact it. This form of "praxis" makes the balance achievable. Using Medicine Wheels as an analytical tool in healing and learning demands the continuous and ongoing reflection of oneself in relation to others, thus balance must be maintained while embracing change. "The teaching and healing process is evolutionary and cyclical in nature, as is the continuum of medicine wheels. It begins with a desire to understand and identify with the balance, wholeness and interconnectedness expressed in the medicine wheel" (Graveline, 1998, p 182).

In order to create the "movement" required by the northern direction, one must re-visit the other directions to achieve a 360 degree vision (Dumont in Stiegelbauer, 1992). By going to the east where one "visions" to transform that which is, one can actively create a better life for oneself and others. "Vision can inform our thinking, willing, feeling, and doing. As such, to be visionary is to be reacting, enacting, and pro-acting" (Graveline, 1998, p. 279). Indigenous people can vision how they can be active in the "creation of oppositional analytical and cultural space" (Mohanty, 1994, p. 148). Visioning allows them to engage in the hopeful utopian thinking necessary for radical transformation (Benhabib, 1992). Once a guiding vision is achieved, strategies can then be planned to help actualize it.

Teachings	East	South	West	North
races of people	red	yellow	black	white
season	spring	summer	fall	winter
time of day	morning	afternoon	evening	night
stages of life	infant	youth	adult	elder
aspects of people	spiritual	physical	emotional	mental
life givers	earth	sun	water	air
medicines	tobacco	sweetgrass	sage	cedar
relatives	plants	animals	swimmers	winged
abilities	vision	time	reasoning	movement
original teachings	kindness	honesty	sharing	strength
negative/fear	inferiority	jealousy	resentment	uncaring
positive/love	discipline	humility	respect	caring
stages of healing	fear	denial	awakening	acceptance
steps in healing	identify	express	understand	change
community development	cultural	economical	social	political
doorkeepers	eagle	deer	buffalo	bear
learning cycle	awareness	understanding	knowledge	wisdom
learning process	see it	relate to it	figure it out	do it

Figure 1: Some teachings of medicine wheels.

Each person then has the responsibility to do the work required to fulfill the vision (Cajete, 1994).

Indigenous people are fighting to actualize their visions for change in the education of their children. A revolutionized world will not "come into existence in a linear way, as the result of a single-minded drive, but in a cyclic, circular way, working in all dimensions of a culture, moving from one position to another, not in reaction but in interaction with other forces" (French in Gould, 1987, p. 18). Agreeably, "the movement from linear models to acknowledgment of the strength of the interconnectedness of the circle is truly a revo-

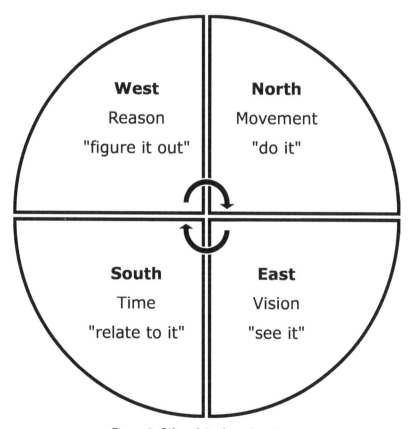

Figure 2: Gifts of the four directions.

lutionary position, one that guides the development of pedagogy and vision for the future" (Graveline, 1998, p. 288).

The Transmission of Medicine Wheel Teachings

A key question that needs to be addressed in the creation of an Indigenous, culturally-relevant educational process is how to create a schooling environment that reflects Indigenous culture and instils traditional values while providing the student with the skills they would need to "survive" in the modern world. Indigenous knowledge thus becomes important to understand. This knowledge becomes crucial to creating a culturally relevant space, pedagogy, and environment for teaching Indigenous children (see Figure 3).

Understanding Indigenous knowledge and world view begins with Medicine Wheel teachings previously discussed: the gifts of the directions (vision, time, reason, movement), the actions of those gifts (see it, relate to it, figure it out, do it), and the learning process (awareness, understanding, knowledge, wisdom). Building from these understandings, Indigenous knowledge embraced by Medicine Wheels can be defined as wholeness, interrelationships, interconnections, and balance/respect. Wholeness requires that one look in entireties – that the whole is greater than the sum of its parts, yet the parts cannot be fully seen until the shape of the whole can be seen. Interrelationship requires that one establish a personal relationship with the "whole" – with all that surrounds them. In addition, one must establish a relationship with their whole being; this includes one's spiritual, physical, mental, and emotional aspects. Interconnections create an environment which is mutually sustaining – where there is a transcending of logic and linear thought to reveal synthesis and dynamic interdependence. Balance and respect provide an order and structure to the whole and all its relationships and interconnections while providing an appreciation for the "awe" of it all.

It is necessary to consider Indigenous knowledge as a collection of knowledge from different Indigenous nations. Indigenous knowledge is therefore culture specific, contained within the local knowledge and world view of the nation. It therefore also has to be ecological, where the knowledge is contained within the land of the geographic location of the nation. Knowledge is also contained within the people of the nation. Indigenous knowledge then becomes personal and generational as there is a process of generational transmission. Indigenous knowledge is epistemological in that each nation determines for itself how it knows what it knows.

While Indigenous world view articulates that Indigenous people need to develop themselves, including their children, in a holistic way which addresses their spiritual, physical, emotional, and mental capacities, they need to address how to transmit learning through all

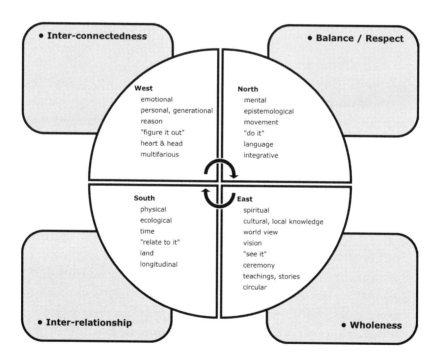

Figure 3: The transmission of Indigenous Knowledge through education.

of those personal aspects. The spiritual can be touched through ceremony, teachings, and stories. The physical can be transmitted through the land, while the emotional aspect can be developed through a balanced connection between the heart and the head. Mental capacities can be developed through ancestral languages and integrative learning.

Wisdom then becomes the goal of any educational process including "living"; to say that one is truly knowledgeable as a person is to say that he or she not only "knows" what is valued by a nation, but that he or she has lived their life in such a way that they have experienced what they know and can therefore be considered wise. Indigenous knowledge and world view is attained by choosing to do what is necessary to obtain multiple perspectives from which to view the world. This in-depth searching for knowledge is what leads to wisdom.

Moving Forward With Hope

Educational spaces need to be inclusive of the experiences, histories, and voices of those on the "margins," including Indigenous people. While the new Ontario Curriculum has attempted to include First Nation, Métis, and Inuit content into the curriculum, it is offered in an "add-on" approach that does not serve the cultural needs of its Indigenous students.

> The inclusion of Indigenous experiences and perspectives is expected, whether or not there is an explicit reference to Indigenous peoples stated in Ministry curriculum document expectations. The provision for inclusion is implicitly embedded within the commitment to ensure that Indigenous peoples see themselves reflected [meaningfully] in the curriculum across all subject areas. (Toronto District School Board, 2006, p. 15)

The First Nation, Métis, and Inuit Education Policy Framework released by the Ontario Ministry of Education (2007) begins to encourage teachers and schools to infuse Indigenous knowledge throughout the curriculum across all grades. The public school system needs to strive toward providing an education for First Nation, Métis, and Inuit students to experience learning from an Indigenous epistemological foundation. Limited, dissected Indigenous knowledge is often shared without placing it in an Indigenous cultural context or process of learning.

It is essential that culturally-appropriate educational spaces be provided for Indigenous children to gain the knowledge, skills, and attitudes needed to "survive" in Canadian and Indigenous communities. Indigenous education has always been about survival. Traditional education consisted of teaching children what they needed to know to survive in the environment that existed for them. "Survival" today requires that First Nation, Métis, and Inuit children have the skills necessary to provide for themselves in the dominant Canadian and global culture, while being strongly grounded in who they are as a First Nation, Métis, or Inuit person and ensuring that the culture of the Indigenous people survives. Providing an educational space whereby First Nation, Métis, and Inuit students have an "identity firmly anchored in the cultural world of their people while at the same time possessing the skills and knowledge required to succeed in the larger society" (Kulchyski et al., 1999, p. xxiv) enables Indigenous students to pursue any goal they choose. This will result in every Indigenous student being rooted in a cultural sense of self.

The perspectives, experiences, and histories of Indigenous peoples is an integral part of the history of Canada and should thus be embedded in anti-discriminatory education. Inclusion is therefore expected whether there are Indigenous students in the school or not as the cultural awareness of all Canadian citizens helps to ensure respectful relations between the Indigenous and non-Indigenous populations.

As a Nation, First Nation, Métis, and Inuit people may not be entirely able to move back to ancestral ways (nor is this necessarily desired), but they may use foundations of the past along with contemporary life to build their futures. To achieve this goal, Indigenous and non-Indigenous people must work together to ensure that every First Nation, Métis, and Inuit student is rooted in a cultural sense of self and that non-Indigenous students have developed an awareness, understanding, and thus respect for Canada's First Peoples. "To heal the future we must first confront the past in the present" (Indigenous student). The following story of the same boy addressed at the beginning of this chapter illustrates the hope there is for the educational system to meet the Indigenous education needs of all its students.

An Indigenous boy, now 16 and in grade 11, enjoys the opportunity to learn in ways conducive to his traditional understandings through an outdoor education program that allows him to learn in experiential and meaningful ways. Of his many experiences in this program, he listens to a leader on a camping trip sing a song with a hand drum. The boy experiences a connection to the drumming and singing as he has been raised with the songs of his people as taught to him by his father who is an Indigenous drummer and singer. With the desire to share his culture and bravery with his non-Indigenous peers, he asks to use the drum to sing an Indigenous song to his class and teachers. In doing so, he invites the only other Indigenous student in the class to join him. Upon receiving the song, his fellow students and teachers are impressed by the cultural sharing and offer admiration and gratitude. The lead teacher even makes the point of telling the boy's father how impressed she was that the boy offered to share of his own volition and how brave it is for him to share of himself in such an intimate way. This experience resulted in shared understandings of what it means to be an Indigenous person in contemporary society and the vital importance of Canadian society knowing its First Peoples.

Notes

1   The term "Indigenous" is used as an inclusive term encompassing all First Nations, Métis, and Inuit peoples in Canada.
2   The term used by Algonquian nations to identify themselves.
3   The choice of *cultural identity* as the appropriate concept here signals the view that Indigenous peoples in Canada share many cultural attributes, and frequently a common history in relation to the larger society, even though there are many specific cultures in the strict sense of the term (Berry, 1999).
4   The First Nation, Metis, and Inuit population grew five times faster than the general population between 2001 and 2006. The Indigenous population is also younger than the non-Indigenous population (Statistics Canada, 2006).
5   Approximately 50% of the Indigenous population are youth. Additionally, the Indigenous population in Canada is growing at twice the rate of the general population.
6   The term "medicine wheel" was established when stone constructions in the shape of wheels were found on Medicine Mountain.

References

Absolon, K. (1994, March). *Building health from the Medicine Wheel: Aboriginal program development.* Paper presented at the meeting of the Native Physician's Association, Winnipeg, MB.

Anderson, D. B. (2002). Preparing to Teach Our Children the Foundations for an Anishinaabe Curriculum. *McGill Journal of Education, 37*(3), 293–307.

Antone, E. (2000). Empowering Indigenous Voice in Indigenous Education. *Canadian Journal of Native Education, 24*(2), 92–101.

Assembly of First Nations (1994). *Breaking the Silence.* Ottawa: First Nations Health Commission.

Battiste, M. (2000). Maintaining Indigenous identity, language, and culture in modern society. In M. Battiste (Ed.), *Reclaiming Indigenous Voice and Vision* (pp. 192–208). University of British Columbia Press.

Bell, D. (2004). *Sharing our success: Ten case studies in Indigenous schooling.* Society for the Advancement of Excellence in Education. Available from http://saee.ca

Bell, N. (2005). *"Just Do It": Providing Anishnaabe Culture-Based Education* (Unpublished doctoral dissertation). Trent University, Peterborough, ON.

Benhabib, S. (1992). *Situating the self: Gender, community, and postmodernism in contemporary ethics.* New York, NY: Routledge.

Berry, J. W. (1999). Aboriginal Cultural Identity. *The Canadian Journal of Native Studies, 19*(1), 1–36.

Black Elk, F. (1982). Observations on marxism and Lakota tradition. In W. Churchill (Ed.), *Marxism and Native America* (pp. 137–157). Boston, MA: South End Press.

Bopp, J., Bopp, M., Brown, L, & Lane, P. (1984). *The sacred tree.* Four Worlds Development Project. Available from http://www.4worlds.org

Cajete, G. A. (1994). *Look to the mountain: An ecology of Indigenous education.* Asheville, NC: Kivaki Press.

Calliou, S. (1995). Peacekeeping actions at home: A Medicine Wheel model for a peacekeeping pedagogy. In J. Barman & M. Battiste (Eds.), *First Nations Education in Canada: The circle unfolds* (pp. 47–72). University of British Columbia Press.

Castellano, M. B. (2004). *Keynote Address.* Presented at a national gathering of the Aboriginal Healing Foundation, Edmonton, AB.

Coggins, K. (1990). *Alternative pathways to healing: The recovery medicine wheel.* Deerfield Beach, FL: Health Communications.

Gould, K. (1987). Feminist principles and minority concerns: Contributions, problems, and solutions. *Affilia, 2*(3), 6–19.

Graveline, F. J. (1998). *Circle works: Transforming eurocentric consciousness.* Halifax, NS: Fernwood Publishing.

Haig-Brown, C., Hodgson-Smith, K. L., Regnier, R., & Archibald, J. (1997). *Making the spirit dance within: Joe Duquette high school and an Aboriginal community.* Toronto, ON: James Lorimer & Company.

Hampton, E. (1995). Towards a redefinition of Indian education. In J. Barman & M. Battiste (Eds.), *First Nations Education in Canada: The Circle Unfolds* (pp. 5–46). University of British Columbia Press.

Hart, M. A. (2002). *Seeking mino-pimatisiwin: An Aboriginal approach to helping.* Halifax, NS: Fernwood Publishing

Hollow Water Community Holistic Circle Healing. (1993). *Position on Incarceration.* Unpublished manuscript.

Kulchyski, P., McCaskill, D., & Newhouse, D. (Eds.) (1999). *In the words of elders: Indigenous cultures in transition.* University of Toronto Press.

Medicine, B. (1993). Prologue to a Vision of Aboriginal Education. *Canadian Journal of Native Education, 20*(1), 42–45.

Miller, J. P. (1993). *The holistic curriculum.* Toronto, ON: OISE Press

Mohanty, C. T. (1994). On race and voice: Challenges for liberal education in the 1990's. In H. Giroux & P. McLaren (Eds.), *Between Borders: Pedagogy and the Politics of Cultural Studies* (pp. 145–166). New York, NY: Routledge.

Odjig-White, L. (1996). Medicine Wheel teachings in Native language education. In S. O'Meara & D. S. West (Eds.), *From Our Eyes: Learnings from Indigenous Peoples* (pp. 107–122). Toronto, ON: Garamond Press.

Ontario Ministry of Education. (1975). *People of Native Ancestry: A resource guide for the primary and junior divisions.*

Ontario Ministry of Education. (2007). *The Ontario First Nation, Métis, and Inuit Education Policy Framework.* Retrieved from http://www.edu.gov.on.ca/eng/aboriginal/fnmiFramework.pdf

Regnier, R. (1994). The Sacred Circle: A process pedagogy of healing. *Interchange, 25*(2), 129–144.

Royal Commission on Aboriginal Peoples (1996). *Report of the Royal Commission on Aboriginal peoples.* Available from http://www.ainc-inac.gc.ca/ap/rrc-eng.asp

Sanderson, J. (1991). *The Cree Way: Traditional Paths to Learning* (Unpublished master' thesis). University of Saskatchewan, Saskatoon.

Schissel, B. & Wotherspooon, T. (2003). *The legacy of school for Indigenous people: Education, oppression, and emancipation.* Oxford University Press.

Statistics Canada. (2001). *Census 2001: Aboriginal Population Profile.* Available from http://www.statcan.ca/bsolc/english/bsolc?catno=94F0043XIE

Statistics Canada. (2006). *Census 2006: Aboriginal Population Profile.* Available from http://www12.statcan.ca/census-recensement/2006/rt-td/index-eng.cfm

Stiegelbauer, S. (1992). *The individual is the community; the community is the world; Native elders talk about what young people need to know.* Paper presented at the meeting of the American Educational Research Association, San Francisco, CA. (ERIC Document Reproduction Service No. ED 249 151).

Toronto District School Board. (2006). *Indigenous Voices in the Curriculum: A guide to teaching Indigenous studies in K–8 classrooms.*

Young, W. (1999). Aboriginal students speak about acceptance, sharing, awareness and support: A participatory approach to change at a university and community college. *Native Social Work Journal, 2*(1), 21–58.

ANCHORING THE MARY CELESTE: SCIENCE, EDUCATION, AND SITUATED ENVIRONMENTAL KNOWLEDGES[1]

16

Steve Alsop & Leesa Fawcett, York University

HOW SHOULD WE SPEAK OF SCHOOLING in Canada? Beyond the Molson brewery list of what it means to be a Canadian, and a statement of geographic enormity, our southerly neighbours can dwell on differentiating our national thoughts and identities. In education, we reflect on distant, yet all too familiar policies: No Child Left Behind and the Education Science Reform Act and the practices of the Institute of Education Science (IES). These all serve in some ways, perhaps, to shape our perspectives. Of course, such reflections can evoke simplistic divisions in an era of many striking similarities. In Canada we are subject to seemingly endless education assessments and desires of improvement. Just like so many other places, our attention has fixated on improving quality through the easily measurable, more often than not. Structures have been put in place that measure, regulate, control, and standardize school curricula as well as assessment procedures, reporting mechanisms, funding formulas, terms and conditions of employment for teachers and other education workers, teacher certification, and teacher education. As Alan Luke (2004) laments, such reforms have given rise to changes that include "devolved school management and business models of education at the local level; universal standardized norm-referenced achievement testing; expanding and often untrained usage of other standardized measures in schools and classrooms; proliferation of compensatory pull-out programmes for dealing with cultural, linguistic, and epistemological diversity; growing expenditure on behavioural management programmes; and voluminous print-based documentation" (p. 1426). The spirit of "No Child Left Behind" is all too easily found within our own national educational boundaries.

It seems that what many of us hold dear in education is under threat by slippery questions of enhanced empirical objectivity – questions which are more often than not framed by the "objectively measurable." It is somehow repetitive to state once more that we "value what we measure," registering another concern about the long-standing torment over the scientificity of educational inquiry. The enhanced status of science in education is not only a curriculum issue; it also profoundly shapes the culture of our institutional practices as educators and researchers as well. A question, as always, is how might we mobilise for change against such seductive and powerful reasoning? How should we speak of science in education in Canada?

This is the focus of our chapter. We discuss science and education both within the curriculum and its cultural influences on the curriculum. We draw on selective literature in science and technology studies (STS) and feminist post-colonial theories to offer some acts of culture jamming through local situated environmental knowledges and practices as sciences. Our argument is that contemporary curriculum questions cannot easily escape discussion of science and its effects on the curriculum, but some of the curriculum discussions in the sciences relating to situated environmental knowledges might offer insight and opportunities to act.

The rhetoric and ideology of western modern science has, of course, been widely discussed and its hostile effects extensively documented. Stanley Aronowitz (1988), for example, writes that "the genius of science, unlike religion or philosophy before Kant, has been its ability to identify the absolute with knowledge or nature" (p. viii). Science fetishisms present us with a strangely comforting, predictable world – a world held apart from troublesome, sometimes confrontational, questions of purpose, values, morality, and aesthetics. To imagine knowledge as certain and real is in many ways securing? The merely possible, on the other hand, resists closure and perhaps preys too readily on vulnerabilities. At the core of such musings are a series of old, well-worn dualisms between nature and culture:

subjects (subjectivism) and objects (objectivism) and the knower versus the known. In the current culture of education, these seem especially important. In part because they can frame not only our dissatisfactions (our problematics) but also haunt our satisfactions and linger behind the scenes as a subtext of our responses.

Anderson and Adams's (2008) work is so delightfully evocative, depicting science using the metaphor of the mysterious Mary Celeste, a seemingly abandoned brigantine merchant ship.2 The Mary Celeste is often thought of as the archetypal ghost ship, a derelict vessel that was found drifting around the globe, powerfully packaged and intact with its origins strangely erased. How do we resist science and education that wanders unaccounted for and unaccountably, like the Marie Celeste, across social, political, and cultural boundaries? Over the past decade, scholars of Science and Technology Studies have sought to understand the mobilities of science in terms such as vectors, "boundary objects," and "immutable mobiles." There are parallel conversations about globalized educational reforms and their local origins, their vectors, arrivals, and influences. In a culture of policies and practices seemingly from "nowhere," we hope to capture a view from "somewhere" (Haraway, 1991). Mobility is an interesting question for education and schooling because in so many ways we exist in an educational era of "nowhere" and "everywhere." Indeed, the word "education" itself has an unnerving generalness, devoiced from a sense of temporality, spirit, ecology, value, and context. It is almost as though we have to keep pinching ourselves to remember that we live and work in unique places – that our practices comprise particular schools and classrooms full of unique learners. With these comments, you can almost hear critical theorists "sharpening their knives," relishing the opportunity of explaining how existing structures serve those in power, who see no reason in upsetting the pedagogical and epistemological traditions of their authority. And there is a persuasive, well-developed argument here. Schooling is, of course, implicated in propping up the natural order of things. Our practices are sharpened to include, exclude, and make invisible. Insightfully, Noel Gough asks, "What invisible mental landscapes are (or might be) shared by curriculum scholars and environmental educators who work transnationally?" (2009, p. 76) The question of curriculum in Canada is, in part, about upsetting this apple cart. To ask of a Canadian curriculum what it produces and reproduces cannot be confined to simple curriculum additions, for it opens up questions at the very heart of schooling itself. Questions at the very heart of our anxieties over the "scientific" in education.

Science Education and Traditional Ecological Knowledges

In science education in Canada (and many other parts of the world) there has been sustained discussion of whose knowledge gets to count as knowledge in the curriculum as well as how can we make the curriculum more representative of multiple cultural knowledge claims. The particular case of local, "environmentally-related knowledges" as science in education has been the focus of much of this recent attention. There are overwhelming reasons to include traditional ecological knowledges (TEK)3 as science education. Generations of indigenous students continue to be marginalised in science education on the basis of cultural identities (Battiste, 2002); TEKs embody environmental awareness and ecological responsibility (Snively & Corsiglia, 2001); epistemic monocultures are likely to be less flexible and more sterile, and there are important economic and vocational arguments regarding future Science, Technology, Engineering, Mathematic (STEM) agendas (Council of Ministers of Education Canada, 1997). This has all been clearly documented in thoughtful and insightful research and scholarship (including Aikenhead, 2001; Ogawa, 1995; Stanley & Brickhouse, 2001). In this chapter we dip into a recent exchange about this topic and the concept of "recalibrating." An influential paper written by van Eijick and Roth (2007) has become the focus of a series of responses (including our own – see Alsop & Fawcett, 2010). The article focuses on the epistemic status of Western modern science (WMS) in science education with the desire to push back its hegemony that renders other knowledges to the peripheral status of "other." The pedagogical question that they explore is how to de-privilege, how to recalibrate WMS in science education. How might we disrupt the threat that science has brought – and continues to bring – to bear on science pedagogical practices?

Van Eijick & Roth's arguments stem from a study of epistemology located in the Northern Pacific coasts of Canada and the United States. In a particular ecological context, they juxtapose narratives of the Coastal Saanich First Nation peoples and their fishing practices and narratives of science and biology in the same location. The upshot of this juxtaposition is that although science and TEK are both forms of knowledges, the artifacts of these knowledges cannot be understood apart from the distinctive cultural-historically determined human activities in which they emerged and consequently are irreducible to each other and thus incommensurate. Such a task as the authors acknowledge has a series of caveats concerning texts, representations, and cultural interpretations. To de-privilege western modern science in science education, Michael van Eijick and Wolff-Michael Roth (2007) advocate utilitarianism, advancing the advantages of embedding epistemic and pedagogical discussions and judgments within particular social, cultural, and local ecological contexts. Their arguments seek to overcome the multicultural-universalism debate, and in search of a way of uniting these well-worn binary positions, they look to develop epistemology that simultaneously entails both "culture" and "physical reality" by rejecting a position of "truth" and adopting utilitarianism as a measure of the validity of knowledge. This position also embodies the dynamic, heterogeneous, and plural nature of products of human beings and understandings. A pedagogical conclusion drawn from this argument is that learners should learn to generate knowledge in pursuit of actions within collaborative, culturally heterogeneous communities with shared/negotiated utilitarian goals. Such a position advocates that science education should adopt local contexts – social, cultural, economic, political, and environmental – in which several literacies are brought to bear on problems and situations of shared concerns and agencies.

Recalibrating the Mary Celeste: Challenging Scientism in Education Reforms

So what might we draw from the clash of discourses on the Pacific coast? How can we recalibrate science in education? From his prison cell in Turin, in 1929, Antonio Gramsci wrote to his wife about his concerns regarding his son's obsession with playing with Meccano4. It has a tendency, he wrote, to make "man rather dry, machine-like and bureaucratic" (Gramsci, 1988, p. 88). He then continued with comments about the dangers of educational principles that determine the "new" and lamenting his son's seeming "obsession," almost "intoxication," with science, technology, and mathematics. In contemporary times this seems so delightfully quaint. While things have certainly changed dramatically since Gramsci's day, such personalised reflections serve to locate science and technology education within the historically emerging concept of hegemony, which is in itself a pause for thought.

Van Ejick and Roth set their article within discussions of Foucaultian "regimes of truth" and the power structures of society. As they note, these arguments extend far beyond the prison to include schools and the minute power relations that constitute our lives. The danger here is that after reading, Foucault regimes seem so entrenched and robust. But the exercise of power, as Foucault (1977) himself comments, always goes hand in hand with resistance. And throughout both papers there is an undercurrent that TEK as science education raises significant opportunities for resistance. Such possibilities stem beyond free-floating oppositional narratives to narratives that might exploit some deep-rooted contradictions in current realities. Edward Said (1993) claims that post-colonial perspectives offer a view from within called "counter-narratives" that disrupt and transform the official natural histories and could question some of the reigning truths in science education. For post-colonial scholar Ilan Kapoor (2003, pp. 566–567), referring to Homi Bhabha's work, however, "there are no relations of power without agency," and power is concerned with "making possible and making trouble, both at once." Perhaps the key question here is what can we trouble in science pedagogy from this standpoint? The environmental activist Starhawk (1987) is always direct. We must become more than victims, she writes, by "actively resisting weapons that culture has devised against the self" (p. 71). To resist, we have some choices: to rebel, to withdraw, and/or to manipulate. The authors of the preceding papers seek in many ways to "manipulate" dominant discourses and practices. These acts of subversion have different referents. They force us to ask how our research and practice might become more strategic in seeking out transformations that we desire. In the following sections we explore three acts that TEKs provoke. In the ghostly spirit of The Mary Celeste, we frame these by extending our nautical metaphor with hope to anchor a powerful vessel with hegemonic cargos, "fetished" origins and invisible alliances.

Captain's log I: Partial perspectives

There is always a danger in discussions of this type of dualisms, of polemic reasoning. Hilary Rose (1997) once commented that "dreams come into existence not through binary confrontations but through multiple conversations and complex alliances" (p. 64). The epistemology and pedagogy that we commit to throughout these discussions is pluralistic and partial; it hopes to attend to many voices, many languages, and many cultures. Of course, such a positioning needs to be especially attendant to those voices that have over time been silenced and overwhelmed, lost in the shadows of dominant historical, socio-political, "natural" orders. Polemics, it is often written, can obscure the richness of dialectical and dialogical reasoning. Such positioning serves, perhaps, to do little more than sustain arguments and reassert established hierarchies. The processes of separation seek to demarcate clean positions and accentuate differences rather than celebrate commonalities, collaborations, and shared concerns. What becomes lost is a sense of diverse hybrid imaginaries, shared common heritages, and ways of making sense of differences. Dualisms immediately raise questions of power and privilege. Who benefits from such divisions, why and how? As the late philosopher and ecofeminist Val Plumwood (2002) observed, dualisms "create a radical discontinuity between the group identified as the privileged 'centre' and those subordinated" (p. 101). Plumwood identified dualisms as sets of interlocking oppressions that police the boundaries against any unlawful flow of ideas across the divide, for example, between culture and nature or science and TEK. In her analysis of the power of dualisms to oppress, she outlines five characteristics of how interlocking oppressions hold power in colonizing practices by: (1) back grounding, (2) radical exclusion, (3) incorporation, (4) instrumentalism, and (5) homogenisation. For instance, Plumwood claims one of the reigning assumptions embedded in the success of dualistic power inequities is to radically exclude or hyper-separate the Other as inferior; this has been the historical treatment of indigenous peoples and their knowledges. At another scale, the homogenization of indigenous people's knowledges has served to erase the place-based specificity and the particular understanding of each unique group.

In his latest book on the politics of nature, Bruno Latour (2004) invites us to start with a dissociation; we are asked to dissociate Science (singular and capitalised) from the sciences (plural and lower case). He then goes on to define Science as the "politicization of the sciences through epistemology in order to render ordinarily political life impotent through the threat of an incontestable nature" (p. 10). This trend is echoed by Raymond Williams's (1980) assertion that in Western culture the word "nature" has evolved into a singular, abstracted, and personified meaning. Williams writes that "just as in religion the moment of monotheism is a critical development, so, in human responses to the physical world, is the moment of a singular Nature" (p. 69). In this case the diverse multiplicity of living processes are rendered down into one essentialist meaning. What happens when this Nature meets that Science? Such a move serves to dissociate the local, discursive, material practices that constitute the practices of the sciences (Rouse, 1996) from the rhetorical threat that Science brings to bear on the exercise of politics as well as the practices of these sciences themselves. With the construct of Science, or Western Modern Science (WMS), there are always problems of essentialism, conversations that slip into the "West versus the rest" dialogs. As Mueller and Tippins (2009), in a response to Eiijick and Roths arguments, comprehensively demonstrate, the genealogy (and contemporary practices) of WMS are neither exclusively Western, nor have they ever been, or will be, especially modern (Latour, 1993). While the dissociation of "Science" from "sciences" has a series of weaknesses (as these are clearly not mutually exclusive), it might help to slightly broaden the question that we are discussing here and in so doing respond to some of the tensions of essentialism.

What we need, above all else, is a science in education that carries with it a notion of the collective/public good. A discourse that in Donna Haraway's words, "insists on a better account of the world," and within this process "it is not enough to show radical historical contingency and modes of construction for everything" (1991, p. 187).

Captain's log II: Localism/Places

Of late, there has been much interest in what has been called the "new localism" in education. Place-based education has a series of high profile advocates (Gruenewald & Smith, 2008; Smith, 2002; Theobald, 1997). In a general sense these approaches adopt local environments – social, cultural, economic, political, and natural – but there are caveats here, and it is important not to be drawn into celebratory hierarchical enactments of old dualisms – nature vs. culture, localism vs. globalism, rural vs. urban, traditional vs. non-traditional. Localism offers many interesting possibilities for science education which, as the previous discussions suggest, include hopes of resisting and challenging globalized knowledges and imperialist cultures. However, bounded places have their limitations, and associated discourses cannot overlook inequalities and boundaries inscribed in the local. It is an open question of when the local becomes parochial (for example). In proposing a radical pedagogy of place, Ruitenberg (2005) critically examines the concept of locality in place-based educational practices and the trap of "topological essentialism" that resides in deterministic notions of locality and unquestioned desirability of rootedness. Local places are not necessarily the conditions to develop "better" identities, "better" pedagogies, "better" epistemologies, and "better" societies. Moreover, there is no localism that is not connected and uncontaminated by globality – after all, in fundamental sense, the local is only intelligible with reference to the existence of the non-local, which, as such, always leaves its imprint. We should be ever careful of not stumbling back into romantic myths of isolation and overlook interdependencies, relationships, and the trans-local.

Van Ejick and Roth's arguments, as their title suggests, are in part built on keeping the "local local." They explore the knowledge applied to salmon fishing practices of Coast Salish peoples at the Northern Pacific coasts of Canada and the United Status. The choice of location, in this regard, is not arbitrary. It is a specific cultural and ecological location to compare and contrast common linguistic and physical artifacts of Saanich people with those of scientists (an evolutionary biologist). As you read their case, what becomes clearly apparent is that location matters in epistemology and pedagogy. This point is all too easy to overlook in an era of globalization and transient "liquid modernity," to use Zygmunt Bauman's (2008) term. Science and technology seem so naturally universal and globalized, but what emerges in Van Eijick and Roth's case study is the power of location. Uncovered in the particular are the experiential situations of knowledge production and use, and this is where global power differentials can subside. There is subversion in the pedagogical act of keeping the local local.

David Greenwood's (2009) work in place-based environmental education critically examines concepts of decolonization and reinhabitation of specific locales by "learning to recognize disruption and injury in person-place relationships, and learning to address their causes" (p. 13) It is this kind of politicized ethical local education that we want to support and celebrate – learning and teaching that are able to hold the historical tension of violent and colonizing practices while imagining and enacting forms of environmentally and socially just ways of living in particular places.

Captain's log III: Beyond utilitarianism

The vast majority of material about TEK is written by outsiders, not indigenous authors, and focuses on the usefulness of TEK – as Reid, Teamey, and Dillon (2004) point out. Reid et al. argue that TEK has an important role to play in improving and deepening environmental education practices, but drawing on Bowers (2001), they too recognize that "centralized, top-down and modernist approaches to education found in the institutions, philosophies and practices of formal, bureaucratized education have trouble with systems of knowledge such as TEK-based approaches to developing ecosystem resilience" (Reid et al., p. 247). A key question they ask is: "What power and privilege is generated, granted, and denied to people based on a particular construction of TEK?" (p. 251).

Dropping anchor

So, perhaps a way to de-privilege Science in science education is within pedagogy of agency set within a specific social and environmental context. To elaborate, Dan Longboat, a Mohawk scholar, used concepts from island biogeography to examine the connections between endangered languages, cultures, and habitats in North America.

What might local, situated knowledges bring to Science and its influences on the Curriculum? Mi'kmaq elder Albert Marshall has developed a theory about Two-Eyed Seeing, which according to Greg Lowan (in press) is about "viewing the world simultaneously through both Western scientific and Aboriginal lenses" which will indeed lead to new visions and narratives. So, how might we subvert the global rhetoric of Science? Feminist science studies critic Donna Haraway talks about "naturecultures," which we believe should guide us in approaching and thinking about a science and education "where the categorical separation of nature and culture is already a kind of violence, an inherited violence anyway" (2000, p. 106). In the process of peacefully making worlds visible, we intend to enact libratory forms of situated environmental knowledges that resist the globalizing effects of Science in part by relying on decolonizing methodologies (Tuhiwai Smith, 1999). To decolonize ourselves requires decolonizing our collective imaginations first. If as Rosi Braidotti (2006) states "the 'imaginary' refers to a set of socially mediated practices which function as the anchoring point, albeit unstable and contingent, for identifications and therefore for identity formations" (p. 86), these practices can lead us to a lagoon to anchor the Mary Celeste for a while. This gives us time to float and reflect on our individual subject positions, our collective yearnings, and dream about what science pedagogy and science in education might become before we hoist the main sail.

Notes

1   Throughout this chapter we use the plural term "knowledges" to emphasise the partial, situated, dynamic, materialistic nature of theorising. Such a position is concordant with a broad array of scholarship in the fields of science and technology studies and feminist postcolonial studies. This position is nicely framed in an essay by Donna Haraway (1991).

2   Built in Nova Scotia in the mid-nineteenth century, the Mary Celeste was originally named *The Amazon* and transported cargos between the West Indies, Central, South America, Canada, and Europe. In 1867, the ship ran aground in Glace Bay, Nova Scotia and was salvaged and then renamed the Mary Celeste. In addition to the ghostly mystery, a reason we have chosen this metaphor connects with the ship's colonial history and its Canadian origins. There is a monument to the ship and her crew at Spencer's Island, Nova Scotia. (The ship is sometimes incorrectly referred to as the *Marie* Celeste, which was the name that Sir Arthur Conan Doyle used in a novel and one of his Sherlock Holmes detective mysteries)

3   We rely on Winona LaDuke's definition of traditional ecological knowledge as the "culturally and spiritually based way in which indigenous people relate to their ecosystems. This knowledge is founded on spiritual-cultural instructions from 'time immemorial' and on generations of careful observation within an ecosystem of continuous residence" (2002, p. 78).

4   Meccano is a brand name of a popular metal construction system. The first sets were developed and sold in the UK during the early 1900s. It is still very popular, particularly in Europe. Indeed, as a child I (Alsop) shared Delio Gramsci's obsession. As a child, I (Fawcett) caught snakes in the backyard instead.

References

Aikenhead, G. (2001). Integrating Western and aboriginal sciences: Cross-cultural science teaching. *Research in Science Education, 31,* 337–355.

Alsop, S. & Fawcett, L. (2010). After this nothing happened. *Cultural Studies in Science Education, 5,* 1027–1045.

Anderson, W. & Adams, V. (2008). Pramoedya's chickens: Postcolonial studies of technoscience. In E. Hackett, O. Amsterdamska, M. Lynch, & J. Wajcman (Eds.), *The handbook of science and technology studies* (3rd ed., pp. 181–205). Cambridge, MA: Harvard University Press.

Aronowitz, S. (1988). *Science as power: Discourse and ideology in modern society*. University of Minnesota Press.

Battiste, M. (2002). *Indigenous knowledge and pedagogy in First Nations education: A literature review with recommendations*. Ottawa: Indian and Northern Affairs.

Bauman, Z. (2008). *Does ethics have a chance in a world of consumers?* Cambridge, MA: Harvard University Press.

Bowers, C. A. (2001). *Education for eco-justice and community*. University of Georgia Press.

Braidotti, R. (2006). *Transpositions: On nomadic ethics*. Cambridge, England: Polity Press.

Council of Ministers of Education Canada. (1997). *Best practices in increasing Aboriginal postsecondary enrolment rates*. Victoria, BC: R. A. Malatest & Associates Ltd.

Foucault, M. (1977). *Discipline & punish: The birth of the prison*. New York, NY: Vintage Books.

Gough, N. (2009). Becoming transnational: Rhizoesemiosis, complicated conversation, and curriculum inquiry. In M. McKenzie, P. Hart, H. Bai, & B. Jickling (Eds.), *Fields of green: Restorying culture, environment and education* (pp. 67–83). Cresskill, NJ: Hampton Press, Inc.

Gramsci, A. (1988). *Prison letters* (H. Henderson, Trans.). London, England: Pluto Press.

Greenwood, D. (2009). *Nature, empire and paradox in environmental education*. Keynote paper presented at North American Association for Environmental Education Research Symposium, Portland, OR.

Gruenwald, D., & Smith, G. (2008). *Place-based education in the Global Age*. New York, NY: Lawrence Erlbaum.

Haraway, D. (1991). Situated knowledges: The science question in feminism and the privilege of partial perspective. In *Simians, Cyborgs, and Women: The Reinvention of Nature* (pp. 183–201). New York, NY: Routledge.

Haraway, D. (2000). *How like a leaf: An interview with Thyrza Nichols Goodeve*. New York, NY: Routledge.

Kapoor, I. (2003). Acting in a tight spot: Homi Bhabha's postcolonial politics. *New Political Science, 25*(4), 561–567.

LaDuke, W. (2002). *The Winona LaDuke reader: A collection of essential writings*. Penticton, BC: Theytus Books.

Latour, B. (1993). *We have never been modern* (Catherine Porter, Trans.). Cambridge, MA: Harvard University Press.

Latour, B. (2004.) *Politics of nature: How to bring the sciences into democracy* (Catherine Porter, Trans.). Cambridge, MA: Harvard University Press.

Lowan. G. (in press). Indigenous environmental education research in North America: A brief review. In M. Brodey, J. Dillon, R. Stevenson, & A. Wals (Eds.), *International handbook of research on environmental education*. New York, NY: Sage Publications.

Luke, A. (2004). Teaching after the market: From commodity to cosmopolitan. *Teachers College Record, 106*(7), 1–14.

Mueller, M., & Tippins, D. (2009). Van Ejick and Roth's utilitarian science education: Why the recalibration of science and traditional ecological knowledge invokes multiple perspectives to protect science education from being exclusive. *Cultural Studies in Science Education, 5*(4), 993–1007.

Ogawa, M. (1995). Science education in a multi-science perspective. *Science Education, 79*, 583–593.

Plumwood, V. (2002). *Environmental culture: The ecological crisis of reason*. London, England: Routledge.

Reid, A., Teamey, K., & Dillon, J. (2004). Valuing and utilizing traditional ecological knowledge: Tensions in the context of education and the environment. *Environmental Education Research, 10*(2), 237–254.

Rose, H. (1997). Science wars: My enemy's enemy is – only perhaps – my friend. In R. Levinson, & J. Thomas (Eds.), *Science today: Problem or crisis* (pp. 51–64). London, England: Falmer.

Rouse, J. (1996). *Engaging science: How to understand its practices and philosophy*. Ithaca, NY: Cornell University Press.

Ruitenberg, C. (2005). Deconstructing the experience of the local: Toward a radical pedagogy of place. In K. Howe (Ed.), *Philosophy of Education* (pp. 212–220). Urbana, IL: Philosophy of Education Society.

Said, E. (1993). *Culture and imperialism*. New York: Knopf.

Smith, G. (2002). Place-based Education: Learning to be where we are. *Phi Delta Kappan, 83*(8), 584–594.

Snively, G. & Corsiglia, J. (2001). Discovering indigenous science: Implications for science education. *Science Education, 85*, 6–34.

Stanley, W. B. & Brickhouse, N. W. (2001). Teaching sciences: The multicultural question revisited. *Science Education, 85*, 35–49.

Starhawk. (1987). *Truth or dare: Encounters with power, authority and mystery*. New York, NY: Harper Row.

Theobald, P. (1997). *Teaching the commons: Place, pride and the renewal of community*. Boulder Co: Westview Press.

Tuhiwai Smith, L. (1999). *Decolonizing methodologies: Research and indigenous peoples*. New York, NY: Zed Books.

van Eijick, M., & Roth, W. M. (2007). Keeping the local local: Recalibrating the status of science and traditional ecological knowledge (TEK) in science education. *Science Education, 91*, 926–947.

Williams, R. (1980). *Problems in Materialism and Culture*. New York, NY: Verso.

CONTRIBUTORS

STEVE ALSOP is a Professor of Education at York University, Canada. He has held a series of academic positions including Associate Dean, Academic Director, honorary professor, and teacher in educational institutions in Canada and the UK. His PhD is in philosophy of education with a specialization in science, technology, and risk. His current research interests include: the personal, social, and political organization of scientific and technological knowledge; environmental and sustainability education; and community and popular education.

GERALDINE BALZER is an Assistant Professor of Curriculum Studies in the College of Education at the University of Saskatchewan. A traveller at heart, she studied at the Universities of Waterloo, British Columbia, and Saskatchewan and worked in Switzerland, Germany, the Northwest Territories, and Nunavut before returning to her prairie roots. While her first love was English literature, her experiences teaching Inuit students led to her interest in decolonizing pedagogies and transformative education. Her teaching focuses on ways of disrupting the hegemony of standard English and embracing the diversity of Englishes within our world, incorporating Aboriginal and postcolonial literature into secondary classrooms, and preparing teachers to be advocates of social justice. Her current research interest is in the transformative impact of service learning.

MARIE BATTISTE, a Mi'kmaw educator from Potlo'tek First Nations, Nova Scotia, is a Professor in the College of Education and Director of the Aboriginal Education Research Centre (AERC) at the University of Saskatchewan. Her research interests are in initiating institutional change in the decolonization of education, in particular humanities, language and social justice policy and power, and postcolonial educational approaches that recognize and affirm the political and cultural diversity of Canada. She is involved in the ethical protection and advancement of Indigenous knowledge, co-authoring *Protecting Indigenous Knowledge and Heritage: A Global Challenge* with J. Youngblood Henderson (Saskatoon: Purich Press, 2000), which received a Saskatchewan Book Award in 2000. She has published widely, including the edited work *Reclaiming Indigenous Voice and Vision*, a special co-edited issue of the *Australian Journal of Indigenous Education*, and senior editor with Jean Barman for *First Nations Education in Canada: The Circle Unfolds*.

NICOLE BELL is Anishnaabe from Kitigan Zibi First Nation in Quebec, Canada and is from the Bear Clan. Dr. Bell has a Master of Education degree from Queen's University (Ontario, Canada) and a Doctor of Philosophy degree from Trent University (Ontario, Canada). Dr. Bell is the founder of an Anishnaabe culture-based school for Aboriginal children in junior kindergarten to grade 12 which provides traditional Anishinaabe world view and values in a contemporary educational context. Dr. Bell is currently an Assistant Professor at Trent University with the School of Education and the Department of Indigenous Studies.

SHEILA L. CAVANAGH is an Associate Professor in Sociology and the Sexuality Studies Coordinator at York University. She does gender and sexuality studies with a focus on feminist, queer, cultural, and psychoanalytic theories. Her scholarship focuses on the social regulation of gender and sexuality in schools; trans studies; museum studies; and film studies. She published *Sexing the Teacher: School Sex Scandals and Queer Pedagogies* with the University of British Columbia Press in 2007 and it was given honourable mention by the Canadian Women's Studies Association. Her second book, *Queering Bathrooms: Gender, Sexuality, and the Hygienic Imagination*, is forthcoming with the University of Toronto Press. Cavanagh has also published in a wide range of refereed journals including: *Sexualities: Studies in Culture and Society*; *Body and Society*; *Social Text*; *Discourse:*

Studies in the Cultural Politics of Education; *Psychoanalysis, Culture and Society*; and *The International Journal of Cultural Studies*.

BRENT DAVIS is a Professor and Distinguished Chair in Mathematics Education in the Faculty of Education at the University of Calgary. His research areas include mathematics teachers' disciplinary knowledge, teacher education, complexity research in education, and teaching and learning of mathematics. His research program focuses on recent developments in the cognitive and complexity sciences. He is also author and co-author of several books, research papers, and essays in a number of academic journals that have addressed mathematics learning and teaching, curriculum theory, teacher education, and action research.

LEESA FAWCETT lives on the Nottawasaga River, where she has raised her family and is involved in community work focusing on resilience, sustainability, and food sovereignty. She is an Associate Dean, Associate Professor, and Coordinator of the graduate Diploma in Environmental and Sustainability Education at the magnificently interdisciplinary Faculty of Environmental Studies, York University.

LUIGI IANNACCI is an Associate Professor in the School of Education and Professional Learning at Trent University in Peterborough, Ontario. He teaches and coordinates courses that focus on language and literacy as well as special needs learners. He has taught mainstream and special education in a range of elementary grades in Ontario. His research interests include first and second language and literacy acquisition, critical multiculturalism, early childhood education, critical disability studies, and critical narrative research. He is the former President of the Language and Literacy Researchers of Canada (LLRC) and the International Society for Educational Biography (ISEB). Luigi can be reached at luigiiannacci@trentu.ca

David W. Jardine is a Professor of Education in the Faculty of Education at the University of Calgary. Recent work includes a forthcoming book entitled *Pedagogy Left in Peace* and a co-authored essay entitled "A Zone of Deep Shadow: Pedagogical and Familial Reflections on 'The Clash of Civilizations'," published in *Interchange: A Quarterly Review of Education*.

Andrejs Kulnieks is an Assistant Professor with the Nipissing University Schulich School of Education at the Muskoka Campus. His research interests include curriculum theory, language arts, literacies, Indigenous Knowledge, and eco-justice environmental education. He has published articles with *Alternative: An International Journal of indigenous Peoples, Canadian Journal of Environmental Studies, EcoJustice Review*, and *Journal of the Canadian Association of Curriculum Studies*.

Linda Laidlaw is an Associate Professor at the University of Alberta in the Department of Elementary Education. Her research interests are in early literacy and the education of young children; as well as diversity and the development of innovative learning environments. She continues to focus on ecological approaches and complexity thinking in curriculum and research.

Dan Roronhiakewen Longboat "He Clears the Sky" belongs to the Turtle Clan of the Mohawk Nation, is a citizen of the Haudenosaunee, is originally from Ohswe:ken (the Six Nations community on the Grand River Territory), and is now living in Peterborough, Ontario. He is currently an Associate Professor in the Department of Indigenous Studies and is the Founder and Director of the Indigenous Environmental Studies Program at Trent University. His areas of research involve cultural knowledge, which serves to support research and development of culturally based courses and integrated science programs focused upon Indigenous human health and the environment, foods and medicines, natural resource restoration, community sustainability, international Indigenous networks, Indigenous languages, cultures and the recognition of traditional life skills and practices.

REBECCA LUCE-KAPLER is Associate Dean of Graduate Studies and Research in the Faculty of Education, Queen's University. Her research interests focus on the integral role of literary practices, particularly writing, in the development of human consciousness and identity. This work has contributed to understanding the normative power of cultural forms and the importance of interpretive reading and writing practices for generative learning and teaching. Her most recent SSHRC research, which involves senior-aged women reading and writing literary memoirs, investigates how literary practices can deepen learning and interpretation of experience. She is the author of *Writing with, through, and beyond the text: An ecology of language* and *The gardens where she dreams.* She is co-author of *Engaging Minds: Changing teaching in complex times.* She gratefully acknowledges the Social Sciences and Humanities Research Council for its ongoing support of her research.

NICHOLAS NG-A-FOOK is an Assistant Professor of curriculum theory at the University of Ottawa (Canada), where he teaches curriculum studies in both the Bachelor of Education and Graduate Studies Program. He is the director of A Canadian Theory Curriculum Project at the University of Ottawa. His research projects focus on curriculum and pedagogy, history of education, and life narratives. He is the author of *An Indigenous Curriculum of Place: The united Houma nation's contentious relationship with Louisiana's educational institutions* (Peter Lang, 2007).

ANNE PHELAN is a Professor in the Department of Curriculum and Pedagogy, and a Research Associate with the Centre for the Study of Teacher Education, at the University of British Columbia. She has published in journals such as the *Journal of Curriculum Studies,*

Teaching and Teacher Education, Curriculum Inquiry, and *Studies in Philosophy of Education.* Her interests lie in the relationship between language, subjectivity, and power, and the dynamic of judgment and responsibility in teaching and teacher education. She is co-editor (with Dr. Jennifer Sumsion) of *Critical Readings in Teacher Education: Provoking Absences.*

SHARON RICH is a Professor and Dean of Education at the Schulich School of Education, Nipissing University. She uses the concept of co-learning as a foundation for her work with teacher educators and students.

TASHA RILEY is an HIV Prevention and Awareness Educator in the Prevention and Awareness Services Department with AIDS Vancouver. Her research considers the significance of teachers' attribution theories on the educational decisions made by teachers. She is an educator and researcher with expertise in teaching and facilitation, project coordination and curriculum development and specializes in anti-oppressive and anti-racist education in the context of HIV/AIDS prevention education and community-based research.

DAVID GEOFFREY SMITH is Professor of Education at the University of Alberta. He researches and teaches in the areas of Curriculum Studies, Globalization Theory, and Wisdom Traditions. Collections of his published papers are available in two volumes, *Pedagon: Interdisciplinary essays in the human sciences, pedagogy and culture* (Peter Lang, 1999), and *Trying to teach in a season of great untruth: Globalization, empire and the crises of pedagogy* (SensePublishers, 2006). Further information is available on his website: http://www.ualberta.ca/~smithdg

HANS SMITS is an Associate Professor in the Faculty of Education at the University of Calgary. He is currently on administrative leave after serving as the Associate Dean of Teacher Preparation for the past five and half years. His research and writing interests are in teacher education and hermeneutic interpretation of teachers' work and curriculum.

DARREN STANLEY is Associate Dean of Graduate Studies, Research and Continuing Education in the Faculty of Education, University of Windsor. His research interests focus on the connections between complex dynamical systems, health and healthy organizations, ecology and ecojustice, and leadership and governance as complex responsive processes. This work has contributed to understanding the underlying conceptual underpinnings, descriptions and images, and pragmatics of living organizations. He has published in the *Journal of Curriculum Theorizing, Complicity: An International Journal of Complexity and Education*; *Paideusis: Journal for the Canadian Philosophy of Education Society*; *Educational Insights*; *Emergence: Complexity and Organization*; and *The Innovation Journal: The Public Sector Innovation Journal.*

DENNIS SUMARA is Dean of Education at the University of Calgary. His research areas include literacy education, teacher education, and curriculum studies. His research program focuses on the study of literary engagement and curriculum, analyses of normative and counter-normative discourses in teacher education, and the theoretical and practical implications of complexity science to the field of education. He is author or co-author of five books, including *Why Reading Literature in School Still Matters: Interpretation, Imagination, Insight*, which won the 2003 USA National Reading Conference's Ed Fry Book Award, and has published many research papers and essays in journals such as *Harvard Educational Review, Educational Theory, Journal of Curriculum Studies*, and the *Journal of Literacy Research.*

KELLY YOUNG is an Associate Professor at Trent University's School of Education and Professional Learning where she teaches English Curriculum methods and foundational courses. Her areas of research include literacy, curriculum theorizing, and leadership in ecojustice environmental education. Her most recent co-edited book (Smale & Young), *Approaches to Educational Leadership and Practice* (Detselig, 2007) challenges contemporary practice in educational leadership. She has published articles in *Language and Literacy: A Canadian Educational E- Journal, Journal of Curriculum Theorizing, EcoJustice Review: Educating for the Commons,* and *Journal of the Canadian Association for Curriculum Studies.*